SO-BDS-961

BUILDING
AN ACTIVE COLLEGE
VOCABULARY

Patricia M. Licklider

John Jay College of Criminal Justice—CUNY

Longman

New York San Francisco Boston
London Toronto Sydney Tokyo Singapore Madrid
Mexico City Munich Paris Cape Town Hong Kong Montreal

To Nancy and Virginia,
From whom the words came, to whom the words go.

Editor-in-Chief: Joseph Opiela
Senior Acquisitions Editor: Steven Rigolosi
Associate Editor: Barbara Santoro
Marketing Manager: Melanie Craig
Supplements Editor: Donna Campion
Production Manager: Denise Phillip
Project Coordination, Text Design, and Electronic Page Makeup: WestWords, Inc.
Cover Design Manager: John Callahan
Cover Designer: Maria Ilardi
Manufacturing Buyer: Lucy Hebard
Printer and Binder: Courier Corp.
Cover Printer: Coral Graphics Services, Inc.

For permission to use copyrighted material, grateful acknowledgment is made to these copyright holders: "The Souks." From *Berlitz Morocco Pocket Guide* By Neil Wilson (revised Robert Ullian), pp. 68–70. Copyright © 2000 Berlitz Publishing Company, Inc. "Assignment Lets Him Hit Nail on the Head" by Scott Smith. From *The Gazette*, Colorado Springs. "Tree at my Window" by Robert Frost. From *Poetry of Robert Frost*, pp. 251–2, edited by Edward Connery Lathem. Copyright 1956 by Robert Frost, © 1928, 1969 by Henry Holt & Co, LLC. Reprinted by permission of Henry Holt and Company, LLC. "The Trees" by Philip Larkin. From Collected Poems by Philip Larkin (edited by Anthony Thwaite) p. 166. Copyright © 1988, 1989 by the Estate of Philip Larkin. Reprinted by permission of Farrar, Straus and Giroux, LLC. "Little Red Riding Hood Revisited" by Russell Baker. From the *New York Times*. Copyright © 1980 by the New York Times Co. Reprinted by permission. *You Just Don't Understand: Women and Men in Conversation* by Deborah Tannen, pp. 23–31. Copyright © 1990 by Deborah Tannen. Reprinted by permission of HarperCollins Publishers, Inc. William Morrow. *Phantoms in the Brain*, by V.S. Ramachandran and Sandra Blakeslee, from *Phantoms in the Brain* by V.S. Ramachandran, M.D., PH.D. and Sandra Blakeslee Copyright © 1998 by V.S. Ramachandran and Sandra Blakeslee. Reprinted by permission of HarperCollins Publishers, Inc. William Morrow.

Library of Congress Cataloging-in-Publication Data
Licklider, Patricia.
    Building an active college vocabulary / Patricia M. Licklider.
      p. cm.
    Includes index.
    ISBN 0-321-08327-X
    1. Vocabulary—Problems, exercises, etc. I. Title.

PE1449 .L53 2001
428.1—dc21

                                        2001029241

Copyright © 2002 by Addison Wesley Longman, Inc.

All rights reserved. No part of this publication may be reproduced, stored in a retrieval system, or transmitted, in any form or by any means, electronic, mechanical, photocopying, recording, or otherwise, without the prior written permission of the publisher. Printed in the United States.

Please visit our website at http://www.ablongman.com

ISBN 0-321-08327-X

1 2 3 4 5 6 7 8 9 10—CRS—04 03 02 01

Brief Contents

Contents

UNIT 6 Post-Tests 349

UNIT 7 Appendix: Additional Word Families
Introduction: More Latin Roots 352

Glossaries

Preface

When students complain that they are poor writers, they often attribute their lack of fluency to not knowing enough "good words." And when they complain that a book they have been assigned to read is "boring," this remark often means that they have not understood it. To weak readers with small vocabularies, many college-level texts seem to be written in a foreign language. Because students entering college who are not avid readers do not have wide reading vocabularies, their writing vocabularies are even more limited. To be successful in college and beyond, students like these need to develop their word hoards. They need help learning words from their reading; they need help using a dictionary and a thesaurus efficiently and profitably; and they need help making their writing vocabulary better. It is to these ends that *Building an Active College Vocabulary* has been written. Its main purpose is to give students a set of skills to help them build the number of words they recognize when reading and listening, as well as the number of words they know well enough to use in writing and speaking. While this book emphasizes the skills, in practicing these skills students also learn many new words. This book thus combines the two kinds of vocabulary-building texts now on the market: those that emphasize the skills for acquiring new words on one's own and those that present word lists for students to acquire immediately.

This text is intended for students who enter college with a reading vocabulary at about a tenth-grade level and with a writing vocabulary that is heavily reliant on generalizations and clichés. But it would also be appropriate for older students interested in increasing their functional reading and writing vocabulary, including those whose first language is not English. Its combination of reading, dictionary, thesaurus, and writing vocabulary skills is not found in any other vocabulary book. It should thus appeal to both reading and writing teachers of students considered developmental, remedial, or basic, as well as to teachers of study skills and of freshman composition who want to enrich their students' awareness of language. Most of the words highlighted for study in the text are cited as twelfth-grade level or higher in *The Living Word Vocabulary: A National Vocabulary Inventory* by Edgar Dale and Joseph O'Rourke. The remaining highlighted words are cited as tenth-grade level. Thus after some weeks of study, students should at least know the meanings of many more words at a higher reading level than that at which they began.

The thesis of this text, which is based on studies of human memory, is that learning new words occurs most successfully when they are in *a memorable context,* particularly one that is meaningful to the learner. For example, new words are more easily learned and remembered if students encounter them in sentences or longer prose paragraphs. Furthermore, if students create for themselves a context for learning a new word, they are even more likely to retain the word longer. Mere lists of unrelated words are difficult to learn and not as likely to be retained. Thus throughout the book, students learn and practice many different ways of putting new words into a memorable context. By experimenting with a variety of context-building strategies, students can find the strategy that works best for them.

Organization and Features

In **Unit One,** "What Surrounds a New Word?", students examine reading passages for clues to the meanings of unfamiliar words. This unit explains and helps students practice the kinds of decoding skills that avid readers develop for themselves over the course of several years. In **Unit Two,** "What Is Inside a New Word?", students learn those prefixes, roots, and suffixes that are reliable clues to the meanings of words in which they appear because they have one unvarying meaning. Then they can use these word parts as another way to decode unfamiliar words and as a way to retain their meaning. Skillful use of a college dictionary is the subject of **Unit Three,** "What Help Is a Dictionary?". Here, unlike other vocabulary texts, *Building an Active College Vocabulary* shows how to spend sixty seconds in the dictionary *after* reading a word's meaning to find a memorable context within which to place the word and its meaning. The emphasis here, then, is on the power of the dictionary beyond the listing of definitions. **Unit Four,** "Playing with Word Parts," returns to prefixes, roots, and suffixes not included in Unit Two, but not because these are necessarily accurate guides to a word's meaning. Rather, students use the general meaning and form of a root, for example, to create a family of related words and then use their common root as a context for remembering them. **Units Five,** "Improving Your Writing Vocabulary," and **Six,** "What Help Is a Thesaurus?" turn to the vocabulary that students feel comfortable using when they write or speak. Unit Five offers advice, for example, on using words new to the writer, on replacing clichés with more specific and precise language, and on using words figuratively. Unit Six discusses that other word book to which students so often turn when at a loss for words, the thesaurus, both in print and on line. The unit examines the limitations of a thesaurus but also its utility as a source of writing ideas, as well as of synonyms. The text thus progresses from the least familiar words and ways of figuring them out to the most familiar.

In addition, every unit contains a **reading selection** from material that college freshmen are likely to be assigned. Three of the authors, for example, are frequently anthologized in readers for first-year writing courses. I have chosen them from books and essays in different disciplines with an eye toward engaging the readers' imagination as well as their word sense. Each reading selection is keyed to the skills examined in its unit, so that students can practice newly acquired word skills on a college-level text. **Mastery Exercises** at the end of each selection help students understand both the meaning and usage of words in the selection, and in so doing, understand more fully the meaning of what the author is saying. Again, the words are examined in a **meaningful context.**

In every unit, the **exercises** provided are extremely varied, from **match-ups** and **fill-in-the-blanks** to **word grids,** to **imaginative play with word origins,** to **small-group work,** to **word replacements,** to **creation of small glossaries,** to brief **writing assignments,** and so on. The variety of the work students can do in the text matches the book's thesis that each learner should find his or her own best way of learning and remembering new words. Individual instructors can also choose to assign the kind of work that they think is most productive for vocabulary-building. The text and exercises can also be self-paced because **many of the answers are provided in the back of the text.**

The *Instructor's Manual* that accompanies the text contains teaching tips as well as additional exercises. This variety of exercise material makes *Building an Active College Vocabulary* stand out among the competition. Every unit has, in addition to the many exercises that accompany the explanations, ample **review exercises** and, following the reading selections, several brief **post-tests.** For those who enjoy using and assigning word lists, an **appendix** provides for self-paced study or for classroom assignment fifteen word lists, each arranged around a Latin root and each followed by exercises.

My constant theme throughout the text is that vocabulary enrichment is an open-ended process, not bound by the end of a semester or of a book. As the tone of the book suggests, this process can be enjoyable and empowering. The suggestions for using memorable contexts, for creating such contexts for themselves, and for enriching the words they use in their own writing are methods students can continue to use long after they have finished their formal schooling. I hope that *Building an Active College Vocabulary* helps them see new words as challenges to be met long after they have completed its exercises.

—Patricia M. Licklider

Acknowledgments

The idea for this book came first from my own students, who feel that if only they knew the right words, success in life would be theirs. If only it were so easy! Nonetheless, they are correct in thinking that a more extensive vocabulary will help them succeed at least in college. They continue to inspire me, even after all these years, with their enthusiasm and willingness to work hard. I hope they find this book useful. I want to thank my college, John Jay College of Criminal Justice, for providing the two half-leaves that enabled me to produce this book. Among the people who helped bring this book to publication, it is Steve Rigolosi, Senior English Editor at Longman Publishers, who deserves the largest *grazie*. It was he who first thought there was something worthwhile in my initial proposals and who worked tirelessly with me through many revisions to make the text as useful and comprehensive as it is. Every textbook writer should have so congenial and tireless an editor to push her along. Jennifer Krasula, Steve Rigolosi's one-time assistant, was helpful to me in many small ways, and for these I thank her. I have been constantly buoyed in the long process of writing by the encouragement and vitality of my colleagues in the English department at John Jay; they make the college an enjoyable place to work, and for their collegiality I thank them as well. I must also thank the dedicated reviewers who assessed and criticized the manuscript at every stage of development:

Kelly Cox, Independence Community College
Bruce Gamble, Owens Community College
Patrick Haas, Glendale Community College
Julie Hanks, Cabrillo College
Maggi Miller, Austin Community College
Katie Smith, Riverside Community College
Pamela Smith, Pellissippi State Technical Community College
Barbara Sussman, Miami-Dade Community College
Jill Wilks, Southern Utah University
Mary Wolting, Indiana University–Purdue University Indianapolis (IUPUI)

Finally, loving thanks go to my husband Roy, both lighthouse and anchor.

—Pat Licklider
New York, NY

"Good words are worth much, and cost little."
George Herbert
1651

UNIT 1

What Surrounds a New Word?

In this Unit, You Will Learn to Look as You Read for Word Meanings in:

For Skills Practice, You Will Read:

When These Skills Aren't Useful, See:

Introduction: Reading to Increase Your Vocabulary

The most effective way to increase your vocabulary is to read often and widely. Learning new words as you read also shows you how they are used. Such words enter the store of vocabulary that you know well enough to recognize, and if you see the words often enough as you read, you will know enough about them to begin using them yourself.

But you might be thinking, How can I learn the meanings of new words in my reading without using a dictionary? Without opening the dictionary, you can often figure out the meaning of a word you don't know from the other, more familiar words around it. These other words are called its *context*. More than half the time, the context contains clues to the meaning of an unfamiliar word. And even when there are no clues at all in the first context, the new word may appear later in a more helpful context. This unit will outline the kinds of clues you can look for in the context. The first are OBVIOUS clues to a word's meaning, and the rest are LESS OBVIOUS clues that require you to play the detective.

"By God, for a minute there it suddenly all made sense!"

Copyright © 2002 by Addison Wesley Longman, Inc.

© The New Yorker Collection 1986 Gahan Wilson from cartoonbank.com. All Rights Reserved.

1

Definitions and Restatements, Examples, Demonstratives: Obvious Clues to Meaning

Definitions and Restatements: The Writer Defines the Word or Says It in Other Words.

> **LOOK FOR**
>
> in other words
> that is to say

What is being DEFINED here?

> *. . . the plant forms both food and oxygen as part of the same process. . . . Chemists call the process of putting together complex substances from simple ones "synthesis" from Greek words meaning "to put together." Since sunlight is essential to oxygen production and therefore to food synthesis the process is called* "photosynthesis" (*"To put together by light").*
>
> Isaac Asimov, *Photosynthesis* (NY: Basic Books, 1968), p. 19

The writer first takes the new word *photosynthesis* apart to define it and then puts these partial meanings together at the end of the sentence, *To put together by light.*

What is being RESTATED here?

> *The most conspicuous physical feature of a Sumerian city was its* ziggurat—*a steep pyramidal mound, artificially built of bricks and earth, upon which rested a temple reached by a long flight of stairs.*
>
> Joseph Swain, *The Ancient World,* vol. 1 (NY: Harper & Row, 1950), p. 76

Here, the new word *ziggurat* is defined in detail by the words following it.

Vocabulary Exercise 1.1

In a textbook you are using for another class, find five words or phrases that are explained with definitions or restatements. Jot them down in your word list or on index cards, learn their meanings, and then without looking at your list or cards, compose definition or restatement sentences of your own for each word. Exchange your sentences and the original definitions/restatements you took from the textbook with those of a classmate. Were you able to explain each word correctly?

Writing Assignment 1.1

Think of a word or phrase that you and your friends or coworkers use but that other people might consider slang or jargon (the special language of a trade or profession). Write a paragraph explaining the meaning of this word or phrase to someone who doesn't understand it. In your paragraph, use a definition or restatement such as those discussed above. Share your paragraph with your classmates. ■

Examples: The Writer Gives a List of Specific Examples of the Unfamiliar Word.

LOOK FOR

for example
for instance
such as
like

Copyright © 2002 by Addison Wesley Longman, Inc.

From the EXAMPLES in this passage, what do you think *tactics* means?

There are two ways to study "presidential power." One way is to focus on the tactics, *so to speak, of influencing certain men in given situations: how to get a bill through Congress, how to settle strikes, how to quiet Cabinet feuds, or how to stop a Suez.*

Richard E. Neustadt, *Presidential Power* (NY: Wiley, 1980), p. 2

The examples of kinds of *tactics* in the *how to* phrases are several actions, so you would be correct to think that *tactics* means *action* or *way of getting something done*.

Vocabulary Exercise 1.2

Go back to the five words/phrases you chose from a textbook for Vocabulary Exercise 1.1. This time, write new sentences for each in which you explain each by giving at least two examples of the word or phrase. Use *for example, for instance, such as,* or *like* to help.

Writing Assignment 1.2

Choose a complex activity that you do well and often, such as driving a car or surfing the Internet. What do you think is the most important quality a person must have in order to do this activity well? Write a paragraph to a classmate who wants to learn this activity. In the paragraph, explain this quality by giving several examples from your own experience that show its importance. For example, if you chose driving a car, you might say that a good driver must have constant awareness. An example of such awareness might be a recent experience in which you had to stop the car quickly in the middle of a street to avoid a pedestrian who was jaywalking. ■

Demonstratives: If an Unfamiliar Noun is Preceded by *This, That, These, Those* or *Such,* Look for the Word's Meaning in What Has Just Come Before it in The Passage.

LOOK FOR

this
that
these
those
such

In the following, what do the sentences before *proselytizing* tell you it means?

Mormons send missionaries out to seek converts even among those already associated with another faith. Since 1960, the church has added more members through conversion than were born into the faith. This vigorous proselytizing *is deeply resented by many non-Mormons.*

Richard T. Schaefer, *Racial and Ethnic Groups,* 7th ed. (NY: Longman, 1998), p. 145

You would be correct to think that *proselytizing* means *seeking or adding converts.*

Writing Assignment 1.3

Go back to the slang or jargon that you chose for Writing Assignment 1.1. But for this assignment, imitate the passage above about Mormons. That is, first write a few sentences describing the actions or attitudes that the word you have chosen refers to, but without using the word itself. Then use *This* or *These* and the word to start a final sentence that says something more about it.

■

Vocabulary Exercise 1.3

Here are some brief passages containing difficult words in italics. Use clues in the rest of the passage to figure out the meaning of the italicized word, and then complete the sentence following the passage so that you give the word's meaning. Look for definitions, restatements, examples, and demonstratives.

1. *Segregation* refers to the physical separation of two groups in residence, workplace, and social functions. Generally, the dominant group imposes segregation on a subordinate group.
                                    Schaefer, p. 22
   You can say that *segregation* exists among people when

   _____

2. We tend to think that the norms we follow represent the "natural" way human beings do things. Those who behave otherwise are judged as being morally wrong. This viewpoint is *ethnocentric,* which means that people think their own culture represents the best, or at least the most appropriate, way for human beings to live.
                  James Spradley & David McCurdy, *Conformity and Conflict: Readings in Cultural Anthropology* (NY: Longman, 1997), p. 4
   A person who is *ethnocentric* believes that

   _____

Copyright © 2002 by Addison Wesley Longman, Inc.

(Continued)

3. If you cross the Sahara, and you fall, by and by vultures circle around you, smelling, sensing your death. They circle lower and lower: they wait. They know. They know exactly when the flesh is ready, when the spirit cannot fight back. The poor are always crossing the Sahara. And the lawyers and bondsmen and all that crowd circle around the poor, exactly like vultures. Of course, they're not any richer than the poor, really, that's why they've turned into vultures, *scavengers,* indecent garbage men.

   James Baldwin, *If Beale Street Could Talk* (NY: Dial Press, 1974), p. 7

   Vultures are called *scavengers* because they

   _____

4. The poor aren't necessarily strongly annoyed at the difference between themselves and the very rich. They might be somewhat bothered by this *disparity,* but they probably are even more upset by differences between themselves and others who are similar to them in background.

   Leonard Berkowitz, *A Survey of Social Psychology* (Hinsdale, IL: Dryden Press, 1975), p. 120

   Another word for *disparity* is

   _____

5. While some central-city neighborhoods are in decline and find it difficult to attract mortgage money, other neighborhoods have experienced *gentrification.* This has been characterized by upper-middle-income and professional people moving into old neighborhoods, refurbishing the houses there, and turning aged apartment buildings into condominiums.

   John J. Harrigan, *Politics and Policy in States and Communities* (NY: Longman), 1998, p. 409

   Gentrification is the process by which

   _____

6. The word *taboo* comes from a Polynesian term meaning prohibition. Breaking a *taboo* or prohibition leads to undesirable consequences or bad luck. Most [baseball] players observe at least a few *taboos.* Some are careful never to step on the chalk foul lines or lines of the batters box.

   George Gmelch, "Baseball Magic," in Spradley & McCurdy, p. 325

   An action would be called *taboo* if

   _____

(Continued)

7. The word *proletariat* entered European languages before the mid-nineteenth century to describe those workers afloat in the labor pool who owned nothing, not even the tools of their labor, and who were becoming "appendages" to the new machines that dominated production.

> Mark Kishlansky, Patrick Geary, & Patricia O'Brien,
> *Civilization in the West, Volume C Since 1789,* 3rd ed.
> (NY: Longman, 1998), p. 766

If you were a member of the *proletariat,* you were

_____

8. The other kind of culture change is borrowing. Borrowing—or *diffusion,* as it is sometimes called—refers to the adoption of something new from another group. Tobacco, for example, was first domesticated and grown in the New World but quickly *diffused* to Europe and Asia after 1492.

> Spradley & McCurdy, p. 349

When we say that the use of a new word or a new food *diffused* throughout an area, we mean that it

_____

9. Paul was tall for his age and very thin, with high, cramped shoulders and a narrow chest. His eyes were remarkable for a certain hysterical brilliance and he continually used them in a conscious, theatrical sort of way, peculiarly offensive in a boy. The pupils were abnormally large, as though he were addicted to *belladonna,* but there was a glassy glitter about them which that drug does not produce.

> Willa Cather, "Paul's Case," in *Youth and the Bright
> Medusa* (NY: Knopf, 1920), pp. 199–200

You can assume that *belladonna* is a type of

_____

10. When men are present, women are "onstage" insofar as they feel they must watch their behavior more. Another possibility is that it was not the presence of men in general that affected this woman's behavior, but the presence of her husband. One interpretation is that she was somehow *cowed,* or silenced, by her husband's presence.

> Deborah Tannen, *You Just Don't Understand* (NY:
> William Morrow, 1990), p. 93

If someone is *cowed* she is

_____

Copyright © 2002 by Addison Wesley Longman, Inc.

2

Repetition, Lists, Repeated Word Patterns: Less Obvious Clues I

Repetition: The Writer Repeats a Familiar Word that Helps Explain an Unfamiliar Word.

From the REPETITION of *suppose* below, what do you think a *supposition* is?

Suppose *his father had heard him getting in at the window and had come down and shot him for a burglar?* Then again, suppose *his father had come down, pistol in hand, and he had cried out in time to save himself, and his father had been horrified to think how nearly he had killed him?* Then again, suppose *a day should come when his father would remember that night, and wish there had been no warning cry to stay his hand?* With this last supposition *Paul entertained himself until daybreak.*

Cather, pp. 210–11

You would be correct to think that a *supposition* is an act of supposing, an imagining.

Writing Assignment 2.1

Pretend that you are a writer of advertisements to be read on the radio. Your assignment is to write a ten-second ad for a new household detergent or a new restaurant in town. Make up its name yourself. In the ad use repeated words or phrases to emphasize the product's or restaurant's excellence.   ■

Lists: The New Word Appears in a List of Other More Familiar Words.

In the LIST of three things below, what do the first two suggest that *paucity* means? Note also that all three were *a great disadvantage*.

Puerto Rico's small size, its small population, and its paucity *of natural resources, especially minerals, were a great disadvantage from the beginning of the colonial period.*

Oscar Lewis, *La Vida* (NY: Random House, 1966), p. xvi

From the repetition of *small* in the other parts of the list, you would be correct to think that *paucity* has something to do with being small, so a word like *scarcity* or *lack* would be close to its meaning.

Repeated Word Patterns: The New Word Has the Same Function or Shape as Another More Familiar Word.

To figure out what *conventionally* means in the next passage, find another word that has the same *-ly* ending, which indicates they are both adverbs in their sentences.

To analyze the problem of obtaining personal power one must try to view the Presidency from over the President's shoulder, looking out and down with the perspective of [his] place. This is not the way that we conventionally *view the office;* ordinarily, *we stand outside it, looking in.*

Neustadt, p. vi

You would be correct to think that *conventionally* is similar in meaning to *ordinarily* because of their similarity in form.

Writing Assignment 2.2

Think of a child's nursery rhyme such as "Humpty Dumpty." Write a paragraph in which you explain how different kinds of repetition in the little poem make it easy for a child to remember. To get you started, one kind of repetition in "Humpty Dumpty" is the repetition of "umpty" in both parts of his name.   ■

Copyright © 2002 by Addison Wesley Longman, Inc.

Vocabulary Exercise 2.1

Here are some brief passages containing difficult words in italics. Use clues in the rest of the passage to figure out the meaning of the italicized word, and then circle the letter of the words following the passage that are closest to it in meaning. Be sure the words make sense in the original passage. Look for repetition and repeated word patterns.

1. All people communicate on several different levels at the same time, but are usually aware of only the verbal dialog and don't realize that they respond to nonverbal messages. But when a person says one thing and really believes something else, the *discrepancy* between the two can usually be sensed. . . . When we find ourselves thinking, "I don't know what it is about him, but he doesn't seem sincere," it's usually this lack of *congruity* between a person's words and his behavior that makes us anxious and uncomfortable.

   > Edward Hall & Mildred Hall, "The Sounds of Silence,"
   > in Spradley & McCurdy, p. 62

   discrepancy
   a. lying
   b. difference
   c. change

   congruity
   a. feeling
   b. satisfaction
   c. agreement

2. It is well known that none of the German nations inhabit cities, or even admit of *contiguous* settlements. They dwell scattered and separate, as a spring, a meadow, or a grove may chance to invite them.

   > Tacitus, *Germania,* in *Sources of the West: Readings in
   > Western Civilization,* 3rd ed., Vol. I, ed. Mark Kishlansky
   > (NY: Addison Wesley Longman, 1998), p. 100

   contiguous
   a. crowded
   b. adjoining
   c. continuous

3. Since a prince must know how to use the character of beasts, he should pick for imitation the fox and the lion. As the lion cannot protect himself from traps, and the fox cannot defend himself from wolves, you have to be a fox in order to *be wary of* traps, and a lion to *overawe* the wolves. Those who try to live by the lion alone are badly mistaken.

   > Niccolo Machiavelli, *The Prince,* in Kishlansky,
   > (NY: Longman, 1998), p. 226

(Continued)

be wary of	**overawe**
a. be afraid of	a. scare
b. destroy	b. run from
c. be on the lookout for	c. befriend

4. He [President Truman] could not feel that he had done his job if he let personal *proclivities* or personal self-interest outweigh what he took to be a presidential duty.

Neustadt, pp. 128–29

proclivities
a. inclinations
b. habits
c. honors

5. And yet, though the elder person was as simply clad as the younger, and as simple in manner too, he had an indescribable air of one who knew the world, and who would not have felt *abashed* at the governor's dinner table, or in King William's court, were it possible that his affairs would call him thither.

Nathaniel Hawthorne, "Young Goodman Brown" in
Mosses from an Old Manse, I (NY: Three Sirens Press,
n.d.), p. 76

abashed
a. welcome
b. silly
c. embarrassed

6. A woman I will call Rebecca, who is generally quite happily married, told me that this [failure to talk to her] is the one source of serious dissatisfaction with her husband, Stuart. . . . For Rebecca, who is accustomed to expressing her *fleeting* thoughts and opinions as they come to her, *saying* nothing means *thinking* nothing. But Stuart does not assume that his passing thoughts are worthy of utterance. He is not in the habit of uttering his *fleeting ruminations,* so just as "naturally" Rebecca speaks her thoughts, he "naturally" dismisses his as soon as they occur to him.

Tannen, p. 83

fleeting	**ruminations**
a. suitable	a. dreams
b. floating	b. thoughts
c. passing	c. bad feelings

7. But there is something else about that paper—the smell! . . . It creeps all over the house.

Copyright © 2002 by Addison Wesley Longman, Inc.

(Continued)

   I find it hovering in the dining room, *skulking* in the parlor, hiding in the hall, lying in wait for me on the stairs.

> Charlotte Perkins Gilman, "The Yellow Wallpaper"
> *The Yellow Wallpaper and other writings*
> (NY: Bantam, 1989), p. 15

skulking
a. sneaking around
b. playing
c. sitting

8. Each of the Great Powers had a *vulnerability,* a geographic Achilles' heel. Germany's *vulnerability* lay in its North Sea ports. German shipping along its only coast could easily be *bottlenecked* by a powerful naval force. Such an event, the Germans knew, could destroy their rapidly growing international trade. What was worse, powerful land forces could "encircle" Germany.

> Kishlansky, Geary & O'Brien, p. 876

vulnerability
a. sense of power
b. weakness
c. self-destructiveness

bottlenecked
a. greatly increased
b. destroyed
c. greatly slowed down

9. During the century from 390 B.C. to 290 B.C., Romans rebuilt their city and *recouped* their losses. They also reorganized their army. . . .

> John McKay, Bennett Hill & John Buckler, *A History of Western Society, Vol. A: From Antiquity to 1590,* 4th ed. (Boston: Houghton Mifflin, 1991), p. 134

recouped
a. forgot
b. mourned
c. got back

10. Superficially, *Walden* is the story of Thoreau's experiment, movingly and beautifully written. It is also an acid indictment of the social behavior of the average American, an attack on unthinking conformity, on *subordinating* one's own judgment to that of the herd.

> John A. Garraty & Mark C. Carnes, *The American Nation, Vol. One: A History of the United States to 1877,* 10th ed. (NY: Longman, 2000), p. 310

subordinating
a. reducing
b. placing lower
c. conquering

3

Contrast, Descriptive Words: Less Obvious Clues II

Contrast: A Writer Contrasts the Unfamiliar Word with Others that Are Better Known.

LOOK FOR words signaling contrast	
instead of	however
more	in contrast
less	on the other hand
than	though
but	although
rather than	

What is *exacerbate* contrasted with in the following passage?

The last several years have been hard on the public image of state courts. A few highly publicized criminal cases left many citizens shaking their heads in ways that seemed to exacerbate *rather than ease the great social conflicts that we have been considering. . . .*

Harrigan, p. 292

Because *exacerbate* is contrasted with *ease,* you would be correct to think that it means the opposite of *ease:* to make worse or to aggravate.

Copyright © 2002 by Addison Wesley Longman, Inc.

Writing Assignment 3.1

Write a paragraph in which you return to the activity you described in Writing Assignment 1.2 to explain it further by saying what doing the activity well is NOT. For example, driving a car well does NOT mean being aggressive on the road. Also say why these negative qualities are undesirable.   ■

Descriptive Words: Other Words Around the Unfamiliar Word May Provide Useful Information, Such as Its Shape, Color, Size, Texture, Purpose, or Value.

Using other words in the following, what sort of thing do you think a *calabash* is?

> The old man greeted me cordially. "Sit down and drink." I accepted a large calabash *full of beer, poured some into a small drinking gourd, and tossed it down.*
> Laura Bohannon, "Shakespeare in the Bush," in Spradley & McCurdy, p.35

From the words *large, full of beer,* and *poured,* you would be correct to deduce that a *calabash* is a big container for liquor. If you wanted more information, your dictionary would tell you that it is a large, bottle-shaped gourd that can be dried and cut open for use as a container. But simply deducing that it is a large container for liquor allows you to keep reading with understanding.

Writing Assignment 3.2

Here are some words that might be used to describe a person: *braggart, prude, oaf.* Look up these words in a dictionary to find their meanings. Then choose one, and write a few sentences in which you describe such a person, displaying her or his nature, but without using the word itself until the very last sentence in which you say, "In short, Mary (or Harry or whatever name you give the person) was a _____."   ■

Vocabulary Exercise 3.1

Here are some brief passages containing difficult words in italics. Once again, use clues in the rest of the passage to figure out the meaning of the italicized word, and then complete the sentence following the passage so that you give the word's meaning. Look for repetition, repeated word patterns, lists, contrast, and descriptive words to help.

(Continued)

1. Josephine was kneeling before the closed doors with her lips to the keyhole, imploring for admission. "Louise, open the door! I beg; open the door—you will make yourself ill. What are you doing, Louise? For heaven's sake open the door."

   "Go away. I am not making myself ill." No; she was drinking in a very *elixir* of life through that open window. . . .

   She arose at length and opened the door to her sister's *importunities*.
   > Kate Chopin, "The Story of an Hour," in R.S. Gwyn,
   > *Fiction: A Longman Pocket Anthology*, 2nd ed. (NY:
   > Longman, 1998), p. 47

   An *elixir* is something you drink that _____
   Importunities are words that

   _____

2. To survive in the world, we have to act *in concert* with others, but to survive as ourselves, rather than simply as cogs in a wheel, we have to act alone.
   > Tannen, p. 28
   When we act *in concert* with others, we are not

   _____

3. How do these images [of the elderly] develop? Partly, we tend to see the elderly only in situations that reinforce the image. For example, physicians see more sick old people, so "all old people are sick." Social workers see only the *indigent;* therefore, "all aged are poor." We see the aged sitting on park benches but do not notice them rushing to and from jobs or volunteer work, so "all old people are inactive with no interests to keep them involved with society."
   > Schaefer, p. 439
   Indigent people are those who

   _____

4 & 5. It [the Supreme Court] cannot, like a legislature or governor or President, *initiate* measures to cure the ills it perceives. It is, as Justice Robert H. Jackson said, "a substantially passive instrument, to be moved only by the *initiative* of litigants." In short, the Court must sit and wait for issues to be presented to it in lawsuits.
   > Anthony Lewis, *Gideon's Trumpet* (NY: Random House,
   > 1974), p. 12
   If a legislator or governor sees something wrong, he or she can
   _____ new laws.

   To take the *initiative* means to _____.

Copyright © 2002 by Addison Wesley Longman, Inc.

(Continued)

6 & 7. For all of my life my mother had been the other: I was aggressive,
she was *passive*. (Perhaps simply reserved?) I was intellectual, she was not.
(Perhaps not given the opportunity?) I was *gregarious*, she was shy.
(Perhaps simply more selective in her attachments?)

> Anna Quindlen, "Mother's Day," from *Living Out Loud*
> (NY: Random House, 1994), p. 100

If a *passive* person got caught up in an argument, she/he would

_____

At a party, a *gregarious* person would

_____

8. Adams . . . was also extremely *straitlaced*. Unlike Franklin, who had two
illegitimate children, he was able to assure his descendants that he had
never wandered from the straight and narrow, before or after his marriage
to Abigail Smith.

> Garraty & Carnes, p. 71

A person who is *straitlaced* would never do the following:

_____

9. Egypt was fortunate in that it was nearly self-sufficient. . . . The Egyptians
. . . had little cause to look to the outside world for their essential needs, a
fact that helps to explain the *insular* quality of Egyptian life.

Geography encouraged isolation by closing Egypt off from the
outside world. . . . Yet Egypt was not completely sealed off. . . .

> McKay, Hill & Buckler, p. 23

A people who lived an *insular* life would be unlikely to

_____

10. I never saw a worse [wall]paper in my life. . . . The color is *repellent*,
almost revolting; a smouldering unclean yellow, strangely faded by the
slow-turning sunlight.

It is a dull yet lurid orange in some places, a sickly sulphur tint in
others.

No wonder the children hated it! I should hate it myself if I had to
live in this room long.

> Gilman, p. 4

A sweater in a *repellent* color is one that you find

_____

Review Exercise I

Here are some passages containing difficult words in italics. Once again, use whatever clues you can find in the rest of the passage to figure out the meaning of each word. Then think of one or two words to express this meaning; be sure that the word or words would fit into the sentence. Write the word or words in the blank following each passage.

1. To the Romans slavery was a misfortune that befell some people, but it did not entail any racial theories. . . . For the talented slave, the Romans always held out the hope of eventual freedom. *Manumission*—the freeing of individual slaves by their masters—became so common that it had to be limited by law.
   McKay, Hill & Buckler, p. 144

   _____

2. The North African Arab states of Morocco, Algiers, Tunis, and Tripoli had for decades made a business of piracy, seizing vessels all over the Mediterranean and holding crews and passengers for ransom. The European powers found it simpler to pay them annual protection money than to crush them. Under Washington and Adams, the United States joined in this *tribute;* while large, the sums were less than the increased costs of insurance for shippers when the protection was not purchased.
   Garraty & Carnes, p. 175

   _____

3. Nearly every day an echo of my mother's mothering *wafts* by me, like the aroma of soup simmering on a stove down the street.
   Quindlen, p. 101

   _____

4. The motivation for the Brown [law]suit came not merely because Black schools were inferior, although they were. Blacks were assigned to poorly ventilated and dilapidated buildings, with overcrowded classrooms and unqualified teachers. Less money was spent on Black schools than on White schools throughout the South in both rural and metropolitan areas. The issue was not such *tangible* factors, however, but the *intangible* effect of not being allowed to go to school with Whites.
   Schaefer, p. 196

   _____

Copyright © 2002 by Addison Wesley Longman, Inc.

(Continued)

5. In the hillside shantytowns that spring up around cities, . . . marriages are brittle, single parenting is the norm, and women are frequently forced into the shadow economy of domestic work in the homes of the rich or into unprotected and oftentimes "scab" wage labor on the surrounding sugar plantations, where they clear land for planting and weed for a *pittance,* sometimes less than a dollar a day.

    Nancy Scheper-Hughes, "Mother's Love: Death Without Weeping," in Spradley & McCurdy, p. 197

---

6. The handsomest of all these fish, and the one most ardently pursued by anglers, is *Morone saxatilis,* the striped bass, . . . It is also by far the best tasting and the most *amenable* to any kind of cooking: poached, baked, grilled, fried, or sliced into sashimi when right out of the water.

    Robert Hughes, *A Jerk on One End: Reflections of a Mediocre Fisherman* (NY: Ballantyne Publishing Group, 1999), p. 32.

---

7. The two categories of differences between the male and female speakers in the videotapes that were most striking to me were what the friends talked about and their body language—how they *oriented* themselves to each other with their bodies and eyes.

    Differences in physical *alignment,* or body language, leap out at anyone who looks at segments of the videotapes one after another. At every age, the girls and women sit closer to each other and look at each other directly. At every age, boys and men sit at angles to each other.

    Tannen, pp. 245–46

---

8. When she abandoned herself a little whispered word escaped her slightly parted lips. She said it over and over under her breath: "Free, free, free!" The vacant stare and the look of terror that had followed it went from her eyes. They stayed keen and bright. Her pulses beat fast, and the *coursing* blood warmed and relaxed every inch of her body.

    Chopin, p. 46

---

9. Unlike common schools, with their democratic overtones, private colleges had at best a *precarious* place in Jacksonian America. For one thing, there

(Continued)

were too many of them. . . . The problem of supply was compounded by a demand problem—too few students. . . . So desperate was the shortage that colleges accepted applicants as young as 11 and 12 and as old as 30.
Garraty & Carnes, p. 319

10. French physiologist Paul Broca (1824–80), a contemporary of Darwin's, countered in 1873 that the skull capacity of the two sexes was very similar and that a case for inferiority could not be based on measurement. But Broca was *atypical*. Most scientific opinion argued in favor of female frailty and outright inferiority.
Kishlansky, Geary & O'Brien, p. 839

Review Exercise II

Each of the pairs of passages below comes from the same book and uses the same difficult word, in italics. Study the context surrounding the word in each passage to help you figure out its meaning. Then answer the question about the word after each pair of passages.

1. (From paragraph 1 of the Douglass reading selection below, on pp. 27–30)

   a. I lived in Master Hugh's family about seven years. During this time, I succeeded in learning to read and write. In accomplishing this, I was compelled to resort to various *stratagems.*

   b. I determined to try to hire my time, with a view of getting money to make my escape. In the spring of 1838, when Master Thomas came to Baltimore to purchase his spring goods, I got an opportunity, and applied to him to allow me to hire my time. He unhesitatingly refused my request, and told me this was another *stratagem* by which to escape. He told me I could go nowhere but that he would get me; and that, in the event of my running away, he should spare no pains in his efforts to catch me.

   Remember the *stratagems* Douglass used to learn to read. What does Master Thomas mean when he says that Douglass's request is "another *stratagem* by which to escape"?

Copyright © 2002 by Addison Wesley Longman, Inc.

(Continued)

2. (Again from Douglass's story of his life as a slave)

   a. In addition to the pain of separation, there was the horrid dread of falling into the hands of Master Andrew. He was known to us all as a most cruel wretch,—a common drunkard, who had, by his reckless mismanagement and profligate *dissipation,* already wasted a large portion of his father's property.

      p. 60

   b. The slaveholders like to have their slaves spend those days [Christmas holidays] just in such a manner as to make them as glad of their ending as of their beginning. Their object seems to be, to disgust their slaves with freedom, by plunging them into the lowest depths of *dissipation.* For instance, the slaveholders not only like to see the slave drink of his own accord, but will adopt various plans to make him drunk. One plan is, to make bets on their slaves, as to who can drink the most whiskey without getting drunk; and in this way they succeed in getting whole multitudes to drink to excess. Thus, when the slave asks for virtuous freedom, the cunning slaveholder, knowing his ignorance, cheats him with a dose of vicious *dissipation,* artfully labelled with the name of liberty.

      p. 85

   What sorts of activities do you imagine a *dissipated* person like Master Andrew doing?

   _____

3. (From Robert Hughes' little book on fishing, *A Jerk on One End:*)

   In Italy, where I lived for a little while in the fishing village of Porto Ercole, there were few fish to catch; even thirty-odd years ago, the waters of the Tyrrhenian Sea were so *depleted* by pollution and relentless dragnetting that a two-pound *dentice* or *spigola* would become the talk of the Bar Centrale. In England, where I settled later, I seldom moved outside London. No fishing there. But after I crossed to New York in 1970, fishing presented itself again.

   The eastern end of Long Island, three hours or less from Manhattan, was one of the world's great fisheries and, though considerably *depleted,* it still is. The angler's year begins in April, when the "cocktail blues"— small bluefish—begin to show up in the bays and the flounder stir from their hibernation on the seabed, and it goes right through to the middle of November, when it gets too cold for me or any but the hardiest to fish from the beaches or from an open boat.

   pp. 30–31

(Continued)

What does it mean to say that a supply of something like fish is *depleted?*

_____

4. (Again from Hughes's book:)
   There was no noble way of taking fish [in ancient Rome], because fish
   themselves weren't noble. Their pursuit was an entirely *plebeian* occupation.
         Hunting was noble, the sport of kings and of gods. . . .
                        p. 64
         But Christ and his first followers, as readers of the Bible well know,
   weren't just fish but fishermen. Four of the apostles (Andrew, James,
   John, and of course Peter) were busy at the tedious task of net mending
   by the Sea of Galilee when Christ recruited them by offering to make
   them "fishers of men"; from then on, the image of the evangelist
   fishing for souls would proliferate throughout the religious imagery of
   the West. It had strong *plebeian* associations. Fishing was work—hard,
   sometimes dangerous, uncertain in its returns, meager in its profits.
                        p. 68
   If noblemen in the ancient Roman Empire hunted, what sort of people
   fished? So then, what might *plebeian* mean?

_____

5. (From Deborah Tannen's book on the differences between male and
   female talk, *You Just Don't Understand:*)

   a. In a study of how women and men talk about their divorces,
      Catherine Kohler Riessman found that both men and women
      mentioned increased freedom as a benefit of divorce. But the word
      "freedom" meant different things to them. When women told her
      they had gained freedom by divorce, they meant that they had
      gained "independence and autonomy." It was a relief for them not
      to have to worry about how their husbands would react to what
      they did, and not have to be "responsive to a *disgruntled* spouse."
      When men mentioned freedom as a benefit of divorce, they meant
      freedom from obligation—the relief of feeling "less confined," less
      "claustrophobic," and having "fewer responsibilities."
                        pp. 40–41
   b. Yet another cartoon shows a wedding cake that has, on the top, in
      place of the plastic statues of bride and groom in tuxedo and gown, a
      breakfast scene in which an unshaven husband reads the newspaper
      across the table from his *disgruntled* wife. The cartoon reflects the

Copyright © 2002 by Addison Wesley Longman, Inc.

(Continued)

enormous gulf between the romantic expectations of marriage represented by the plastic couple in traditional wedding costume, and the often disappointing reality represented by the two sides of the newspaper at the breakfast table—the front, which he is reading, and the back, at which she is glaring.

p. 82

Describe the feelings and/or facial expressions of a *disgruntled* person.

---

6. (Again, from Tannen's book:)

   a. Some men are further frustrated because, as one put it, "When am I supposed to read the morning paper?" If many women are *incredulous* that many men do not exchange personal information with their friends, this man is *incredulous* that many women do not bother to read the morning paper.

   p. 82

   b. Keeping friends up to date about the events in one's life is not only a privilege; for many women it is an obligation. One woman explained that she didn't enjoy telling the story of her breakup with her boyfriend over and over, but she had to, because if she had failed to inform any of her close friends about such an important development, they would have been deeply hurt when they found out. . . . The woman, furthermore, was *incredulous* when she learned that her boyfriend had not told anyone at all about their breakup. He had gone to work, gone to the gym, and played squash with his friends, all as if nothing had happened to change his life.

   p. 98

What might be some synonyms for *incredulous*?

---

7. (And yet again from Tannen's book:)

   a. Both status and connection are ways of being involved with others and showing involvement with others, although those who are focused on one may not see the other as a means of involvement. Men are more often inclined to focus on the *jockeying* for status in a conversation: Is the other person trying to be one-up or put me down? Is he trying to establish a dominant position by getting me to do his bidding? Women are more often attuned to the negotiation of connections: Is the other person trying to get closer or pull away?

(Continued)

Since both elements are always present, it is easy for women and men to focus on different elements in the same conversation.

p. 38

b. Girls don't give orders; they express their preferences as suggestions, and suggestions are likely to be accepted. Whereas boys say, "Gimme that!" and "Get outta here!" girls say, "Let's do this," and "How about doing that?" Anything else is put down as "bossy." They don't grab center stage—they don't want it—so they don't challenge each other directly. And much of the time, they simply sit together and talk. Girls are not accustomed to *jockeying* for status in an obvious way; they are more concerned that they be liked.

p. 44

What are boys and men doing when they are *jockeying* for status? How is what they do similar to what *jockeys* who ride race horses do in a race?

---

8. (From a discussion of slavery in *The American Nation* by Garraty and Carnes:)

a. Well-managed plantations yielded annual profits of 10 percent and more, and, in general, money invested in southern agriculture earned at least a modest return. Considering the way the workforce was *exploited,* this is hardly surprising. Recent estimates indicate that after allowing for the cost of land and capital, the average plantation slave "earned" cotton worth $78.78 in 1859. It cost masters about $32 a year to feed, clothe, and house a slave. In other words, almost 60 percent of the product of slave labor was expropriated by the masters.

p. 353

b. One southern white woman tended a dying servant with "the kindest and most unremitting attention." Another, discovered crying after the death of a slave she had repeatedly abused, is said to have explained her grief by complaining that she "didn't have nobody to whip no more."

Such diametrically conflicting sentiments often existed within the same person. And almost no white Southerners had any difficulty *exploiting* the labor of slaves for whom they felt genuine affection.

p. 356

c. Slaves had strong family and group attachments and a complex culture of their own, maintained, so to speak, under the very noses of their masters. By a mixture of subterfuge, accommodation, and passive resistance, they erected subtle defenses against *exploitation,* achieving a sense of community that helped sustain the psychic integrity of individuals.

Copyright © 2002 by Addison Wesley Longman, Inc.

(Continued)

In these three different words, *exploited, exploiting,* and *exploitation,* the verb *exploit* appears. What does it mean to *exploit* someone else's work? Replace *exploited, exploiting,* and *exploitation* in the above passages with other words that you think mean somewhat the same thing. Be sure the sentences make sense with your words in them.

---

9. & 10. (From a discussion, also in *The American Nation,* of American humor in the early nineteenth century:)

The clash between the desire of the few for a "high" culture and the simpler tastes of the majority led James Fenimore Cooper to conclude that Americans would be forever "wanting in most of the high tastes, and consequently in the high enjoyment." But other writers were not so sure, and some, rather than despair over the cultural incongruities, found in them a rich source of humor.

They were hardly the first to do so. The comic potential in *juxtaposing* high ideas and low reality had been exploited by the Greek playwright Aristophanes; by Rabelais, the creator of *Gargantua;* and by Cervantes in *The Adventures of Don Quixote*—all, incidentally, works available in mid-century America. William Byrd and Benjamin Franklin had both used the differences between the pretensions of colonial sophisticates and the ways of common folk to good comic effect. But the possibilities of this kind of humor were greatly enlarged in the Jacksonian era. Where else was there a country theoretically based on equality whose inhabitants were so strikingly varied?

One of the first writers to exploit the comic aspects of Jacksonian democracy was Seba Smith, a newspaperman from Portland, Maine. Smith's fictional creation, Major Jack Downing, was a Jackson man from a part of the country suspicious of both the general's politics and his intelligence. Smith had Major Downing accompany the president on his 1833 tour of New England, which included, among other adventures, an appearance at Harvard to receive an honorary degree. In the presence of so many learned gentlemen with political views contrary to his own, Downing advised the president "jest to say nothing, but look as knowing as any of them." Which was what Jackson did, even when faced by snickering "sassy students." "The General stood it out like a hero," the major assured readers, "and got through very well."

A writer who turned the possibilities of "Down East" humor to more telling satirical effect was James Russell Lowell, author of the *Biglow Papers,* which began appearing in 1847. Lowell *juxtaposed* Hosea Biglow, a Yankee farmer of "homely common-sense heated up

(Continued)

by conscience," and Birdofredum Sawin, a scoundrel hoping to turn a profit on his patriotism. . . .

    The Old Southwest provided another locale for *juxtaposing* the genteel and the vulgar. Life in the region provided chroniclers with more than enough violence to capture the attention of their "gentle readers."
pp. 323–324

Note that in each use above of the verb *juxtapose*, two qualities or characters are involved. Mention one of these pairs. What might it mean to *juxtapose* these qualities or characters? How might this meaning be related to the root *pose*, which is inside *juxtapose*?

_____

_____

11. Note that the verb *exploit* appears again in the long passage about American humor just quoted. Find the two uses of *exploit* in the passage. Does the meaning you decided on for *exploit* in the passages about slavery also fit these uses of the word here? Or is *exploit* used differently here?

_____

Reading 1

The following is most of Chapter VII of the autobiography of Frederick Douglass, who was born a slave in 1818 but later escaped to freedom and then worked tirelessly against slavery. He was a brilliant, powerful speaker, appearing throughout the North and in Europe. He continued to deliver this antislavery message by writing his autobiography, which he did three times over the course of his life. But the first version, *Narrative of the Life of Frederick Douglass, An American Slave: Written by Himself,* published in 1845, was the most successful, selling over 11,000 copies immediately and later translated into several other languages. This excerpt is from this first version. In it Douglass describes how as a young slave he secretly taught himself to read and write. Slaveholders considered it a crime to educate slaves because education would make them want to be free.

    Several words in the passage have been italicized. If they are unfamiliar to you, use all you have learned about context to figure out their meaning. Then answer the questions after the passage. The paragraphs are numbered for your convenience.

Copyright © 2002 by Addison Wesley Longman, Inc.

1   I lived in Master Hugh's family about seven years. During this time, I succeeded in learning to read and write. In accomplishing this, I was compelled to resort to various *stratagems*. I had no regular teacher. My mistress, who had kindly commenced to teach me, had, *in compliance with* the advice and direction of her husband, not only ceased to instruct, but had set her face against my being instructed by any one else. It is due, however, to my mistress to say of her, that she did not adopt this course of treatment immediately. She at first lacked the *depravity* indispensible to shutting me up in mental darkness. It was at least necessary for her to have some training in the exercise of irresponsible power, to make her equal to the task of treating me as though I were a brute.

2   My mistress was, as I have said, a kind and tender-hearted woman; and in the simplicity of her soul she commenced, when I first went to live with her, to treat me as she supposed one human being ought to treat another. In entering upon the duties of a slaveholder, she did not seem to *perceive* that I *sustained to* her the relation of a mere *chattel,* and that for her to treat me as a human being was not only wrong, but dangerously so. Slavery proved as injurious to her as it did to me. When I went there, she was a pious, warm, and tender-hearted woman. There was no sorrow or suffering for which she had not a tear. She had bread for the hungry, clothes for the naked, and comfort for every mourner that came within her reach. Slavery soon proved its ability to *divest* her of these heavenly qualities. Under its influence, the tender heart became stone, and the lamb-like disposition gave way to tiger-like fierceness. The first step in her downward course was her ceasing to instruct me. She now commenced to practice her husband's *precepts.* She finally became even more violent in her opposition than her husband himself. She was not satisfied with simply doing as well as he had commanded; she seemed anxious to do better. Nothing seemed to make her more angry than to see me with a newspaper. She seemed to think that here lay the danger. I have had her rush at me with a face made all up of fury, and snatch from me a newspaper, in a manner that fully revealed her *apprehension.* She was an *apt* woman; and a little experience soon demonstrated, to her satisfaction, that education and slavery were *incompatible* with each other.

3   From this time I was most narrowly watched. If I was in a separate room any considerable length of time, I was sure to be

suspected of having a book, and was at once called to give an account of myself. All this, however, was too late. The first step had been taken. Mistress, in teaching me the alphabet, had given me the "inch," and no precaution could prevent me from taking the "ell."

4   The plan which I adopted, and the one by which I was most successful, was that of making friends of all the little white boys whom I met in the street. As many of these as I could, I converted into teachers. With their kindly aid, obtained at different times and in different places, I finally succeeded in learning to read. When I was sent on errands, I always took my book with me, and by doing one part of my errand quickly, I found time to get a lesson before my return. I used also to carry bread with me, enough of which was always in the house, and to which I was always welcome; for I was much better off in this regard than many of the poor white children in the neighborhood. This bread I used to *bestow* upon the hungry little *urchins,* who in return, would give me that more valuable bread of knowledge. I am strongly tempted to give the names of two or three of those little boys, as a *testimonial* of the gratitude and affection I bear them; but *prudence* forbids;—not that it would injure them; but it might embarrass them; for it is almost an unpardonable offence to teach slaves to read in this Christian country. It is enough to say of the dear little fellows, that they lived on Philpot Street, very near Durgin and Bailey's ship-yard. I used to talk this matter of slavery over with them. I would sometimes say to them, I wished I could be as free as they would be when they got to be men. "You will be free as soon as you are twenty-one, but I am a slave for life! Have not I as good a right to be free as you have?" These words used to trouble them; they would express for me the liveliest sympathy, and *console* me with the hope that something would occur by which I might be free.

5   I was now about twelve years old, and the thought of being a slave for life began to bear heavily upon my heart. Just about this time, I got hold of a book entitled "The Columbian Orator." Every opportunity I got, I used to read this book. Among much of other interesting matter, I found in it a *dialogue* between a master and his slave. The slave was represented as having run away from his master three times. The *dialogue* represented the conversation which took place between them, when the slave was retaken the third time. In this *dialogue,* the whole argument in behalf of slavery was brought

Copyright © 2002 by Addison Wesley Longman, Inc.

forward by the master, all of which was disposed of by the slave. The slave was made to say some very smart as well as impressive things in reply to his master—things which had the desired though unexpected effect; for the conversation resulted in the voluntary *emancipation* of the slave on the part of the master.

6   In the same book, I met with one of Sheridan's mighty speeches on and in behalf of Catholic *emancipation*. These were choice documents to me. I read them over and over again with *unabated* interest. They gave tongue to interesting thoughts of my own soul, which had frequently flashed through my mind, and died away for want of utterance. The moral which I gained from the dialogue was the power of truth over the conscience of even a slaveholder. What I got from Sheridan was a bold *denunciation* of slavery, and a powerful *vindication* of human rights. The reading of these documents enabled me to utter my thoughts, and to meet the arguments brought forward to sustain slavery; but while they relieved me of one difficulty, they brought on another even more painful than the one of which I was relieved. The more I read, the more I was led to *abhor* and detest my enslavers. I could regard them in no other light than a band of successful robbers, who had left their homes, and gone to Africa, and stolen us from our homes, and in a strange land reduced us to slavery. I *loathed* them as being the meanest as well as the most wicked of men. As I read and *contemplated* the subject, behold! that very discontentment which Master Hugh had predicted would follow my learning to read had already come, to torment and sting my soul to *unutterable anguish*. As I *writhed* under it, I would at times feel that learning to read had been a curse rather than a blessing. It had given me a view of my wretched condition, without the remedy. It opened my eyes to the horrible pit, but to no ladder upon which to get out. In moments of agony, I envied my fellow-slaves for their stupidity. I often wished myself a beast. I preferred the condition of the meanest reptile to my own. Any thing, no matter what, to get rid of thinking! It was this everlasting thinking of my condition that tormented me.

Mastery Exercises

1. How can you tell that Douglass did not like to use *stratagems* to learn to read and write? What would he have preferred instead? What do you think *stratagems* are?

2. Why did Douglass's mistress stop teaching him?

3. What words does Douglass use in Par. 2 to describe his mistress when he first went to live with her? These words are opposed to *depravity* (Par. 1), which is described as necessary for her to shut Douglass up *in mental darkness*. Given these clues, what might *depravity* mean?

4. At first, she treated Douglass as a human being as opposed to *mere chattel*. Given its contrast with *human being* and the descriptive word *mere*, what might *chattel* mean?

5. In Par. 2, Douglass describes how slavery changed his mistress. Given his description, what other word could you substitute for *divest*?

6. Given your answer to #2 above, what might *her husband's precepts* be? What other word could you use for *precepts*?

7. *Apprehension* can mean either *fear and dread of the future* or *the act of learning*. Which meaning do you think best fits Douglass's mistress snatching a newspaper from him?

8. At the end of Par. 2, Douglass says his mistress "was an *apt* woman." Look at the rest of that sentence, and then choose from among these meanings of *apt* the one you think he means: *ready; likely; suited to a purpose; intelligent.*

9. Given the way his mistress's attitude toward teaching a slave to read changes, say in other words what it means for education and slavery to be *incompatible* with each other.

10. Why does Douglass take bread with him when he leaves the house to run errands? What does he do with it? What are *urchins*?

11. The word *testimonial* is similar to *testimony*. Why does Douglass wish he could name the little boys who helped him learn to read?

12. Why doesn't he name them? Note the contrast, indicated by *but*, between Douglass's desire to name the little boys and his *prudence*. What might be another word for *prudence*?

13. The little boys felt sorry for Douglass, so they *consoled* him with the hope that he too might be free some day. The word *consoled* must

Copyright © 2002 by Addison Wesley Longman, Inc.

(Continued)

therefore be something people do when they feel sorry for someone else. Name one or two such things.

14. If you are not sure what a *dialogue* is, note how it is described in Par. 5. Here is another bit of information to help you understand what a *dialogue* is: In Unit 2 of this book, you will learn that the word part *log-* means *word* or *speech.*

15. What might be the "desired though unexpected effect" of a slave's intelligent argument with his master against slavery? That is, what would the slave want but not expect to receive from his master? Douglass calls it "voluntary *emancipation.*" What was Lincoln's *Emancipation* Proclamation?

16. In Par. 6, Douglass describes the dialogue and speeches in "The Columbian Orator" as "interesting," "impressive," "mighty," "choice." So he read them "over and over with *unabated* interest." What kind of interest might that be?

17. Sheridan, whose speeches Douglass read, was obviously against slavery, so what would Sheridan be doing when he made a "bold *denunciation*" of it? Slavery in this same sentence is linked with "human rights." Would Sheridan be *for* or *against* human rights? So what would he be doing when he *vindicated* them?

18. What happened to Douglass the more he read? Given the fact that he links the verb *abhor* with the verb *detest* when describing his feelings towards his enslavers, you would be correct to assume that the two verbs are similar in meaning. A few lines later, he says he "*loathed* them as being the meanest as well as the most wicked of men." What might be another word for *loathed* here?

19. Douglass writes that his discontentment with being a slave would "torment and sting" his soul. Both verbs are about the inflicting of pain or "*unutterable anguish.*" Note that the less difficult word *utter* is inside *unutterable*, and, as you will see in Unit 2, *un-* means *not* or *the opposite of.* So what kind of pain or *anguish* did Douglass feel?

20. Given Douglass's description of his suffering from thinking about slavery, what might you guess that *writhed* means? (The first three letters of *writhed* rhyme with *rye.*)

A Final Word on Contexts

What can you do if there are NO clues to the meaning of an unfamiliar word in its context?

- Look up such a word if an author uses it more than once and you still can't figure it out or if it is crucial to your understanding of an entire passage.

If you stop to look up every new word whose context is not helpful, you may lose your train of thought and will have to start reading the passage over again. After a while, reading will become a burden rather than a pleasure.

- Don't panic. Remember that the more you read the same author, the more familiar you will become with that author's vocabulary.

Authors will probably repeat words related to their subject, as well as other, more general words and turns of phrase that they like to use. For example, in *Gideon's Trumpet,* a book about a case brought before the Supreme Court, Anthony Lewis uses many legal terms, such as *litigant, jurisdiction,* and *statute.* And he also regularly uses such nonlegal words as *contention, incorporate,* and *corrosive.* The more times you run across a new word like these in your reading, the better you will know it because, each time it appears, the word has a different context with different, additional clues to its meaning and usage, as in Review Exercise II.

- Finally, if the context is not helpful, try using a word's parts as clues to its meaning.

In the next unit, you will explore these clues to meaning that are INSIDE a word.

Copyright © 2002 by Addison Wesley Longman, Inc.

Unit 1

Post-Test 1

Here are some unfinished analogies using words highlighted in this unit, in italics. Finish the analogies using what you remember about the meanings of these words.

EXAMPLE: *photosynthesis* : plants :: cooking : humans

(The dots in an analogy should be read in this way: Photosynthesis **is to** plants **as** cooking **is to** humans. In other words, the first word is related to the second word in the same way that the third word is related to the fourth; photosynthesis is the way that plants make food, and cooking is a way that humans make food.)

1. *taboo* : forbidden :: permission : _____

2. *bottleneck* : traffic :: bloodclot : _____

3. *tangible* : *intangible* :: physical : _____

4. *diffused* : floodwaters :: _____ : speech

5. to *initiate* : _____ :: to turn on : to turn off

6. *segregation* : a mail sorter :: _____ : food blender

7. *indigent* : soup kitchen :: _____ : 4-star restaurant

8. *tactics* : chessgame :: battle plan : _____

9. *gentrification* : slum :: _____ : smashed car fender

10. *exacerbate* : add fuel to the fire :: _____ : put out the fire

Unit 1
Post-Test 2

Here in Column A are other words highlighted in this unit. In the blank next to each, write the word from Column B that is most nearly its *opposite*.

Column A	Column B
1. fleeting _____	encouraged
2. contiguous _____	relaxed, loose
3. gregarious _____	permanent
4. subordinating _____	unashamed
5. straitlaced _____	secure
6. cowed _____	broad-minded
7. precarious _____	placing higher
8. abashed _____	attractive
9. insular _____	shy
10. repellent _____	separated

Copyright © 2002 by Addison Wesley Longman, Inc.

Unit 1

Post-Test 3

In a paragraph 6–8 sentences long, summarize below the story Frederick Douglass tells in Reading 1, pages 21-23. Then give it a title that highlights its main point.

_____

_____

_____

_____

_____

_____

_____

_____

_____

_____

_____

_____

_____

_____

_____

Unit 1

Post-Test 4

Here are some of the highlighted words from Reading 1. Circle the letter of the word next to each that best fits its meaning as Frederick Douglass uses it. In case you want to look back at the reading, the paragraph of each word is provided.

1. depravity (par. 1) a) intelligence b) corruption c) desire

2. chattel (par. 2) a) tool b) child c) possession

3. divest (par. 2) a) unclothe b) take away from c) distract from

4. precepts (par. 2) a) rules b) beliefs c) decisions

5. bestow (par. 4) a) give to b) hide from c) leave to

6. urchins (par. 4) a) orphans b) poor boys c) delinquents

7. console (par. 4) a) predict b) warn c) comfort

8. dialogue (par. 5) a) written argument b) written talk c) written condemnation

9. vindication (par. 6) a) defense b) attack c) defeat

10. abhor (par. 6) a) be afraid of b) avoid c) hate

Copyright © 2002 by Addison Wesley Longman, Inc.

UNIT 2

Words in Focus
root
prefix
suffix

What Is Inside a New Word?

In this Unit, You Will Learn to Find Word Meaning in:

You Will Also See:

For Skills Practice, You Will Read:

Introduction: Word Parts as Clues to Meaning

When you find an unfamiliar word in your reading, you can sometimes use not only the context surrounding the word but also the parts of the word itself to figure out its meaning. There are three kinds of word parts:

- Roots
- Prefixes
- Suffixes

A root carries the most meaning. It is a syllable or syllables or an independent word that carries the basic dictionary meaning of a word. A root cannot be broken apart any further and still carry a meaning. Roots are nouns, verbs, adjectives, and adverbs, or they once were in the languages from which English borrowed them. These parts of speech carry more meaning than pronouns, prepositions, conjunctions, and other connecting words.

Prefixes, which are word parts added to the beginnings of words, also carry meaning, but not as much, as we shall see in Chapters 7 and 15. Prefixes are like prepositions. In fact, some prefixes can be prepositions on their own (*in-* can be *in,* for example), and many prefixes once were prepositions in Greek or Latin, the languages from which English borrowed them. Suffixes—word parts that are added to the ends of words—carry even less meaning than prefixes, as we shall also see later in Chapters 8 and 16–17.

"My instructor said my vocabulary was execrable. I wonder what he meant by that?"

© 2000 Frank Cotham from cartoonbank.com. All Rights Reserved.

ex- prefix for *out of, away from,* + *sacer,* root meaning *sacred* + *-able,*
suffix meaning *able* = *execrable: able to be cursed, detestible; very bad*

Copyright © 2002 by Addison Wesley Longman, Inc.

4

Roots

The root of a word may be the whole word:

bird
large
hand

Or the root may be part of a word and have prefixes, suffixes, or other roots attached to it:

birdlike
enlarge
handy

The roots in each of these words are words in their own right, but many other roots cannot stand alone. For example:

cran- in *cranberry*
boysen- in *boysenberry*
logan- in *loganberry*

The last examples show that sometimes two roots are put together, or compounded, to make one word. There are a great many compound words in English. Some are even made of two independent words:

birdhouse
largehearted
handcuff

Vocabulary Exercise 4.1

Each noun in the left-hand column below can be combined with one or more words in the right-hand column to form compound words like *birdhouse* and *birdseed*. In the space provided, create as many compound words as you know by combining a word from the first column with one from the second. There are at least fifteen or twenty possible combinations all together.

back	ache
bed	burn
day	light
head	line
heart	long
life	rest
sun	side
	time

Writing Assignment 4.1

Compare the compound words you formed for the preceding exercise with those of a classmate. Then together with your classmate, write down some rules you followed in making the compound words. If English is your first language, you are probably not conscious of these rules because you learned them automatically when you learned to speak English as a child, so you and your classmate will have to think hard to bring them to your conscious mind. Here are some questions to get you started: Do the names of body parts go first or second in a compound word? What are some other kinds of nouns that must go first? What kinds must go second? If you learned English as a second or third language, you probably learned these rules consciously. Write down the ones you know for forming compound words in English.

Copyright © 2002 by Addison Wesley Longman, Inc.

Vocabulary Exercise 4.2

Now make compound words beginning with the adjectives below. Choose five or more of the adjectives and in the space provided, write all the compound words you can think of that start with each one. Can you think of any compound words that *end* with the adjectives too? If so, write these down as well. Try to think of at least two compounds for each adjective. If you like, work with a classmate on this exercise to come up with as many compounds as possible.

EXAMPLE: large   largehearted
                      large-scale
                      Congressman-at-large

bare   hot
blue   new
brown   red
deep   soft
high   strong

_____

_____

_____

_____

_____

Spelling Box

Be careful to distinguish between the following compound words (*already*) and their uncompounded cousins (*all ready*), which have a different meaning. As you read aloud a sentence containing the uncompounded version of such pairs, you can pause in between the two words without destroying meaning, and each word is accented. You can also sometimes put another word in between the two words, as in the following examples.

(Continued)

Compounds	Separate Words
already	*all ready*
altogether	*all together*
anymore	*any more*
everyday	*every day*
into	*in to*
maybe	*may be*
sometime	*some time*

We are not *altogether* happy with the proposal you have made. (*Altogether* means *entirely*)

We are going to submit an alternative proposal *all together*. We are going to submit an alternative proposal *all of us together*. (*All together* are two separate words meaning *the whole group*.)

Your coming to work a half-hour late is becoming an *everyday* occurrence. (*Everyday* is an adjective meaning *regular*.)

You have been coming to work a half-hour late *every day* this week. You have been coming to work a half-hour late *every single day* this week. (*Every day* are separate words, a noun and an adjective.)

Maybe this movie will win an Academy Award. (*Maybe* means *perhaps*.)

This movie *may be* the best-directed film of the season. This movie *may well be* the best-directed film of the season. (*May be* are two separate words, a verb phrase.)

Writing Assignment 4.2

On your own paper, compose a sentence or two using each of the words in the two columns of the Spelling Box for which there are no examples. That is, write a sentence using *already* and another sentence using *all ready*, being careful to use each correctly. If necessary, look up a word in a dictionary. ■

The same root can appear in different words but not always with the same specific meaning. For example, *come* is a root in *outcome, comedown,* and *income.* In each of these words, you can see the general meaning of *come—to move from here to there*—but this general meaning has developed into something more specific in each word. *Income* for example, is something that

Copyright © 2002 by Addison Wesley Longman, Inc.

comes in, but the word usually refers more specifically to money that comes in to a person at regular intervals. The ideas of money and regular intervals are not in the root or the prefix by themselves.

Thus you can guess at the general meaning of a word from the meaning of its root and prefixes and suffixes, but the sum of the meanings of all these parts may NOT be the word's meaning at all. Another problem with looking at a word's parts to figure out its meaning is that the longer word may contain a shorter word that has nothing to do with its meaning. For example, the word *hallucination* has nothing to do with a *hall*.

Despite these drawbacks, however, you can still help yourself unlock the meaning of an unfamiliar word by looking for shorter words, or roots, inside it. If you then combine this information with other information you find in the context surrounding the word, you can help yourself even more. In fact, the word's context can also help you decide whether or not a smaller word inside it is really a part of its meaning.

Vocabulary Exercise 4.3

Here are some difficult words that contain shorter words that are clues to the meanings of their longer cousins. Each word contains one such root. Underline it.

EXAMPLES: <u>advantag</u>eous hyper<u>active</u>

1. marginal	11. periodical
2. amateurish	12. elongation
3. juxtaposition	13. ascertained
4. quintessential	14. meritorious
5. impassioned	15. personification
6. metaphysical	16. constraint
7. normalization	17. riverine
8. dramaturgy	18. acidulous
9. equipoise	19. polarization
10. correlate	20. infanticide

Vocabulary Exercise 4.4

Here are some more difficult words that contain shorter words that are clues to their meaning. But in each of these words there are two or more roots, one after the other or one inside the other. Write out each word or root you find.

EXAMPLES: copyright <u>copy right</u> (two roots)
reenactment <u>enactment, reenact, enact, act</u> (four roots)

1. afterthought_____

2. oppressive_____

3. freakishly_____

4. antiestablishment_____

5. disheartened_____

6. dewlap_____

7. stealthiness _____

8. foolhardy_____

9. precautionary_____

10. unpremeditated_____

11. browbeat_____

12. inextinguishable_____

13. overindulgent_____

14. half-witted _____

15. developmental _____

16. managerial _____

17. loggerheads _____

18. untrustworthiness _____

19. harpsichord_____

20. Orientalism_____

Copyright © 2002 by Addison Wesley Longman, Inc.

Writing Assignment 4.3

Carefully read over an essay you have written recently, looking for compound words (words that have shorter words inside them that are related to them in meaning). Make a list of these words. Choose five of them, and write a sentence or two explaining how you think each word is related in meaning to the smaller word inside it. For example, the word *copyright* contains both *copy* and *right* because it refers to an author's right to make copies of what she has written. ■

Vocabulary Exercise 4.5

Look at the words in italics below. Find smaller words inside them. Now use these smaller words, together with the other words in the sentences, to figure out the meanings of the italicized words. Thus you will be using both the words' roots and their contexts to figure out what they mean. Write what you think the italicized word means in the blank following each sentence.

1. Because of inflation, we have to be careful to live within our budget, so we have to cut out some *marginal* expenses, like going to the movies and taking swimming lessons.

   _____

2. After training so enthusiastically for six months, Cooper was really *disheartened* because he did not qualify for the varsity team.

   _____

3. Weeks before his complete collapse, Jennings had behaved *freakishly*, constantly surprising and annoying his family and friends.

   _____

4. The burglars were such masters of *stealthiness* that they managed to carry off the valuables on the first floor without waking any of us sleeping on the second floor.

   _____

5. My mother claims that it is her right as a grandparent to be *overindulgent* to my children. She says that I am their parent, so I should discipline them, not she.

   _____

(Continued)

6. Besides stopping mail and newspaper deliveries while they were on vacation, the Browns installed a timer to turn their lights on every night as an added *precautionary* measure.

   _____

7. One aspect of an *oppressive* government is that it limits freedom of speech by censoring newspapers and magazines and by preventing anyone from making a public speech on forbidden subjects.

   _____

8. The investigator for the insurance company *ascertained* the dollar amount of fire damage by carefully examining the burned-out building.

   _____

9. With deeply moving words and powerful gestures, the defense attorney made an *impassioned* plea to the jury to find the defendant not guilty.

   _____

10. Although the actors had been guided by a competent director, they gave an *amateurish* performance of *Hamlet* last night.

    _____

Copyright © 2002 by Addison Wesley Longman, Inc.

Vocabulary Exercise 4.6

Underline the root words in the longer words below. Then, using these roots as clues to the meanings of the longer words, choose the word or phrase from the list next to each word that you think is closest in meaning to that word. Circle the letter of the word you choose.

EXAMPLE: <u>acid</u>ulous: a. eager   (b.) slightly sour   c. agreeable

1. marketable   a. noticeable   b. physical   c. fit to be sold

2. elongation   a. a period of time   b. the ability to speak well   c. a lengthening

3. bullheaded   a. stubborn   b. important   c. red

4. problematical   a. possible, likely   b. wasteful, spendthrift   c. uncertain, questionable

5. exactitude   a. overemphasis   b. the quality of being precise   c. the quality of being appropriate

6. self-assertive   a. humble   b. aggressive   c. in control of oneself

7. noteworthiness   a. the quality of being without value   b. the quality of being musical   c. the quality of being outstanding

8. hatchery   a. a place where knives are sharpened   b. a place where hats are sold   c. a place where fish or poultry eggs are hatched

9. riverine   a. a soft, sweet, pulpy fruit   b. near the banks of a river   c. a fierce, meat-eating animal living in cold climates

10. byword   a. homeward   b. a familiar saying   c. something near at hand

5

Using Roots Carefully

Words are sometimes tricky creatures. A great many words have shorter words inside them,

> But these shorter words are not always true roots and may have nothing to do with the meaning of the longer words.

For example, the word *fastidious* has no relation to *fast;* the word *hallucination* has nothing to do with *hall;* the word *bustled* is completely different from either *bust* or *bus*. In fact, there are probably just as many words in English that contain shorter words unrelated to them in meaning as there are words containing roots that are related.

You can decide whether or not you have a true root word inside a longer, unfamiliar word by looking at the rest of the word and the context in which it appears. If the context does not help, use a dictionary.

> A small word inside a longer one can be helpful if you combine it with information you can gather from its context.

Copyright © 2002 by Addison Wesley Longman, Inc.

Vocabulary Exercise 5.1

The italicized words in the following sentences contain the shorter words in parentheses after each sentence. Use the rest of the sentence in which the longer word appears to help you decide whether the short word is or is not related in meaning to the longer one. If it is related, circle it. If it is not, cross it out.

EXAMPLES: The cat in the television commercial was so *fastidious* that he would eat only one kind of cat food. (~~fast~~)

Cursing the referee is considered *unsportsmanlike* behavior. (sportsman)

1. Before the cotton cloth is dipped into the dye, it is treated with a *fixative* called a mordant so that the dye will stick to the cloth.   (fix)

2. The author of this biography of President Franklin Roosevelt *manifests* her admiration of him in her repeated praise of his social services programs.   (man)

3. He grew up in Middleton, a tiny *hamlet* fifty miles north of Portland. (ham)

4. The sunken ship was covered with a heavy *incrustation* of seaweed, barnacles, and other forms of sea life.   (crust)

5. To the three *dimensions* of space, length, width, and height, Einstein in his theory of relativity added a fourth *dimension,* time.   (dime)

6. The dwarf Rumpelstiltskin let out a *demoniacal* wail of rage when he realized he had been defeated by the queen.   (demon)

7. When you get a cold, your body's reaction is *analogous* to warfare: it sends its soldiers, the white corpuscles, to battle the invading germs in the nose and throat.   (log)

8. Harcourt hadn't seen any of his family in ten years; this *alienation* was caused by his own feelings of failure.   (alien)

9. When Doug entered college, his head was full of *unformulated* desires for some sort of career that would be both interesting and well-paying. (form)

10. The actress has accused the writer of a popular book about Hollywood of being a *scandalmonger* for claiming that she had used sex as a way to fame.   (scandal)

11. If you base your conclusions on *fallacious* reasoning, then your conclusions will be faulty too.   (fall)

(Continued)

12. The *largess* of the millionaire Andrew Carnegie, who felt that everyone, no matter who, should be able to read, is responsible for many of the free public libraries in the United States.   (large)

13. The excellence of the new reading and writing curriculum for the middle school shows the careful thought, thorough research, and *painstaking* care of the teachers who put it together.   (pains)

14. My *fortuitous* encounter with you in the train station yesterday brought back many pleasant memories of last summer.   (fort)

15. The ease with which Mark makes friends acts as a *counterbalance* to his wife's shyness.   (balance)

16. The old man told his grandchildren that his most important *legacy* to them would not be money or property, of which he had little, but the family's good name and self-respect.   (leg)

17. In the famous "To be or not to be" speech, Hamlet admits the fear of what comes after death. Except for that fear, who would put up with all of life's troubles when he "might his *quietus* make with a bare bodkin [dagger]"?   (quiet)

18. During certain periods the patient talked and talked without *surcease,* even when she was all by herself   (cease)

19. He told one *ribald* joke after another, and even those who blushed at his indecencies also laughed.   (rib)

20. Her words were so *cuttingly* sarcastic and insulting that I felt like crying.   (cut)

Copyright © 2002 by Addison Wesley Longman, Inc.

Writing Assignment 5.1

Choose five sentences from the preceding exercise that are NOT clues to the meaning of the longer words in italics. Look up the longer words in a dictionary so you are sure of their meaning. Then imagine that you are an eighth-grade teacher. Using the meanings of the sentences in which the longer words appear, briefly explain to your students why each of the shorter words cannot be roots of the longer words. Suggest what a better guess of the word's meaning would be by referring to each word's context.

EXAMPLE: The cat in the television commercial was so *fastidious* that he would eat only one kind of cat food. (fast)

This sentence is talking about a cat who is very picky about what he eats. It says nothing about how the cat moves, so the word FAST can't have anything to do with the word FASTIDIOUS. You could more safely guess that FASTIDIOUS means something like PICKY.

Vocabulary Exercise 5.2

The italicized words in the following sentences contain smaller words that may or may not be clues to their meanings. Find at least one shorter word inside each italicized word. Then using the rest of the sentence, decide if the shorter word is or is not a clue to the meaning of the longer word. If it is, use this root and the rest of the sentence to guess at the meaning of the longer word. Write your guess in the space following the sentence, and explain how you arrived at your guess. If the shorter word is not a clue to meaning, write NO in the space instead.

EXAMPLE: Cursing the referee is considered *unsportsmanlike* behavior.
SPORTS

UNSPORTSMANLIKE probably means acting badly, not like a good SPORT because the sentence is about cursing the referee, which is a bad way to act when you're playing SPORTS.

1. Archeologists are especially careful to preserve any *artifacts* they dig up. Even bits of broken pottery are kept as possible clues to the kind of people who made them.

(Continued)

_____

_____

2. The suspension and fine that players will have to pay for joining a fight on the court are *punitive* but not excessive. They should be enough to discourage players from emptying the bench whenever a fight breaks out.

_____

_____

3. In the fable about the race between the tortoise and the hare, the hare lost, despite his ability to run very fast, because he was a *laggard:* he assumed he would win and took a nap during the race.

_____

_____

4. Everything and everyone—even the dog—were stretched out in *lassitude,* worn out by the heat and humidity.

_____

_____

5. Several of the mayor's recent speeches in which he talked mostly about problems in the state, not the city, made it *patent* to even the most casual observers that he was planning to run for higher office.

_____

_____

6. The general issued a *directive* to the army units in the west to attack at dawn because his scouts reported that the enemy was massing there.

_____

_____

7. There is usually a brief stopping point shortly after the start of a play when *latecomers* waiting in the lobby are allowed to take their seats.

_____

_____

Copyright © 2002 by Addison Wesley Longman, Inc.

(Continued)

8. Among meerkats, a kind of mongoose in South Africa, one animal stands *sentinel* on his hind legs, looking all around for signs of danger, while the rest of his family looks for food.

_____

_____

9. The reason that all love songs say mostly the same things is that the experience of love is *ineffable*. Roses and hearts and sweet words don't come close to saying what a lover feels for the beloved.

_____

_____

10. The *ill-timed* arrival of reinforcements after the enemy had succeeded in breaking through our defenses cost us the battle.

_____

_____

11. In the American League, a player called the *designated* hitter, or DH, is allowed to go to bat in place of the pitcher. In the National League, pitchers have to go to bat for themselves.

_____

_____

12. The parents of the boys who vandalized the school have to pay *restitution* to repair or replace what was destroyed.

_____

_____

13. My salary for the first job I had after high school was so small that I could barely support myself, and at the end of every month I had such a *shortfall* that I used to pray someone would invite me to dinner so I could eat for free.

_____

_____

(Continued)

14. Dan's old friend from college invited Dan to join him in a new business venture at an *opportune* time, since at the time, Dan was not only bored with his job but wanted more independence as well.

15. The "Fitz" in the name "Fitzgerald," the "Ben" in "Ben Gurion" and the "son" in "Johnson" all mean "son of." Such *patronymics* date back to a time when most people had only a first name and had to be distinguished from others with the same name.

16. The guards of the Tower of London, who are very impressive when dressed in full *regalia*—red, white and black outfits dating from the sixteenth century—are called "Beefeaters."

17. The letters of reference in your file are all *testimonials* to your good character and strong work habits.

18. At the recent parent-teacher conferences, Jimmy's teacher told us that he has a very *lackadaisical* attitude toward reading, and she suggested that we read with him every night instead of letting him watch television.

19. Because Yolanda is ambitious and works hard for promotions and pay raises, Chuck thinks she is *materialistic*. He says that all she talks about is money. But I disagree. I think Chuck is just envious.

Copyright © 2002 by Addison Wesley Longman, Inc.

20. The Greek philosophers Plato and Aristotle were teacher and student, but Aristotle's ideas are not merely *offshoots* of his teacher's. Unlike Plato, Aristotle taught that one should observe nature closely before drawing theoretical conclusions.

_____

_____

Dictionary Exercise 5.1

Look up in a dictionary the meanings of the words for which you wrote NO in the preceding exercise. In the space after each NO, write a brief summary of each word's meaning. You will return to these words in Unit 3.

6

Greek and Latin Roots with Fixed Meanings

Most of the roots we have been talking about so far are English words in their own right. The word *margin,* for example, is in *marginal,* and the word *continent* is inside *intercontinental.* Now we will work with roots that are not English words but were nouns or adjectives in Greek or Latin. Many of the words made with the Greek roots in particular tend to be scientific or scholarly in nature, perhaps because English speakers have often used old Greek words to name new ideas, discoveries, and inventions. But these roots are significant for another reason:

These roots have one unvarying meaning in whatever words they appear.

Some of these roots, listed below, can be used only in the first part of a word, some only in the last part, and some in both places, as indicated by the dashes before and after the roots. Many can be combined with each other to form compound words, like *telephone* and *philanthropy.*

Root	Meaning	English Examples
-anthrop(o)-	man	*anthro*pology, phil*anthropy*
auto-	self	*auto*mobile
ben(e)-	well, good	*bene*fit
biblio-	book	*biblio*graphy
bio-	life	*bio*logy
-centr-	center	*centr*alize, con*centr*ic
-chron(o)-	time	*chrono*logy, syn*chron*ize
chrom(o)-	color	*chromo*some
-cracy	rule by, government by	demo*cracy*

Copyright © 2002 by Addison Wesley Longman, Inc.

Root	Meaning	English Examples
-crat	one who supports government by _____	democrat
-cosm(o)-	order, harmony; hence, the universe	cosmos, cosmetics, microcosm
-gram-	writing, or gram	grammar, kilogram
-graph(y)	writing	graphic, biography
heter(o)-	different	heterosexual
homo-	same	homosexual
hydr(o)-	water	hydroelectric power
-latry	worship of	idolatry
-log(o)-, -logy, -logue	speech, words, or the study of	catalog, monologue, logarithm, neurology
macro-	long, large	macrocosm
micro-	small	microscope
metr-, -meter, -metry	a measure of _____	thermometer, geometry
multi-	many	multicolored
omni-	all	omnibus
orth(o)-	straight, right	orthopedist
-path(o)-	feeling, suffering	pathetic, sympathy, pathology
pan-	all, entire	panorama, Pan-American
-phil(o)-	love of	philosophy, Anglophile
-phobia or -phobe	hate, fear of or one who hates or fears	claustrophobia, Anglophobe
-phon(o or e)-	sound, voice	phonograph, telephone
-photo-	light	photograph, telephoto lens
poly-	many, much	polygon
proto-	first, original	prototype
pseudo-	false	pseudonym
psych(o)-	the mind, mental processes, soul	psychology, psychic
-scop-	seeing	scope, microscope
tel(e)-	far off, at a distance	television
–the(o)-	god	theology, atheist

Vocabulary Exercise 6.1

Answer the following questions, using the list of roots above together with the contexts surrounding the italicized words.

1. Why is a person who gives other people large sums of money called a *philanthropist?*

   _____

2. If a *monogamous* society allows only one wife to each husband, how many wives can a husband in a *polygamous* society have?

   _____

3. Why do you think *cosmetics,* that is, lipstick, makeup, eye shadow, etc., are so named?

   _____

4. If a *herbivorous* animal eats only plants, and a *carnivorous* animal eats only meat, why are we humans called *omnivorous?*

   _____

5. If we say that a people like the Dutch or Swiss are *polyglot,* what are we saying about their knowledge of languages? (*-glot* means *tongue.*)

   _____

6. Why does an *orthodontist* put braces on children's teeth?

   _____

7. Why do you think *television* is so called?

   _____

8. What is special about a *hydroplane?*

   _____

9. Who writes a person's *autobiography?*

   _____

10. Why is a satellite that calculates distances from its orbit around the earth an example of *telemetry?*

    _____

Copyright © 2002 by Addison Wesley Longman, Inc.

(Continued)

11. Where does the god worshipped by a *pantheist* dwell?

_____

12. Why do we say that a company like Coca Cola is a *multinational* corporation?

_____

13. What do you think a *bibliophile* would collect as a hobby?

_____

14. What does a *microbiologist* study?

_____

15. How much power does one who is *omnipotent* have?

_____

16. Why is a tumor that is not cancerous and that will not cause death called *benign*?

_____

17. What does a *psychoanalyst* analyze?

_____

18. If we said that the people who live in another country were *xenophobic*, what would we mean? (*xeno-* means *stranger, foreigner.*)

_____

19. What kind of head cold is a *chronic* cold?

_____

20. When Mary Ann Evans wrote the novel *Silas Marner*, she signed to it the name George Eliot. Why is George Eliot called her *pseudonym*?

_____

21. If we say that a leader is an *autocrat*, do we mean that he acts (1) gently, (2) bossily, or (3) wisely?

22. What is wrong with someone who is a *psychopath*?

_____

(Continued)

23. What do the names that early European explorers gave two groups of islands in the Pacific Ocean, *Micronesia* and *Polynesia*, mean? (*-nesia* means *island*.)

_____

24. Why are the earth's land, air, and water sometimes given the single name of *biosphere?*

_____

25. If someone were working on a project concerning Communist *ideology,* what would she be doing?

_____

Vocabulary Exercise 6.2

Using what you have learned about the words in the preceding exercise, consider the possible synonyms for each listed in Column B below, and underline those that you think are closest in meaning to the words in Column A.

EXAMPLE: philanthropist   a) wise man
 b) benefactor
 c) woman-chaser

1. bibliophile   a) librarian
 b) rare book seller
 c) eager reader

2. psychopath   a) comedian
 b) madman
 c) freak

3. pseudonym   a) family name
 b) faker
 c) pen name

4. omnipotent   a) supreme
 b) almighty
 c) kingly

Copyright © 2002 by Addison Wesley Longman, Inc.

(Continued)

5. polyglot

    a) speaks many languages
    b) is a linguist
    c) gluttonous

6. ideology

    a) dictatorship
    b) study of government
    c) set of concepts

7. benign

    a) harmless
    b) deadly
    c) generous

8. xenophobic

    a) prejudiced
    b) afraid of the foreign
    c) timid

9. chronic

    a) long-lasting
    b) heavy
    c) well-timed

10. autocrat

    a) self-reliant person
    b) motivated leader
    c) dictator

Writing Assignment 6.1

This is a small-group exercise, so you will need to work with two or three of your classmates to answer this question: What are some fields of study whose names contain one or more of the roots covered in this chapter? To find out, do some research in the catalogue of your own or another college or university, or in the course offerings of some large science departments in your institution. Each person should choose five different names that contain a root from the list on pages 57–58. Look up these names in a college dictionary to find out what the rest of each name means in Greek or Latin. Then write a small "Glossary of Fields of Study" by putting together all the names and root meanings your group has compiled. Such a glossary would be useful for entering freshmen to read. ■

Vocabulary Exercise 6.3

This exercise is also for a small group of three or four people. Your task is to imagine some new inventions or ideas and then to make up names for them by combining various roots from the list on pages 57–58 and from the glossary you compiled for Writing Assignment 6.1. You may also want to use some prefixes from Chapter 7. Write down the name and a brief description of each new idea/invention to share with other classmates. Be imaginative, even funny. But be sure to use the roots properly. That is, observe the rules for where in a word a root may appear. Here's an example: someone who loves to watch television might be called a "telephile."

Copyright © 2002 by Addison Wesley Longman, Inc.

7

Prefixes with Fixed Meanings

A prefix (from *pre-* meaning *before* and *fix*) is a syllable or syllables added to the beginning of another word or root to change its meaning.

> Some, but not all, prefixes are accurate clues to the meanings of longer words to which they are attached.

Prefixes are often old Greek and Latin prepositions that were added to Greek, Latin, or English words many years ago. Here are a few examples:

English Preposition	Latin Prefix	English Word
in	in-	*in*clude
over	super-	*super*intendent
under	sub-	*sub*marine
with	com-	*com*bine
to	ad-	*ad*joining
through	per-	*per*colate

(For a more complete list, see Glossary, pages 387–388.)

Sometimes a prefix can be removed from a word to which it is attached, which we shall call its *root,* and the root is still a word. For example, the prefix *dis-* can be removed from *disown, disappear* and *disapproval,* and these would still be words. But in many others, we cannot. For example, we cannot remove *dis-* from *dispel, disperse,* and *disrupt.* Many of the words in this second group came into English from French or Latin with their prefixes already attached, and like all words in a living language, they had already undergone some change in meaning.

So, even if you learn what it meant originally in Latin,

> A prefix may no longer have its original meaning in the English word you are trying to figure out.

But there are some prefixes that can be very useful to you in your reading because they have one unvarying meaning which contributes to the meaning of the words in which they appear. If you combine the meaning of one of these prefixes with other information from a word's context, you can increase your understanding of the word—and without a dictionary. Here, then, for you to memorize are some of these useful prefixes.

Prefix with One Meaning	*Meaning*	*English Example*
ante-	in front of, previous to	*ante*room, *ante*date
circum-	around	*circum*navigate
contra-	against, opposite to	*contra*diction (but not in *contract*)

The later French form of this prefix also entered English as *counter,* a verb or prefix meaning *to oppose* or *opposing, contrary,* as in *counterclockwise, counteract.*

equi-	equal	*equi*distant
extra-	outside of	*extra*curricular (but not in *extract*)
hyper-	over, excessive	*hyper*active
inter-	between	*inter*planetary (but not in *internal*)
intra- OR intro-	within, into, in	*intra*mural (but not in *intransitive*) *intro*duce
mal-	bad	*mal*adjusted (but not in *male, mallet*)
mis-	wrong, bad	*mis*fit (but not in *miser, mission*)

In a very few words, the prefix *mis-* means *hating.* The most common are *misanthropist,* someone who hates all people, and *misogynist,* someone who hates women.

Copyright © 2002 by Addison Wesley Longman, Inc.

non-	not	*non*sense
retro-	backwards	*retro*active
sym-		*sym*pathetic
OR	together with,	
syn-	at the same time as	*syn*onym

Vocabulary Exercise 7.1

Using the list of prefixes above, answer the following questions.

1. What kind of voyage did Magellan make when he *circumnavigated* the globe?

   _____

   _____

2. If someone described the title character in Shakespeare's *Richard III* as a *malcontent*, what might she mean?

   _____

   _____

3. How does *intravenous* feeding differ from feeding someone with a spoon? (*ven-* means *vein*.)

   _____

   _____

4. Why might a person who is *hypercritical* be hard to live with?

   _____

   _____

5. If the *prospect* of some event is *looking forward* to it, what does it mean to think of an event in *retrospect*?

   _____

   _____

(Continued)

6. What tasks might a police chief assign to a *counterterrorist* group of officers?

   _____

   _____

7. What does an anthropologist mean when she says that two tribes have *intermarried?* _____

   _____

8. If an *extrovert* is more interested in the outside world than in his own feelings, what is an *introvert?*

   _____

   _____

9. What does a history book mean when it says that the sinking of the Titanic *antedated* the development of radar?

   _____

   _____

10. On March 21 and September 21, daylight lasts twelve hours, and so does darkness. Why then are these two days called the *equinox?* (*nox* means *night.*)

    _____

    _____

11. What did the Scoutmaster mean when he told his Scouts to *synchronize* their watches before setting off on the hike? (*chron-* means *time.*)

    _____

    _____

12. If a mayoral candidate said that taxes were a *nonissue*, what would she mean?

    _____

    _____

13. What do we mean when we say that some action *contravenes* the law?

    _____

    _____

Copyright © 2002 by Addison Wesley Longman, Inc.

(Continued)

14. Why are a headache, a stuffy nose, and a sore throat called *symptoms* of a cold?

_____

_____

15. What sorts of pranks at Halloween might be called *malicious* mischief?

_____

_____

16. If two countries have signed a *nonaggression* pact, what have they agreed upon?

_____

_____

17. What sorts of things do people who say they have *extrasensory* perception (ESP) claim to know?

_____

_____

18. What would it mean to receive a raise in pay that is *retroactive* to January 1?

_____

_____

19. If you were looking through a telescope for a small star that you know is *equidistant* from two bright stars you've already located, where would you look for the small star?

_____

_____

20. Why would her family be unhappy if a young woman's marriage was a *misalliance*?

_____

_____

Now in the following exercise, consider some prefixes that are based on the numbers in Greek and Latin.

Vocabulary Exercise 7.2

Use your understanding of the groups of words listed below on the left to guess at the *number* represented by their prefixes in italics. Then write the words next to the number on the right represented by their prefixes. In some cases, two different prefixes in two different groups of words represent the same number. One group is written in as an example. Check the table of number prefixes on the following page when you have completed this exercise.

a. *quin*tuplets, *quin*tet

b. *uni*corn, *uni*cycle, *uni*ty

c. *cent*ury, *cent*ipede, *cent*igrade

d. *oct*agon, *oct*opus, *oct*ave

e. *bi*focals, *bi*cycle, *bi*weekly

f. *quadr*angle, *quadri*lateral

g. *sept*et, *sept*uagenarian

h. *tri*angle, *tri*plets, *tri*o

i. *dec*ade

j. *sex*tuplets, *sex*tet

k. *du*al, *du*plicate, *du*et

1. _____

_____

2. _____

_____

3. _____

_____

4. _____

_____

5. _____

_____

6. _____

_____

7. _g. septet, septuagenarian_

8. _____

_____

10. _____

100._____

Copyright © 2002 by Addison Wesley Longman, Inc.

Check your answers against the complete list of number prefixes below.

Number Prefix	Meaning	English Example
uni- mono-	single, one	unicorn monologue
bi- du-	twice, two, double	bicentennial dual
tri- quadri-	three four	triple quadrilateral
pent- quin(t)-	five	Pentagon quintuplets
sext- sept- oct- dec-, deca-	six seven eight ten	sextet September October December

(Be careful with this prefix because it is very close to the much more common prefix *de-,* which has several, very different meanings.)

cent-	hundred	cent, century
mille-, milli-	thousand	millennium, millipede
demi- hemi- semi-	half	demigod hemisphere semicircle

Vocabulary Exercise 7.3

Answer the following questions, using the preceding list of numerical prefixes to figure out the meanings of the italicized words.

1. How many sides does a *quadrilateral* shape have? Name one such shape.

_____

2. How would a *demitasse* cup compare in size with a regular coffee cup?

_____

3. Why is it harder to ride a *unicycle* than a *bicycle*?

_____

(Continued)

4. The first books of the Bible are called the *Pentateuch.* How many books are there in the *Pentateuch?*

_____

5. How many musicians make up a *sextet?* What would the sextet be called if one more musician joined it?

_____

6. What part of a meter is a *millimeter?*

_____

7. How many men would a *centurion* in the ancient Roman army command?

_____

8. The *biathlon, pentathlon* and *decathlon* are all special multiple sports events in the Olympic Games. How many sports does each contain?

_____

9. How many legs does a camera *tripod* have?

_____

10. If you *bisect* a pie, how many parts will it have? (-*Sect* means *cut.*)

_____

11. How many units does a *duplex* apartment have? A *triplex* apartment?

_____

12. How many wives does a *monogamist* have? A *bigamist?*

_____

13. How many *hemispheres* does a globe representing the earth have?

_____

14. If you *quintuple* your investment of $100 in the stock market, how much money have you made?

_____

15. Why are *September, October,* and *December* not accurate names for those months in our present-day calendar?

_____

Copyright © 2002 by Addison Wesley Longman, Inc.

The last two prefixes we will look at in this chapter vary somewhat in meaning, but they are still very useful to know generally: *in-* and *un-*. The first one, *in-,* changes its spelling to match the first letter of the root to which it is attached. See the Spelling Box below.

Prefix	Two Meanings	English Examples
in-, also spelled en-, il-, im-, ir-	1. not	*in*efficient, *il*legitimate *im*mature, *ir*responsible
	2. within, inside	*in*carnation, *en*thusiasm, *il*luminate, *ir*rigation
un-	1. not	*un*likely, *un*fortunate
	2. the opposite of	*un*seat, *un*tie

Spelling Box

Before we continue, pause to examine one peculiarity of *in-:*

- It changes its spelling according to the first letter of the root it begins.

It is too difficult to say such combinations as **inlegal, *inmature, *inresponsible,* so these consonant combinations changed gradually to the more easily pronounced **double consonants** that we see in *illegal, immature,* and *irresponsible.* Once you know that this prefix in one of these variant spellings is part of a word, it will be easier for you to remember to spell the word with **double consonants.**

- Remember that *in-* + a root beginning with *l, m,* or *r* = *ill—, imm—, irr —.*

Before roots that begin with *b, p,* or *ph,* this prefix also changes to *im-* and sometimes to *em-* for the same reason: Words like **inbecile, *inpress* and **inphasis* would be too hard to pronounce, but *imbecile, impress* and *emphasis* are not. And *embarrass* and *employ* are easy to say also.

For other prefixes that also cause **double consonants,** see page 163 in Unit 4.

*The * before a word or phrase indicates that this item does not exist in regular usage.

Vocabulary Exercise 7.4

Circle the prefix in each of the following words, and say which of the prefix's two meanings it has in that word. Check the word in your dictionary if you are not sure.

EXAMPLE: undress un- means the opposite of TO DRESS

 1. inflexible_____

 2. uncertainty_____

 3. unpack_____

 4. immodest_____

 5. implant_____

 6. undecided_____

 7. irreligious_____

 8. illogical_____

 9. unfold_____

10. irrigate_____

Vocabulary Exercise 7.5

Add the prefix *in-* or *un-* to each of the following words to make other English words. Be sure you change the spelling of *in-* as required by the words it prefixes. Use your dictionary to be sure you have made existing words. Then after each word you create, say which of the two meanings of *in-* or *un-* the prefix gives to the word. Again, check your dictionary to be sure.

EXAMPLE: legal illegal il- means NOT

 1. equality_____

 2. migrate_____

 3. substantial (make two words)_____

_____

Copyright © 2002 by Addison Wesley Longman, Inc.

(Continued)

4. tangible_____

5. cover_____

6. workable_____

7. literate_____

8. pressed (make two words)_____

_____

9. touched_____

10. tangle (make two words)_____

_____

8

Suffixes with Fixed Meanings

Most suffixes in English are useful not for helping us figure out the meaning of an unfamiliar word, but only for telling us what part of speech the word is. For example, the common suffix *-tion* tells us a word is a noun: *translation, inspiration.* But a few suffixes do carry some meaning, usually brought with them from Latin or Greek. These are listed here according to the parts of speech they signify:

Suffixes	Meanings	Examples
Verb		
-fy	to make or cause _____	beauti*fy,* glori*fy,* terri*fy*
Nouns		
-ability,	ability to be or do _____	dur*ability* (ability to be durable)
-ibility		cred*ibility* (ability to be credible)
-ard, -art	one who does something too much	drunk*ard,* bragg*art*
-cide	killing, killer	homi*cide,* parri*cide*
-ee	a person who is _____ *or* a thing that is like _____	employ*ee,* goat*ee*
-er, -ar, -or, -eer, -ier, -yer, -ster	one who does _____ OR is connected with _____	employ*er,* begg*ar,* don*or,* volunt*eer,* law*yer,* young*ster*
-ification	a making or causing of _____	glor*ification,* beaut*ification*

Copyright © 2002 by Addison Wesley Longman, Inc.

Suffixes	Meanings	Examples
-ics	the art or science of _____ OR typical actions/qualities of _____	opt*ics*, phys*ics*, acrobat*ics*, characterist*ics*
-onym	name or word	syn*onym*, ant*onym*

Adjectives

-able, -ible	able to _____	dur*able*, cred*ible*
-acious	full of _____	cap*acious*, aud*acious*
-fic	making, causing _____	terri*fic*, horri*fic*
-ish, -like	like a _____	child*ish*, child*like*
-less	without	home*less*, defense*less*
-onymous	about a word or name	an*onymous*, syn*onymous*
-ose	full of _____ OR possessing the qualities of _____	verb*ose*, grandi*ose*
-ward, -wards	in the direction of _____	home*ward*, back*wards*

Vocabulary Exercise 8.1

Complete the rewriting of the sentences below by changing the italicized words to nouns ending in noun suffixes from the list above. The beginnings of these nouns are filled in for you. Use your dictionary if you are unsure how a word is spelled.

EXAMPLE: There are ten *people standing* on the bus.

There are ten <u>standees</u> on the bus.

1. In civil wars, *brothers kill brothers*. In civil wars there is fratri_____.

2. Dacron's *ability to be washed* makes it a suitable fabric to combine with cotton. Dacron's wash_____ makes it a suitable fabric to combine with cotton.

3. Stainless steel *can endure* very high temperatures, making it good for cookware. Stainless steel's dur_____ under very high temperatures makes it good for cookware.

(Continued)

4. He is *too dull* to learn physics. He is such a dull_____ he can't learn physics.

5. The baby is pretty even *without* hair. The baby is pretty even hair_____.

6. Martha Hutchins is *being trained* as a lay analyst. Martha Hutchins is a train_____ in lay analysis.

7. The author does not want his *name* used. The author wants to remain an_____.

8 & 9. The contractor is coming next week *to modify* the entrance so that it is *accessible* to the handicapped. The contractor is coming next week for the mod_____ of the entrance to improve its access_____ to the handicapped.

10. The boys aimed their homemade rocket *into the sky*. The boys aimed their homemade rocket sky_____.

Vocabulary Exercise 8.2

Figure out the meanings of the following words by using the meanings of their suffixes, prefixes, and roots. The meanings of some roots are provided in parentheses following the words. It will help you to remember the part of speech signaled by a word's suffix: verb, noun, or adjective.

1. homonym_____

2. infanticide_____

3. rectify (*rect-*, straight)_____

4. invincible (*vinc-*, to conquer)_____

5. voracious (*vora-*, to devour)_____

6. nullify (*null-*, none)_____

7. sluggard (*slug*, to walk heavily and slowly)_____

8. irascible (*ira*, anger)_____

9. patronymic (*patr-*, father)_____

10. sagacious (*sagax,* wise, intelligent)_____

Copyright © 2002 by Addison Wesley Longman, Inc.

(Continued)

11. waspish_____

12. sanctify (*sanct-*, holy)_____

13. matricide (*mater, matri-*, mother)_____

14. inscrutable (*scrut-*, to examine carefully)_____

15. pacify (*pax, pacis*, peace)_____

Vocabulary Exercise 8.3

Fill in the blanks in the following sentences with one of the words from the preceding exercise, using the contexts surrounding the blanks and the words' suffixes and roots to help you choose. No word is used more than once.

1. Rip Van Winkle's wife was always nagging and yelling at him for not being more successful. While his farm fell into ruin and his children went in rags, he would escape to his favorite inn to drink and talk with his pals. Who could blame his wife for being _____ and _____?

2. Julius Caesar was a very capable military leader and politician. But he was also a fine writer. When he took his Roman army north to fight and _____ the fierce tribes of Gaul, he recorded his experiences in *The Gallic Wars,* noted for their masterly descriptions of warfare. In his famous remark, "I came, I saw, I conquered," we see not only his _____ military career, but also his clear and simple style.

3. Many Native American tribes today have been able to _____ the misdeeds of European settlers by reclaiming land promised to them hundreds of years ago in treaties. Several tribes have then built gambling casinos on this land, reaping great profits from the _____ appetites of gamblers.

4. The Greek god Apollo _____ed a beautiful spot called Delphi high in the mountains of central Greece and set his prophetess there to speak his prophecies. People came from all over Greece to seek her sound advice and _____ counsel. But often her remarks were mysterious and _____, and the priests who cared for the holy place had to interpret them.

Vocabulary Exercise 8.4

Using what you have learned about the words in the two preceding exercises, consider the other words in italics listed next to them in Column B below. Underline the words in Column B that you think contain the same root as the word in Column A. To help you, some of the meanings of the words in Column B are provided.

EXAMPLE: sluggard: *slugabed* (someone who stays in bed past
                                  the proper time)
                            slugfest (a fight with heavy blows)
                            sluggish (lazy and slow-moving)

Column A	Column B
1. irascible:	*irate* (angry) *irrational* (without reason) *ire* (anger)
2. sagacious:	*saga* (long poem about heroes) *sage* (wise old man) *sag* (sink down)
3. voracious:	*carnivore* (a meat-eater) *vortex* (a whirlpool) *herbivore* (a plant-eater)
4. sanctify:	*sanctimony* (pretended holiness) *sanctuary* (a sacred place; a shelter) *sanguine* (of the color of blood)
5. invincible:	*convince* *vinegar* *wince* (to flinch)
6. matricide:	*maternal* (motherly) *mathematics* *matriarchy* (society in which descent is traced through mothers)
7. rectify:	*correct* *rectitude* (moral uprightness) *reckoning* (an itemized bill)

Copyright © 2002 by Addison Wesley Longman, Inc.

(Continued)

8. inscrutable: *scrutiny* (careful examination)
                      scrupulous (conscientious, moral)
                      scrutinize (to examine carefully)

9. infanticide: *infantile* (immature, childish)
                      infancy (babyhood)
                      infamy (an evil reputation)

10. pacify: *pacifist* (someone opposed to
                         conflict, especially war)
                      pacemaker (one who sets the pace;
                         an electrical device to steady
                         one's heartbeat)
                      pacifier (a nipple-shaped device for
                         babies to suck on)

Spelling Box

The noun suffix *-er*, which usually refers to people who do or are connected with something, such as *worker, winner, islander*, is sometimes spelled *-or* and occasionally spelled *-ar*, *-eer*, *-ier*, *-yer*, or *-ster*, as in *donor, beggar, volunteer, clothier, lawyer*, and *youngster*. These alternate spellings often came into English from French versions of the words, and the French in turn came from the Latin. *-Eer, -ier, -yer*, and *-ster* are easy to remember since these endings are clearly pronounced as they are spelled. But you won't get much help remembering whether to use *-er*, *-or* or *-ar* since these endings are all pronounced the same. So if you are unsure how to spell any of the words in the following exercise, make up a silly, personal way of remembering the correct suffix.

Spelling Exercise 8.1

Form a noun by adding *-er, -or, -ar, -eer, -ier, -yer*, or *-ster* to the following words. To be sure you have used the correct suffix, exchange your list with a classmate and check each other's spellings in a dictionary. For every one you misspell, devise a clever or silly way to remember the correct spelling.

(Continued)

1. credit_____

2. auction_____

3. labor_____

4. trick_____

5. lie_____

6. conquer_____

7. engine_____

8. foreign_____

9. cash_____

10. invest_____

11. finance_____

12. visit_____

13. chariot_____

14. gang_____

15. pamphlet_____

16. act_____

17. carry_____

18. New York_____

19. execute (accent the new noun on the second syllable)_____

_____

20. jury_____

Copyright © 2002 by Addison Wesley Longman, Inc.

Dictionary Exercise 8.1

Many family names that are very common in America and other English-speaking countries are *-er* words. These names, like *Baker,* once told you a person's occupation. Some of these names are listed below. Use your dictionary to find out what occupation or job each name once designated. You may need a large, unabridged dictionary for some of the oldest names.

1. Sawyer_____

2. Webster or Weber_____

3. Carter_____

4. Cooper_____

5. Brewster or Brewer_____

6. Barker_____

7. Wheeler or Wheelwright_____

8. Baxter_____

9. Cutler_____

10. Fuller or Walker_____

11. Spencer_____

12. Porter_____

13. Miller_____

14. Hopper_____

15. Parker_____

Writing Assignment 8.1

What are the roots of the name of your hometown? of the neighboring communities? of your state? Try to find out why one or some of the names were given and what they once meant by consulting dictionaries and histories of the area. For more help, ask older relatives or a local librarian about the origins and stories of the names. You may discover some interesting and amusing surprises. Share your findings with your friends and classmates by writing an essay on one or more of these names.   ■

Copyright © 2002 by Addison Wesley Longman, Inc.

Review Exercise I

Look in the words on the left for the prefixes, roots, and suffixes you have learned in this unit. Use the meanings of these word parts to match the words to the meanings in the right-hand column. Write the letters of their meanings next to the words.

1. equity _____

2. symbiosis _____

3. nonconformist _____

4. telephoto lens _____

5. phonetics _____

6. orthography _____

7. homogenized _____

8. photomicrograph _____

9. hydrophobia _____

10. pentangle _____

a. a picture taken through a microscope

b. correct spelling

c. fairness; justice

d. someone who does not act in harmony with generally accepted beliefs and practices

e. excessive fear of or aversion to water

f. thoroughly blended into one liquid

g. the living together of two dissimilar things for their mutual benefit

h. the science that studies the sounds of speech

i. a geometrical figure with five angles

j. a camera attachment allowing you to take pictures of objects at a distance

Review Exercise II

Using your knowledge of the word parts in this unit, answer the following questions about the italicized words. Wherever possible, use the meanings of the word parts in your answers.

1. Why are intelligence tests called *psychometric*?

_____

(Continued)

2. If two people who felt *antipathy* toward each other were to meet, how would you expect them to act?

   _____

3. When talking about blood pressure, which word would a doctor use to describe high blood pressure, *hypertension* or *hypotension?*

   _____

4. If someone says that astrology, that is, using the positions of stars and planets to predict a person's future, is *pseudoscience,* would you take her attitude to be a) belief, b) uncertainty, or c) disbelief?

   _____

5. If your child's teacher says that your child's behavior in class is *incorrigible,* what would you understand him to mean? (*corri-* is the same root as in *correct.*)

   _____

6. What does it mean to say that the two sides of a face are *symmetrical?*

   _____

7. You have had a heart attack, and your doctor tells you that your heart has suffered *irreversible* damage. What does he mean?

   _____

8. What does a *philologist* love?

   _____

9. How old would you expect a *centenarian* to be?

   _____

10. What might cause your refrigerator to be *malodorous?*

   _____

Copyright © 2002 by Addison Wesley Longman, Inc.

Review Exercise III

Here are some words with prefixes of unchanging meaning from Vocabulary Ex. 6.1 that you should know well enough to use yourself. Cover their meanings in the right column, and compose a sentence using each word. Use your knowledge of their prefixes to remind you of the words' meanings. After each group, uncover the meanings to see if you remembered the words correctly. If you did, you should be able to replace the word in your sentence with its meaning.

EXAMPLE: noncombatants <u>International law outlaws killing any</u> <u>NONCOMBATANTS during a war. TEST: International law outlaws killing any</u> <u>CIVILIANS during a war.</u>

Verbs

1. to circumnavigate   to sail around
2. to intermarry   to wed someone from another group
3. to antedate   to happen at an earlier time
4. to synchronize   to make (some things) operate at the same time
5. to contravene   to go against

Adjectives

1. intravenous   into a vein
2. hypercritical   too critical
3. extramarital   outside of marriage
4. retroactive   going back to a time before
5. equidistant   exactly between two points or things

Nouns

1. extrovert   an outgoing, sociable person
2. introvert   a person turned inward to his own thoughts
3. malcontent   a dissatisfied person
4. equinox   one of two days in the year when daylight and
                            darkness are equal in duration
5. prospect   a future outlook; a landscape or scene
6. retrospect   a looking back, used with *in*
7. misnomer   a wrong name
8. misalliance   an unsuitable or wrong marriage
9. symptom   a sign of illness
10. malpractice   improper or negligent treatment by a doctor

Review Exercise IV

Recall your spelling work with word pairs like *already* and *all ready* and with the various spellings of the prefix *in-*. Some of the italicized words below are spelled incorrectly. Cross out the wrong spellings, and write the correct spellings in the space provided.

1. The members of the soccer team were *already* to go when I arrived.

   _____

2. Chris says she doesn't want to handle the club's money *anymore*.

   _____

3. The umpire is supposed to be an *inpartial* judge of the players' moves in the game.

   _____

4. The little boy had been told never to let a stranger *into* the house.

   _____

5. The little boy had been told never to let a stranger come *into* the house.

   _____

6. John always acts *inmature* around girls his age.

   _____

7. The bank said I had *insufficient* funds to cover my checks.

   _____

8. Why don't you come up and visit me *sometime*?

   _____

9. For *sometime* now, I have been expecting you to visit me.

   _____

10. My handwriting is so poor that it is often *illegible*.

   _____

Copyright © 2002 by Addison Wesley Longman, Inc.

Reading 2

Russell Baker is a journalist who won a Pulitzer Prize for his humorous, satirical comments about political and social events and conditions, published as his *Observer* columns in the *New York Times*. The following reading is one of these columns.

In this unit, we have been working with word parts that can help you figure out the meanings of difficult words. In this essay, Russell Baker deliberately *misuses* difficult, Latinate words to make fun of the unnecessarily complicated language that bureaucrats in government, business, and the professions often use. He does this by "translating" a children's story into that sort of English. His version of the story is full of long words, unnecessary repetitions, gender neutral terms (like "senior citizen" for "old woman"), and jargon. The results are often ridiculous and suggest that writers should choose plainer words when these better suit their audience.

"It's a neat idea for a book, Mr. James, but there's way too many big words."

© The New Yorker Collection 1994 Danny Shanahan from cartoonbank.com. All Rights Reserved.

Your task as you read is to figure out the meanings of difficult, unfamiliar words, using both the information about word parts in this unit and any clues to the words' meanings in their contexts, as well as your knowledge of the original fairy tale. After you have understood Baker's version, "translate" it back again into English that a child could understand. Your version should also be shorter than Baker's. If you are not familiar with the story, do this exercise with a classmate who is.

Little Red Riding Hood Revisited
by Russell Baker

1   In an effort to make the classics accessible to contemporary readers, I am translating them into the modern American language. Here is the translation of "Little Red Riding Hood":

2   Once upon a point in time, a small person named Little Red Riding Hood initiated plans for the preparation, delivery and transportation of foodstuffs to her grandmother, a senior citizen residing at a place of residence in a forest of indeterminate dimension.

3   In the process of implementing this program, her incursion into the forest was in midtransportation process when it attained interface with an alleged perpetrator. This individual, a wolf, made inquiry as to the whereabouts of Little Red Riding Hood's goal as well as inferring that he was desirous of ascertaining the contents of Little Red Riding Hood's foodstuffs basket, and all that.

4   "It would be inappropriate to lie to me," the wolf said, displaying his huge jaw capability. Sensing that he was a mass of repressed hostility intertwined with acute alienation, she indicated.

5   "I see you indicating," the wolf said, "but what I don't see is whatever it is you're indicating at, you dig?"

6   Little Red Riding Hood indicated more fully, making one thing perfectly clear—to wit, it was her grandmother's residence and with a consignment of foodstuffs that her mission consisted of taking her to and with.

7   At this point in time the wolf moderated his rhetoric and proceeded to grandmother's residence. The elderly person was then subjected to the disadvantages of total consumption and transferred to residence in the perpetrator's stomach.

Copyright © 2002 by Addison Wesley Longman, Inc.

8   "That will raise the old woman's consciousness," the wolf said to himself. He was not a bad wolf, but only a victim of an oppressive society, a society that not only denied wolves' rights, but actually boasted of its capacity for keeping the wolf from the door. An interior malaise made itself manifest inside the wolf.

9   "Is that the national malaise I sense within my digestive tract?" wondered the wolf. "Or is it the old person seeking to retaliate for her consumption by telling jokes to my duodenum?" It was time to make a judgment. The time was now, the hour had struck, the body lupine cried out for decision. The wolf was up to the challenge. He took two stomach powders right away and got into bed.

10   The wolf had adopted the abdominal-distress recovery posture when Little Red Riding Hood achieved his presence.

11   "Grandmother," she said, "your ocular implements are of an extraordinary order of magnitude."

12   "The purpose of this enlarged viewing capability," said the wolf, "is to enable your image to register a more precise impression upon my sight systems."

13   "In reference to your ears," said Little Red Riding Hood, "it should be noted with the deepest respect that far from being underprivileged, their elongation and enlargement appear to qualify you for unparalleled distinction."

14   "I hear you loud and clear, kid," said the wolf, "but what about these new choppers?"

15   "If it is not inappropriate," said Little Red Riding Hood, "it might be observed that with your new masticating products you may even be able to chew taffy again."

16   This observation was followed by the adoption of an aggressive posture on the part of the wolf and the assertion that it was also possible for him, due to the high efficiency ratio of his jaw, to consume little persons, plus, as he stated, his firm determination to do so at once without delay and with all due process and propriety, notwithstanding the fact that the ingestion of one entire grandmother had already provided twice his daily recommended cholesterol intake.

17   There ensued flight by Little Red Riding Hood accompanied by pursuit in respect of the wolf and a subsequent intervention on the part of a third party, heretofore unnoted in the record.

18   Due to the firmness of the intervention, the wolf's stomach underwent ax-assisted aperture with the result that Red Riding Hood's grandmother was enabled to be removed with only minor discomfort.

19   The wolf's indigestion was immediately alleviated with such effectiveness that he signed a contract with the intervening third party to perform with grandmother in a television commercial demonstrating the swiftness of this dramatic relief for stomach discontent.

20   "I'm going to be on television," cried grandmother.

21   And they all joined her happily in crying, "What a phenomena!"

Mastery Exercises

1. "Translate" Baker's story into simple words that a child could understand. You will need to eliminate unnecessary elaborations, so your version will be much shorter than Baker's. For example, the first line of the story could be simplified this way: "Once upon a time, a little girl named Little Red Riding Hood decided to bring some goodies to her grandmother, an old woman who lived in a large forest." Also be sure to use Baker's version of the story's ending. Work with a classmate if you like.

2. Here are some complicated phrases from Baker's essay. Underline any roots, prefixes, or suffixes that you think are clues to their meanings.
    attained interface (par. 3)
    a mass of repressed hostility intertwined with acute alienation
        (par. 4)
    An interior malaise (par. 8)
    their elongation and enlargement (par. 13)
    a subsequent intervention (par. 17)
    stomach discontent (par. 19)

3. List and restate in plain English five difficult or unclear phrases from the essay that do not contain easy word-part clues to their meaning but that you could figure out because you know the original story. In these cases, the original story is the *context* that helps you understand Baker's "translation." Also say how you figured out what the phrases mean.

Copyright © 2002 by Addison Wesley Longman, Inc.

(Continued)

EXAMPLE: *displaying his huge jaw capability* opening his big mouth—
Clues: the wolf is trying to scare Red, and the words huge jaw are clear
indications of what Baker means.

_____

_____

_____

_____

_____

_____

_____

_____

_____

4. Most professions (law, medicine, etc.) and trades (electricians, computer
   programmers, etc.) have specialized vocabularies called *jargon* with
   words and word combinations that are unfamiliar to people outside
   those fields. There are also specialized vocabularies in various sports,
   games, and clubs. Baker uses among others jargon from law (*an alleged
   perpetrator*, par. 2), psychology (*a mass of repressed hostility intertwined
   with acute alienation*, par. 4), and sociology (*a victim of an oppressive
   society, a society that not only denied wolves' rights, but actually boasted of
   its capacity for keeping the wolf from the door*, par. 8).

   What specialized vocabulary from work or play whose words may be
   unfamiliar to some of your classmates do you know? If you know such a
   vocabulary, compose a brief glossary of its specialized words and
   phrases, together with their "translations" into ordinary English that
   your classmates can understand. This activity is also one that can be
   done well by a small group whose members all know the jargon you
   plan to explain. For example, three students who know a great deal
   about computers or who are skilled in karate or who know the
   parliamentary rules for conducting meetings could join together for this
   project.

Unit 2

Post-Test 1

Match the word parts on the left with their meanings on the right. Then write next to each a word containing that word part.

1. -ible _____   a. killing, killer

2. phono- _____   b. straight, right

3. sym- _____   c. without

4. -path- _____   d. the opposite of

5. -cide _____   e. all

6. retro- _____   f. to make ___

7. theo- _____   g. outside of

8. ortho- _____   h. bad

9. circum- _____   i. writing

10. -fy _____   j. one who supports government by

11. bene- _____   k. in the direction of

12. inter- _____   l. backwards

13. -less _____   m. around

14. mal- _____   n. sound, voice

15. -graph _____   o. feeling, suffering

16. -crat _____   p. between

17. extra- _____   q. together with, at the same time as

18. omni- _____   r. able to

19. un- _____   s. god

20. -ward _____   t. well, good

Copyright © 2002 by Addison Wesley Longman, Inc.

Unit 2

Post-Test 2

Using what you have learned about roots, prefixes and suffixes in this unit, underline the correct meaning of each word below.

1. ascertain:
   a) to sharpen
   b) to learn for sure
   c) to belong to as a proper part

2. retroactive:
   a) effective before a set date
   b) reflecting on the past
   c) pulling back an army

3. shortfall:
   a) Indian summer
   b) going a roundabout way
   c) failure to come up to what's needed

4. directive:
   a) the plan for performing a play
   b) a rule or regulation
   c) accurate, to the point

5. autocrat:
   a) a dictator
   b) a self-taught person
   c) a self-propelled machine

6. laggard:
   a) someone who is slow, late
   b) someone who doesn't have what is needed
   c) someone who has little to say

7. xenophobic:
   a) fearful of heights
   b) fearful of anything foreign
   c) obsessive

8. contravene:
   a) to plan, devise
   b) to speak out against
   c) to violate, go against

9. philanthropist:
   a) one who has many love affairs
   b) one who gives money to help others
   c) one who studies language

10. rectify:
    a) to make a ruin, to destroy
    b) to make miserable
    c) to make right

Unit 2

Post-Test 3

In the following words, circle any prefixes, roots, and suffixes covered in this unit. Then write their meanings in the spaces provided.

1. bifocals_____

2. infallible_____

3. monochromatic_____

4. personification_____

5. extramarital_____

6. polyphony_____

7. telescope_____

8. macroeconomics_____

9. anticlimax_____

10. synthesis_____

11. polytheist_____

12. eponymous_____

13. heterogamous_____

14. untranslatable_____

15. postmodern_____

16. pentameter_____

17. centrifugal_____

18. microbiology_____

19. orthopedics_____

20. insecticide _____

Copyright © 2002 by Addison Wesley Longman, Inc.

UNIT 3

What Help Is a Dictionary?

In this Unit, You Will Learn to Remember New Words by:

Also Spelling Tips   113

For Skills Practice, You Will Read:

Introduction: Mental Pictures and Other Memory Aids

> Create mental pictures for new words.

Have you ever been introduced to someone at a party and then half an hour later been embarrassed to find that you have forgotten the person's name? Unfortunately, unlike the White Queen in *Through the*

Looking-Glass, our memory only works in one direction. Memory experts say that it is very difficult to remember a fact, like a name or a date or a word, if it is completely isolated from any other fact. To help you remember someone's name, for example, they suggest you make an immediate connection between the name and something unusual about the person as soon as you are introduced. For example, Mary Appleton might have cheeks as red or round as apples. The same is true for learning new words. If you create your own personal *context* for a new word, that is, your own *related material,* you are much more likely to remember it later. You can create your own *context* by:

- Making an immediate connection between the word and an image in which part of the new word appears
- Remembering together words that share a prefix, root, or suffix
- Using 60 seconds in the dictionary when you look up the word to find a context

Briefly, to use the first method, you create a mental picture of the word's meaning, using a part of the word in the picture; the funnier or stranger the picture the better. For example, for the word *bellicose,* which means *warlike,* you might imagine a *bell* with two bell-ringers *warring* over which one will get to ring the bell. This method works

Copyright © 2002 by Addison Wesley Longman, Inc.

"I don't understand you," said Alice. "It's dreadfully confusing!"

"That's the effect of living backward," the Queen said kindly; "it always makes one a little giddy first—"

"Living backward!" Alice repeated in great astonishment. "I never heard of such a thing!"

"—but there's one great advantage in it, that one's memory works both ways."

"I'm sure *mine* only works one way," Alice remarked. "I can't remember things before they happen."

"It's a poor sort of memory that only works backward," the Queen remarked.

best when you can see a smaller word inside the new word, whether or not the smaller word is the longer word's root. Try this method on the following words.

Vocabulary Exercise

Think up a mental picture for remembering the following difficult words and their meanings. Build a picture around the word's meaning, putting a part of the word inside your picture. Then in the space following each word, write a phrase or sentence that describes your picture, again using the word's meaning. Suggestions for pictures follow the words, but feel free to use others.

EXAMPLE: *meander,* to wander aimlessly: <u>A winding lovers' lane for ME AND HER to wander together.</u>

1. *dearth,* a lack of (*earth?*)_____

2. *refurbish,* to make like new (*fur?*)_____

3. *bombastic,* using inflated, high-sounding language (*bomb?*)

   _____

4. *preponderance,* superiority in power, strength, amount (a *pound?*)

   _____

5. *atrophy,* a wasting away (*trophy?*)_____

6. *redoubtable,* awesome, fearsome (*table?*)_____

7. *denunciation,* an open condemnation (*nun?*)_____

8. *diatribe,* bitter, abusive criticism (*tribe?*)_____

9. *histrionic,* overly dramatic, theatrical (*hiss?*)_____

10. *polemic,* an argument, especially one that attacks an opinion (*pole?*)

    _____

But if you already know what a part of a new word means, rather than thinking up an image, it is just as easy to use the part as your context for remembering the word. For example, if you already know that *belli-* in the word *belligerent* means *war,* it is easy to remember that *bellicose* means *warlike.* In Unit 2, you practiced learning words that share word parts, and you will do more of this kind of vocabulary building in Unit 4.

The third method of remembering new words, the 60-Second Memory Aid, is the main work of this unit. You will see that a few extra seconds in the dictionary after looking up a new word can help you find a context for remembering it.

Copyright © 2002 by Addison Wesley Longman, Inc.

9

Survey Your Dictionary

If you can, for work in this unit:

Words in Focus
scrutiny
scrutinize

Use a dictionary called a *college* or *desk* dictionary.

Such a book will be hardcover, about 6 inches by 9 inches and about 3 inches thick. It will usually have thumb indentations marked with the letters of the alphabet for easy opening. Such dictionaries are more useful than pocket-sized dictionaries, which do not give all the information that you may want to know about a particular word, nor will they list as many words as you may need. These pocket-sized word books are good to carry with you to school or work to check spelling or common usage problems, but use a college dictionary for more extensive work in your home or library.

Even college dictionaries do not contain all the words in the language. The dictionaries that contain all the words are called *unabridged,* that is, not shortened. These larger dictionaries are readily available in libraries if you want to do more extended word play.

Once you have chosen a dictionary for your own use, get acquainted with it. Give it some careful *scrutiny,* that is, close examination.

Dictionary Exercise 9.1

Browse through the explanatory meaning in the introduction, and find answers to the questions below.

1. What does your dictionary use to separate the syllables of a word? Dots? Dashes? Spaces? Some other device?

   _____

2. Where in the entry for a particular word does your dictionary tell you how to pronounce it?

   _____

3. Does your dictionary put a guide to pronunciation of vowels and consonants on every page? If so, where on the page is this guide? Pick a page at random. The guide will look something like this: fat, āpe, bâre, cär, . . . or this: ă pat, ā pay, âr care, ä father, or this \a\ ash \ā\ ace \ä\ mop mar.

   _____

4. How does your dictionary tell you which syllable in a word is stressed more than the other syllables? A heavy accent mark like this ′? **Heavy black type?** Underlining? Some other device?

   _____

5. What abbreviations does your dictionary use to tell you that a word is a transitive or intransitive verb?

   _____

6. In what kind of order does a dictionary list the different meanings of a word: the most common meaning first, or the oldest meaning first?

   _____

7. Where in the entry of a particular word does the dictionary put its history, called its *etymology*?

   _____

8. What are some of the usage labels your dictionary uses for words that are appropriate only to a certain level of speech, such as slang words?

   _____

Copyright © 2002 by Addison Wesley Longman, Inc.

(Continued)

9. What are the guide words at the top of the second page of your dictionary? What are the guide words at the top of the last page of *z* words?

   _____

10. Does your dictionary have any special glossaries or guides in the back? If so, what are they?

    _____

11. Look up the word *scrutiny,* and read through your dictionary's entry for it. How many ways does it say *scrutiny* can be pronounced? Pronounce each out loud. Consult the pronunciation guide to find another word with the same *u* sound.

    _____

12. What part of speech is *scrutiny?* Look at its verb form, *scrutinize,* listed above it. What endings can *scrutinize* take?

    _____

13. How many different meanings or definitions does your dictionary give for *scrutiny?* Write out the definition that best fits its use in the following sentence: An ethics committee keeps public officials under careful *scrutiny.*

    _____

14. Does your dictionary give explanations of the differences among some words and their synonyms? For example, are any synonyms of *scrutiny* or *scrutinize* listed and explained after the definitions? If so, what are they? Or does your dictionary tell you to **see** another word like *examine?*

    _____

With a little practice, you will be able to find a word in your dictionary in 30, even 20 seconds. For the following exercise, get together with two other classmates. Your group should have two college dictionaries to use.

Dictionary Exercise 9.2

For this exercise, you need to work with two other classmates. Pretend that you and one classmate are in a contest to see who can find a word in the dictionary more quickly. The third classmate chooses a word for both of you to look up and decides who wins. Repeat three times. Then change roles till all three of you have had a chance to play the referee. Here are some words to use:

profligate, farthingale, subaltern, marmoset, lagniappe, guano, zealot, impinge, dactyl

Writing Assignment 9.1

After doing Dictionary Exercise 9.2 with your two classmates, discuss with them some tips that you would give another student for finding words in a dictionary quickly. Then write a paragraph on one tip addressed to a new student whose dictionary skills are weak. The other two students should write paragraphs on other tips. Organize your three paragraphs into one brief essay. Share it with another group of students. ■

Dictionary Exercise 9.3

Look up in your dictionary the words below to see which of the many meanings of each word is marked with a special usage label, such as *Slang, Obsolete,* or *British.* Write the label and meaning in the space after the word.

EXAMPLE: conduct (noun) <u>Obsolete meaning: a guide or escort</u>

1. crank (noun)_____

2. clout (noun)_____

3. pill (noun)_____

4. favor (noun)_____

5. guy (noun)_____

6. boot (noun)_____

Copyright © 2002 by Addison Wesley Longman, Inc.

(Continued)

7. period_____

8. bonny_____

9. slavish_____

10. nice_____

Dictionary Exercise 9.4

What advice, if any, does your dictionary give about using the following words? Summarize the advice in the lines provided.

EXAMPLE: awful <u>Though some people object to using AWFUL to mean EXCEEDINGLY GREAT, it has been used with that meaning in casual writing since the late 1700s, so it's okay in casual writing.</u>

1. irregardless

_____

2. alright

_____

3. ain't

_____

4. aggravate

_____

5. unique

_____

10

The 60-Second Memory Aid

Take a minute to give a new word a context.

Words in Focus
pathos
deference

With practice, it takes only 20 to 30 seconds to look up an unfamiliar word in a dictionary! While you have the dictionary open to the word, why not spend an extra 20 to 30 seconds looking for something besides its meaning that will help you remember it? Any information you learn about the word becomes the *context* within which you store it in your memory. The more unusual or interesting or amusing the bits of information you choose as memory aids the better. Once you have read the unfamiliar word's definition and understood it, spend a few more seconds to make a connection between that meaning and one or more of the following:

- The word's pronunciation
- The word's origins
- Memorable words in the definition
- An idiomatic expression using the word
- The word's synonyms
- The word's antonyms
- Other words with the same root
- A more familiar word on the same page

For one minute or less, you will have acquired a new word and a context for remembering it. With a few more seconds of your time, you can make the memory aids even stronger by writing them on an index card. Put the new word and the bits of information you chose to remember it by on one side and its meaning on the other. Every so often, flip through your cards, learning the meanings of the new words from the contexts you have created for them.

Copyright © 2002 by Addison Wesley Longman Publishers

Here is an extended example of how the 60-Second Memory Aid works. In the following discussion of Shakespeare's play *King Lear,* imagine that you are not sure what the italicized words mean:

> When King Lear's daughters lock him out of their houses on a cold and stormy night, Lear's "wits begin to unsettle." How could his daughters be so ungrateful? The *pathos of King Lear's condition is increased a few scenes later by the* deference *he shows to a naked madman, Tom O'Bedlam.*

In a typical college dictionary, *Merriam Webster's Collegiate Dictionary,* tenth edition, the entry for the word *pathos* looks like this:

pa . thos \ ′pā thäs, -thȯs, -thōs, *also* ′pa-\ n [Gk, suffering, experience, emotion, fr. *paschein* (aor., *pathein*), to experience, suffer; perh. akin to Lith *kȩsti* to suffer] (1591)
1 : an element in experience or in artistic representation evoking pity or compassion
2 : an emotion of sympathetic pity

You look immediately at the definitions, since it is the *meaning* of *pathos* that you need to know. Both the first and second meanings fit the description of King Lear. Ordinarily, you would at this point snap the dictionary shut and forget about *pathos.* Wait! Spend a few more seconds to put it in some memorable context.

- Look at the word's pronunciation: the first syllable is stressed and rhymes with *pay.* Perhaps you can think of other words to rhyme with *pathos.* Rhyme is a powerful memory aid.
- Look at the word's origins: *pathos* is Greek for suffering. That seems perfectly reasonable and clear, but perhaps not unusual enough to remember it by.
- Look at the word's definitions. Here you may find another word that you know better and that you could link in your memory with *pathos.* One meaning is *an emotion of sympathetic pity.* Perhaps the fact that both *pity* and *pathos* begin with *p* or that *sympathetic* contains the same root, *path-* will help you remember *pathos.* Or there may be a word in the definitions or in a list of the word's synonyms that is also unfamiliar to you, like *evoking.* Though it may seem strange, it will be easier for you to remember two new words linked together than if you learn each one in isolation.
- Look at the words defined just before and just after the word you looked up. Are any related to it in meaning or origin? *Merriam Webster's Collegiate Dictionary* lists some that are related to *pathos* in meaning, but these are also rather difficult and unusual: *pathologist, pathology,* and *-pathy.* You may prefer a more common word, such as *pathetic,* the adjective derived from *pathos.* You will also see words spelled similarly but unrelated in meaning to your word, like *pathway.* Perhaps you can

think of an unusual or amusing mental image linking one of these words to *pathos:* On the *pathway* to madness, King Lear arouses *pathos.*

Now if you look up *deference,* you would find an entry like this:

def . er . ence \ ˈde-fə-rən(t)s, ˈdef-rən(t)s\ *n* (1660) **:** respect and esteem due a superior or an elder; *also* **:** affected or ingratiating regard for another's wishes *syn* see HONOR —**in deference to :** in consideration of

Both definitions here fit the sense of the passage about King Lear. Now how can you remember the word and its meaning?

Dictionary Exercise 10.1

Using the definition for *deference* above and your own dictionary, answer the following questions. Then choose one of these bits of information to remember its meaning, or make up another memory aid that is amusing or odd.

1. The word *defer* is listed just before *deference.* Look up *defer* in your dictionary. It is really two verbs with different meanings. Which one of these verbs is related to *deference,* the first or the second? What is its meaning?

   _____

   _____

2. Which syllable of *defer* is stressed? Which syllable of *deference* is stressed?

   _____

3. Think of other words that have the same root and pronunciation pattern as *defer* and *deference* by thinking of words that rhyme with them, such as *prefer* and *preference.* Try running through the consonants in the alphabet. There are two other common pairs.

   _____

4. Look at the origins of the version of *defer* that is related to *deference.* What Latin word (or words) does it come from? How is the Latin related to the English meaning of *defer?*

   _____

   _____

Copyright © 2002 by Addison Wesley Longman, Inc.

(Continued)

5. What synonyms does your dictionary give for *deference*?

_____

6. What kind of person would *you* show *deference* to? Perhaps you can use this person as a memory aid. Would you show the same person *reverence* or *homage*, two possible synonyms for *deference*?

_____

7. What idiomatic expression or expressions are listed under *deference*? Have you ever heard it (or them) before? Write a sentence using the expression(s).

_____

The answers to one or more of the questions above could be your own memory aid for the new word. The more you practice this 60-Second Memory Aid, the easier it will become. The exercises in the rest of this unit help you try out some of these memory aids in greater detail.

Writing Assignment 10.1

Look up in your dictionary the word *mnemonic* and the name *Mnemosyne*, an ancient Greek goddess. Both come from the Greek word for *memory*. (The 60-Second Memory Aid is a *mnemonic device*.) The Greeks considered the goddess Mnemosyne to be the mother of the nine Muses, who were the patron goddesses of all the arts and sciences. In what ways is *memory* the basis (the mother) of the arts and sciences? Write an essay in which you explore the importance of memory in one or two arts and sciences. Choose those with which you are somewhat familiar.   ■

11

Using a Word's Pronunciation

Learn new words by connecting their unusual pronunciation with their meaning.

Words in Focus
interpolate
epitome

Some words are not used very much in conversation, so you may not know how to pronounce them when you run across them in your reading. For example, the verb *interpolate,* which means *to insert new material into a piece of writing,* is not pronounced like other words beginning with *inter-.* Some, like *interfere* and *interrupt,* stress the last syllable, while others, like *interview* and *interval,* stress the first syllable. But *interpolate* is pronounced *in • ter′ • po • late.* The odd stress on the second syllable is like an abrupt break in a text, which is what an *interpolation* is!

Also, the spelling of some words is rather different from their pronunciation. Thus you might not recognize such words when you come across them in your reading, even though you have heard them spoken before. For example, the spelling of *epitome,* which means *one that is the best representative of a whole class,* suggests that it ends in a silent *e* and should therefore be pronounced to rhyme with *home.* But the word has a pronunciation closer to its original Greek than to English. It is pronounced *e • pi′ • to • me* with the last *e* rhyming with *me.* To remember this word, you might create a short sentence using its unusual pronunciation: Marilyn Monroe is *to me* the *epitome* of sex appeal.

Copyright © 2002 by Addison Wesley Longman Publishers

Dictionary Exercise 11.1

Here are some words that are not often used in spoken English or that have spellings that do not seem to fit their pronunciation. They are grouped according to similarities in their sounds. Look up each in your dictionary, write it out in syllables, and circle the stressed syllable. If the word has two or more stresses, circle the syllable that gets the heaviest stress. Finally, create a short sentence to connect the word's pronunciation to its meaning, or to connect a word or words to a more familiar word with related sound and/or meaning. Some suggestions for connections you might make follow some words.

EXAMPLE: *aurora borealis,* the northern lights au • (ror)• a bor • e •(al)• is
When they were in Alaska, LAURA and ALICE saw the AURORA BOREALIS.

1. *naive,* lacking sophistication, naturally simple

   _____

2. *naivete,* the quality of being naive

   _____

3. *guerrilla,* an irregular soldier who tries to surprise the enemy (Connect to *gorilla?* to another word beginning with *gu?*)

   _____

4. *guise,* outward appearance; false appearance (Connect with *disguise* or *guerrilla?*)

   _____

   _____

5. *unanimity,* total agreement (Connect to *unanimous?*)

   _____

6. *quay,* a wharf

   _____

7. *queue,* a line of people (Connect to *quay?*)

   _____

8. *strident,* harsh and grating in sound (Connect to *strike* or *striking?*)

   _____

(Continued)

9. *wrangle,* to quarrel noisily (Connect to another word beginning with *wr-*?)

_____

_____

10. *ptomaine,* a kind of poison

_____

11. *pterodactyl,* extinct flying reptile (Connect to *ptomaine?* to another word beginning with a silent *p* like *psychology?*)

_____

12. *dichotomy,* division into two contradictory parts

_____

13. *didactic,* instructive (Connect both *di-* words to another *di-* word like *dialogue?*)

_____

_____

14. *demur,* to object

_____

15. *demure,* modest, shy; pretending shyness

_____

(Keep the sound of *demur* separate from *demure* by making a sentence contrasting them.)

_____

Copyright © 2002 by Addison Wesley Longman, Inc.

Dictionary Exercise 11.2

First, look up each of the words below in your dictionary, write it out in syllables, and circle the stressed syllable. But this time, devise your own memory aid for learning each word and its meaning. Write this aid as a phrase or sentence. Again, you might connect a word's pronunciation to its meaning, or you might pair words that share a sound or that are different in sound though similar in spelling. And once again, some words with similar or opposed sounds are listed together.

1. *precipice,* a steep cliff

   _____

2. *precipitous,* very steep; rushed, hasty

   _____

3. *hierarchy,* a group of people organized and classified by rank or authority

   _____

4. *hieroglyphics,* ancient Egyptian writing in which figures and symbols represent words

   _____

5. *heinous,* extremely wicked, abominable

   _____

6. *heir apparent,* an heir who is next in line for a title

   _____

7. *reconnoiter,* to make a preliminary survey, usually for military purposes

   _____

8. *reconnaissance,* a survey, a reconnoitering

   _____

9. *recreant,* faithless, disloyal; a faithless, disloyal person

   _____

10. *reprobate,* a morally unprincipled person

    _____

(Continued)

11. *impugn,* to oppose or attack someone as false, to criticize

_____

12. *pugnacious,* eager to fight, combative

_____

13. *paradigm,* an example or model

_____

14. *projectile,* something fired or projected forward, like a bullet

_____

15. *apocalypse,* a prophetic revelation; *cap.,* the last book of the New Testament, also known as Revelations

_____

16. *apropos,* appropriate, pertinent, relevant

_____

17. *panacea,* a cure-all

_____

18. *physiognomy,* general facial features, esp. regarded as revealing character

_____

19. *gnash,* to grind (teeth) together

_____

20. *gnome,* a fairy-tale dwarf; a maxim or moral

_____

Copyright © 2002 by Addison Wesley Longman, Inc.

Spelling Box

For some words with letters that are not pronounced or that are hard to hear, like the *c* in *muscle* and the *n* in *condemn,* pair each in your memory with a closely related word in which the silent letter IS pronounced. Pair *muscle* with *musCular* and *condemn* with *condemNation,* for example. Note

(Continued)

that in both these words and several of the following, the silent letter in a word will be pronounced when you add a suffix to it:

column	→	colum**N**ist
condemn	→	condem**N**ation
damn	→	dam**N**ation
design	→	desi**G**nate
hypocrisy	→	hypocr**I**tical
muscle	→	mus**C**ular
paradigm	→	paradi**G**matic
phlegm	→	phle**G**matic
sign	→	si**G**nature
solemn	→	solem**N**ity
strength	→	stron**G**

Writing Assignment 11.1

What should we call you? Imagine that you are writing an essay on your full name, and in the process, you decide to explain how your full name should be pronounced. In your explanation, write out your name in syllables, as your dictionary would do it. Then explain what syllable in each part of your name is stressed. Finally, explain how the parts of your name sound by offering words or syllables with which they rhyme. Save this work because you will use it later in Chapter 13. ■

12

Using a Word's History

Use a new word's unusual history to remember its meaning.

Words in Focus

etymology
carouse
manipulate

Another rich source of contexts for remembering new words is word history, called *etymology.* In a college dictionary, the history of many words can be found in square brackets following the word's pronunciation and part of speech or after all the word's definitions. (Pocket-sized dictionaries almost never give word histories.) A word's original meaning and the changes in that meaning over the centuries are often interesting, strange, and even funny. The more unusual and amusing the word's history, the easier it will be for you to remember the word.

For example, the word *carouse,* meaning *to drink heavily, to take part in a hilarious drinking party,* comes from the German words *gar aus,* meaning *completely out,* from *gar austrinken, to drink completely out, to drain a glass.* The English phrase *all out,* as in the sentence "We went *all out* for the last party," is similar in meaning and usage to the German *gar aus.* That history may be interesting enough for you to remember the meaning of *carouse.*

"Holy cow, do you always carry a dictionary?"

Copyright © 2002 by Addison Wesley Longman Publishers

Some English words are traced back to Old English, spoken from the fifth to the mid-twelfth centuries, or to Middle English, spoken from the mid-twelfth to the fifteenth centuries. Others are traced back to a word in French, Latin, Greek, or another language. A few can be traced even further back than ancient Greek, Latin, or Old English to the parent language of them all, called Indo-European. Writing did not exist for the speakers of Indo-European, so etymologists have figured out Indo-European words or roots of words from the evidence of all the languages that have developed from it. These Indo-European words and roots are marked with asterisks to show that they are educated guesses. Sometimes, only a part of a word, often its root, can be traced back farther than its other parts.

For even more information about a word's etymology than your college dictionary provides, try the *Oxford English Dictionary,* nicknamed the OED. This monumental work is thirteen volumes long and took over 70 years to compile. It is also available now on CD-ROM. Unlike other unabridged dictionaries, it lists the meanings of a word beginning with the oldest written example and date. It also provides quotations illustrating how a word has been used over the centuries.

Familiarize yourself with the kind of etymological info your dictionary provides.

Before going on to the exercise below, read through the histories of a few common words. Look up *but,* for example. Does your dictionary use the symbol < which means *comes from?* Or does it use *fr.,* the abbreviation of *from?* Or does it simply list the Middle English and then the Old English ancestors of *but?* Now look up *street.* Note that this word can be traced back all the way through Old English to Latin. Check your dictionary's list of abbreviations for the meanings of the abbreviations you find in these word histories. For example, what does *LL* mean? Or *OF?*

Dictionary Exercise 12.1

Look up the etymology of the following words. What is the oldest word and its meaning to which your dictionary traces each? What language does this old word belong to? Use an asterisk if the word is Indo-European.

EXAMPLE: maiden **maghu-, meaning YOUNGSTER in Indo-European*

(Continued)

1. strike_____

2. mail (the kind from the post office)_____

3. mail (armor, as in *coat of mail*)_____

4. library_____

5. orange_____

6. skill_____

7. paradise_____

8. silk_____

9. jade (the green stone)_____

10. ethic_____

> The vocabulary of English is extremely large and varied.

This variety is one of its most important assets. Although English, in its structure and common words, is grouped with Germanic languages (like German, Dutch, Danish), a majority of its words come from Latin, the language of the Roman Empire, and many from Latin through French, the language of the Norman Conquest of England. In addition, English freely borrows words from other languages with which its speakers come into contact and makes these words its own, as you can see below.

> English is more international than any other modern language.

Dictionary Exercise 12.2

For this exercise, work with two classmates, each of whom has a college dictionary. Each person should look up one of the words in each group of three words below. Who can find out most quickly the common language from which all three come?

EXAMPLE: moccasin, moose, tomahawk Algonquian (Native American tribe)

Copyright © 2002 by Addison Wesley Longman, Inc.

(Continued)

  1. balcony, piano, umbrella_____

  2. alligator, mosquito, vanilla_____

  3. bazaar, pajamas, shawl_____

  4. boss, cookies, etch_____

  5. genius, necessary, private_____

  6. garage, gourmet, routine_____

  7. czar, intelligentsia, mammoth_____

  8. bungalow, jungle, thug_____

  9. barbecue, hurricane, tobacco_____

 10. soy, tea, typhoon_____

 11. alcohol, algebra, coffee_____

 12. kindergarten, noodles, waltz_____

 13. amok (as in *to run amok*), bamboo, gingham_____

 14. pecan, raccoon, skunk_____

 15. ass (the animal), slogan, whiskey_____

 16. cabal, cherub, sapphire_____

 17. gesture, nerve, picture_____

 18. egg, scalp, skin_____

 19. delta, kinetic, pyramid_____

 20. chocolate, coyote, tomato_____

Writing Assignment 12.1

Pick a country or culture that has brought to the United States distinctive kinds of food and the words connected with its *cuisine* or style of cooking. Choose any cuisine with which you are very familiar. Make a list of at least 5 words for kinds of food or dishes introduced to America by immigrants from that country/culture. Then write a long paragraph praising that cuisine and explaining what kind of food or dish each word refers to and what the word itself means in the original language. You can look up the words in your

(Continued)

dictionary or go to someone more knowledgeable than you are about that culture and language to find out what the words mean.

EXAMPLE: SPAGHETTI, introduced by Italians, consists of long strings of PASTA, which is itself a PASTE or dough made of flour and water. Spaghetti is usually served with a sauce, often made with tomatoes. The word SPAGHETTI comes from SPAGO, Italian for STRING. SPAGHETTI means literally LITTLE STRINGS. ■

If you stop for a minute to make your own link between a new word's origin and its present meaning, turning etymology into a game, you will be creating a highly memorable context for the word. For example, the word *manipulate* comes from the Latin *manipulus,* meaning *a handful.* How might *manipulate* have come to mean *to handle with skill, especially in an unfair way* as in the following sentence?

The embezzler had *manipulated* the bank's books for years before he was caught.

You could make your own chain of connection with this kind of reasoning: Something you can hold in your hand (a handful) is easily controlled by your hand. Easy control can develop into skillful control—of the bank's books, for example. With enough skill, you can take advantage of others who lack your skill, like the bank's officers.

> Create a story to connect a word's origin and its current meaning.

Vocabulary Exercise 12.1

Here are some English words and meanings and the foreign words to which they can be traced. How do you think the modern English word came to have its current meaning? In the space following each pair of words, give your own explanation or story connecting the older word and its modern descendant. Use your imagination rather than your dictionary.

EXAMPLE: *obvious,* evident, easy to see *from* Latin *ob-*, against, across + *via*, way, road

If something is across the road, in your way, then you have to notice it. It's easy to see, or OBVIOUS.

Copyright © 2002 by Addison Wesley Longman, Inc.

(Continued)

1. *nonchalant,* without enthusiasm, showing a cool lack of concern *from* Latin *non,* not + *calere,* to be warm

    _____

2. *dissipated,* indulging in pleasure to excess *from* Latin, *dis-,* apart, away from + *sipare,* to throw

    _____

3. *jeopardy,* risk, danger, peril *from* French *jeu,* game + *parti,* divided—a game with even chances on both sides

    _____

4. *eccentric,* odd, peculiar, unconventional *from* Greek *ek-,* out of + *kentron,* the center

    _____

5. *insidious,* working to spread harm in a stealthy way, slyly deceitful *from* Latin *insidere,* to lie in wait for

    _____

6. *candor,* sincerity, impartiality, frankness *from* Latin *candor,* whiteness, radiance *from* Latin *candere,* to be white, shine

    _____

7. *scruple,* a feeling of doubt about what is right, a misgiving *from* Latin *scrupulus,* a small, sharp stone, as in a person's shoe

    _____

8. *lethargy,* a great lack of energy *from* Greek *lethargia,* forgetfulness *from* *Lethe,* the river of forgetfulness in the underworld

    _____

9. *manifest,* evident, obvious to the senses *from* Latin *manu* + *festus,* struck by the hand

    _____

10. *metaphor,* an implied comparison, a figure of speech in which one thing is spoken of as if it were another thing *from* Greek *meta,* over + *pherein,* to carry

    _____

Dictionary Exercise 12.3

Here are some words with unusual, strange, or even amusing histories. Look up each in your dictionary, read through its history, and then summarize it briefly in the space provided by answering these questions: (a) To what older word and its meaning can the word be traced? (b) What is one meaning of the modern word? (c) What story can you tell to connect the two meanings?

EXAMPLE: atone _Older meaning: AT + ONE, to be AS ONE, to be in harmony with. When you ATONE, you make up for some sin or wrongdoing. You make two people ONE by bringing together yourself as wrongdoer and the person you wronged._

1. supercilious

   _____

2. filibuster

   _____

3. hermit

   _____

4. ostracize

   _____

5. pavilion

   _____

6. shibboleth

   _____

7. pariah

   _____

8. meretricious

   _____

9. nostalgia

   _____

Copyright © 2002 by Addison Wesley Longman, Inc.

(Continued)

10. cynical

_____

11. chortle

_____

12. juggernaut

_____

13. boggle

_____

14. jovial

_____

15. lackadaisical

_____

16. satire

_____

17. kowtow

_____

18. tawdry

_____

19. hassle

_____

20. fulminate

_____

Writing Assignment 12.2

Review the 20 words in the preceding exercise to see which you might be able to use in the same sentence if you were writing a description or story. When you have 5 or 6 pairs, compose a sentence or two for each pair about any subjects you like in which you use the two words appropriately. For more help on a word's usage, check your dictionary again. If you like, you may use another form of a word, changing a noun to a verb, for example. Here is a sample sentence:

EXAMPLE: When Margaret first arrived in Canada from Jamaica, she felt NOSTALGIC for the warm Caribbean, but the friendliness of her JOVIAL employers helped her adjust.

■

Copyright © 2002 by Addison Wesley Longman, Inc.

13

Using a Word's Cognates

Link a new word with its cousin or *cognate*.

Words in Focus

cognate
fiasco
writhe

Another way of using a new word's origins to help you remember it is to pair it in your mind with another more familiar word that is its *cognate.* Cognates are words that can be traced back to the same older word, but they entered the language at different times or developed under different circumstances.

For example, the words *flask* and *fiasco* both come from a medieval Latin word meaning *bottle. Flask* came into English a very long time ago, perhaps during the last years of the Roman Empire. It meant *bottle* then, and it still does. The Latin word continued to be used in Italy, and it developed into *fiasco,* the modern Italian word for *bottle.* The Italian phrase *fare fiasco,* literally, *make a bottle,* was borrowed by English speakers to refer to a failure or breakdown, especially on the stage. For example, "The new musical comedy at the Arco Theater is a *fiasco.*" What's the connection between *bottle* and *breakdown?* Perhaps because a bottle breaks, a fiasco has come to mean a complete breakdown or failure. The connection between *flask* and *fiasco* can help you to remember *fiasco.*

Not all cognates have been borrowed from another language. Some cognates can develop within the same language. That is, two modern English words may come from the same Old English word. For example, the Old English verb *writhan,* meaning *to twist,* became both *writhe,* meaning *to twist or contort the body,* and *wreath,* flowers or leaves twisted into a circlet. Another example: the verb *answer* is a cognate of the verb *swear.* Both come from Old English *sweran,* meaning *to swear, assert. Swear* is the direct descendant of *sweran,* and *answer* comes through the intermediate Old English word *andswarian,* meaning *to swear against, to reply.* If your dictionary tells you at the end of its information about a word's origins to "see" another word, that other word is probably its cognate.

Dictionary Exercise 13.1

The following sets of words are cognates. Look up the less familiar, italicized word in your dictionary, and find in its etymology the older word from which this word and its cognate(s) have developed. In the space provided, (a) write this original word, the language it belongs to, and its meaning. Then (b) briefly define the italicized cognate(s) in each set. Finally, (c) compose a sentence in which you connect the italicized word(s) to its more familiar cognate.

EXAMPLE: police—*politics*
      (a) FROM Greek POLITES, CITIZEN and POLIS, CITY
      (b) POLITICS is the science or art of governing citizens.
      (c) Sometimes the POLICE department gets caught up in POLITICS.

1. gentle—*jaunty*

2. trench—*trenchant*

3. amuse—*muse* (verb)

4. sentimental—*sentient*

Copyright © 2002 by Addison Wesley Longman, Inc.

(Continued)

5. trunk—*truncated*

_____

_____

_____

6. wreck—*wreak*

_____

_____

_____

7. slack—*slake*

_____

_____

_____

8. German—*germane*

_____

_____

_____

9. jealous—*zealous*

_____

_____

_____

10. dragon—*rankle*

_____

_____

_____

(Continued)

11. increase—*accrue*

_____

_____

_____

12. enclose—*cloister*

_____

_____

_____

13. clove (the spice)—*cloy*

_____

_____

_____

14. peaceful—*pacific*

_____

_____

_____

15. punish—*punitive*

_____

_____

_____

16. flute—*flout*

_____

_____

_____

Copyright © 2002 by Addison Wesley Longman, Inc.

(Continued)

17. threat—*throes*

_____

_____

_____

18. fine (adj.)—*finesse*

_____

_____

_____

19. comrade—*camaraderie*

_____

_____

_____

20. terror—*deter*

_____

_____

_____

Dictionary Exercise 13.2

Here are more sets of cognates, but this time, both words in a set are likely to be unfamiliar to you. Look up these words, and in the space provided, write (a) a brief definition of each word and (b) the source word of both, the language this older word belongs to, and its meaning. Finally, (c) compose a sentence or two in which you connect the cognates in some memorable way, perhaps by relating them to their origins. You will be writing a small paragraph about each pair.

EXAMPLE: feign—figment To FEIGN means to pretend or to make up, invent; a FIGMENT is something made up by the imagination, as in the phrase "a FIGMENT of your imagination." Both words come from the Latin verb FINGERE,

(Continued)

meaning to form or shape. Sentence: <u>At night, the child was afraid of the</u>
<u>FIGMENTS of his imagination, like the monster under his bed, and he FEIGNED</u>
<u>sickness so his mother would stay in his room.</u>

1. opportune—importune

_____

_____

_____

_____

_____

2. venerate—venereal

_____

_____

_____

_____

3. repress—reprimand

_____

_____

_____

_____

4. undulate—redundant

_____

_____

_____

_____

Copyright © 2002 by Addison Wesley Longman, Inc.

(Continued)

5. countenance—continence

_____

_____

_____

_____

_____

6. reprisal—reprieve

_____

_____

_____

_____

_____

7. taint—tinge

_____

_____

_____

_____

_____

8. salutary—salubrious

_____

_____

_____

_____

_____

(Continued)

9. cognizance—cognition

_____

_____

_____

_____

_____

10. salient—salacious—sally

_____

_____

_____

_____

_____

Writing Assignment 13.1

What is the history of your own name, first, middle, and last? For an essay about your name, explain in one or more long paragraphs the origins of your full name. First look up your first and last names in your college dictionary, in an unabridged dictionary in the library, or in a dictionary of the language from which your name was taken. (Or speak to older relatives about your names' possible meanings.) Then write your paragraph(s) about the following, being sure to organize your thoughts in a logical way:

- What your name means in English or in the language from which it was taken
- Other names or words with which your name(s) are cognate or otherwise related
- Why you have the name you do
- Any family stories related to your name

Finally, return to the work you did for Writing Assignment 11.1 on page 114. Figure out a way of including that information on how to pronounce your name into this work on its history. ■

Copyright © 2002 by Addison Wesley Longman, Inc.

Review Exercise I

Using your knowledge of the words highlighted in this unit, answer the following questions using some of these italicized words. Wherever possible, use the meanings of the words in your answers.

1. What does it mean to put a small matter like a failing grade on an exam in a larger *context*?

   _____

2. Why might you *defer* to someone else in a class discussion?

   _____

3. If a biographer gives careful *scrutiny* to the letters written by the person he is writing about, what is he doing?

   _____

4. A movie critic has just called the latest action thriller film a *fiasco*. What does she mean?

   _____

5. What would a *mnemonic* device be good for?

   _____

6. If someone says that Fred Astaire is the *epitome* of grace, what is she saying about his dancing?

   _____

7. When a chiropractor (pronounced kī′ rō prăk tr) *manipulates* someone's spinal column, what is he doing?

   _____

8. Some friends invite you to *carouse* with them. What can you expect if you do?

   _____

9. Why would a newspaper columnist be upset if, without her knowing it, her editor *interpolated* remarks in her column?

   _____

10. In which of these track-and-field sports would you be likely to find people *writhing*? Explain. running, wrestling, long-jumping

    _____

Review Exercise II

Circle any letters in the italicized words in the questions below that are silent when the words are pronounced correctly. Then briefly answer the questions.

EXAMPLE: What are some *signs* of a coming head cold? sore throat, sneezing, runny nose

1. Why might a fire inspector *condemn* a house?

   _____

2. What sound is heard when someone *gnashes* his teeth?

   _____

3. Why might you expect to find people *wrangling* in a courtroom?

   _____

4. What would it mean if a politician campaigned under the *guise* of a reformer?

   _____

5. If a person *impugns* your integrity, what is she doing?

   _____

6. The word *phlegmatic* comes from the word *phlegm,* and can be used to describe a kind of person. What kind of person might be a *phlegmatic* man unmoved by tears?

   _____

7. What would a teacher mean if she held up a student's paper as a *paradigm* of good research methods?

   _____

8. When people in England make a *queue* at a bus stop, what are they doing?

   _____

9. If a senator is called a *redoubtable* champion of universal health care, what kind of supporter is he?

   _____

10. If a neighbor told you that he had bought some *gnomes* to put on his lawn, what would you expect to see?

    _____

Copyright © 2002 by Addison Wesley Longman, Inc.

Review Exercise III

Match the words in Column A with their cognates in Column B. Then on your own paper, write a sentence using one or both of each pair of cognates.

EXAMPLE: pacific—peaceful The PACIFIC Ocean looked very PEACEFUL the first time I saw it.

Column A	Column B
1. trunk_____	a. sally
2. enclose_____	b. redundant
3. comrade_____	c. tinge
4. undulate_____	d. truncated
5. taint_____	e. deter
6. punish_____	f. camaraderie
7. reprisal_____	g. rankle
8. salient_____	h. cloister
9. dragon_____	i. punitive
10. terror_____	j. reprieve

Review Exercise IV

How well do you remember the words with interesting etymologies that you studied in this unit? Match the words in Column A below with the meanings of the original words from which they developed.

EXAMPLE: lethargy—the Greek river of forgetfulness

Column A	Column B
1. candor_____	a. butterfly
2. meretricious_____	b. lightning
3. fulminate_____	c. a sharp stone in your shoe
4. manifest_____	d. sea shell
5. filibuster_____	e. to be white or shine
6. supercilious_____	f. thrown away
7. pavilion_____	g. prostitute
8. dissipated_____	h. struck by a hand
9. scruple_____	i. freebooter
10. ostracize_____	j. eyebrow

Reading 3

Here is a selection from *Phantoms in the Brain* by V.S.Ramachandran and Sandra Blakeslee. Dr. Ramachandran is a *neurologist,* that is, a doctor specializing in the workings of the brain and nervous system. In this book, he and his co-author discuss patients who have suffered damage to their brains that produces unusual behavior. These cases have helped Dr. Ramachandran and other researchers figure out the complex workings of the brain.

Some difficult words are in italics. You may already know or be able to figure out the meanings of many of these. Look for the following among the italicized words:

1. Technical words that the authors **define** or **restate**
2. Words you can figure out from **other clues** in their **context**

Copyright © 2002 by Addison Wesley Longman, Inc.

3. Words containing **word parts** that are clues to their meaning
4. Words you can't figure out and need to look up in a **dictionary**

   Put a check ✓ next to all the italicized words you **can** figure out.

from Phantoms in the Brain
by V.S.Ramachandran, M.D., Ph.D. and Sandra Blakeslee

1   A man wearing an enormous *bejeweled* cross dangling on a gold chain sits in my office, telling me about his conversations with God, the "real meaning" of the *cosmos* and the deeper truth behind all surface appearances. The universe is *suffused* with spiritual messages, he says, if you just allow yourself to tune in. I glance at his medical chart, noting that he has suffered from temporal *lobe* epilepsy since early adolescence, and that is when "God began talking" to him. Do his religious experiences have anything to do with his temporal lobe seizures?

2   An amateur athlete lost his arm in a motorcycle accident but continues to feel a "phantom arm" with vivid sensations of movement. He can wave the missing arm in midair, "touch" things and even reach out and "grab" a coffee cup. If I pull the cup away from him suddenly, he yelps in pain. "Ouch! I can feel it being wrenched from my fingers," he says, *wincing*.

3   A nurse developed a large blind spot in her field of vision, which is troubling enough. But to her dismay, she often sees cartoon characters *cavorting* within the blind spot itself. When she looks at me seated across from her, she sees Bugs Bunny in my lap, or Elmer Fudd, or the Road Runner. Or sometimes she sees cartoon versions of real people she's always known.

4   A schoolteacher suffered a stroke that paralyzed the left side of her body, but she insists that her left arm is *not* paralyzed. Once, when I asked her whose arm was in the bed lying next to her, she explained that the limb belonged to her brother.

5   A librarian from Philadelphia who had a different kind of stroke began to laugh uncontrollably. This went on for a full day, until she literally died laughing.

6   And then there is Arthur, a young man who sustained a terrible head injury in an automobile crash and soon afterward claimed that his father and mother had been replaced by duplicates who looked

exactly like his real parents. He recognized their faces, but they seemed odd, unfamiliar. The only way Arthur could make sense out of the situation was to assume that his parents were impostors.

7   None of these people is "crazy"; sending them to psychiatrists would be a waste of time. Rather, each of them suffers from damage to a specific part of the brain that leads to *bizarre* but highly characteristic changes in behavior. They hear voices, feel missing limbs, see things that no one else does, deny the obvious and make wild, extraordinary claims about other people and the world we all live in. Yet for the most part they are *lucid*, rational and no more insane than you or I. . . .

8   These patients, whose stories you will hear in detail, are our guides into the inner workings of the human brain—yours and mine. Far from being curiosities, these *syndromes* illustrate fundamental principles of how the normal human mind and brain work, shedding light on the nature of body image, language, laughter, dreams, depression and other *hallmarks* of human nature. Have you ever wondered why some jokes are funny and others are not, why you make an explosive sound when you laugh, why you are inclined to believe or disbelieve in God, and why you feel *erotic* sensations when someone sucks your toes? Surprisingly, we can now begin to provide scientific answers to at least some of these questions. Indeed, by studying these patients, we can even address lofty "philosophical" questions about the nature of the self: Why do you endure as one person through space and time, and what brings about the *seamless* unity of subjective experience? What does it mean to make a choice or to will an action? And more generally, how does the activity of tiny *wisps* of protoplasm in the brain lead to conscious experience?

9   Philosophers love to debate questions like these, but it's only now becoming clear that such issues can be tackled experimentally. By moving these patients out of the clinic and into the laboratory, we can conduct experiments that help reveal the deep architecture of our brains. Indeed, we can pick up where Freud left off, *ushering* in what might be called an era of experimental *epistemology* (the study of how the brain represents knowledge and belief) and *cognitive neuropsychiatry* (the *interface* between mental and physical disorders of the brain), and start experimenting on belief systems, consciousness, mind-body *interactions* and other hallmarks of human behavior.

Copyright © 2002 by Addison Wesley Longman, Inc.

10   I believe that being a medical scientist is not all that different from being a *sleuth*. In this book, I've attempted to share the sense of mystery that lies at the heart of all scientific pursuits and is especially characteristic of the *forays* we make in trying to understand our own minds. . . .

11   To help you get a feel for this way of doing science, consider these colorful cases—and the lessons drawn from them—taken from the older neurological literature.

12   More than fifty years ago a middle-aged woman walked into the clinic of Kurt Goldstein, a world-renowned neurologist with keen *diagnostic* skills. The woman appeared normal and conversed *fluently;* indeed, nothing was obviously wrong with her. But she had one extraordinary complaint—every now and then her left hand would fly up to her throat and try to strangle her. She often had to use her right hand to wrestle her left hand under control, pushing it down to her side—much like Peter Sellars portraying Dr. Strangelove. She sometimes even had to sit on the murderous hand, so intent was it on trying to end her life.

13   Not surprisingly, her primary physician decided she was mentally disturbed or hysterical and sent her to several psychiatrists for treatment. When they couldn't help, she was dispatched to Dr. Goldstein, who had a reputation for diagnosing difficult cases. After Goldstein examined her, he established to his satisfaction that she was not *psychotic,* mentally disturbed or hysterical. She had no obvious neurological *deficits* such as paralysis or exaggerated reflexes. But he soon came up with an explanation for her behavior: Like you and me, the woman had two cerebral *hemispheres,* each of which is specialized for different mental capacities and controls movement on the opposite side of the body. The two hemispheres are connected by a band of fibers called the *corpus callosum* that allows the two sides to communicate and stay "in sync." But unlike most of ours, this woman's right hemisphere (which controlled her left hand) seemed to have some *latent* suicidal tendencies—a genuine urge to kill herself. *Initially* these urges may have been held in check by "brakes"—*inhibitory* messages sent across the corpus callosum from the more rational left hemisphere. But if she had suffered, as Goldstein *surmised,* damage to the corpus callosum as the result of a stroke, that inhibition would be removed. The right side of her brain and its murderous left hand were now free to attempt to strangle her.

14   This explanation is not as far-fetched as it seems, since it's been well known for some time that the right hemisphere tends to be more emotionally *volatile* than the left. Patients who have a stroke in the left brain are often anxious, depressed or worried about their prospects for recovery. The reason seems to be that with the left brain injured, their right brain takes over and frets about everything. In contrast, people who suffer damage to the right hemisphere tend to be blissfully *indifferent* to their own predicament. The left hemisphere just doesn't get all that upset. . . .

15   When Goldstein arrived at his diagnosis, it must have seemed like science fiction. But not long after that office visit, the woman died suddenly, probably from a second stroke (no, not from strangling herself). An autopsy confirmed Goldstein's suspicions: Prior to her Strangelovian behavior, she had suffered a massive stroke in her corpus callosum, so that the left side of her brain could not "talk to" nor exert its usual control over the right side. Goldstein had unmasked the dual nature of brain function, showing that the two hemispheres are indeed specialized for different tasks. . . .

16   Sometimes a tiny brain *lesion*—damage to a mere speck of cells among millions—can produce far-reaching problems that seem *grossly* out of proportion to the size of the injury. For example, you may think that memory involves the whole brain. When I say the word "rose," it evokes all kinds of associations: perhaps images of a rose garden, the first time someone ever gave you a rose, the smell, the softness of petals, a person named Rose and so on. Even the simple *concept* of "rose" has many rich associations, suggesting that the whole brain must surely be involved in laying down every memory trace.

17   But the unfortunate story of a patient known as H.M. suggests otherwise. Because H.M. suffered from a particularly *intractable* form of epilepsy, his doctors decided to remove "sick" tissue from both sides of his brain, including two tiny seahorse-shaped structures (one on each side) called the *hippocampus,* a structure that controls the laying down of new memories. We only know this because after the surgery, H.M. could no longer form new memories, yet he could recall everything that happened before the operation. Doctors now treat the hippocampus with greater respect and would never knowingly remove it from both sides of the brain.

Copyright © 2002 by Addison Wesley Longman, Inc.

18   Although I have never worked directly with H.M., I have often seen patients with similar forms of amnesia resulting from chronic alcoholism or *hypoxia* (oxygen starvation in the brain following surgery). Talking to them is an *uncanny* experience. For example, when I greet the patient, he seems intelligent and *articulate,* talks normally and may even discuss philosophy with me. If I ask him to add or subtract, he can do so without trouble. He's not emotionally or psychologically disturbed and can discuss his family and their various activities with ease.

19   Then I excuse myself to go to the restroom. When I come back, there is not a glimmer of recognition, no hint that he's ever seen me before in his life.

20   "Do you remember who I am?"

21   "No."

22   I show him a pen. "What is this?"

23   "A fountain pen."

24   "What color is it?"

25   "It's red."

26   I put the pen under a pillow on a nearby chair and ask him, "What did I just do?"

27   He answers promptly, "You put the pen under the pillow."

28   Then I chat some more, perhaps asking about his family. One minute goes by and I ask, "I just showed you something. Do you remember what it was?"

29   He looks puzzled. "No."

30   "Do you remember that I showed you an object? Do you remember where I put it?"

31   "No." He has absolutely no recollection of my hiding the pen sixty seconds earlier.

32   Such patients are, in effect, frozen in time in the sense they remember only events that took place before the accident that injured them neurologically. They may recall their first baseball game, first date and college graduation in elaborate detail, but nothing after the injury seems to be recorded. For example, if post accident they come upon last week's newspaper, they read it every day as if it were a brand-new paper each time. They can read a detective novel again and again, each time enjoying the plot and the surprise ending. I can tell them the same joke half a dozen times, and each time I come to the punch line, they laugh heartily (actually, my graduate students do this too).

33   These patients are telling us something very important—that a tiny brain structure called the hippocampus is absolutely vital for laying down new memory traces in the brain (even though the actual memory traces are not stored in the hippocampus). They illustrate the power of the *modular* approach: In helping narrow the scope of inquiry, if you want to understand memory, look at the hippocampus. And yet, as we shall see, studying the hippocampus alone will never explain all aspects of memory. To understand how memories are retrieved at a moment's notice, how they are edited, *pigeonholed* (sometimes even censored!), we need to look at how the hippocampus *interacts* with other brain structures such as the frontal lobes, the *limbic system* (concerned with emotions) and the structures in the brain stem which allow you to attend selectively to specific memories. . . .

34   These historical examples and case studies *gleaned* from my notes support the view that specialized *circuits* or *modules* do exist, and we shall encounter several additional examples in this book. But other equally interesting questions remain and we'll explore them as well. How do the modules actually work and how do they "talk to" each other to generate conscious experience? To what extent is all this *intricate circuitry* in the brain *innately* specified by your genes or to what extent is it acquired gradually as a result of your early experiences, as an infant interacts with the world? (This is the ancient "nature versus nurture" debate, which has been going on for hundreds of years, yet we have barely scratched the surface in *formulating* an answer.) Even if certain circuits are *hard-wired* from birth, does it follow that they cannot be altered? How much of the adult brain is *modifiable?*

Copyright © 2002 by Addison Wesley Longman, Inc.

Mastery Exercises

1. The reading contains several examples of technical words whose meaning is given in definitions or restatements, for example, the two in par. 9. Among the other *underlined* words, find three that are defined in the text, and write them here.

   _____

   _____

2. The meanings of several *underlined* words can be at least partly figured out because examples are given to illustrate what they mean, or other simpler words describe them, or a demonstrative like "these" and "that" points to their meaning. For example, *bizarre* in par. 7 is illustrated by the actions in the sentence following it. Write in this space two examples of any other *underlined* words that are explained by examples, descriptions, or demonstratives pointing to their meaning. Next to each, write what you think it means.

   _____

   _____

3. Several *underlined* words contain roots, prefixes, or suffixes we examined in Unit 2 as definite clues to a word's meaning. Write five of them here.

   _____

   _____

4. List below 10 of the *underlined* words whose meanings you do not know or cannot figure out from any clues inside the words or in their context. Look them up in your dictionary, write a brief definition next to each, and then find a memory aid for the word in its pronunciation, its history, or its cognates. For example, the pronunciation of "latent" (par. 13) as "lā-tint" may be memorable; "hallmarks" has an interesting history, and "erotic" is related to "Eros," Greek god of love.

   _____

   _____

   _____

(Continued)

_____

_____

_____

_____

_____

_____

_____

_____

5. In a brief paragraph, summarize, in your own words as much as possible, the reasons why Dr. Ramachandran studies people who have had brain injuries.

_____

_____

_____

_____

_____

_____

_____

_____

_____

_____

Copyright © 2002 by Addison Wesley Longman, Inc.

Unit 3

Post-Test 1

Circle the syllable in each of the following words in Column A that is stressed when the word is pronounced correctly. Then match the word to its meaning in Column B.

Column A	Column B
1. precipitous_____	a. appropriate, pertinent, relevant
2. unanimity_____	b. a prophetic revelation
3. apropos_____	c. a cure-all
4. reconnoiter_____	d. very steep; rushed, hasty
5. naive_____	e. to make a preliminary survey
6. apocalypse_____	f. eager to fight, combative
7. panacea_____	g. a morally unprincipled person
8. precipice_____	h. unsophisticated
9. pugnacious_____	i. total agreement
10. reprobate_____	j. a steep cliff

Unit 3

Post-Test 2

How many of the following adjectives in Column A, all words that were highlighted in this unit, do you now know? Match each with its meaning in Column B. Then write sentences using five of the adjectives and describing a person. Here is the beginning of such a sentence to get you started: A_____ person is/would. . . .

EXAMPLE: dissipated: indulging in pleasure to excess <u>A DISSIPATED person</u> <u>would spend his time enjoying himself in sensual pleasures, not working or caring</u> <u>about others.</u>

1. nonchalant_____   a. peace-loving

2. eccentric_____   b. doubting, sneering at others'
                                    sincerity

3. bellicose_____   c. showing a cool lack of concern

4. cynical_____   d. odd, peculiar, unconventional

5. lackadaisical_____   e. passionately pursuing something

6. jovial_____   f. warlike, combative

7. insidious_____   g. modest, shy

8. pacific_____   h. slyly deceitful

9. zealous_____   i. good-humored, jolly

10. demure_____   j. lacking energy, spirit

_____

_____

_____

_____

_____

_____

Copyright © 2002 by Addison Wesley Longman, Inc.

Unit 3

Post-Test 3

Below are some phrases and idioms using some of the highlighted words in this unit. Explain the meaning of each by using it in a sentence in the space provided.

EXAMPLE: a *trenchant* remark <u>After the prosecutor's TRENCHANT remark about the defendant's alibi, the defendant agreed to accept a plea bargain.</u>

1. in the *throes* of a divorce

   _____

   _____

2. *flout* the law

   _____

   _____

3. a *venereal* disease

   _____

   _____

4. a severe *reprimand*

   _____

   _____

5. benefits that will *accrue*

   _____

   _____

6. an argument that is *germane* to the issue

   _____

   _____

7. to *slake* your thirst

   _____

   _____

(Continued)

8. to *wreak* havoc

   _____

   _____

9. a *jaunty* tune

   _____

   _____

10. a *cloying* scent

   _____

   _____

11. an *opportune* moment

   _____

   _____

12. *punitive* measures

   _____

   _____

Copyright © 2002 by Addison Wesley Longman, Inc.

UNIT 4

Playing with Word Parts

In this Unit, You Will Learn to Create Families of Related Words with:

You Will also Learn to Use Suffixes to:

For Skills Practice, You Will Read:

Introduction: Creating Word Families

As you have seen in earlier units, word parts are useful for figuring out and remembering unfamiliar words. But roots, prefixes, and suffixes can be useful in building an active vocabulary in another way. Once you have learned one new word, you can often use it to build around it a whole family of words, all resembling one another. A single word can thus help you learn many others.

We started to create such a family of words in Chapter 10 around *pathos*, based on the Greek root *path-*, feeling, suffering. We could add more members to this family by using this root and the prefixes in Chapter 7 and suffixes in this unit:

feeling with (someone)	*without feeling*	*feeling inside for (someone)*
sym- + *pathetic* = *sympathetic*	*a-* + *pathetic* = *apathetic*	*in-* + *pathetic* = *empathetic*
sym- + *-pathy* = *sympathy*	*a-* + *-pathy* = *apathy*	*in-* + *-pathy* = *empathy*
sym- + *-pathize* = *sympathize*		*in-* + *-pathize* = *empathize*

Learning these words as a family with a common root meaning and spelling gives you a very rich context for remembering them. In this unit, you will be creating other word families in the same way.

"No, wait a minute. I'm King. You're Rex."

© The New Yorker Collection 1990 Warren Miller from cartoonbank.com. All Rights Reserved.

Copyright © 2002 by Addison Wesley Longman, Inc.

14

Common Latin Roots

More than half the words in English come, one way or another, from Latin. And because many of these Latinate words appear more often in writing or formal speech than in everyday talk, they are often less familiar. They are "fancy," while the purely English words are "plain." For example, to describe a person we know, we might use the purely English word *fat*, but in writing, we might use the fancier Latinate word *corpulent* or *rotund*. Here are a few other plain and fancy alternatives:

Word in Focus
Latinate

Plain English	*Latinate English*
to breathe	to respire
live or die	exist or expire
roundabout way	circuitous route
dogs and cats	canines and felines
a loving husband	an amorous spouse

The roots in this chapter are all Latin in origin. But unlike the roots in Chapter 6, the original meanings of these roots are not always obvious in the English words that contain them. Why learn them, then?

- Learning Latin roots will give you a sense of control over the Latinate words you find in your reading.

Once you learn the meaning of a new word containing one of these Latin roots,

- You can use the root to remember that meaning.
- You can build a whole family of words that contain the same root and use their similarities as a memory aid.
- You will be better able to understand the subtle differences among synonyms so that you will know when to use *corpulent* or *rotund,* for example, instead of *fat*.

Vocabulary Exercise 14.1

In the space on the right, explain how the meaning of the common Latin root of the following groups of words can be seen in the current meaning of each word in the group. That is, make up a connection between the two. You may need to use your knowledge of prefixes and other roots from Unit 2. Try to use the meaning of the Latin roots in your explanations. Brief definitions of less familiar words are provided. Use the root and the other words in the group as memory aids for learning the new words as you go along.

EXAMPLE: *sati(s)-*,   1. satisfy <u>to fulfill someone's wishes or to be enough</u>

enough   2. satiate: <u>to satisfy an appetite fully, to feed an appetite more than enough</u>

-dic(t)-
say, tell

1. diction_____

2. prediction_____

3. dictator_____

4. dictum: a strong opinion_____

_____

5. benediction: a blessing_____

_____

-pung-; -punct-
to prick;
a point, dot

6. pungent: sharply painful (odors)_____

_____

7. punctual_____

8. punctuation_____

9. punctilious: very careful about behavior and manners

_____

10. compunction: uneasiness caused by guilt

_____

-anim(a)-
mind, spirit

11. animation_____

12. animosity: active hatred_____

_____

Copyright © 2002 by Addison Wesley Longman, Inc.

(Continued)

13. equanimity: composure, an even temper

_____

14. magnanimous: generous and forgiving (*magn-* = large)

_____

15. pusillanimous: cowardly (*pusill-* = very small)

_____

-fide-
faith; to trust, rely on

16. confide_____

17. fidelity: faithfulness

_____

18. infidel: an unbeliever

_____

19. diffidence: shyness, timidity

_____

20. fiduciary: held in trust

_____

domest-, domin-
house, head of house

21. domestic_____

22. dominate_____

23. domineering_____

24. domicile: residence

_____

25. dominion: a self-governing country

_____

Vocabulary Exercise 14.2

Here are some more Latin roots and some English words that contain them. This time, in addition to writing a brief phrase explaining how each word's root meaning can still be seen in its current meaning, think of 2–3 other

(Continued)

words you know that contain the same root. Write these in the spaces following each group. Think of words that rhyme or that are longer versions of the words in the list. Once again, use your knowledge of prefixes and other roots from Unit 2. And once again, use the root and other words in a group as memory aids for learning the new words as you go along.

EXAMPLE: *-cor(d)-*   record: <u>something that is a record can be thought</u>
heart, mind <u>over in your mind—other words are recording,</u>
<u>recorder, discord</u>

-spect-
see, look at

1. spectacle_____

2. specter: a ghost_____

3. perspective_____

4. prospects_____

5. circumspect: careful_____

_____

_____

-scrib(e)-, -script-
write, written

6. scribble_____

7. scripture_____

8. postscript_____

9. circumscribe: to enclose, restrict

_____

_____

10. conscription: a drafting of people into an army

_____

_____

-grad(e), -gress
step, walk, go

11. graduate_____

12. degrade_____

13. retrograde: retreating_____

_____

Copyright © 2002 by Addison Wesley Longman, Inc.

(Continued)

14. digress: wander off the subject

   _____

15. transgression: a sin

   _____

   _____

   _____

-man(u)-
hand

16. maneuver_____

17. manufacture_____

18. manure_____

19. manage_____

20. manifest: v., to show; adj., easy to see

   _____

   _____

   _____

   _____

-mand-, -mend-
literally, to give into
someone's hands;
to entrust, order

21. command_____

22. demand_____

23. commend: mention favorably_____

   _____

24. mandate: an order

   _____

25. mandatory: compulsory

   _____

   _____

   _____

Dictionary Exercise 14.1

Each group of words below, arranged alphabetically, should appear on the same page or two of your dictionary, either preceding or following the italicized word. Look up each italicized word to find out which of the other words in its group *begins* with the *same* root. Underline those that do. Then write the common root and its meaning in the blank. You will have to look at the definition and origin of each word to determine its root. Often, you will find that words containing the same root sound similar too.

EXAMPLE: *problematic*—probe, <u>problem</u> <u>problematical</u> Greek-PROBLEMA, obstacle (Note that the *o* in *probe* is pronounced ō, while the *o* in the others is ä.)

1. *jocular*—jockey, jocose, jocularity, jodhpurs

   _____

2. *patent*—pate, paten, patency, paternal

   _____

3. *inviolate*—inviolable, inviolacy, invisible, invocation

   _____

4. *guile*—guild, guileless, guillotine, guilt

   _____

5. *designee*—design, designate, designation, designing

   _____

6. *conglomerate*—congest, congestion, conglomeration, conglutinate

   _____

7. *necromancy*—necrology, necrophilia, necrosis, necropolis

   _____

8. *maxim*—maxilla, maximum, maximize, maxwell

   _____

9. *languid*—language, languish, languor, languorous

   _____

Copyright © 2002 by Addison Wesley Longman, Inc.

(Continued)

10. *fumigate*—fumble, fume, fumigation, funambulist

_____

Dictionary Exercise 14.2

Here are some common English words followed by Latinate synonyms and their Latin roots. Use your dictionary to look up the synonyms for two purposes:

1. Examine the definitions, examples, and usage notes to figure out the differences between the synonyms: When might we use one instead of another? Then following your dictionary's advice about usage, write a sentence using each synonym.

2. Write down any other words you see in the dictionary that contain the same root as each synonym.

EXAMPLE: Synonyms for *weak:*

infirm (from *infirm-*, not firm, strong)
This part of the hospital is for elderly, infirm patients. Other words: infirmity, infirmary.

decrepit (from *decrep-*, cracked, broken down)
The rocking chair I saw at the yard sale is really decrepit. Other words: decrepitude.

Synonyms for *talkative* or *wordy:*

1. verbose (from *verb-*, word)

_____

2. loquacious (from *loqui-*, to speak)

_____

3. garrulous (from *garri-*, to chatter)

_____

4. voluble (from *volv-*, *volu-*, to turn)

_____

(Continued)

5. effusive (from *effus-*, poured out)

_____

6. prolix (from *prolixus*, poured forth)

_____

Synonyms for *fat:*

7. corpulent (from *corp-*, body)

_____

8. rotund (from *rotund-*, round)

_____

9. obese (*obedere*, to eat away)

_____

10. portly (from *port-*, to carry)

_____

Writing Assignment 14.1

Explore for yourself the flexibility of English by looking at the various meanings that a common word, like the noun *root*, has acquired over the centuries. Look up this noun in your dictionary, and make a brief list of its meanings, starting with the most basic, *the underground portion of a plant.* Then write a few paragraphs explaining how you think the other meanings developed out of this basic meaning. Consider a fellow classmate as your reader. Group together the meanings that seem to belong together, and vary your sentence openings to keep your reader's interest. ■

Copyright © 2002 by Addison Wesley Longman, Inc.

Vocabulary Exercise 14.3

How many of the Latin roots in this chapter can you remember? Without looking back, jot down the meaning of each root below and give two English words derived from it.

1. -spect-_____

2. corp-_____

3. -scrib(e)-, -script-_____

4. man(u)-_____

5. -dic(t)-_____

6. -fide-_____

7. -pung-, -punct-_____

8. -verb-_____

9. -mand-, -mend-_____

10. -grad-, -gress_____

11. -anim(a)-_____

12. -cord-_____

13. satis-_____

14. domest-, domin-_____

Vocabulary Exercise 14.4

Now see how many of the following Latinate words you remember from this chapter. Briefly define each word, using the meaning of its root if you can.

1. verbose_____

2. transgression_____

3. perspective_____

4. diffidence_____

5. equanimity_____

(Continued)

6. animosity_____

7. dictum_____

8. punctilious_____

9. retrograde_____

10. circumscribe_____

11. circumspect_____

12. mandate_____

13. effusive_____

14. domicile_____

15. manifest_____

16. satiate_____

17. infidel_____

18. benediction_____

19. compunction_____

20. decrepit_____

Copyright © 2002 by Addison Wesley Longman, Inc.

15

Common Prefixes

Words in Focus
allude
elude
abject

Before we go on to more work with roots, it will be helpful to study the common Latin prefixes that appear in many words with Latin origins, like those in the last chapter. We discussed in Chapter 7 prefixes that have one unvarying meaning no matter where they appear (*mono-* = *one,* for example). But the common prefixes in this chapter come with several warnings:

- They often have *several* meanings, not one.
- It is often *difficult to recognize* these meanings because words containing the prefixes have changed so much over the years.
- The prefixes often have several *different* spellings.

But if you are willing to use your dictionary now and then, some knowledge of these prefixes can be helpful because:

- You can see how Latinate words are *put together*—prefix + root + suffix— and how the Latin meanings of these word parts have contributed to current meanings, thus helping you remember a new word.
- When you can take a word apart, prefix, root, suffix, you can also build for yourself *a family of words,* all containing the same root but with different prefixes before it and different suffixes after it.
- This knowledge of prefixes can help your spelling, for many of the words containing them have *double consonants* because of them.
- Knowing the different prefixes and their general meanings can help you *distinguish* between similar English words.

For example, can you distinguish between *allude* and *elude?* They share the Latin root *-lude,* meaning *playing, mocking,* but their prefixes are different. *Allude* comes from *ad-, to,* so if you *allude to* something, you make an indirect reference *to* it. But *elude* comes from *ex-, away from,* and the original Latin meant to take *away from* someone at play, so if you *elude* others, you have escaped *from* them through trickery. Also, there are two *l*'s in *allude* because *ad-* + *lude* = *allude,* but only one in *elude* because the prefix *ex-* drops the *x* before an *l*. (See the Spelling Box on page 163.)

Or suppose you look up *abject,* a word that is new to you. The dictionary tells you that *abject* means *miserable, wretched: ab-* is a prefix meaning *down, away,* while *-ject* comes from the Latin *jacere,* meaning *to throw.* Thus as a memory aid, you could say that someone who is *abject* (miserable) is *thrown down.* With this root and a knowledge of common prefixes, you can also create a whole family of words. Read through the following list of common prefixes, making words you already know by combining some with *-ject,* as in *abject.* Included are two prefixes from Unit 2, *in-* and *inter-,* because they are so frequently joined to Latin roots. (Check your list of *-ject* words against the one after the list, page 162.)

Prefixes and their Various Spellings	*Broad Meaning*	*Examples*
ab-, abs-, a-	away from, down	abject, abstract, aversion
ad-, ac-, af-, ag-, al-, an-, ap-, ar-, as-, at-	to, toward, near	adjoin, accept, affair, aggravate, allure, annihilate, approve, arrive, associate, attain
com-, con-, col-, cor-, co-	with, together	combine, commute, companion, conduct, collect, correct, cooperate
de-	away from; down; entirely; OR the opposite of	deceive, decline, defunct, defrost
dis-, di-	away from; not; OR the opposite of	dismiss, dishonest, disunity, divide, divert
ex-, ec-, ef-, es-, e-	out of, from; forth; beyond; away from	expel, excess, eccentric, effect, escape, elect
in-, im-, il-, ir-,	in, into; OR not	infer, immigrate illegible, irresponsible
inter-	among, between, together with	interchange, interact
ob-, oc-, of-, op-, o-	toward; before; against; upon; OR entirely	obtain, obscure, occur, offer, oppose, omit

Copyright © 2002 by Addison Wesley Longman, Inc.

Prefixes and their Various Spellings	Broad Meaning	Examples
per-	through; OR thoroughly	perceive, persuade
post-	after; later; OR behind	postgraduate, postscript, postnasal
pre-	before, in front of	presuppose, precedent
pro-	before, ahead of; on behalf of; OR favoring	progress, pronoun, prolabor
re-	back; again; anew	repay, reassign
sub-, suc-, suf-, sug-, sum-, sup-, sur-, sus-	under; lower; less than; OR forming part of	subdivision, succeed, suffer, suggest, summon, support, surrogate, suspend, sustain
trans-	across; over; through;	transact, transcend, transport

Words with *-ject*

You can form these words, mostly verbs, by combining *-ject* with some of these prefixes:

dejected, literally, *thrown down;* now means *depressed, sad* (not as sad as *abject*)

eject, lit., *to throw out*

inject, lit., *to throw into;* now means *to introduce,* OR *force into the skin*

interject, lit., *to throw between,* that is, *to interrupt*

object, with the stress on the second syllable, a verb meaning *to oppose* (lit., *to throw against);* with the stress on the first syllable, it is a noun meaning *thing*

project, lit., *to throw forward;* with the stress on the second syllable, it is a verb; with the stress on the first syllable, it is a noun meaning a *plan or scheme*

reject, lit., *to throw back*

subject, with the stress on the second syllable, a verb meaning *to bring under someone's control* (lit., *to throw under);* with the stress on the first syllable, it is a noun, one of whose meanings is *someone under another's control*

Spelling Box

Before we continue, pause to examine one peculiarity of some of these prefixes:

- They change their spelling according to the first letter of the root they begin.

We already noted this peculiarity for the prefix *in-* in Chapter 7. Another example from the list above is the prefix *ad-*. The original Latin of *affect* would have been *ad-* + *facere*, but the combination of *-d* and *-f* (**adfacere*) is very hard to pronounce, and over time, the *-d* changed to *-f*. The same change to a **double consonant** for easier pronunciation of *ad-* occurred with many other consonants, *c, g, l, n, p, r, s,* and *t,* as noted in the various spellings for *ad-* in the list on page 161 above.

The same change to a **double consonant** occurred with the prefixes *com-, ex-, in-, ob-,* and *sub-:*

> *com-* + *duct* = co**N**duct
> *ex-* + *centric* = e**C**centric
> *in-* + *migrate* = i**M**migrate
> *ob-* + *pose* = o**P**pose
> *sub-* + *gest* = su**G**gest

This spelling peculiarity will be a great help to you in learning to spell many words containing these prefixes, for they often **double the consonants,** the first for the prefix, the second for the root: *accumulate* has two *c*'s, one for the prefix, the other for the root. There are exceptions (for example, *ex-* does not always change to *ec-* when a root starts with *c*, as in *excess, except, excel*). So it is best to learn to spell a hard word from the dictionary and then to use the prefix only as a memory aid.

Copyright © 2002 by Addison Wesley Longman, Inc.

Spelling Exercise 15.1

Here are some words that are often misspelled. What prefix does each word contain to explain its double consonants? Circle the prefix as it appears in the word. Use your dictionary if you need help.

EXAMPLE: (ac)cumulate

1. accustomed
2. sufficient
3. committee
4. occasion
5. appearance
6. irresistible
7. efficient
8. supplement
9. oppression
10. illiterate

Vocabulary Exercise 15.1

Form words by combining each set of prefixes and roots below. All the words you will create have double consonants, as explained in the Spelling Box above.

EXAMPLE: com- + lateral = _collateral_

1. in + mature = _____

2. com- + rection = _____

3. ex- + face = _____

4. ad- + surance = _____

5. ob- + cupation = _____

6. in- + lusion = _____

7. sub- + plant = _____

8. ad- + lusion = _____

9. com- + loquial = _____

10. ob- + portunity = _____

Dictionary Exercise 15.1

Look up the following words in your dictionary. What is the origin of each word that explains the spelling of the underlined consonants?

EXAMPLES: 1.   i<u>mm</u>igrate _This word comes from the prefix IN- and the word MIGRATE._

2.   i<u>m</u>agine _This word comes from the Latin IMAGO, which has no prefix._

1. i<u>r</u>idescent _____

_____

2. a<u>pp</u>aratus _____

_____

3. co<u>ll</u>eague _____

_____

4. co<u>l</u>ony _____

_____

5. e<u>c</u>onomy _____

_____

6. su<u>cc</u>umb _____

_____

7. a<u>c</u>ademy _____

_____

8. a<u>cc</u>omplish _____

_____

9. o<u>p</u>eration _____

_____

10. o<u>pp</u>osite _____

_____

Copyright © 2002 by Addison Wesley Longman, Inc.

Spelling Box

You can remember the difference between some commonly confused words if you pay attention to their prefixes and their meanings. For example, *access*, meaning *a way of approaching*, comes from *ad-, to, toward* + *cedere, to go*. So an *access* road is one *going to* a place. But *excess*, meaning *a quantity that is more than enough*, comes from Latin *ex-, out of, beyond* + *cedere, to go*. Something that is an *excess*, or *excessive*, goes beyond what is necessary. In the same way, you can distinguish *accept* from *except*, and *accede* from *exceed*.

Dictionary Exercise 15.2

In the following pairs of confusing words, how do the meanings of their prefixes help you distinguish one from the other? Look them up in your dictionary, and write a brief explanation of their differences, following the example in the Spelling Box above.

1. allusion—illusion

   _____

2. elicit—illicit

   _____

3. descent—dissent

   _____

4. eminent—imminent

   _____

5. precede—proceed

   _____

6. persecute—prosecute

   _____

7. amused—bemused

   _____

(Continued)

8. disinterested—uninterested

_____

9. & 10. assure—ensure—insure

_____

_____

Dictionary Exercise 15.3

Using the explanations you wrote in the preceding exercise, underline the correct word in parentheses for each sentence below.

1. I recognized the (allusions, illusions) to Shakespeare's play *Hamlet* in the Steve Martin film *LA Story*.

2. The quiz show host tried to (elicit, illicit) tension from the contestant by stressing how much money she could win.

3. Some Americans claim (descent, dissent) from the Puritans who came to America on the Mayflower in 1620.

4. The local people think that this nuclear power plant is in (eminent, imminent) danger of leaking radioactive gases into the atmosphere.

5. The judge told the defense attorney to (precede, proceed) with his cross-examination.

6. It is difficult to (persecute, prosecute) a defendant for murder when the body of the murder victim has not been found.

7. The party-goers were so (amused, bemused) with alcohol that they didn't hear the doorbell ringing and ringing.

8. Former President Jimmy Carter has often been invited to developing countries as a/an (disinterested, uninterested) observer of their first elections.

9. I often buy generic drugs if my pharmacist (assures, insures) me that they are just as effective as name brands.

10. Those people living in the floodplain of the river find it almost impossible to (ensure, insure) their homes against flood damage.

Copyright © 2002 by Addison Wesley Longman, Inc.

Now that you have practiced using the prefixes that change their spelling, let's return to our work with the full list of prefixes and some roots to which they are attached.

Vocabulary Exercise 15.2

Make words (mostly verbs) by combining each of the following roots with any of the prefixes on pages 161–162. Write down only those words that you are certain exist. Check your dictionary for words about which you are unsure. In some cases, a few less familiar words have been provided for you. The number following each root tells you how many words you can make all together with that root and the prefixes. Learn the meaning of each root as you go along.

EXAMPLE: -lay (to lay, leave, let) 4 *allay, delay, inlay, relay*

1. -mit (send) 8 _____

   _____

   (Yes, make a word with *re-;* also, *ex-* and *ob-* drop their consonants with this root.)

2. -duct (lead, led) 4 _____

   _____

3. -fer or -fere (bring) 10 _____

   _____

   _____ (What two prefixes begin the word *proffer?*)

4. -port (carry) 8 _____

   _____

   _____ (Yes, you can make words with *com-* and *dis-*.)

5. -pel (push) 6 _____

   _____ (Yes, you can make a word with *re-*.)

6. -tain (hold) 8 _____

   _____

(The *i* in *inter-* changes to *e* here.)

(Continued)

7. -claim (cry out, call) 6 _____

_____

(Yes, you can make words with both *de-* and *dis-*.)

8. -sist (set, stand) 8 _____

_____

(After the *x* in *ex-*, drop the first *s* in *-sist;* you can also make a word with *sub-*.)

9. -struct (build) 4 _____

10. -cept, -ceive (take) 5 with -cept, and 4 with -ceive _____

_____

_____ (Make 2 words with *con-* and one with *pre-*.)

Vocabulary Exercise 15.3

Here are some sentences containing some of the less familiar words you formed in Vocabulary Exercises 15.1 and 15.2. Use the context in which each word appears and its root and prefix to guess at the word's meaning. Write your guess in the space after the sentence. You will be working with these words in the next chapter, so don't worry if your guesses here are not totally on target.

1. The bill from the moving company asked us to *remit* payment to their Boston office.

_____

2. After my quarrel with the company over an error in my bill, the manager *proffered* me an apology.

_____

3. After the party for my son's fifth birthday, Mandy's parents wanted to know how she had *comported* herself. I was too embarrassed to tell them that she had caused a minor riot over some cupcakes.

_____

Copyright © 2002 by Addison Wesley Longman, Inc.

(Continued)

4. Over the centuries, the elements—rain, wind, air pollution—have *effaced* the details from the Parthenon, the famous temple to Athena in Athens. But its awesome design and structure can still be appreciated.

   _____

5. Snakes *repel* many people because they are thought to be slimy and dangerous.

   _____

6. The union members voted against the officers who had misspent the union's funds and *supplanted* them with the two men who had uncovered the fraud.

   _____

7. Wherever they went in the week after they returned from their triumph in the Final Four, the basketball players were greeted with great *acclaim*. Everyone in the state seemed to know and honor them.

   _____

8. Polonius, the king's councilor in *Hamlet*, gives his son some wise *precepts* to guide his behavior when he goes away to Paris.

   _____

9. The substance heparin can dissolve blood clots that might otherwise *obstruct* the flow of blood through the veins and arteries.

   _____

10. There is a difference between the *colloquial* language you use when writing a letter to a friend and the more formal language you use in a research paper.

   _____

11. The Greek orator Demosthenes used to walk along the seashore, his mouth full of pebbles, *declaiming* speeches over the roar of the waves.

   _____

12. A cell phone *emits* a radio signal when you turn it on and dial a number. This signal is then relayed by antennas in the cell phone's area to the telephone you dialed.

   _____

(Continued)

13. The children ran in and out of the fountain, laughing and *disporting* themselves all afternoon. Some were playing tag through the water, while others were dancing and squealing with delight.

_____

14. Until he was discovered by Brahms and other music notables, the Czech composer Antonin Dvorak barely *subsisted* on his salary as an organist in Prague.

_____

15. Twelve juniors will be *inducted* into the honor society this evening, the greatest number ever to be admitted in a single year.

_____

Writing Assignment 15.1

The traditional names of the parts of speech in English all come from Latin word parts. Together with a classmate, compose for eighth graders a glossary of these terms, listed below, using their Latin origins to explain what they mean. Refer to your dictionary for more help.

TRADITIONAL PARTS OF SPEECH

noun, from Latin: *nomen* (name)
pronoun, from Latin *pro-* + *nomen*
verb, from Latin *verbum* (word)
adjective, from Latin *ad-* + *-ject* (thrown, added)
adverb, from Latin *ad-* + *verbum*
preposition, from Latin *pre-* + *positio* (to place, a placing)
conjunction, from Latin *con-* + *junct-* (to join, a joining)
interjection, from Latin *inter-* + *-ject*

Copyright © 2002 by Addison Wesley Longman, Inc.

16

Common Suffixes

We can take the building of word families a step further by using suffixes. As discussed in Chapter 8, suffixes, unlike roots and many prefixes, do not tell us a great deal about the meanings of words. But they are important because:

Words in Focus
objective
subjective
admit

- Suffixes tell us what part of speech a word is.
- Suffixes distinguish from each other words that contain the same root.

For example, many of the *-ject* verbs become nouns when we add the noun suffix *-ion:*

ejection, injection, interjection, objection, projection, rejection, subjection

If we add the adjective suffix *-ive* to the *-ject* verbs instead, we can form two adjectives that have acquired opposite meanings:

objective and *subjective*

The first refers to reality that exists outside a person's mind and over the years has come to mean *fair-minded, impartial.* The second refers to the view of reality of some particular person and over the years has come to mean *influenced by one's own thoughts and feelings.*

Changing the suffixes from *-ive* to the noun ending *-ivity* gives us the nouns *objectivity* and *subjectivity,* the state or quality of being objective or subjective. These two nouns are very different in meaning from the nouns ending in *-ion, subjection* and *objection.* Thus, if you know what parts of speech different suffixes create, you will be able to recognize different forms of words you already know.

Now let's play with suffixes and some of the other words you formed from Latin roots in Vocabulary Exercise 15.2, page 168. The first word we can make with the root *-mit* and a prefix is *admit.* If we look up *admit* in the dictionary, we find just before and after it some related words:

admissibility, admissible, admission, admissive, admittance, admittedly

This long list suggests that the *-mit* family may be quite large. Perhaps the other *-mit* words you have made can take the same suffixes as *admit*. Let's form a grid to see if this is true. Some of the various suffixes of the words formed from *admit* are listed across the top of the grid, and the other members of the *-mit* family are listed down the left side. We can combine each word on the left with the suffixes across the top to fill in the boxes of the grid. An X appears in any box of the grid when no such word exists. For example, no such word as *commissible* is in the dictionary, so an X appears in the box under the *-ible* suffix and across from *commit*.

	-ible, adjective *-ibility*, noun *-ibly*, adverb	*-sion*, noun	*-ive*, adjective	*-ance*, noun
commit	X	commission	X	X
emit	X	emission	emissive	X
omit	omissible	omission	omissive	X
permit	permissible permissibility permissibly	permission	permissive	X
remit	remissible	remission	X	remittance
submit	submissible	submission	submissive	X
transmit	transmissible transmissibility	transmission	transmissive	X

Why do some words in a particular family take some suffixes while others do not? That is, why don't we have English words to fill the boxes marked with X in the grid above?

> Words came into English directly from Latin or indirectly through French, and they were each borrowed at somewhat different times for different meanings.
> Some words fell into disuse, while others acquired different, more specialized meanings later on.

For example, there was once an adjective *submiss*, meaning *humble, obedient*, but it was eventually replaced by *submissive*. Yet we still use the old adjective *remiss*, meaning *careless, negligent*.

Copyright © 2002 by Addison Wesley Longman, Inc.

> English is a very flexible language with a very large vocabulary; it easily tolerates the use of old words in new ways or new words altogether.

For example, the word *transmission* still has the general meaning of *the act of transmitting,* but it has also acquired a more specialized meaning; a car's transmission, that is, the part of the car that *transmits* engine power to the wheels. Words in a living language, especially one as flexible as English, are constantly changing according to the needs of their users.

As we noted at the start of this chapter, different suffixes on the same root signal different meanings. So to be sure of the meaning of a word with a familiar root but an unfamiliar suffix, you need to look it up in a dictionary or search for clues to its meaning in its context. For example, the adjective suffix *-ive* has a very general meaning of *tending to _____.* Thus, *permissive* can mean *tending to permit,* but nowadays, it is more often used to mean *giving **too much** permission, being lenient.* We can't see this common meaning in the suffix alone. However:

> Learning to manipulate suffixes as we have done with prefixes and roots gives you a sense of power over Latinate words.
> In the process, you build a whole family of related words as a strong memory aid for the less familiar words among them.

Vocabulary Exercise 16.1

Here are some of the words of the *-mit* family. Use each word in a sentence. Meanings for less familiar words are provided. For more help, use your dictionary.

1. admissible

   _____

2. commission

   _____

3. intermittent, stopping and starting again

   _____

(Continued)

4. emission, something that is sent forth, like polluting gases

_____

5. submissive, obedient

_____

6. remit, to cancel; to send back

_____

7. permissible

_____

8. permissive

_____

9. transmit

_____

10. noncommittal, won't say yes or no

_____

The following exercises are a series of grids like the one on page 173. Each grid allows you to build a family of words with a common Latin root. The questions following each grid then allow you to play with some of the words in the grid so that you have more than one context in which to remember them. As in the earlier grid, fill in each blank of a grid with the word in the left-hand column as it would be spelled with the suffix above it. You will not need to use your dictionary. Again, if a common English word cannot be made with that suffix, an X appears in the appropriate space. The first few blanks in each grid are filled in for you as examples. Learn the meaning of each Latin root as you complete its grid. As you work through the grid questions, also learn the words from the grid that are unfamiliar to you.

Copyright © 2002 by Addison Wesley Longman, Inc.

GRID I		
-fer to carry, bear, bring		
Verbs, No Suffix	**Nouns, *-ence***	**Adjectives, *-ential* (*showing* ____ *ence*)**
confer	conference	X
defer (to postpone; to submit to out of respect)	(submission, courteous yielding to another's opinions)	
differ		
infer (to draw a conclusion)		
interfere		X
offer	X (But *offering* is a noun.)	X
prefer		
refer		
suffer	sufferance (the capacity to tolerate pain; permission given by failure to prohibit) (*Suffering* is another noun from *suffer*.)	X
transfer		X

Grid I Exercise

1. All the verbs in the left-hand column are stressed on their second syllables, except *differ, offer,* and *suffer.* What is there about the spelling of all three words that might explain their stresses?

   _____

2. What kind of treatment is *preferential treatment?* Who might be given it in a college's admissions process?

   _____

3. *Infer* is different from *imply,* a word with which it is often confused. George *implies* something by his actions or words, not stating it directly, and Gracie *infers* what he means from his actions or words. George makes an *implication* by his actions, but Gracie draws an *inference* from them.

(Continued)

Fill in the blanks below with the correct word, chosen from the words in parentheses following each sentence.

Martha _____ that I had lied to her when I talked to her on the phone about the party. (inferred, implied)

From her tone of voice, though, I _____ that she had forgiven me. (inferred, implied)

4. What were the original meanings of the prefix and root of *differ?* Go back to page 161 for the prefix's meanings. How might *differ* have come to mean *to be unlike?*

   _____

5. In the word *referee,* the suffix *-ee* means a person who is *referred to.* In what sense is a *referee* in a sport a person who is referred to?

   _____

6. Something that would normally not be allowed—such as eating lunch in class—may be allowed *on sufferance,* that is, just because it has not been openly forbidden. List two other things that might happen *on sufferance.*

   _____

Spelling Box

Note that all the nouns in Grid I end in *-ence,* except for *sufferance.* There is no rule for whether a word should end in *-ence* or *-ance.* You simply have to MEMORIZE the correct spelling. It is helpful to keep together in your mind words that have the same ending, like *conferEnce, differEnce, inferEnce, referEnce* and so on, but to think up a special way—the sillier the better—to remember the one that doesn't fit. For example, you can *suffer* if you have *Ants* in your *pAnts,* so spell it *sufferAnce.*

Copyright © 2002 by Addison Wesley Longman, Inc.

GRID II *-duce, -duct* to lead; led			
Verbs, No Suffix	**Nouns, *-tion***	**Adjectives, *-tive* *-cible, -tible***	**Adjectives,**
conduce (to tend, contribute)	X	conducive (favorable; leading toward)	X
conduct (to control, lead, transmit)	(transmission, usually of electricity)		
deduce (to conclude by reasoning) AND deduct (to subtract)			(Make 2 adjs.)
educe (to draw out, elicit, extract)	X	X	
induce (to persuade; to cause; to infer)	X (But inducement)	X	
induct (to install; to admit as a member)			X
introduce (to present; recommend; bring in; open)		(Also, introductory)	X
produce (to create, make)			X
reduce (to lessen)			
seduce (to lead astray, lure into bad conduct)			

Grid II Exercise

1. What *inducements* to attend his college might a recruiter for a college basketball team offer to talented high school players?

_____

2. What happens at an *induction* ceremony?

_____

(Continued)

3. What kind of person would be a more profitable employee of a company, a *productive* one or a *seductive* one?

_____

4. In what sense is a bribe a *seduction?*

_____

_____

5. Lightning rods are put atop buildings because they are *conductive.* They lead electricity safely to the ground. *Conducive* has a broader meaning of being helpful, contributing to. What are some things that might be *conducive* to a good night's sleep?

_____

6. *Inductive* reasoning is the opposite of *deductive* reasoning. *Induction* draws out of particular examples some general conclusion, while *deduction* applies a general statement to particular examples. What type is the following bit of reasoning?
All men must die.
Socrates is a man.
Therefore, Socrates must die.

_____

Writing Assignment 16.1

Choose five words from Grids I and II that were unfamiliar to you before you worked through these pages. Write a sentence or two using each one. If you need more help with meaning and usage, consult your dictionary. ∎

Copyright © 2002 by Addison Wesley Longman, Inc.

GRID III		
-claim, -clam- to cry out, call		
Verbs, No Suffix	**Nouns, *-clamation***	**Adjectives, *-clamatory***
acclaim (to greet with loud approval, applaud)	acclamation	acclamatory
declaim (to deliver a speech; to speak loudly)		
disclaim (to give up claim to; disown; deny)	(Also, disclaimer—a denial of a claim)	X
exclaim (to cry out; speak suddenly)		
proclaim (to announce officially, declare)		X
reclaim (to rescue; reform; to make land capable of cultivation)		X
claim (to demand as one's right; to deserve; assert)	X (But clamor—loud outcry; public protest; any loud noise)	X (But clamorous)

Grid III Exercise

1. More than words in the other grids, these words show in their present meanings a clear connection to the meanings of their Latin prefixes and root. For example, *acclaim* comes from *ad-* (to) and *-claim* (cry out). It means to greet with loud approval, to *cry out to* someone. It is also a noun meaning vigorous applause. Show how the meanings of *disclaim* and *proclaim* are also closely related to the meanings of their Latin prefixes and root.

   _____

   _____

2. In English words, stressed syllables usually alternate with unstressed ones; it is very unusual to find three unstressed syllables in a row. In words more than three syllables long, there are usually two stresses, one heavier than the other.

(Continued)

See how this works: circle the syllable in each of these words that gets the heaviest stress when spoken, and underline the syllable that gets the next heaviest stress:

> ex • cla • ma • tion   dec • la • ma • tion
> ex • clam • a • to • ry   de • clam • a • to • ry

Why is the position of the heaviest stress in *exclamation* and *declamation* different from that in their adjective forms, *exclamatory* and *declamatory*?

_____

_____

3. If the spokeswoman for the mayor issues a *disclaimer* about a rumor concerning contributions to the mayor's campaign fund, what is she saying?

_____

_____

4. Why do we call this mark, !, an *exclamation point*?

_____

5. What are mining companies supposed to do when they take care of land *reclamation*?

_____

6. Explain why the name of Abraham Lincoln's famous statement freeing the slaves, the *Emancipation Proclamation*, sounds like poetry. Give two reasons._____

_____

7. How do you think the verb *claim* came to mean *to demand as one's right*? Use the meaning of the Latin root as your starting point.

_____

_____

8. Consider the meaning of *claim* (preceding question), and then underline the meaning of the adjective *clamorous* that seems most suitable, remembering that *claim, clamor* and *clamorous* are closely related:

   a. uncontrollably violent
   b. happily and excessively noisy
   c. crying out urgently and insistently

Copyright © 2002 by Addison Wesley Longman, Inc.

GRID IV -port, to carry			
Verbs, No Suffix	**Nouns, *-ment***	**Nouns, *-ation***	**Adjectives, *-able***
comport (to behave in a certain way; agree with)	comportment	X	X
deport (to expel from a country; to behave in a certain way)			
disport (to amuse, entertain)	X	X	X
export (to carry goods out of a country)	X		
import (to bring into a country; to mean)	X (But importance)		(Also important)
purport (pur- from pro-, to mean; claim; profess)	X	X	X
report (to give an account of)	X	X	
support (to keep steady; strengthen; favor)	X	X	
transport (to carry from one place to another; to enrapture)	X		

Grid IV Exercise

1. Which of the nine verbs in the left-hand column can also be used as nouns? (A noun can fill the following blank: The _____ is good.) Check your dictionary if you are unsure.

_____

The nine verbs are usually all stressed on their second syllables. When we use them as nouns, all but two of them move the stress to the first syllable:

EXAMPLES: My uncle's company *exPORTS* plumbing supplies.   (*export* as verb) His *EXports* go mostly to South America.   (*export* as noun)

(Continued)

Which two of the nine keep the stress on the second syllable? Underline them. Again, consult your dictionary if you are unsure.

2. What meaning do the verbs to *comport* and to *deport* share?

_____

3. The words *import* and *export* are opposites when they both refer to moving goods from one country to another. They appear in the nouns *importation* and *exportation*. But *import* is also the root of another, more widely used noun, *importance*. What adjective corresponds to the noun *importance*?

_____

4. Like *import, deport* also has two meanings and a different noun for each. If *deportment* means a person's way of behaving, what does *deportation* mean? Check your dictionary.

_____

5. The verb *purport* implies that there is something fake about what is being *purported*. For example, we might say that a politician *purports* to be in favor of campaign funding reform, but he still accepts big donations to his campaign fund. So his claims cannot be honest. Look up the noun version of *purport* in your dictionary. Does it carry this same feeling of dishonesty? What other words are closest to it in meaning?

_____

6. What would we mean if we said that a defendant's claim of innocence is *insupportable*?

_____

Copyright © 2002 by Addison Wesley Longman, Inc.

Writing Assignment 16.2

Choose five words from Grids III and IV that were unfamiliar to you before you worked through these pages. Write a sentence or two using each one. If you need more help with meaning and usage, consult your dictionary.   ∎

GRID V *-pel, -puls(e)* to push			
Verbs, No Suffix	**Nouns, *-pulsion***	**Nouns, *-pulse***	**Adjectives, *-pulsive***
compel (to force; to get by force)		X	
dispel (to scatter, drive away, disperse)	X	X	X
expel (to drive out by force; to dismiss)		X	X
impel (to push forward; to force, urge)	X (But impulse)		
propel (to push; to drive onward, forward)		X	X
repel (to drive back; to refuse; to resist)			
Other Related Verbs			
appeal (to make an urgent request; to take a lawsuit to a higher court)	The grid above is rather short, but there are three other verbs listed to the left that come from the same Latin roots. Their histories are somewhat different from the *-pel* words above, so they do not form the same nouns and adjectives.		
repeal (to withdraw officially, cancel)			
push (to press against a thing so as to move it, etc.)			

Grid V Exercise

1. All of the verbs from *compel* to *repel* contain the Latin root's meaning of *force by pushing*. A wind, for example, can *dispel* the clouds. We can also use some of these words to talk about the power of feelings and other spiritual forces. Write a sentence in which you use the verb *dispel* to describe what love or ambition can push away.

   _____

   Now write another sentence saying what sort of person *repels* you.

   _____

(Continued)

2. The adjective *compulsive* usually refers to people and their behavior, while another adjective, *compulsory*, refers to things that *compel*. Fill in each blank below with the correct adjective.

   Matt is a boring companion because he is such a _____ talker.

   The new tax law makes the filing of separate forms _____ for all married couples.

3. English spelling requires us to double the final *-l* in the verbs from *compel* to *repel* before we add *-ed* or *-ing* or any other suffix starting with a vowel: *compelled, dispelling.* We must do this to make sure that the *-e* before the *-l* is correctly pronounced to rhyme with the *ell* in *bell.* If we didn't double the *l,* we would be correct in pronouncing the *-e* as *ee.* That is, **compeled* would be pronounced as **compeeled.* Why don't we have to double the *-l* in *appeal* and *repeal* also?

   _____

   _____

4. The noun *pulse* comes from the same Latin root as *compulsion* and the other *-pulse* words. What is the connection between the root's meaning, *to push,* and our *pulse?*

   _____

5. We can add the suffix *-ant* to *propel* and *-ent* to *repel,* doubling the *l* before them: *propellant, repellent.* Use the meanings of the root and prefix to explain what a coat does if it is *water-repellent* and what an insect *repellent* is.

   _____

   _____

6. One of the meanings of the adjective *appealing* is *attractive.* How is this meaning related to the meaning of the verb *appeal, to make an urgent request?*

   _____

7. The verb *push* has been an English word for such a long time that it has been combined with many other English words in such compound words

Copyright © 2002 by Addison Wesley Longman, Inc.

(Continued)

and idiomatic expressions as *push-button* and *push off*. Together with another classmate, make a list of other compounds and idiomatic expressions using *push*. (An idiomatic expression is a group of words that means something different when used together than if each word were used by itself. For example, *to push off* means to *leave, depart:* "I'll be *pushing off* now." We can also use *push* and *off* separately, not as an idiom, meaning to force something away: The dog licked my face until I *pushed* her *off*.) Arrange the *push* compounds and expressions in two lists: things or actions that push (as in *I'll be pushing off now*) and things or actions that get pushed (*push-button*).

Spelling Box

Doubling a Final Consonant

We stated briefly in question 3 above part of a spelling rule for adding suffixes to words like *compel* and *dispel*. We must DOUBLE the final consonant under these three conditions:

- The word ends in one consonant preceded by one vowel: *drag, stun*
- The word is only one syllable OR is stressed on the last syllable: *shop, o-mit′*
- The suffix begins with a vowel: *-art, -ing, -ed, -ant,-* ible

Watch how this works in the following examples: *dragging, stunned, shoppers, omitting, braggart, forgettable*. If you have problems with doubling consonants in such words, memorize the three conditions above, and then practice, practice, practice.

Spelling Exercise 16.1

Combine the following words and suffixes, carefully applying the rule above. Be sure ALL THREE conditions are present before doubling the final consonant.

1. flat + en = _____

   flat + er = _____

2. pair + ed = _____

   purr + ing = _____

3. occur + ed = _____

   occur + ence = _____

4. despair + ing = _____

   dishevel + ed = _____

5. admit + edly = _____

   adopt + ing = _____

6. propel + er = _____

   prosper + ous = _____

7. forget + ful = _____

   forget + ing = _____

8. control + able = _____

   convert + ible = _____

9. top + less = _____

   top + ing = _____

10. red + ness = _____

    red + ening = _____

Copyright © 2002 by Addison Wesley Longman, Inc.

GRID VI *-sist* to stand; to set		
Verbs, No Suffix	**Nouns, *-ance* or *-ence***	**Adjectives, *-ant* or *-ent***
assist (to help, aid)		
consist (to be made up of; to be contained in; to be in harmony with)	(Also *consistency*)	
desist (to stop, cease)	X	X
exist (to be, have reality, occur)		
insist (to take and maintain a stand; to demand strongly)		
persist (to refuse to give up in the face of opposition)	(Also *persistency*)	
resist (to withstand, oppose, fight)		(Also *resistible*)
subsist (to continue to live, remain alive)		

Grid VI Exercise

1. Only two of the eight verbs in the left-hand column take the suffixes *-ance* and *-ant* instead of *-ence* and *-ent*. Which are they? Check your dictionary if you are not sure. Then figure out a silly way to remember the spellings._____

   _____

2. A *cease and desist order* is an order issued by some agency like the Federal Trade Commission that commands a company to stop actions that the agency considers unfair or illegal. Look up both *cease* and *desist* in your dictionary. Do you think they mean exactly the same thing? Why or why not?

   _____

   _____

(Continued)

3. Using the Latin meaning of its prefix and root, explain how you think *assist* came to mean *to help, aid*.

———————————————————————————————

———————————————————————————————

4. Two of the adjectives in the grid, *consistent* and *resistible,* can take the prefix *in-*. Write out the words with this prefix attached. Be careful about their spelling (see the Spelling Box on page 163 for help). What does *in-* mean in each word?

———————————————————————————————

———————————————————————————————

5. One thing can be *consistent* with another—that is, stand with or be in harmony with another—as a newspaper's views may be *consistent* with your own views. How can something like someone's behavior or attitude toward others be *consistent* in *itself*?

———————————————————————————————

6. What do we mean when we say that a family is living on a bare *subsistence* level?

———————————————————————————————

7. The adjectives *resistant* and *resistible* are different in meaning. Something or someone is *resistant* if it/she can fight off something else. A fabric can be *water-resistant.* Something/someone is *resistible* if someone else is able to fight it/her off. So the offer of a cigarette may be *resistible* by someone who is determined never to smoke again. Fill in the following blanks with the appropriate adjective.
Despite all my efforts, Marcia remained _____ to the idea of running for club president.
After getting food poisoning once from some shrimp I ate, I find the offer of a shellfish dinner totally _____.

Copyright © 2002 by Addison Wesley Longman, Inc.

Writing Assignment 16.3

Choose a modern invention that you know well, such as the cell phone, television, personal computer, modern recording devices, specialized automobiles, modern weapons, and so on. Make a list of at least 8–10 words connected with the invention that are new words created from older word parts or old words that have acquired new meanings because of the invention. Examples of new words that have been created from older word parts are *computer* and *ultrasound;* examples of old words that have acquired new meanings are *cassette* and *cell phone*. Write explanations of the words for people who know only a little English, but who are familiar with Latin roots (perhaps they speak Spanish or French as their first language). Refer when you can to any Latin roots of the words, and if you think it would be helpful, to their prefixes and suffixes as well. Use your dictionary for help.   ■

Vocabulary Exercise for Grids I-VI

Here are some questions about words drawn from all the grids you have just completed. See if you can answer them by remembering the italicized words from the grid. When in doubt, look first at the root and prefix of a word, and then look back at the other words in its grid before consulting your dictionary.

1. If a senator publishes a *disclaimer* that he is associated with a company being investigated for illegal practices, what is he saying?

   _____

2. The word *missive* is an old and rather fancy name for which of the following? (Consider its Latin root.)

       a strainer   a married woman   a letter

3. What do you do to *disport* yourself?

   _____

4. Why might you describe a child as *insufferable?*

   _____

5. Which of the following could be called a *duct?* (Consider this word's Latin root.)

       a fingernail   a blood vessel   a tooth

(Continued)

6. When you act on *impulse,* you act unexpectedly because of a sudden feeling or whim. Is an *impulsive* person the same as a *compulsive* one? Explain. (Consider the prefixes.)

_____

_____

7. Why do you think such expressions as *Oh! Well! Ouch!* and *Darn it!* are called *interjections?*

_____

_____

8. During the Vietnam War, a group of anti-war protestors might set up a *persistent clamor* outside an *induction* center. What would they have been doing and where?

_____

_____

9. Because Columbus thought that the world was round, he concluded that he could reach India by sailing west. Sir Isaac Newton is said to have come up with the principle of gravity after an apple fell on his head. Was Columbus reasoning *inductively* or *deductively?* Why? How about Newton? Why?

_____

_____

10. Which two of the sentences below are closest to each other in meaning? Explain.

   a. Mario *claims* to be a friend of the governor.
   b. Mario *prefers* to be a friend of the governor.
   c. Mario *disclaims* being a friend of the governor.
   d. Mario *purports* to be a friend of the governor.
   e. Mario *persists* in being a friend of the governor.

_____

_____

Copyright © 2002 by Addison Wesley Longman, Inc.

Review Exercise I for Chapters 14–16

Refer to pages 161–162 for the common prefixes we have been working with in this unit so far. How many verbs can you make with each of the following Latin roots by combining them with those prefixes? Run through the prefixes for each root. The number in parentheses is the number of possible verbs with that root and the prefixes.

EXAMPLE: *-pend* (to hang or weigh)
append, depend, expend, impend, suspend

1. *-vert* (to turn) (8)_____

    _____

2. *-tend* (to stretch) (6)_____

    _____

3. *-fect* (to make, do) (4)_____

    _____

4. *-pose* (to put, place) (10)_____

    _____

5. *-tract* (to pull, drag) (9)_____

    _____

Review Exercise II for Chapters 14–16

The words in the following groups of words contain the same Latin root. In each word, circle the root and prefix(es), if there are any. A few words have two prefixes. Then choose one of the words in each group whose meaning you best remember, and write a sentence using it.

1. admissible, permissive, noncommittal

    _____

2. deportment, insupportable, comport

    _____

(Continued)

3. postscript, scripture, circumscribe

_____

4. fidelity, infidel, diffidence

_____

5. dispel, compulsory, repellent

_____

6. exclamation, disclaimer, acclaim

_____

7. infer, preferential, deference

_____

8. animosity, equanimity, magnanimous

_____

9. pungent, punctuation, compunction

_____

10. inducements, seductive, conducive

_____

Review Exercise III for Chapters 14–16

Copyright © 2002 by Addison Wesley Longman, Inc.

In the left-hand column below are verbs from Chapters 14–16. Match each verb with the definition in the right-hand column closest to it in meaning.

1. infer _____	a. replace
2. persecute _____	b. interrupt
3. dissent _____	c. stray from the subject
4. persist _____	d. praise
5. digress _____	e. conclude from evidence
6. commend _____	f. block
7. interject _____	g. hold firmly to a purpose
8. elude _____	h. disagree
9. supplant _____	i. oppress, ill-treat
10. obstruct _____	j. cleverly escape

Review Exercise IV for Chapters 14–16

Here are some adjectives from Chapters 14–16. Underline as many of the nouns following each one that could be described by that adjective.

EXAMPLE: submissive: <u>child</u>   tree   <u>horse</u>

1. compulsory: desires   exams   uniforms
2. pungent: mountain   garbage   perfume
3. abject: wealth   poverty   laws
4. seductive: dance   song   punishment
5. repellent: personality   odor   meal
6. objective: estimate   opinion   anger
7. impulsive: commute   journey   kiss
8. persistent: telephoning   hiding   questioning
9. clamorous: appeal   thoughts   judgment
10. deferential: diagnosis   treatment   disease
11. prolix: infant   politician   speech
12. circumspect: lawyer   banker   football player

Review Exercise V for Chapters 14–16

Fill in each blank below with a noun from the list that best fits the sentence's meaning. Some nouns should be used more than once.

acclaim	animosity	compunction	domicile	equanimity
manacles	prospects	specter	transgression	infidel

1. Jamison accepted his sentence to 15 years with calm _____, and as he was led away in _____, he glanced over at his mother and smiled.

2. When the two boys who had been quarreling came into the principal's office, she could feel their _____ toward each other. She wanted to help them resolve their conflict themselves, but she had no _____ about calling their parents if they could not or would not.

3. The _____ of getting better than a minimum-wage job for a high school graduate with no college experience are pretty slim.

4. The _____ of inflation like the bloated prices we saw in the sixties and seventies has not yet reared its ugly head.

(Continued)

5. Once Martha had gone off to Europe, she no longer felt any
   _____ about writing to John to break off their
   relationship. Somehow, doing it was a lot easier from a distance.

6. Census-takers will try to contact residents in every
   _____ in the nation, but they admit that they may fail
   to count homeless people.

7. An international literary prize such as the Nobel Prize for Literature can
   bring instant _____ to writers little known outside
   their own countries.

8. The Crusades were religious wars of Christians against Moslems with
   each side calling the other _____. The Christians wanted
   to punish the Moslems for what Christians saw as the Moslem
   _____ against the holy city of Jerusalem, which the
   Moslems held, and the Moslems wanted to push the Christians back to
   Europe where they came from.

9. Despite the public _____ in which he was held for
   his novels and stories, Hemingway felt himself a failure in later life and
   committed suicide. The _____ of the loss of his powers
   looming ahead of him was too frightening for him to face.

10. It is difficult not to feel some _____ against a critic
    who has given your work a bad review, especially if the review is widely
    read.

Copyright © 2002 by Addison Wesley Longman, Inc.

Review Exercise VI for Chapters 14–16

Correct any of the following words that are misspelled. Watch for the prefixes that change their spelling in different words.

1. obportunity_____

2. imigrate_____

3. occasion_____

4. accomodate_____

5. efficient_____

6. suround_____

7. apropriate_____

8. interrupt_____

9. excessive_____

10. adcustomed_____

17

Playing with Suffixes

English has many suffixes that tell us little about what a word means. Why pay any attention to them, then? For two reasons:

Words in Focus
induce/
inducement
induct/
induction

If you can manipulate new words by adding different suffixes to them, you will gain more control over the words and will have more ways of remembering them.

For example, in Grid II, page 178, you learned two words with the same prefix and root: *induce,* meaning *to persuade; to cause,* and *induct,* meaning *to introduce into.* A good way of distinguishing them in your memory is to learn that *induce* can be made into a noun by adding the suffix *-ment,* while *induct* becomes a noun when you add *-tion.* An *inducement* is something that leads someone to act, while an *induction* is someone's introduction into an organization.

Knowledge of suffixes will also give you greater flexibility in your writing.

For example, consider this sentence:

The acrobats flew like birds on the trapeze and amazed *the audience.*

If you want to emphasize the audience's reaction, you could change *amazed* to the noun *amazement* and put that part of the sentence first. (You will need to add words to fit the new sentence.):

To the amazement of the audience, *the acrobats flew like birds on the trapeze.*

OR   To the audience's amazement, *the acrobats flew like birds on the trapeze.*

Just as you can change many verbs to nouns if you know suffixes, you can do the reverse, changing nouns to verbs. Consider the sentence on top of the next page:

Copyright © 2002 by Addison Wesley Longman, Inc.

The police chief's main objective is the recruitment *of more minority officers.*

To give the police chief more action, try changing the noun to a verb:

> *The police chief's main objective is* to recruit *more minority officers.*

OR   *The police chief* wants to recruit *more minority officers.*

(Note that the words *the* and *of* are omitted and *to* is added in the revised sentences.)

You can practice this suffix process in the following exercises.

"Your vocabulary is enlarged."

© The New Yorker Collection 1994 Frank Cotham from cartoonbank.com. All Rights Reserved.

Vocabulary Exercise 17.1

Rewrite the sentences below by changing the italicized verbs to nouns ending in *-ment*. First drop verb endings so that you use the infinitive or dictionary form of the verb. Then add *-ment* to make the noun. You may also have to add other words to fit the noun into the sentence. Do not add to or subtract from the meaning of a sentence when you rewrite it. Some rewritings are provided to help you.

EXAMPLE: The grand jury has *indicted* three officials for income tax evasion.

indicted → indict + -ment = indictment

The grand jury has handed down the <u>indictment</u> of three officials for income tax evasion.

1. Famous athletes often make money by *endorsing* various products on television.
   Famous athletes often make money from their _____ of various products on television.

2. The Bill of Rights attached to our Constitution *embodies* the unalienable rights that Jefferson wrote about in the Declaration of Independence.
   The Bill of Rights attached to our Constitution is the _____ of _____.

3. The movie has such a good story to tell and such strong acting that it doesn't have to be *embellished* any further with special effects.
   The movie has such a good story to tell and such strong acting that it doesn't need any further _____ with special effects.

4. A college dictionary is *abridged;* that is, it omits many technical and seldom used words. An unabridged dictionary is more than twice as thick.
   A college dictionary is an _____; that is, it omits many technical and seldom used words. An unabridged dictionary is more than twice as thick.

5. If parents automatically *disparage* every opinion a teenager expresses because they think he is too immature to have opinions, he feels justified in becoming angry.
   Parents' automatic _____ of every opinion a teenager expresses because they think he is too immature to have opinions makes him feel justified in becoming angry.

Copyright © 2002 by Addison Wesley Longman, Inc.

(Continued)

6. Dorothy and her friends the Scarecrow, the Tin Man, and the Cowardly
   Lion were totally *disillusioned* when they found that the celebrated
   Wizard of Oz was just an ordinary man with a noise-making machine.
   Dorothy and _____ felt total

   _____

   _____

7. At Lexington and Concord, the American Revolution began when
   British troops first *engaged* American militiamen. The British Redcoats
   sustained 273 casualties, while fewer than 100 Americans died.
   At Lexington and Concord, the American Revolution began with the first
   _____ of British troops with American
   militiamen. The British Redcoats sustained 273 casualties, while less than
   100 Americans died.

8. Mrs. Johnson filed a suit against Hubert because Hubert constantly
   harassed her about her dog. He screamed at her when the dog barked,
   threw rocks at her windows, and even tried to shoot the dog with a BB
   gun.
   Mrs. Johnson filed a suit against Hubert because of his constant
   _____ about her dog. He screamed
   at her when the dog barked, threw rocks at her windows, and even tried
   to shoot the dog with a BB gun.

9. The gambling charges against Collins were dismissed because his lawyer
   proved that he had been *entrapped* by the undercover police.
   The gambling charges against Collins were dismissed because his lawyer
   proved _____ by the undercover police.

10. To further *aggrandize* himself as France's "Sun King," Louis XIV, who
    once said, "L'état, c'est moi—I am the state," built the sumptuous
    palace of Versailles and had elaborate gardens planted around it.
    For the further _____ of
    himself, Louis XIV, who once said, "L'état, c'est moi—I am the state,"
    built the sumptuous palace of Versailles and had elaborate gardens planted
    around it.

Vocabulary Exercise 17.2

Use the contexts of the sentences above and the roots of the italicized words to figure out the meanings of the words as they are used in the sentences. Underline the meaning next to each word that you think is closest.

1. endorsing: supporting   signing   using
2. embodies: represents   gives form to   includes
3. embellished: weighted down   dressed up   complicated
4. abridged: shortened   judged unfairly   simplified
5. disparage: laugh at   make little of   disown
6. disillusioned: disgusted   made unhappy   freed from a false idea
7. engaged: defeated   fought with   met
8. harassed: persecuted   shouted at   annoyed
9. entrapped: fooled   lured into danger   caught
10. aggrandize: celebrate   make known   make greater

Spelling Box

In the next vocabulary exercise, some of the changes you are asked to make are of verbs ending in *-ate* to nouns ending in *-ation,* so it is appropriate to mention here the rule for adding suffixes like *-ation* to words with a final *e:*

- Drop a final *e* before a suffix that starts with a vowel:

  come + -ing = coming   settle + -ing = settling
  type + -ist = typist   eliminate + -ation = elimination

- Keep the final *e* before a suffix that starts with a consonant:

  arrange + -ment = arrangement   definite + -ly = definitely
  shame + -ful = shameful   love + -ly = lovely

- BUT some words keep their *e* to prevent confusion:

  dye + -ing = dyeing (different from dying)

- And others keep it to prevent mispronunciation.

  For example, many words ending in *-ce* or *-ge* KEEP the final *-e* before a suffix starting with *a, o,* or *u* so that the *c* and *g* keep their "soft" sounds as in *race* and *rage.*

  notice + -able = noticeable   courage + -ous = courageous
  change + -able = changeable   outrage + -ous = outrageous
  BUT: notice + -ing = noticing   change + -ing = changing

Copyright © 2002 by Addison Wesley Longman, Inc.

Spelling Exercise 17.1

Combine the following words and suffixes according to the preceding rule.

1. entice + -ing _____

2. believe + -able _____

3. care + -less _____

4. care + -ing _____

5. judge + -ing _____

6. judge + -ment _____

7. civilize + -ation _____

8. recede + -ing _____

9. legalize + -ation _____

10. isolate + -ation _____

Spelling Exercise 17.2

First pronounce each of the following words out loud. Does the *c* or *g* in each one have a "soft" sound as in the words *race* and *rage*? Then *-e* or *-i* should follow the *c* or *g*. Or does the *c* or *g* have a "hard" sound as in *carrot* and *go*? Then *a, o,* or *u* should follow the *c* or *g*. Using this guide, underline each word's correct spelling. Check your dictionary when you are unsure.

1. outrageous, outragous   6. elegant, elegent

2. allegance, allegiance   7. vengance, vengeance

3. judicious, judicous   8. financial, financal

4. knowledgable, knowledgeable   9. religous, religious

5. embracable, embraceable   10. eligable, eligible

Spelling Exercise 17.3

Here are some words that you may not know. Figure out how they are pronounced by remembering that *c* and *g* have a "soft" sound when *e* or *-i* follow them, as in *race* and *age*, but they have a "hard" sound when *a, o,* or *u* follow them, as in *can, got,* and *gutter.* Write *soft* after words with a soft *c* or *g* and *hard* after words with a hard *c* or *g.* To help you pronounce them, the stressed syllable in each word is capitalized, and meanings are provided. Use the words' sounds and meanings to learn the words as you go along.

1. GENocide: the systematic killing of a whole people
2. LANguor: listlessness, lack of vitality (the *u* in *languor* is silent)
3. viCISSitudes: the ups and downs of fortune in one's life
4. beLEAguer: to besiege by encircling, as with an army
5. condesCENding: talking down to those below you, patronizing, haughty
6. larGESSE: generous giving
7. LAcerate: to tear or wound jaggedly (the *a* in the first syllable rhymes with *bad*)
8. laCONic: saying much in a few words
9. VAgary: an odd or unexpected action, oddity (the *a* in *VA-* rhymes with *may*)
10. rogues' GALlery: a collection of photos of criminals (the *u* in *rogues'* is silent)

Vocabulary Exercise 17.3

Rewrite the sentences below by changing the italicized *-ation* nouns to verbs or the italicized verbs to *-ation* nouns. You may have to add words like *the, of,* or *to,* but do not add to or subtract from the MEANING of a sentence when you rewrite it. The beginnings of a few rewritings are provided to help you.

EXAMPLE: When was the Democratic Party *formed*?

When did the <u>formation of the Democratic Party occur</u>?

1. How does water *evaporate*?
   What causes the _____

Copyright © 2002 by Addison Wesley Longman, Inc.

(Continued)

2. The soil and climate of southern Italy are good for *cultivating* olive trees.
   The soil and climate of southern Italy are good for the_____

   _____

3. This copy machine may be *imitated,* but it will never be *duplicated.*
   There may be _____ of this copy machine, but_____

   _____

4. This book is a careful *delineation* of some little understood aspects of
   George Washington's personality.
   This book carefully_____

5. The *generation* of enough electrical power for a million more homes
   makes the proposed dam very attractive.
   The proposed dam is very attractive because it will_____

   _____

6. To improve his relationship with Congress, the President needs someone
   on his staff to *mediate* disputes and misunderstandings between his office
   and Congress.
   To improve his relationship with Congress, the President needs someone
   on his staff for the_____

   _____

7. In this report, I am only *speculating* about the possibility of humans
   traveling to Mars, not *advocating* our doing it next week or even next year.
   This report is my_____

   _____

8. The *proliferation* of books and other printed materials has been so great
   in recent years that libraries are having trouble keeping their collections
   up to date.
   Books and other printed materials have _____ so much

   _____

9. Hamlet's "To be or not to be" speech *articulates* his fear of death, a fear
   we all share but seldom express so openly. But he speaks it only to himself,
   so no one else in the play understands his feelings.

(Continued)

The _____ of his _____ in

Hamlet's _____ is a fear _____

_____

10. The widow was awarded two million dollars as *compensation* for the death
of her husband in the traffic accident. The money should help *mitigate* her
sense of loss.

    The widow was awarded two million dollars to_____

    _____

    The money should help the_____

11. Calling each other names is an *exacerbation* of your bad feelings for each
other. Why not call in a third person for the *arbitration* of your dispute?

    _____

    _____

12. When you are sad about failing an exam, you always ask me to
commiserate. But I find it hard to sympathize with you because you
usually *procrastinate* studying till the last minute.
When you are sad about failing an exam, you always ask for my_____

    _____

    But I find it hard to sympathize with you because of your _____

    of studying till the very last minute.

13. People go to expensive spas hoping for *rejuvenation* in a few days, even
though they have not paid attention to their health in years. But to
purge from the body cholesterol and the effects of years of smoking and
heavy drinking takes a lot longer than a few days.

    _____

    _____

    _____

    _____

Copyright © 2002 by Addison Wesley Longman, Inc.

(Continued)

14. The first suspect was released because two co-workers *corroborated* his alibi for the night of the robbery. The time punched on his timecard further *substantiated* his alibi.

    _____

    _____

    The time punched on his timecard was a_____

15. The governor's *vacillation* over whether or not to run for reelection has led to his *alienation* from the rest of the Democrats, who want a more committed candidate.
    Because the governor is _____,
    he is_____

Vocabulary Exercise 17.4

Use the contexts of the sentences above plus any knowledge you have of a word's root and prefix to figure out the meanings of the following words as they are used in the sentences above. Underline the meaning you think is closest.

1. delineation:	accurate description	exploration	full disclosure
2. generation:	transfer	production	possibility
3. to mediate:	make up	settle	cover up
4. speculating:	considering	playing with	discarding
5. advocating:	warning against	supporting	criticizing
6. proliferation:	deterioration	rapid increase	importance
7. articulates:	outlines	expresses in words	conceals
8. compensation:	revenge	payment	reward
9. mitigate:	lessen	work against	increase
10. exacerbation:	moderating	aggravating	counteracting
11. arbitration:	resolution	analysis	definition
12. commiserate with:	argue with	help	feel sorry for
13. procrastinate:	give excuses	go to sleep	put off
14. rejuvenation:	new life	strengthening	restoration of youth
15. purge:	substitute	cleanse	restore
16. corroborated:	supported	denied	excused
17. substantiated:	questioned	allowed	proven
18. vacillation:	arguing	deciding	wavering
19. alienation:	rejection	separation	support

Vocabulary Exercise 17.5

What verbs are inside the following -*ation* nouns? Be careful: the verbs do not all end in -*ate*. Hint: you can put *to* in front of a verb, as in the examples. When you are unsure, look up the -*ation* nouns in your dictionary to see what verbs they are related to.

EXAMPLES: inclination to incline   application to apply

1. relaxation_____

2. revelation_____

3. adaptation_____

4. occupation_____

5. sterilization_____

6. improvisation_____

7. provocation (Hint: change the *c* to *k*.)_____

8. denunciation_____

9. insinuation_____

10. inflation_____

Writing Assignment 17.1

Choose four words from the preceding exercise whose meaning is unfamiliar or unclear to you. You may choose either the noun or the verb form. Look them up in your dictionary if you have not already done so. Then write sentences on your own paper using each word correctly. ■

After working through the last seven exercises, you now know that the suffixes -*ment* and -*ation* are for nouns. Review the grids you worked on in Chapter 16, pages 172–191. Here is a list of common noun suffixes. Which ones have you already used in Chapter 16? Underline them.

Copyright © 2002 by Addison Wesley Longman, Inc.

-ability, -ibility	-ism
-acity	-ment
-ance, -ancy	-mony
-ence, -ency	-ness
-ation, -tion, -sion	-ship
-dom	-tude
-ery	-ty, -ity
-hood	-ure

Vocabulary Exercise 17.6

Combine each word in the left-hand column below with the appropriate suffix in the right-hand column to form a noun. Hint: a noun is a word you can put after *the, a,* or *an* and before *of,* as in the example. Use each suffix only once, except for #10, the word *correct.*

EXAMPLE: adult + -hood = adulthood (the adulthood of a horse)

1. friend _____   -ness

2. command _____   -dom

3. deliver _____   -(t)ion

4. elect _____   -ment

5. martyr _____   -tude

6. alcohol _____   -ance

7. bake _____   -ity

8. exact + i- _____   -ship

9. authentic _____   -(e)ry

10. correct (make 3 nouns, one with an added *i-*) -ism

_____

If we grow up learning English as children, we learn how to change a word from one part of speech to another by adding or subtracting a suffix, and we also learn that words that sound and look alike when they are one part of speech do not always take the same suffixes when used as another part of speech. In fact, they may not take any suffixes at all.

For example, we learn that the noun version of the verb *decide* is *decision,* but the noun version of *reside* is not **resision* but *residence.* The noun for *erase* is *erasure,* but the noun for *chase* is *chase* (no suffix needed at all). Add to your own mastery of suffixes by working through Vocabulary Exercise 17.7, in which words that look and sound alike do not necessarily take the same suffixes.

Spelling Box

For some of the words in the next exercises, you will need to remember this rule:

- A final *-y* preceded by a consonant becomes *-i* before any ending **except** *-ing* because *-ing* already begins with an *-i.*

> happy + ly = happily   carry + ed = carried
> lonely + ness = loneliness   hurry + ed = hurried

In words like *marrying,* the *-y* is needed to make us pronounce the second syllable of *marry.* Without the *-y, marrying* would be the same as *mar + ing: marring.*

> carry + ing = carrying   hurry + ing = hurrying

Spelling Exercise 17.4

Combine the following words and endings, following the rule above.

1. hasty + ly _____

2. lazy + ness _____

3. try + ing _____

4. convey + ing _____

5. convey + ance _____

6. worry + ed _____

7. pretty + er _____

8. rally + ed _____

9. rally + ing _____

10. delay + ing _____

Copyright © 2002 by Addison Wesley Longman, Inc.

Spelling Exercise 17.5

What is the original word to which a suffix has been added to form the longer words below? You may want to review the Spelling Box in Chapter 16, page 186.

EXAMPLES: happily *happy*   batted *bat*

1. caring _____

2. tarred _____

3. tarrying _____

4. parted _____

5. partied _____

6. curtseyed _____

7. eying _____

8. gripped _____

9. griped _____

10. cuter _____

Vocabulary Exercise 17.7

Each group of italicized words below can be changed in the same way from verbs to nouns. The first pair of each group shows you how the rest of the group changes. Fill in the blanks in each group with the appropriate noun and the rest of each phrase. Note that you may have to add or remove little words like *to* when you rewrite a phrase. Dotted lines separate the groups from one another. Learn new words by grouping them in your mind with others in their group that you already know. Use their rhyming as a memory aid.

EXAMPLES: to *acquaint* yourself with a new class: *ACQUAINTANCE with a new class* to *disturb* the peace: *a DISTURBANCE of the peace*

1. to *rely* on the government: a *reliance* on the government

2. to *ally* with Japan: an _____ with Japan

3. to *comply* with the law: _____ with the law

4. to *defy* the law: _____ of the law

----

5. to *try* a new product: a *trial* of a new product

6. to *deny* the rumor: _____ of the rumor

7. to *espy* a secret meeting: an _____ of a secret meeting

(Continued)

8. to *defile* the park: a *defilement* of the park

9. to *revile* the soldier by calling him a traitor: the
   _____ of _____

   _____

10. to *derail* a train: the _____ of _____

----

11. to *connive* with the lawyer to avoid taxes: a *connivance* with the lawyer to avoid taxes

12. to *contrive* means to invent: a _____ is an

    _____

----

13. to *revive* an old song: a *revival* of an old song

14. to *survive* a fire: _____ from the fire

----

15. to *submerge* in the pool: *submersion* in the pool

16. to *convert* from oil to gas heat: a _____ from_____

17. a toy to *divert* a baby: a toy as a _____ for the baby

18. to *immerse* yourself in your work: your_____

----

19. to *converge* at the intersection: a *convergence* at the intersection

20. to *diverge* from the norm: a _____

21. to *emerge* from the cocoon as a butterfly: _____

22. to *resurge* or rise again: a _____ or rising again

----

23. to *acquiesce* or to agree silently: *acquiescence* or silent agreement

24. to *coalesce* or grow together: a _____ or
    growing together

25. to *effervesce* or to be lively: _____ or being lively

Copyright © 2002 by Addison Wesley Longman, Inc.

Of course, there are a great many nouns in English that have none of these suffixes. In fact, English is so versatile in its use of words that the same word without adding suffixes at all can be a noun in one sentence and an adjective in another, or a verb in one place and a noun in another. For example, if you are referring to a group of people who have the same quality, you can use a particular adjective as a noun to describe them:

The merciful *shall be shown mercy.*
The meek *will inherit the earth.*

Now here are some examples of common words that can be either nouns or verbs: *walk, talk, call, cook, drive:*

Verbs	*Nouns*
He *walks* to school every day.	The *walk* to school is long.
She *talks* to her mother every day.	I had a long *talk* with my mother today.
The baby-sitter *called* the children in.	The director sent out a *call* for child actors.
Can Tomas *cook* his own dinner?	Too many *cooks* spoil the broth.
Fred *drives* a bus for a living.	The *drive* in the country was refreshing.

When you look up a new word in your dictionary, note whether or not it can be used as more than one part of speech. If it can, then by learning the word, you will have acquired two meanings for the "price" of one word. Try alternating the same word as different parts of speech in the following exercises, and use this double nature of the words to help you remember those that are unfamiliar to you. To help you, review these quick ways of distinguishing nouns, verbs, and adjectives from one another:

- A noun in English is any word that can be used after *a, an,* or *the.*
- A verb is a being or action word that can be used after *to* and that usually changes its spelling to indicate a change in time. (*to drive;* Last week we *drove. . . .*)
- An adjective is a word that can fill this blank: a/an _____ thing/person. (a *pretty* thing, an *elegant* lady)

Dictionary Exercise 17.1

Look up the words below in your dictionary and write in the blanks (a) one of their meanings as a verb and (b) one of their meanings as a noun. Then write two sentences on your own paper using each word twice, first as a verb and then as a noun.

(Continued)

EXAMPLE: taint verb: <u>to corrupt</u> noun: <u>contamination, stain</u>

taint as verb: <u>Though she lived in a crime-ridden neighborhood, it did not</u> <u>TAINT her innocence.</u>

taint as noun: <u>Once a public official has been accused of wrongdoing, even if</u> <u>he is innocent, it is hard for him to get rid of the TAINT of dishonesty.</u>

1. temper   verb: _____   noun: _____

2. exploit   verb: _____   noun: _____

3. pique   verb: _____   noun: _____

4. barter   verb: _____   noun: _____

5. ebb   verb: _____   noun: _____

6. rebuff   verb: _____   noun: _____

7. lapse   verb: _____   noun: _____

8. dupe   verb: _____   noun: _____

9. lampoon verb: _____   noun: _____

10. quibble verb: _____   noun: _____

Vocabulary Exercise 17.8

How well do you know the words in the preceding exercise? Fill in each blank in the sentences below with one of the ten VERBS in that exercise. Each word is used only once.

1. The author _____ for hours with her editor over the best title for her new murder mystery. Should it be called *Body Language* or *Body English*?

2. The wounded man _____ into unconsciousness before he could tell the police what had happened.

3. The severity of my father's demand for obedience was always _____ by his enthusiastic support for my achievements.

4. In the early 17th century, the Dutch and the Lenape Indians _____ about $24 worth of goods for the island of Manhattan.

5. There are enough different movies showing at the mall to _____ the interest of anyone.

Copyright © 2002 by Addison Wesley Longman, Inc.

(Continued)

6. Several elderly people living alone have been _____ by a pair of swindlers who have gone through the neighborhood pretending to be selling life insurance.

7. To preserve the earth for our children, we must learn to _____ its resources without destroying them forever.

8. We took a long, leisurely walk down the beach watching the tide slowly _____.

9. Late-night TV talk show hosts often _____ public figures to make us laugh.

10. When Columbus tried to get financial support for his proposed voyage to find the western passage to the East Indies, he was _____ by everyone except King Ferdinand and Queen Isabella of Spain.

Vocabulary Exercise 17.9

Here again in Column A are the words from the two preceding exercises. Next to each is another word in Column B that shares ONE meaning with the word in Column A. Look up each word in Column B to find the meaning it shares with the word in A. Write this shared meaning in Column C. (You will discover that many of the words in Column B can ALSO be used as either verbs or nouns, like those in A.)

Learn the meaning of each unfamiliar word as you go along by finding a memory aid in the dictionary, or by forming a silly or humorous image for the word in your mind, or by grouping together the words from all three columns.

EXAMPLES: a taint (noun)   a smear   <u>Both are stains.</u>
               to taint (verb)   to corrupt   <u>Both actions make something
                                               or someone turn bad.</u>

A	B	C
1. his bad *temper* (noun)	her good *humor*	_____
2. to *exploit* (verb)	to *avail* yourself of	_____
3. to *pique* my interest (verb)	to *intrigue* me	_____
4. the *barter* of goods (noun)	the *traffic* in drugs	_____
5. to *ebb* away (verb)	to *decline*	_____

(Continued)

6. to *rebuff* his advances (verb)   to *snub* him   _____

7. a *lapse* of duty (noun)   a *slip* of the tongue   _____

8. to *dupe* foolish men (verb)   to *gull* foolish men   _____

9. a *lampoon* of the mayor   a *satire* of the mayor   _____

10. to *quibble* over details   to *cavil* over details   _____

After all this work with changing parts of speech and with suffixes, it is time to examine some words that are often confused with each other because they are the same EXCEPT for their suffixes. In each case, a change in suffix makes a great change in the meaning of the root. A very well-known example of this kind of confusion is that between the nouns *principal*, meaning the head of a school, and *principle*, meaning a basic truth. Do you have trouble with this pair? If so, think up a good memory aid. A common one is this: Your school's princiPAL is your PAL. If you have trouble distinguishing between any of the following pairs of words, think up a memory aid for at least one of the confused words, the sillier and more visual the better.

Vocabulary Exercise 17.10

In each of the following pairs of words, the first will probably be well known to you, while the second, which differs only in its suffix, may be quite unfamiliar. Use the context of the sentence containing the second word to figure out its meaning, and write a synonym for it in the blank that could be substituted for it in the sentence. Then write a sentence using the first, more familiar word.

EXAMPLE: *prejudiced*   *prejudicial*

The analysis of the DNA in the blood found on the defendant's clothes was *prejudicial* to his case. When he and his lawyer realized this effect of the physical evidence, they decided to accept a plea bargain and not let the case go to the jury. damaging, detrimental

The graffiti written on the temple walls show that whoever wrote them is PREJUDICED against ethnic minorities.

Copyright © 2002 by Addison Wesley Longman, Inc.

(Continued)

1. *official   officious*
   The Vargas's neighbor was an *officious* busybody who often volunteered
   to help when no help was needed or wanted.

   _____

2. *responsible   responsive*
   Our congresswoman is very *responsive* to calls from her constituents,
   especially when they are having trouble with the regulations of the
   Immigration and Naturalization Service, because her own parents were
   immigrants, and she knows how complicated the regulations can be.

   _____

3. *reliable   reliant*
   Migrating geese flying in a V-formation are *reliant* on both the goose at
   the head of the V and on each other's honking to keep them on track to
   their destination.

   _____

4. *confident   confidant* (male) and *confidante* (female)
   In Shakespeare's play, Hamlet tells his secret suspicions of his uncle the
   king to Horatio, his close friend and *confidant*. He rejects two other
   friends, Rosencrantz and Gildenstern, when they try to gain his
   confidence because he knows they are working for his uncle.

   _____

5. *special   specious* (pronounced spē′-shəs)
   Hamlet's uncle, King Claudius, puts on a *specious* show of grief for the
   sudden death of his brother, whom he murdered, but in private,
   Claudius is tormented with guilt.

   _____

6. *personal   personnel*
   When unemployment is very low, we have a very difficult time finding
   qualified *personnel* to staff the lowest paying positions in the company.
   And if we do find qualified people, they often move on in a few months
   to better paying jobs.

   _____

(Continued)

7. *captive   captious*

The boy's aged father was a *captious* critic of his son's every move: nothing Rafael did, not his earning good grades nor pitching well on the baseball team, was good enough for the old man. But because his father was ill, Rafael never lost his temper.

_____

8. *council   counsel*

Rafael's coach *counseled* him at almost every practice about his game, his studies, his friends, his whole life, so that Rafael considered him his second father.

_____

9. *preferable   preferential*

In hiring new officers, the city will give *preferential* treatment to applicants who live within the city limits even if their test scores are somewhat lower than out-of-town applicants since officers who are city residents are more likely to treat other residents as they themselves would like to be treated.

_____

10. *negligent   negligible*

I earned such a *negligible* amount of money last year at my part-time job that I won't have to pay any income tax on it, and I will get a refund from the IRS of the money that was withheld from my paycheck every week. It's a small amount, but it should pay for some of my college texts next semester.

_____

Vocabulary Exercise 17.11

The pairs of words italicized in the sentences below may all be unfamiliar to you. They look similar to each other but, like those in the preceding exercise, they too have different meanings because of their different suffixes. Figure out this difference by considering the words' roots and by reading the context in which each word appears. If you need more help, look up the word pairs in your dictionary. Then in the blank after each sentence, provide a synonym or a rephrasing that could replace each italicized word in its sentence.

Copyright © 2002 by Addison Wesley Longman, Inc.

(Continued)

EXAMPLE: *respectable*   *respective*

"This is a *respectable* hotel," said the security man to the drunken guests. "Please lower your voices." <u>reputable, decent</u>

The director shouted above the hubbub, "Will everyone please move to their *respective* spots on the stage for the start of Act II?" <u>their own spots, their</u> <u>particular spots</u>

1. *censor*   *censure*
   In 1934, the motion picture industry adopted the Hays Code by which producers *censored* any scenes filmed by their studios that they considered sexually explicit.

   _____

   The judge was *censured* by the Bar Association because he often made offensive remarks about defendants in the presence of the jury.

   _____

2. *appreciative*   *appreciable*
   To the delight of the *appreciative* audience, the singer performed two encores after her performance.

   _____

   There is an *appreciable* difference between the standard fees charged by health maintenance organizations (HMOs) and the actual cost of medical care.

   _____

3. *indigent*   *indigenous* (in pronouncing these, remember that -*ge*- is
                     "soft" as in *germ*)
   In order to qualify for a room in this nursing home, the woman has to be truly *indigent;* that is, she must not have enough income to pay for her own care.

   _____

   Anthropologists in the early twentieth century like Frank Boaz and Margaret Mead traveled to many out-of-the-way places around the world to study their *indigenous* peoples, who had often had very little contact with white people before.

   _____

(Continued)

4. *chastise* (pronounced chas-tīz′)   *chasten* (pronounced chā′-sin)
Sea captains routinely *chastised* crewmen with whippings when they
caught their men stealing from the ships' stores of food or rum.

After his girlfriend told him that his jokes were in poor taste, especially
when he told them to her mother, Carlos, *chastened* by her rebuke,
seldom spoke to her mother again.

---

5. *congenial*   *congenital*
Shayla found a small, secluded beach on the other side of the island that
would be a most *congenial* spot for a picnic. It was both private and
beautiful.

A harelip is a *congenital* defect in which a child is born with a split in the
upper lip and palate; like many other *congenital* defects, it can be
repaired by surgery in the first months of a baby's life.

---

6 & 7. *incredible*   *incredulous*   AND   *credible*   *credulous*
People believe the most *incredible* things, such as alien abductions, just
because they see them presented as fact on television. Such people are
truly *credulous.*

I gave Bill an *incredulous* stare when he said he knew what would
happen to him next year because he had read his stars. How could he
consider astrology *credible?*

---

8. *contentment*   *contention*
We sat back from the table and sighed with *contentment,* having eaten
our way through a turkey, all the trimmings, and two pies.

The International Olympic Committee is filled with *contention* over the
best way to test athletes for drugs. Some members want random blood
tests, while others argue for tests only on the day of an event.

Copyright © 2002 by Addison Wesley Longman, Inc.

(Continued)

9. *indignation   indignity*

The commuter raged with *indignation* when his train broke down for the third time in a week. "Why can't they run the trains the way I run my company?" he roared.

_____

Family members visiting relatives in this prison suffer the *indignity* of strip searches before they can enter the visitors lounge.

_____

10. *diversity   diversion*

You can see the wide *diversity* of the rose family in this garden: hybrid tea roses, antique roses, and bush roses in colors from pure white to deepest red.

_____

Pickpockets often work in teams. While one member sets up a *diversion*, such as spilling a drink on the victim to distract him, the other steals his wallet.

_____

11. *perceptive   perceptible*

Dr. Kinsella is a very *perceptive* analyst. She saw right through my lies and other feeble defenses and helped me see through them too.

_____

There is a *perceptible* difference between the way my car rides with these super shock absorbers and the way it rode on the old regular ones. Can you feel the difference in the back passenger's seat as well?

_____

12. *pertinent   pertinacious*

When you answer the essay question on *Ethan Frome,* be sure to refer to *pertinent* parts of the novel to support your argument.

_____

The salesman in that car dealership was so *pertinacious* about selling us the newest model car that he refused to take "No" or even "Maybe" for an answer. We felt trapped by his sales pitch.

_____

(Continued)

13. *contemptible   contemptuous*

    At the start of Dickens' story *A Christmas Carol,* Scrooge is a *contemptible* self-centered old miser who treats his employee and others so badly that we despise him.

    _____

    When two men come to his office to ask for donations to the poor, Scrooge is *contemptuous* of their efforts on behalf of the poor. "Are there no prisons? Are there no workhouses?" he shouts.

    _____

14. *stimulus   stimulant*

    The promise of an athletic scholarship if he could improve his grades was the *stimulus* that spurred Jack to study during his last year in high school.

    _____

    Caffeine is the most widely used *stimulant* in America today. Who could be alert through the day at work without coffee, tea or a cola drink?

    _____

15. *ostentatious   ostensible*

    The French phrase "nouveau riche (pronounced nü-vō-rēsh′), the newly rich," is used to describe someone who has earned great wealth rather than inheriting it and who makes an *ostentatious* display of that wealth, buying yachts, mansions, fancy cars, and jewels as if to prove his worth.

    _____

    When Ms. Smith was fired from her job with the IRS, the *ostensible* reason, said her supervisor, was that she was not a team player, but everyone knew it was retaliation against her for having testified in Congress about abuses within the IRS.

    _____

16. *sublime* (rhymes with *lime*)   *subliminal* (second syllable rhymes with *limb*)

    When Charles Darwin first saw the great untouched forests of South America on his voyage aboard the *Beagle,* he wrote in his journal that they were *sublime,* so magnificent that anyone standing in them had to believe there was more to man than mere breath.

    _____

Copyright © 2002 by Addison Wesley Longman, Inc.

(Continued)
The advertising images passed so quickly across the television screen that they were almost *subliminal:* Afterward, I wondered, Was that a man or a woman dancing? What was this person wearing? Why was I supposed to buy it?

17. *enormousness   enormity*
The *enormousness* of the dinosaur Tyrannosaurus Rex can be seen in the twenty-five-foot tall skeleton on display in the museum.

The *enormity* of the crimes of the Roman emperor Caligula led to his assassination before he was thirty.

18. *momentary   momentous*
Have you ever run into an acquaintance someplace where you would not normally see her and had a *momentary* lapse of memory: What is her name? Where do I know her from? After a few awkward seconds, you remember, Ah, the receptionist at the dentist's office!

Jim's graduation from college was a *momentous* occasion because he had succeeded despite his acute dyslexia. He thanked all his friends and family who had helped by reading his texts to him.

19. *authoritative   authoritarian*
The science writer presents a great deal of evidence from the most *authoritative* sources that the universe is expanding. She cites numerous experiments and quotes several renowned physicists.

Among his friends, Tal was very easy-going and pleasant, but at home with his wife and children, he adopted an *authoritarian* manner that allowed no disobedience.

(Continued)

20. *epigram   epigraph*

Oscar Wilde was a very witty playwright and poet whose many *epigrams*, such as "I can resist everything except temptation," take up several columns in collections of famous quotations.

_____

As an *epigraph* to precede Chapter One of his book about mental illness, the psychiatrist used "Nothing human is alien to me," a quotation from the Latin writer Terence.

_____

How skilled are you now at manipulating suffixes to change verbs to nouns and nouns to verbs? Try out your skill by completing the following three exercises without looking back in the chapter.

Vocabulary Exercise 17.12

Turn the following verbs into nouns ending in *-ation*.

1. flirt _____
2. discolor _____
3. visit _____
4. consult _____
5. fix _____
6. compute _____
7. found _____
8. conserve _____
9. dramatize _____
10. authorize _____

Copyright © 2002 by Addison Wesley Longman, Inc.

Vocabulary Exercise 17.13

Now turn the following nouns into verbs by removing their noun suffixes and making other changes in spelling when necessary.

1. fulfillment   _____

2. isolation   _____

3. deportation   _____

4. construction   _____

5. continuance   _____

6. empowerment_____

7. enunciation   _____

8. drudgery   _____

9. extension   _____

10. glorification   _____

Vocabulary Exercise 17.14

Correct the spelling of the following words. Three words are already correct.

1. couragous   _____

2. fortunatly   _____

3. truely   _____

4. satisfying   _____

5. arguement   _____

6. definitly   _____

7. desireable   _____

8. managable   _____

9. peaceable   _____

10. sincerly   _____

18

More Play with Word Families

In the last chapter, you built up your word muscles by playing around with nouns and verbs. Now try playing around with nouns and adjectives. In which sentence below are *red* and *blue* nouns? (See page 212 if you can't remember how to pick out nouns.)

Words in Focus
joy/joyous
curiosity/curious

1. The *red* in the sunset was spectacular. It obscured the *blue* of the sky.
2. The *red* sunset was spectacular. It obscured the *blue* sky.

The same words that are nouns in #1 are adjectives describing other nouns in #2. What happens to the noun *joy* in #4 below?

3. A wedding day should be full of *joy*.
4. A wedding day should be *joyous*.

The suffix *-ous* makes the noun an adjective. What happens to the noun *curiosity* in #6 below?

5. We were full of *curiosity* about our new neighbors.
6. We were very *curious* about our new neighbors.

Here, removing the noun suffix *-ity* reveals the adjective inside the noun *curiosity*. To repeat Chapter 17:

> Playing with different forms of new words helps you gain control over them.
> It also gives you greater flexibility in your writing as you look for the best way of expressing your ideas.

Copyright © 2002 by Addison Wesley Longman, Inc.

Writing Assignment 18.1

On your own paper, write a sentence using each of the following words as a noun. Then exchange your sentences for a classmate's, and rewrite the classmate's sentences changing the words from nouns to adjectives. The second sentences will often be harder to write, and you will probably have to add words to do so.

EXAMPLE: summer   *Many more tourists visit the national parks in the SUMMER. →*
Many more tourists visit the national parks in the SUMMER months.

1. orange
2. glass
3. paper
4. country
5. college

6. hundred
7. office
8. amateur
9. iron
10. American

Vocabulary Exercise 18.1

Here are some more difficult words, italicized in sentences below, that can be used as both nouns and adjectives. In these sentences, they are adjectives. Use the context of each sentence to choose the meaning of the unfamiliar adjectives from the list following each sentence. As you proceed, learn words that are new to you by putting each into a memorable context for yourself.

EXAMPLE: My idea is not entirely *novel* or revolutionary, but it does save time.

   a. fictitious
   b. new
   c. strong

1. My cousin's *fledgling* software company, just six months old, helps small businesses design web pages.

   a. old-fashioned
   b. exciting
   c. new

(Continued)

2. She came to the funeral dressed in black, but her insincerity was *patent*. She was almost laughing with triumph. (Pronounce *patent* pā′-tənt.)

   a. shining
   b. obvious
   c. controversial

3. Many ancient peoples believed that blind people were *clairvoyant*, as if inner vision made up for their lack of sight.

   a. unusually perceptive
   b. especially blessed
   c. capable of magic

4. At the start of the planting season every year, the Hopi in colorful regalia and masks dance their *ritual* corn dance following ancient ways to ensure that they are in harmony with nature.

   a. repetitive
   b. ceremonial
   c. rigid

5. On the issue of improving public education, we should not be practicing *partisan* politics. We should all work together, no matter what our party.

   a. democratic and open
   b. one-sided
   c. selfish

6. When he saw the strength of the prosecution's case against him, Comden's defense attorney thought it *expedient* for him to accept a plea bargain and exchange a lesser prison sentence for a confession and information about Comden's accomplices. (Pronounce *expedient* ex-pē′-dē-ənt.)

   a. advantageous
   b. understandable
   c. ridiculous

7. After Malcolm won the lottery, he lived a *profligate* lifestyle for about a year, buying a mansion on the shore, outfitting himself in handmade suits and shoes, acquiring a string of fancy cars, and decking out his girlfriend in diamonds. But then he settled down into the same sort of modest life he had lived before. (Pronounce *profligate* prä′-fli-gət.)

   a. extremely profitable
   b. wildly extravagant
   c. highly unusual

Copyright © 2002 by Addison Wesley Longman, Inc.

(Continued)

8. I find that the best *soporific* activity for me is to read something light for a few minutes before I turn off the lamp. I am usually sound asleep in ten minutes. (Pronounce *soporific* sä-pə-ri′-fic.)

   a. relaxing
   b. leisure
   c. sleep-causing

9. Though he and his men were marooned in Antarctica till the ice melted, Shackleton displayed a *stoic* lack of concern for pain and hardship. (Pronounce *stoic* stō′-ik.)

   a. calm
   b. passionate
   c. cold

10. Falstaff had a truly *epicurean* love for the joys of the flesh, especially liquor. Nothing, not even battle, stood in the way of his pursuit of sensuous delights. (Pronounce *epicurean* e-pi-kyü-rē′-ən.)

    a. cowardly
    b. selfish
    c. pleasure-seeking

Writing Assignment 18.2

To help you learn the italicized adjectives in the preceding exercise, here they are again on the left with one of their antonyms (opposites) on the right. Imagine two people or things or circumstances that could be contrasted by the two antonyms, and write a sentence or two using the two words to show this contrast. The first is done as an example. Use your own paper for the sentences.

1. novel—run-of-the-mill Michelle and her teammates won first prize at the science fair for their NOVEL use of computer graphics to show the life cycle of a frog. Their exhibit stood out among the fifteen other RUN-OF-THE-MILL exhibits.
2. fledgling—mature
3. patent—hidden
4. clairvoyant—unseeing
5. partisan—impartial

(Continued)

6. expedient—impractical
7. profligate—thrifty
8. soporific—exciting
9. stoic—emotional
10. epicurean—self-denying

Many nouns become adjectives with the suffix *-ous: joy + -ous = joyous.* It means generally *having, full of, characterized by* _____. This ending is related to *-ose*, which we saw in Chapter 8, page 76, means *full of,* as in *verbose, full of words.* Note how nouns change to such adjectives in the following exercise.

Vocabulary Exercise 18.2

Change the nouns in the first column below to adjectives by adding *-ous.* Follow additional spelling directions where they occur. Learn the meanings of unfamiliar words as you go along by forming your own memorable context.

1. moment
   _____
   (of utmost importance)

2. peril (danger)   _____

3. advantage   _____

----

4. space (in this group,   spacious
   change the final *e* to *i.*)

5. grace   _____

6. malice (desire to harm others)   _____

7. caprice (a sudden turn of mind, a whim)   _____

8. sacrilege (a violation of
   something sacred)   _____

----

9. fame (in this group the *e* disappears)   famous

10. disaster   _____

11. ridicule   _____

Copyright © 2002 by Addison Wesley Longman, Inc.

(Continued)

12. virtue   _____

13. wonder   _____

- -

14. envy (in this group,   envious
    the final *y* changes to *i*)

15. harmony   _____

16. ceremony   _____

17. acrimony (bitterness)   _____

18. parsimony (stinginess)   _____

19. sanctimony (pretended holiness)   _____

20. pity   piteous (note the unusual *e*)

Vocabulary Exercise 18.3

Use the contexts of the following passages to decide which of the adjectives in the preceding exercise belongs in each blank. Write the word you choose in the blank. Again, use these contexts to help you learn new words.

1. Writing obscene words all over the tombstones in the local cemetery was a _____ act. Whoever did it should be arrested and punished. (More than one word can fill this blank.)

2. The debate over what to do when the local landfill can take no more garbage was filled with _____ and harsh words. The council president could hardly maintain order.

3. To survive only on Social Security benefits, many elderly people must live very _____ lives, spending money only on the bare necessities.

4. The kitten high up the old oak tree let out a _____ cry for help, but no one was strong enough to climb the tree and retrieve it.

5. Graduation from college is a _____ day for students who needed more than four or five years to complete their degrees because they had to work to put themselves through school.

(Continued)

6. Surveys of job-related accidents and deaths show that one of the most _____ jobs in the United States is that of a firefighter. Besides the obvious dangers of exposure to fire and falling debris, firefighters often suffer from smoke inhalation.

7. In Nathaniel Hawthorne's story *Young Goodman Brown,* the main character discovers, or thinks he discovers, that all the good and holy citizens of his town are really _____ hypocrites.

8. Tornadoes are particularly _____ acts of nature; they can touch down and destroy one street of a town but leave the next street unharmed. Weather forecasters have great difficulty in warning people about a tornado's exact path.

9. My neighbors are prejudiced against people who are not exactly like them. They have been passing around really _____ gossip about a couple who just moved in across the street from them.

10. Todd's MA degree in public policy put him in a _____ position when he applied for a job in the office of a U.S. Representative from his state. None of the other applicants had that credential.

Vocabulary Exercise 18.4

Now turn the tables and change the adjectives in the first column below to nouns by following the examples of *enormous* and *enormity* for the first seven blanks and *curious* and *curiosity* for the last six.

1. enormous   enormity

2. ambiguous (having more than one
   possible meaning, uncertain)   _____

3. barbarous (cruel; uncivilized)   _____

4. continuous   _____

5. garrulous (talkative)   _____

6. hilarious   _____

7. sonorous (having a full, rich sound) _____

8. ubiquitous (present everywhere)   _____

Copyright © 2002 by Addison Wesley Longman, Inc.

(Continued)

  9. curious   curiosity

10. generous   _____

11. impetuous (acting quickly   _____
     without thought, impulsive)

12. luminous (full of light)   _____

13. monstrous   _____

14. nebulous (cloudy, unclear)   _____

15. pompous (self-important, behaving   _____
     in too showy a manner)

16. scrupulous (conscientiously honest _____
     and upright)

Vocabulary Exercise 18.5

Use the contexts of the following passages to decide which of the nouns and adjectives in the preceding exercise belongs in each blank. Write the word you choose in the blank. Again, use these contexts to help you learn new words.

1. The fortune-teller's answers to my questions were so _____ that I could interpret them in whatever way I wanted.

2. She was a person who often acted on impulse. If she wanted a new dress, she bought it, almost without thinking. If she met a person she liked, that person became her instant best friend. But her _____ could also make you an instant enemy.

3. The _____ of Lizzie Borden's crime made her an instant legend. How could a young woman have killed both her parents with an ax? (More than one word would fit this blank.)

4. What do teenagers find to talk about for so many hours over the telephone? After spending a day together at school, my son and his closest friend then talk for an hour on the phone. Will they outgrow all this _____?

5. The old couple said they had seen an unidentified flying object. This UFO was a round, flat disk that radiated a soft blue light. It was so _____ that it lit up all the ground around it as it came closer.

(Continued)

6 & 7. After the volcano erupted, a _____ cloud of ash drifted from it. The cloud spread thousands of miles, and for days after the eruption the sun was hidden in its gray mass. The entire area within a 100-mile radius of the volcano was covered with a _____, light gray ash.

8. In old imperial China, the binding of young girls' feet was a _____ custom. It cruelly prevented their feet from growing normally and forced them to stay close to home all their lives. (More than one word would fit this blank.)

9. The violin is a stringed instrument with a high, colorful sound. The viola is a somewhat larger instrument with a somewhat deeper sound. The cello is even larger and makes a deep, _____ music.

10. If you took a year's leave of absence, you would be breaking the _____ of your service to the company and would lose your seniority as well. When you returned, you would have to start all over again to build up a record of unbroken service.

Vocabulary Exercise 18.6

Do you know the adjectives and nouns introduced in the first part of this chapter well enough to use them in your own writing? To check your knowledge of some of these words, write a brief phrase or sentence to describe or answer the following, as in the example. Repeat the italicized word in your response where possible. Write the responses with a classmate if desired.

EXAMPLE: Briefly describe a *momentous* occasion in your life thus far.
Flying to London for the first time was MOMENTOUS for me because I had never flown before.

1. What would a *gracious* hostess say after you spilled spaghetti on her rug?

_____

2. What might a *malicious* co-worker who disliked you say about you behind your back?

_____

Copyright © 2002 by Addison Wesley Longman, Inc.

(Continued)

3. How might a *capricious* child act in a new playground?

   _____

4. Why do people think it is *sacrilegious* to write graffiti on a church, synagogue, or mosque?

   _____

5. What are some flattering ways of saying that a person is *parsimonious?*

   _____

6. Why might a *sanctimonious* man attend religious services?

   _____

7. If a friend asks you how her new haircut looks, and you give the *ambiguous* reply, "It looks nice," what are two different meanings your reply could have?

   _____

8. If you forget to pay your auto insurance bill, what would the insurance company be doing if it broke the *continuity* of your insurance coverage?

   _____

9. Why might you describe a taxicab driver as *garrulous?*

   _____

10. Why would it be expensive for a company to have *ubiquitous* ads for its products?

    _____

11. How can *impetuosity* be a positive trait for an artist to possess?

    _____

12. Describe briefly a bride who looks *luminous.*

    _____

13. Why would a *nebulous* idea about how to solve quadratic equations be a disadvantage on an algebra test?

    _____

(Continued)

14. What qualities does a person who is considered a *pompous* ass possess?

_____

15. A person elected treasurer of a club should be *scrupulous*. Why?

_____

The adjective suffix *-acious,* as we saw in Chapter 8, page 76, means *full of,* and adjectives with this ending can often become nouns ending in *-acity.* Thus *capacious, full of room or space,* goes with *capacity.* There are a great many such adjectives in English, and the following acquaints you with some.

Vocabulary Exercise 18.7

Fill in the blanks below with nouns or adjectives as needed, using *capacious, capacity* as examples. Unusual forms are filled in for you.

Adjectives	Nouns
capacious (roomy)	capacity
audacious (bold, daring)	_____
_____	efficacy (effectiveness)
_____	fallacy (mistake in reasoning)
pugnacious (*pugna-*, to fight)	_____
_____	rapacity (*rape-*, to seize, rape)
perspicacious (*per-* + *spec-*)	_____
_____	salacity (*salax,* lustful)
tenacious (*ten-*, to hold)	_____
_____	veracity (*verax,* truth)
mendacious (*mendax,* liar)	_____

Copyright © 2002 by Addison Wesley Longman, Inc.

Vocabulary Exercise 18.8

Use the parts (roots, prefixes and suffixes) of the words above and their contexts
in the sentences below to figure out what the words mean. In the blank after the
sentence, write the meaning of each word as used in the sentence.

1. She has a great *capacity* for friendship. You can tell from the many
   different kinds of people who are her friends.

   _____

2. In my *capacity* as chairman, I have decided to call a meeting. In your
   capacity as secretary, you must locate a room for the meeting and notify
   the members.

   _____

3. The doctor is a firm believer in the *efficacy* of daily exercise. She advised
   me to jog or cycle for twenty minutes every morning.

   _____

4. An *efficacious* breast cancer drug is still needed. The drugs now available
   are only partially helpful and have nasty side effects.

   _____

5. The *audacity* of a speaker condemning her listeners astonishes me. How
   can a person who has been invited here to speak to us turn around and
   ridicule her audience?

   _____

6. Your reasoning in this essay is *fallacious* and unsound. You cannot argue
   that the world is flat simply because it looks flat.

   _____

7. The *pugnacity* of the fierce Yanomama Indians of South America is
   extraordinary. Periods of violent war are more common in their society
   than times of peace.

   _____

8. He is a *rapacious* old man who still has the first dollar he ever earned.
   That's why we call him Scrooge.

   _____

(Continued)

9. My daughter's first-grade teacher is so *perspicacious* that in the first month of school he was able to see that she needed glasses to see the front of the room. Neither my husband nor I had noticed.

   _____

10. The movie was so *salacious* that even today's movie audiences who are so used to sexually explicit scenes were shocked by it.

   _____

11. The lawyer questioned the witness's *veracity*. After all, the witness was a close friend of the defendant and would want to protect her.

   _____

12. In Tennessee Williams' play *Cat on a Hot Tin Roof,* everyone in Big Daddy's family is accused of *mendacity:* everyone, except his favorite son, keeps trying to get on his good side because he is so rich.

   _____

13. To succeed in the professional theater, besides having a great deal of talent, one needs to be *tenacious,* never giving up despite rejection after rejection.

   _____

Writing Assignment 18.3

Choose ten nouns and adjectives from Vocabulary Exercise 18.7 that are new to you. Reviewing all the information about each word in this chapter, write a sentence using each one correctly. For further information about a word, look it up in your dictionary. Use your own paper for the sentences. ■

For more work changing words from one part of speech to another, see Chapter 23 in the next unit.

Copyright © 2002 by Addison Wesley Longman, Inc.

Review Exercise I for Chapters 17–18

In the left-hand column below are some words discussed in the last two chapters. Match each one with its meaning in the right-hand column. When a word can be two different parts of speech, the part of speech you should consider is indicated.

1. stimulus _____   a. speak badly of
2. repudiation _____   b. persecution
3. impetuosity _____   c. go along with
4. mitigate _____   d. one who endures calmly
5. disparage _____   e. waver, hesitate
6. harassment _____   f. alleviate, moderate
7. rebuff (verb) _____   g. whatever stirs to action
8. vacillate _____   h. snub, push aside
9. acquiesce _____   i. impulsiveness
10. stoic (noun) _____   j. disowning, rejection

Review Exercise II for Chapters 17–18

Here are some adjectives from Chapters 17–18. In the blanks, write a synonym for each. Then match each with its antonym on the right.

1. garrulous _____   a. chaste, modest
2. partisan _____   b. gullible
3. incredulous _____   c. humble
4. ostentatious _____   d. clear, definite
5. expedient _____   e. uncommon, hard to find
6. acrimonious _____   f. laconic, silent
7. salacious _____   g. impractical
8. ambiguous _____   h. pleasant, agreeable
9. pompous _____   i. impartial, neutral
10. ubiquitous _____   j. modest, simple

Review Exercise III for Chapters 17–18

Change each word below into a different part of speech by adding a suffix or changing the suffix it has. Be careful about spelling the word you write. Then write a sentence using either word.

1. endorse _____

2. speculation _____

3. respect _____

4. comply _____

5. disaster _____

6. denounce _____

7. exacerbation _____

8. divert _____

9. purge _____

10. appeasement _____

Review Exercise IV for Chapters 17–18

Here are some adjectives from Chapters 17–18. Underline as many of the nouns following each one that could reasonably be described by that adjective.

EXAMPLE: appreciative: <u>child</u>   <u>audience</u>   sense

1.	barbarous:	comment	behavior	warriors
2.	efficacious:	remedy	dream	painkiller
3.	contemptible:	manner	amateur	liar
4.	sanctimonious:	smile	sneer	attitude
5.	patent:	intention	remorse	invention
6.	condescending:	woman	meeting	privilege
7.	profligate:	savings	spending	earnings
8.	indigent:	laborers	families	hopes
9.	novel:	reading	idea	project
10.	authoritative:	weapons	voice	source
11.	scrupulous:	conscience	leader	lawyer
12.	laconic:	speech	reply	cowboy

Copyright © 2002 by Addison Wesley Longman, Inc.

Reading 4

Here is a selection from *You Just Don't Understand: Men and Women in Conversation*, Deborah Tannen's book on the differences between the ways men and women communicate. These differences in conversational style lead to misunderstandings between the sexes. Consider how these differences have shown up in your own conversations with the opposite sex.

As you read, be especially aware of the words and word parts we have examined in this unit. For more help with unfamiliar words, remember what you learned in Unit 1 about figuring out the meanings of unfamiliar words from their contexts and what you learned in Unit 2 about word parts with unvarying meaning. You may want to review those units briefly before beginning. In her explanations, Tannen often uses difficult words over and over again, and she intersperses explanations with particular examples. So you can figure out the meanings of the difficult words both from the different contexts in which they appear and from the examples. Some difficult words are italicized for your particular attention.

Different Words, Different Worlds

1   Many years ago I was married to a man who shouted at me, "I do not give you the right to raise your voice to me, because you are a woman and I am a man." This was frustrating, because I knew it was unfair. But I also knew just what was going on. I *ascribed* his unfairness to his having grown up in a country where few people thought women and men might have equal rights.

2   Now I am married to a man who is a partner and friend. We come from similar backgrounds and share values and interests. It is a continual source of pleasure to talk to him. It is wonderful to have someone I can tell everything to, someone who understands. But he doesn't always see things as I do, doesn't always react to things as I expect him to. And I often don't understand why he says what he does.

3   At the time I began working on this book, we had jobs in different cities. People frequently expressed sympathy by making comments like "That must be rough," and "How do you stand it?" I was inclined to accept their sympathy and say things like "We fly a lot." Sometimes I would reinforce their concern: "The worst part

is having to pack and unpack all the time." But my husband reacted differently, often with irritation. He might respond by de-emphasizing the inconvenience: As academics, we had four-day weekends together, as well as long vacations throughout the year and four months in the summer. We even benefited from the intervening days of uninterrupted time for work. I once overheard him tell a *dubious* man that we were lucky, since studies have shown that married couples who live together spend less than half an hour talking to each other; he was implying that our situation had advantages.

4   I didn't object to the way my husband responded—everything he said was true—but I was surprised by it. I didn't understand why he reacted as he did. He explained that he sensed *condescension* in some expressions of concern, as if the questioner were implying, "Yours is not a real marriage; your ill-chosen profession has resulted in an unfortunate arrangement. I pity you, and look down at you from the height of *complacence,* since my wife and I have avoided your misfortune." It had not occurred to me that there might be an element of *one-upmanship* in these expressions of concern, though I could recognize it when it was pointed out. Even after I saw the point, though, I was inclined to regard my husband's response as slightly odd, a personal *quirk.* He frequently seemed to see others as *adversaries* when I didn't.

5   Having done the research that led to this book, I now see that my husband was simply *engaging* the world in a way that many men do: as an individual in a *hierarchical* social order in which he was either one-up or one-down. In this world, conversations are *negotiations* in which people try to achieve and maintain the upper hand if they can, and protect themselves from others' attempts to put them down and push them around. Life, then, is a contest, a struggle to preserve independence and avoid failure.

6   I, on the other hand, was approaching the world as many women do: as an individual in a network of connections. In this world, conversations are *negotiations* for closeness in which people try to seek and give *confirmation* and support, and to reach *consensus.* They try to protect themselves from others' attempts to push them away. Life, then, is a community, a struggle to preserve *intimacy,* and avoid isolation. Though there are *hierarchies* in this world too, they are *hierarchies* more of friendship than of power and accomplishment.

Copyright © 2002 by Addison Wesley Longman, Inc.

7   Women are also concerned with achieving status and avoiding failure, but these are not the goals they are **focused** on all the time, and they tend to pursue them in the *guise* of connection. And men are also concerned with achieving involvement and avoiding isolation, but they are not **focused** on these goals, and they tend to pursue them in the *guise* of opposition.

8   Discussing our differences from this point of view, my husband pointed out to me a distinction I had missed: He reacted the way I just described only if expressions of concern came from men in whom he sensed an awareness of *hierarchy*. And there were times when I too disliked people's expressing sympathy about our commuting marriage. I recalled being offended by one man who seemed to have a leering look in his eye when he asked, "How do you manage this long-distance romance?" Another time I was annoyed when a woman who knew me only by reputation approached us during the intermission of a play, discovered our situation by asking my husband where he worked, and kept the conversation going by asking us all about it. In these cases, I didn't feel put down; I felt intruded upon. If my husband was affected by what he perceived as claims to superior status, I felt these sympathizers were claiming inappropriate *intimacy*.

Intimacy and Independence

9   **Intimacy** is key in a world of connection where individuals *negotiate* complex networks of friendship, *minimize* differences, try to reach *consensus,* and avoid the appearances of superiority, which would highlight differences. In a world of status, **independence** is key, because a primary means of establishing status is to tell others what to do, and taking orders is a marker of low status. Though all humans need both *intimacy* and independence, women tend to focus on the first and men on the second. It is as if their life-blood ran in different directions.

10   These differences can give women and men differing views of the same situation, as they did in the case of a couple I will call Linda and Josh. When Josh's old high-school chum called him at work and announced that he'd be in town on business the following month, Josh invited him to stay for the weekend. That evening he informed Linda that they were going to have a houseguest, and that

he and his chum would go out together the first night to shoot the breeze like old times. Linda was upset. She was going to be away on business the week before, and the Friday night that Josh would be out with his chum would be her first night home. But what upset her the most was that Josh had made these plans on his own and informed her of them, rather than discussing them with her before extending the invitation.

11   Linda would never make plans, for a weekend or an evening, without first checking with Josh. She can't understand why he doesn't show her the same courtesy and consideration that she shows him. But when she protests, Josh says, "I can't say to my friend, 'I have to ask my wife for permission'!"

12   To Josh, checking with his wife means seeking permission, which implies that he is not independent, not free to act on his own. It would make him feel like a child or an *underling*. To Linda, checking with her husband has nothing to do with permission. She assumes that spouses discuss their plans with each other because their lives are *intertwined,* so the actions of one have consequences for the other. Not only does Linda not mind telling someone, "I have to check with Josh"; quite the contrary—she likes it. It makes her feel good to know and show that she is involved with someone, that her life is bound up with someone else's.

13   Linda and Josh felt more upset by this incident, and others like it, than seemed warranted, because it cut to the core of their primary concerns. Linda was hurt because she sensed a failure of closeness in their relationship: He didn't care about her as much as she cared about him. And he was hurt because he felt she was trying to control him and limit his freedom.

14   A similar conflict exists between Louise and Howie, another couple, about spending money. Louise would never buy anything costing more than a hundred dollars without discussing it with Howie, but he goes out and buys whatever he wants and feels they can afford, like a table saw or a new power mower. Louise is disturbed, not because she disapproves of the purchases, but because she feels he is acting as if she is not in the picture.

15   Many women feel it is natural to consult with their partners at every turn, while many men automatically make more decisions without consulting their partners. This may reflect a broad difference in *conceptions* of decision making. Women expect decisions to be

Copyright © 2002 by Addison Wesley Longman, Inc.

discussed first and made by *consensus*. They appreciate the discussion itself as evidence of involvement and communication. But many men feel *oppressed* by lengthy discussions about what they see as minor decisions, and they feel hemmed in if they can't just act without talking first. When women try to *initiate* a *freewheeling* discussion by asking, "What do you think?" men often think they are being asked to decide.

16   Communication is a continual balancing act, juggling the conflicting needs for *intimacy* and independence. To survive in this world, we have to act *in concert with* others, but to survive as ourselves, rather than simply as *cogs* in a wheel, we have to act alone. . . .

Asymmetries

17   If *intimacy* says, "We're close and the same," and independence says, "We're separate and different," it is easy to see that *intimacy* and independence *dovetail* with connection and status. The essential element of connection is *symmetry:* People are the same, feeling equally close to each other. The essential element of status is *asymmetry:* People are not the same; they are differently placed in a *hierarchy.*

18   This *duality* is particularly clear in expressions of sympathy or concern, which are all potentially *ambiguous*. They can be interpreted either *symmetrically,* as evidence of fellow-feeling among equals, or *asymmetrically,* offered by someone who is one-up to someone who is one-down. Asking if an unemployed person has found a job, if a couple has succeeded in conceiving the child they crave, or whether an untenured professor expects to get tenure can be meant—and interpreted, regardless of how it is meant—as an expression of human connection by a person who understands and cares, or as a reminder of weakness from someone who is better off and knows it, and hence as *condescending*. The latter view of sympathy seems self-evident to many men. For example, a handicapped mountain climber named Tom Whittaker, who leads groups of disabled people on outdoor expeditions, remarked, "You can't feel sympathetic for someone you admire"—a statement that struck me as not true at all.

19   The *symmetry* of connection is what creates community: If two people are struggling for closeness, they are both struggling for the same thing. And the *asymmetry* of status is what creates contest: Two people can't both have the upper hand, so *negotiation* for status is *inherently adversarial. . . .* Once I identified these *dynamics,* however, I saw them all around me. The puzzling behavior of friends and co-workers finally became comprehensible.

20   Differences in how my husband and I approached the same situation, which previously would have been mystifying, suddenly made sense. For example, in a jazz club the waitress recommended the crab cakes to me, and they turned out to be terrible. I was uncertain about whether or not to send them back. When the waitress came by and asked how the food was, I said that I didn't really like the crab cakes. She asked, "What's wrong with them?" While staring at the table, my husband answered, "They don't taste fresh." The waitress snapped, "They're frozen! What do you expect?" I looked directly up at her and said, "We just don't like them." She said, "Well, if you don't like them, I could take them back and bring you something else."

21   After she left with the crab cakes, my husband and I laughed because we realized we had just automatically played out the scripts I had been writing about. He had heard her question "What's wrong with them?" as a challenge that he had to match. He doesn't like to fight, so he looked away, to soften what he felt was an *obligatory counterchallenge:* He felt *instinctively* that he had to come up with something wrong with the crab cakes to justify my complaint. (He was fighting for me.) I had taken the question "What's wrong with them?" as a request for information. I *instinctively* sought a way to be right without making her wrong. Perhaps it was because she was a woman that she responded more favorably to my approach.

22   When I have spoken to friends and to groups about these differences, they too say that now they can make sense of previously *perplexing* behavior. For example, a woman said she finally understood why her husband refused to talk to his boss about whether or not he stood a chance of getting promoted. He wanted to know because if the answer was no, he would start looking for another job. But instead of just asking, he *stewed* and

Copyright © 2002 by Addison Wesley Longman, Inc.

fretted, lost sleep, and worried. Having no others at her disposal, this wife had fallen back on psychological explanations: Her husband must be insecure, afraid of rejection. But then, everyone is insecure, to an extent. Her husband was actually quite a confident person. And she, who believed herself to be at least as insecure as he, had not hesitated to go to her boss to ask whether he intended to make her temporary job permanent. . . .

23   Yet another woman said she finally understood why her fiancé, who very much believes in equality, once whispered to her that she should keep her voice down. "My friends are downstairs," he said. "I don't want them to get the impression that you order me around."

24   That women have been labeled "nags" may result from the *interplay* of men's and women's styles, whereby many women are inclined to do what is asked of them and many men are inclined to resist even the slightest hint that anyone, especially a woman, is telling them what to do. A woman will be inclined to repeat a request that doesn't get a response because she is convinced that her husband would do what she asks, if he only understood that she **really** wants him to do it. But a man who wants to avoid feeling that he is following orders may *instinctively* wait before doing what she asked, in order to imagine that he is doing it of his own free will. Nagging is the result, because each time she repeats the request, he again puts off fulfilling it.

Mastery Exercises

1. Note that Tannen uses many difficult words over and over again. Often the same root word appears as different parts of speech. Such repetition means that you have many different sentences to use as *contexts* for understanding the meanings and uses of these words. Look at the contexts in which the following words appear. Then choose as many of the meanings for each listed on the right that fit Tannen's use of the word. Note that different words with the same root, like the first two, *hierarchical* and *hierarchies,* should also share root meanings.

Par. 5: *hierarchical*   a. orderly
                              b. arranged from top to bottom
                              c. challenging
                              d. power-giving

(Continued)

Par. 6: *hierarchies*
(used twice)

    a. systems
    b. ranked arrangements
    c. challenges
    d. displays of power

Par. 4: *adversaries*

    a. opposites
    b. dangers
    c. opponents
    d. enemies

Par.19: *adversarial*

    a. contrasting
    b. dangerous
    c. opposing
    d. hostile

Pars. 17 & 19: *asymmetry*
(See also *asymmetrically*
in Par. 18)

    a. imbalance
    b. inequality
    c. war
    d. difference in rank

Pars. 17 & 19: *symmetry*
(See also *symmetrically*
in Par. 18)

    a. balance
    b. equality
    c. peace
    d. similarity in rank

2. Since Tannen is *contrasting* the ways men and women communicate, you may find that you can figure out the meanings of many of the difficult words she uses by their place in her contrast. This is the case, for example, with the contrasted words *asymmetry* and *symmetry,* highlighted in the preceding question. Thus her purpose in writing provides clues to the meanings of the words she uses.

    Use Tannen's contrast, as well as any roots, prefixes and suffixes and any other clues in the italicized words' contexts, to answer the following about some of Tannen's words.

    a. In 3 sentences, summarize Pars. 5–7 in your own words. Then offer a synonym for *guise* in Par. 7.

_____

_____

_____

_____

Copyright © 2002 by Addison Wesley Longman, Inc.

(Continued)

    b. In Par. 12, what is the difference between the way Linda feels about checking with her husband Josh and the way he feels about checking with her? What, then, is an *underling*?

_____

    What does *intertwined* mean?

_____

    c. In Par. 15, why do women LIKE discussing a big decision before making it? Why do men DISLIKE it?

_____

    What, then, does it mean to make a decision *by consensus*? (This word is also used in Pars. 6 and 9.)

_____

    What might be a synonym for *oppressed*?

_____

    What sort of a discussion is *freewheeling*?

_____

3. Tannen also often says the same thing two or three times in different words to make her point clear. If an unfamiliar word occurs in such a sentence, you can use the other, more familiar words that say the same thing to figure out its meaning. Try this strategy with the following:

    a. In Par. 4, Tannen describes her husband's response as *slightly odd, a personal quirk*. What do you think a *quirk* is?

_____

    b. In Par. 6, Tannen says that in women's conversations, they *try to seek and give confirmation and support, and to reach consensus*. What might be a synonym for *confirmation*?

_____

    c. In Par. 22, a woman's husband *stewed and fretted, lost sleep, and worried*. What do you think *stewed* means?

_____

(Continued)

How is a person who is *stewing* similar to a *stew* cooking on a stove?

_____

4. Tannen's examples of people she knows help explain what she means. You can also use these examples to figure out some of her difficult words.

a. In Pars. 3 and 4, she describes the contrasting ways in which she and her husband used to react to people's comments about their long-distance relationship. Summarize her husband's explanation of why he reacted with irritation. Then say what you think *condescension* and *complacence* mean.

_____

_____

_____

_____

(For more help, see the word *condescending* in Par. 18.)

b. In Pars. 20 and 21, how does Tannen's husband respond to the waitress's question? Why?

_____

So what do you think *obligatory* means?_____

_____

What is a *counterchallenge*?_____

_____

What is another way of saying *instinctively*?_____

_____

Copyright © 2002 by Addison Wesley Longman, Inc.

Unit 4
Post-Test 1

Find the roots in the following words by crossing out any prefixes and suffixes you recognize from work in this unit. Then jot down in the blank next to each word two or three other words that contain the same root but that have different prefixes and/or suffixes.

    EXAMPLE: ~~per~~mi̶s̶s̶i̶o̶n̶ _submit, commission, intermittent_

1. sufferance_____

2. impulsive_____

3. postscript_____

4. construction_____

5. irresistible_____

6. allay_____

7. insupportable_____

8. receptive_____

9. inducement_____

10. exclamation_____

Unit 4

Post-Test 2

From each pair of frequently confused words below, choose the correct word to fill in the blank. Use the context of the sentence in which the blank occurs to help you decide.

1. Mugging the elderly is a particularly (contemptuous, contemptible) crime.

2. The first European settlers in New England were known not only as Puritans but also as (Dissenters, Descenders) because they did not agree with the practices of the Church of England.

3. There is a small but (perceptive, perceptible) difference in the taste of lemons and limes.

4. It is hard to believe that every disappearing act the magician performed in last night's show was an (allusion, illusion).

5. The (ostentatious, ostensible) reason why Ermina called Ellen was to congratulate her on her engagement; the real reason was to find out who her fiancé is.

6. Tonight's speaker is an (eminent, imminent) journalist who received the Pulitzer Prize for her series of articles on health care.

7. Because the novels of Solzhenitsyn were (censored, censured) by the Soviet government, only a few Russians read them in hand-printed copies passed secretly from one person to another.

8. Columbus called the (indigent, indigenous) people of the Caribbean island where he first landed "Indians" because he thought he had reached the East Indies.

9. The old man was so (amused, bemused) by the antics of his grandson that he didn't even hear the call to dinner.

10. A colorfully dressed band of bagpipers, playing a happy march tune, (preceded, proceeded) the graduates into the auditorium.

Copyright © 2002 by Addison Wesley Longman, Inc.

Unit 4

Post-Test 3

Underline the correct spelling of each word below. Then if the word has a prefix that accounts for its double consonants, write this prefix in the space next to the words.

1. imature, immature_____

2. acomplish, accomplish_____

3. economy, ecconomy_____

4. comission, commission_____

5. imagine, immagine_____

6. coloquial, colloquial_____

7. opression, oppression_____

8. referee, refferee_____

9. difidence, diffidence_____

10. operate, opperate_____

Unit 4

Post-Test 4

Return to the Russell Baker "translation" of the story of Little Red Riding Hood at the end of Unit 2, page 89. In his retelling of the story, Baker has substituted a great many Latinate words for simpler native English words. In these Latinate words you can often find roots, prefixes and suffixes examined in this unit. List ten different words from the Baker piece that contain one or more word parts studied in this unit. Circle these word parts and then list two or three other words you know with these same parts. Identify the paragraph number from which you take each word.

EXAMPLE:

Par. 1: accessible ac- in acceptable, -cess in success, -ible in permissible

1. _____

2. _____

3. _____

4. _____

5. _____

6. _____

7. _____

8. _____

9. _____

10. _____

Unit 4

Post-Test 5

Return to the selection from *You Just Don't Understand* on pages 240–46. In about 6–8 sentences, explain what Deborah Tannen says is the main reason why men and women often have trouble talking to each other. In your explanation, use some of the difficult words italicized in the reading.

Copyright © 2002 by Addison Wesley Longman, Inc.

UNIT 5

Improving Your Writing Vocabulary

In This Unit, You Will Learn How to Improve Your Writing Vocabulary By:

You Will also Learn:

For Skills Practice, You Will Read:

Introduction: Words in Your Writing Vocabulary

So far in this book, we have been discussing improving your vocabulary by:

- Learning new words from their contexts (Unit 1)
- Using a knowledge of word parts to learn new words (Units 2 and 4)

- Building contexts for new words with a dictionary and word families (Units 3 and 4)

Now that you are equipped with ways of learning unfamiliar words in your reading and with mnemonic devices for remembering the new words you do look up in a dictionary, you can turn to improving the words you use in your writing. This will be the work of the next two units. In Unit 5 you will see how to make your writing more vivid, specific, original and clear by using familiar words and a dictionary. You will discover some ways of avoiding overused words and of using ordinary words in unusual ways. But the unit begins with some advice for using words that are brand new in your vocabulary. For as you move words from your passive memory, that is, words you can recognize in reading, to active use in speaking and writing, they become truly your own.

Copyright © 2002 by Addison Wesley Longman, Inc.

Frank and Ernest

© 1999 Thaves / Reprinted with permission. Newspaper dist. by NEA, Inc.

19

Using New Words

As you increase your reading vocabulary, you will be tempted to start using some new words in your writing, thus making them truly yours. When you use a new word,

Word in Focus
malapropism

> Be bold, but not too bold.

You may know a word's meaning, but not the different ways in which it can be used. Sometimes, your dictionary will help you learn how a word is used by comparing the meanings and uses of several synonyms together, but oftentimes, it will not. We learn how a word is used by hearing or reading other people's use of it many times. Hence the need for caution if you have seen the new word in use only once. To help you be bold, but not too bold, in using new words in your writing, observe these rules of thumb:

- If you can define the word correctly without using a dictionary, use the word.
- Use only a few new words at once.
- Proofread your final draft for words that seem strange to you.
- Ask another reader to react to your use of the new word.

You may still make mistakes. But it is better to try new words, even at the risk of making a mistake, than to continue using familiar words that are no longer adequate for the more complex and subtle ideas you will want to express.

Vocabulary Exercise 19.1

Mrs. Malaprop is a humorous character in Richard Sheridan's 18th-century play *The Rivals*. She makes frequent mistakes with words she doesn't know well. In fact, her name, which comes from French words meaning inappropriate, has entered English to mean a humorously wrong word use. In the *Frank and Ernest* comic strip by Thaves that opens this unit, Malaprop Man is a modern version of Sheridan's character. The words he misuses, which are from computer talk, all *sound* like the words he means.

Get together with one or two classmates, and make a list of the *malapropisms* in the comic. Start by looking in the title panel, where Thaves reminds us of the usual introduction of another superhero in the italicized malapropisms: "Look! Up in the Sky! It's *Absurd!* It's *Inane!* It's 'Malaprop Man'! A.K.A. 'The *Creped* Crusader.'" Then write down the words Malaprop Man *means* to say. Which one of the malapropisms do you find the most amusing? Why? Share your list and reactions with the rest of your classmates.

_____

_____

_____

_____

_____

Vocabulary Exercise 19.2

Now here are some of the original Mrs. Malaprop's *malapropisms*, in italics. Like those of Malaprop Man, they are words that sound like the words she means. In many cases, the mistake contains the same root as the word she means. What word do you think she means in each case? Once again, you may want to work with one or two classmates. Write in the blanks provided.

1. In Act I, Mrs. Malaprop is trying to get her niece Lydia to give up her young lover: "But the point that we would request of you is, that you will promise to forget this fellow—to *illiterate* him, I say, quite from your memory."

_____

Copyright © 2002 by Addison Wesley Longman, Inc.

(Continued)

2–9. When her friend Sir Anthony asks what education she would give a young girl, Mrs. Malaprop says, " I would by no means wish a daughter of mine to be a *progeny* of learning; I don't think so much learning becomes a young woman. . . . I would send her, at nine years old, to a boarding-school, in order to learn a little ingenuity and *artifice.* Then, sir, she should have a *supercilious* knowledge in accounts;—and as she grew up, I would have her instructed in *geometry,* so that she might know something of the *contagious* countries; but above all, Sir Anthony, she should be mistress of *orthodoxy,* that she might not misspell, and mispronounce words so shamefully as girls usually do; and likewise that she might *reprehend* the true meaning of what she is saying. This, Sir Anthony, is what I would have a woman know;—And I don't think there is a *superstitious* article in it."

_____

_____

_____

10. Of Sir Anthony's polite son, Mrs. Malaprop says in Act III, "He is the very *pineapple* of perfection."

_____

11–13. She tells how upset she is that Lydia has continued to see a lover whom Mrs. Malaprop thinks is unworthy: "Oh! it gives me the *hydrostatics* to such a degree. I thought she had *persisted* from corresponding with him; but, behold, this very day I have *interceded* another letter from the fellow; I believe I have it in my pocket."

_____

14. In her most famous malapropism, Mrs. Malaprop thus describes Lydia's stubbornness: "Oh, there's nothing to be hoped for from her! She's as headstrong as an *allegory* on the banks of the Nile."

_____

15. When Lydia compares her lover to the man Mrs. Malaprop wants her to marry, Mrs. Malaprop warns her, "No *caparisons,* miss, if you please. *Caparisons* don't become a young lady."

_____

Vocabulary Exercise 19.3

Like Mrs. Malaprop, several characters in Lewis Carroll's books *Alice's Adventures in Wonderland* and *Through the Looking-Glass* often say one thing when we—and Alice—expect them to say another. Unlike Mrs. Malaprop, however, Carroll's characters mean exactly what they say, but we hear them as "mistakes" that are really word jokes called *puns*. Here from *Alice's Adventures in Wonderland*, for example, is the description of their education by the Mock Turtle and the Gryphon. After reading it, pick out for yourself the words that are puns, and then in the blank lines below, write down what you think we—and Alice—*expected* to hear. Once again, you may wish to work with a classmate or two on this exercise.

"When we were little," the Mock Turtle went on at last, more calmly, though still sobbing a little now and then, "we went to school in the sea. The Master was an old Turtle—we used to call him Tortoise—"

"Why did you call him Tortoise, if he wasn't one?" Alice asked.

"We called him Tortoise because he taught us," said the Mock Turtle angrily; "really you are very dull!"

"You ought to be ashamed of yourself for asking such a simple question," added the Gryphon; and then they both sat silent and looked at poor Alice, who felt ready to sink into the earth. At last the Gryphon said to the Mock Turtle, "Drive on, old fellow! Don't be all day about it!" and he went on in these words. . . .

"I only took the regular course."

"What was that?" inquired Alice.

"Reeling and Writhing, of course, to begin with," the Mock Turtle replied; "and then the different branches of Arithmetic—Ambition, Distraction, Uglification, and Derision."

"I never heard of 'Uglification,'" Alice ventured to say. "What is it?"

The Gryphon lifted up both paws in surprise. "Never heard of uglifying!" it exclaimed. "You know what to beautify is, I suppose?"

"Yes," said Alice doubtfully; "it means—to—make—anything—prettier."

"Well, then," the Gryphon went on, "if you don't know what to uglify is, you *are* a simpleton."

Copyright © 2002 by Addison Wesley Longman, Inc.

"Once," said the Mock Turtle at last, with a deep sigh, "I was a real Turtle."

(Continued)

Alice did not feel encouraged to ask any more questions about it, so she turned to the Mock Turtle, and said, "What else had you to learn?"

"Well, there was Mystery," the Mock Turtle replied, counting off the subjects on his flappers,—"Mystery, ancient and modern, with Seaography; then Drawling—the Drawling master was an old conger eel, that used to come once a week; he taught us Drawling, Stretching, and Fainting in Coils."

"What was *that* like?" said Alice.

"Well, I can't show it to you, myself," the Mock Turtle said: "I'm too stiff. And the Gryphon never learned it."

"Hadn't time," said the Gryphon; "I went to the Classical master, though. He was an old crab, *he* was."

"I never went to him," the Mock Turtle said with a sigh; "he taught Laughing and Grief, they used to say."

"So he did, so he did," said the Gryphon, sighing in his turn, and both creatures hid their faces in their paws.

(Continued)

"And how many hours a day did you do lessons?" said Alice in a hurry to change the subject.

"Ten hours the first day," said the Mock Turtle, "nine the next, and so on."

"What a curious plan!" exclaimed Alice.

"That's the reason they're called lessons," the Gryphon remarked; "because they lessen from day to day."

This was quite a new idea to Alice, and she thought it over a little before she made her next remark. "Then the eleventh day must have been a holiday?"

"Of course it was," said the Mock Turtle.

_____

_____

_____

_____

_____

_____

_____

_____

These exercises in malapropisms and puns may suggest that it is relatively easy to confuse one word with another when both are fairly new to you. Yes, it is inevitable that you will make some mistakes as you learn how to use new words. But the possibility of error shouldn't deter you from using the words appropriate to your topic, even when they are quite new. It is especially important to learn to use the words that are particular to the field of study in which you plan to major or in which you hope to work. Just as your understanding of a new word you find in your reading becomes stronger when the word is repeated later in the same reading, so too will your grasp of the meanings and uses of the new words you try in your writing become firmer the more you try them out. Expect another reader to correct you when you try new words. In fact, *ask* another reader to correct you when you make vocabulary errors. Learning when *not* to use a word is just as important as learning when to use it.

Copyright © 2002 by Addison Wesley Longman, Inc.

Vocabulary Exercise 19.4

From a few pages in a textbook you are reading for a course in your field of special interest or your major, make a list of words and phrases that seem significant in the field. Ask a person knowledgeable in that field, such as a professor or a college senior majoring in that field, to read through your list and cross out any words that are not significant in the field. Then for the words and phrases remaining, (a) jot down synonyms or brief definitions, and then (b) write a sentence or two using each correctly. Ask the same professor or senior to read your sentences to see if you have used the words as they should be used. Continue adding to your list of words as you read and study further.

Writing Assignment 19.1

Like comic-strip writers and Lewis Carroll, comedians often purposely use the wrong words to get a laugh. In the Marx Brothers' movie *Duck Soup*, Chico, on trial for treason, asks his defender Groucho a question:

"What is it has a trunk but no key, weighs 2000 pounds, and lives in a circus?"

The judge yells out, "That's irrelevant!"

"Irrelevant," says Chico, "that's the answer. There's a whole lotta relephants in the circus."

"That kind of testimony we can eliminate," says the judge.

"That'sa fine. I'll take some," says Chico.

"You'll take what?"

"A lemonade, a nice cold glass of lemonade."

In a paragraph or two, explain why you think mistakes like these and the ones that Mrs. Malaprop, Malaprop Man, and the Mock Turtle and Gryphon make are funny. What makes us laugh when we hear or read them?   ■

For more work on deciding how and where to use unfamiliar words, see the work in Unit 6 with the thesaurus.

20

Varying Nouns and Adjectives

We can divide the very common words in English into two large types:

Word in Focus
trite

CONNECTING or FUNCTION WORDS to join our ideas together

Articles (*the, a, an*)
Conjunctions (such as *and, but, therefore, because*)
Prepositions (such as *to, for, by*)
Pronouns (such as *I, you, this*)

CONTENT WORDS to express most of what we mean

Nouns (such as *woman, car, meeting*)
Verbs (such as *make, do, have*)
Adjectives (such as *good, bad, ugly*)
Adverbs (such as *really, truly, elegantly*)

Because content words carry the burden of our meaning in a piece of writing, they need to be vivid and precise. Let's consider the noun *thing*. *Merriam Webster's Collegiate Dictionary* lists twenty-five different meanings for this word. No wonder the word is overused! Look up *thing* in your own dictionary, and read through its many meanings.

Copyright © 2002 by Addison Wesley Longman Publishers

Vocabulary Exercise 20.1

Choose ten of the meanings of *thing* listed in your dictionary. Then in the spaces below, write a brief sentence using *thing* for each of these ten meanings. To be sure that each use of *thing* is distinct from the others, replace *thing* with a synonym appearing in the definition. For example, one definition of *thing* is *an inanimate object,* as in this sentence:

EXAMPLE: Darlene carefully examined all the THINGS in her mother's room, trying to decide which one she loved most. (Here, we could replace *things* with *objects.*)

Write your own sentences here:

_____

_____

_____

_____

_____

_____

_____

_____

_____

_____

   We say that overused words like *thing* are *trite,* from the Latin word meaning *worn out, rubbed away.* Trite words and expressions are comfortable, like old shoes, but they lack freshness and originality. Go back to the sentences you just wrote above. Make each more vivid and precise by replacing *thing* either with a synonym that is more specific and precise, or with one or more examples of the *things* you mean. For example,

Darlene carefully examined all the KEEPSAKES in her mother's room. . . .

   OR

Darlene carefully examined all the PHOTOGRAPHS AND KNICKKNACKS in. . . .

Consider another extremely common word, the adjective *good*. The word *good* has a general feeling of approval. If you say something is good, we know that you think it is as it should be, or is better than average. But there are many specific ways in which experiences, objects, or people can be *good,* and using words that are more specific than *good* can help you express what you mean more effectively. Here is an exercise to help make you aware of the many meanings of the word *good.*

Vocabulary Exercise 20.2

Look up the word *good* in your dictionary and read through its meanings. Read each sentence below to see which meaning of the word is meant. Then write after each sentence the meaning or synonym for *good* that is most appropriate to the sentence. Each sentence uses a *different* meaning.

EXAMPLE: John would be a *good* salesman. successful

1. A pitchfork is good for digging very hard soil.

   _____

2. Green vegetables are good for you.

   _____

3. Their homemade bread is good.

   _____

4. Thor called me a liar and ruined my good name.

   _____

5. The children tried to be good during the story hour.

   _____

6. My grandmother was a truly good woman. She always thought of others before herself.

   _____

7. Mindy and Tamara are really good friends.

   _____

Copyright © 2002 by Addison Wesley Longman, Inc.

(Continued)

8. The students had a good time on the class outing to the zoo.

_____

9. The men I hired to paint the house did a good job.

_____

10. The train station is a good mile from our apartment.

_____

Writing Assignment 20.1

Think of an experience you have had that you consider "good." What details about this experience could you describe for fellow readers that would help them enjoy it vicariously? (*Vicariously* means that through your description, they can pretend to be in your place having the experience for themselves. In Latin, *vicis* means *change, place,* or *stead,* so through your description, your reader can pretend to be in your place.)

Write a paragraph about 6–8 sentences long describing your experience, but without using the word *good.* Try to avoid using any of the most common synonyms for *good* as well. Rather than telling us what you think of the experience, let the details you describe convey your attitude.   ■

Now try the same sort of substitution with an antonym of *good,* the word *bad.* Like its opposite, *bad* also carries a general feeling, but of course the feeling is one of disapproval. Something that is bad is not as it should be or is worse than average. Like its antonym, the word *bad* has many, more specific uses.

Vocabulary Exercise 20.3

Look up the word *bad* in your dictionary and read through its meanings. Then read each sentence below to see which meaning of the word is meant. Then write after each sentence the meaning or synonym for *bad* that is most appropriate to the sentence. Each sentence uses a different meaning.

EXAMPLE: Santa Claus knows if you've been good or *bad*. misbehaving

1. Don't curse me because I brought you bad news._____

2. This meat smells as if it has gone bad._____

3. Mark writes well, but his spelling is bad._____

4. I really feel bad about missing the last game._____

5. You can go to prison for writing bad checks._____

6. Fifty years ago, bad boys were sent to reformatories._____

7. The flu made Emily feel so bad that she had to go to bed._____

8. The last bad storm caused a flood in the valley._____

9. Construction sites are bad places for children to play in._____

10. Prohibition was a bad law because it could not be enforced.

Writing Assignment 20.2

Think of a morally corrupt, truly evil character you know from a book or movie. Choose a real villain. Describe the character for your classmates, but use the person's appearance, expressions, way of talking, actions, or any other suitable details to convey evil. Don't use the word *bad,* and try to avoid its synonyms as well. As in Writing Assignment 20.1, rather than telling us what you think of the villain, let the details you choose paint the picture of a *bad* person. ■

It is difficult, even for experienced writers, to avoid using trite words. These words are so common and comfortable that we often use them without thinking. They allow us to concentrate on our train of thought until

Copyright © 2002 by Addison Wesley Longman, Inc.

we have it down on paper. But, once a thought is down on paper, you can make it clearer, more precise, more vivid, and more interesting by:

> Rereading it looking for very general, overused nouns and adjectives like *thing, person, people, society, good, bad, nice, pleasant, interesting, awful, terrible* and the same words and phrases used over and over again, and
>
> Thinking up synonyms or examples of these words to use instead. Or look them up in your dictionary, not just for synonyms but also for other ideas you could use.

Vocabulary Exercise 20.4

Here is a brief essay praising life in a city. Read through it once to discover what it says. Then reread it, looking particularly at its nouns and adjectives. Leave alone the organization of ideas, the ideas themselves, and the sentence structure at this point, and consider ONLY the choice of words. Then answer the questions following it. The sentences are numbered to help you.

[1]My experiences when visiting the city have all been full of fun and excitement. [2]There are so many things to do there and so many places to go. [3]I think the city has everything except a quiet country atmosphere. [4]It's a great learning experience because it is full of museums and many different cultures. [5]Also, both day and night life are exciting.

[6]Like any other place, the city also has its bad points. [7]These include the crowds of people, the garbage, and of course the noise. [8]Of course, living in the city is not for everyone. [9]I know many people who find the city very hectic and would rather not go there at all. [10]Then there are people who love the city, but they say, "It's a nice place to visit, but I wouldn't want to live there." [11]But I guess it really can't be too bad since so many other people choose to live in the city and love it. [12]They love all the good things that the city has to offer and are not bothered by its bad parts.

[13]One reason for the city's excitement is its variety. [14]There are many people all working at different jobs and doing their own thing, while in small towns it seems that everyone does the same things. [15]If you are a person who likes the security of a small place with familiar faces and if you don't like extra excitement, then you shouldn't live in the city. [16]If you already live in the city and don't

(Continued)

like it as much as you once did, you should try living in a small town for six months. [17]Then you would probably look forward to moving back to the city. [18]A temporary escape from all the people and noise can be good for you, but you will soon get bored and want to come back to the excitement of the city.

1. The writer of this essay relies heavily on several nouns that have very broad, general meanings and uses. *Thing* or *things* is one such noun. Find and list three others:

   _____

2. Think of more specific words to replace the following phrases. Refer to your earlier work with alternative ways of saying *thing*.
   many things to do (sentence 2)_____
   all the good things (sentence 12)_____
   doing their own thing (sentence 14)_____
   does the same things (sentence 14)_____

3. How might you paint a picture in words that show the excitement of a big city? Write a sentence that could follow sentence 1 that describes some particular city event, activity, or experience that could be exciting. But don't use the word *exciting* or *excitement*.

   _____

   _____

4. Refer to the work you did with the word *bad*. Which meaning of *bad* do you think the writer is using in sentences 6, 11, and 12?

   _____

   Write a suitable synonym for *bad* next to each of the following examples from sentence 7:_____
   the crowds of people_____
   the garbage_____
   the noise_____

5. What other particular aspects of a city might be considered *bad* in any of its meanings? List as many bad aspects as you can, and next to each one, write the meaning of *bad* that is suitable for it.

   EXAMPLE: traffic congestion: This is bad because it is unpleasant or disagreeable.

   _____

Copyright © 2002 by Addison Wesley Longman, Inc.

(Continued)

_____

_____

_____

6. So that you don't leave this exercise with a bias against city life, refer to your earlier work with the adjective *good*. Which of its meanings do you think the writer is using in sentence 12?
   In sentence 18?_____
   What other meanings of *good* could you also apply to a city?

_____

_____

7. List all the aspects of city life that the writer thinks are *good*. Then list as many other *good things* in a city as you can think of. Next to each, write several examples of the *good thing*.

   EXAMPLE: a variety of restaurants: French, Italian, Thai; bistros, steak houses, tea shops

_____

_____

_____

_____

8. Review the bad aspects of the city that you listed in #5 above. Now consider them in contrast to or comparison with life in a small town or suburb. List below one contrasting or similar aspect of life in a small town or suburb for each bad aspect of life in a city.

   EXAMPLE: City: traffic congestion/Small town: usually not much traffic except when workers leave the local factory or when tourists arrive

_____

_____

_____

_____

_____

Writing Assignment 20.3

Now that you have worked on the trite words in the essay on page 268, rewrite the essay so that its descriptive language is much more detailed and vivid. You need not change the essay's organization or the point it makes unless you want to, but do avoid overused words. ◼

You can use your dictionary to help you come up with additional ideas for a piece of writing. For example, consider the noun *people,* used over and over in the essay above to refer to different groups of men and women. The meanings your dictionary gives for such a word can lead you to think about different kinds of people to discuss in the essay. Here, for example, is definition 5 of *people* in *Merriam Webster's Collegiate Dictionary:*

a body of persons that are united by a common culture, tradition, or sense of kinship, that typically have common language, institutions, and beliefs, and that often constitute a politically organized group

This definition suggests that people can be grouped in several ways. Now go back to page 268 and reread sentences 13–14 about the city's variety. The writer mentions only one way in which the *people* vary—namely, in their jobs. The definitions above suggest other ways: culture, tradition, sense of kinship, language, and so on. These possible differences among city dwellers give the writer material for two or three more sentences exploring variety. Look up *people* in your own dictionary and read through its definitions. Do they lead you to think about any other remarks you could make about the variety of city dwellers?

Vocabulary Exercise 20.5

Another often repeated word in the essay on page 268 is *excitement.* Look up both *excitement* and its verb *excite* in your dictionary. Read through the definitions to find suggestions for specific kinds of excitement you could add to the essay. Jot these down in the spaces below.

_____

_____

Copyright © 2002 by Addison Wesley Longman, Inc.

(Continued)

_____

_____

_____

_____

_____

_____

> Use your dictionary as a source of writing ideas.

If the dictionary gives you no new ideas for varying a commonly used noun, then think up *examples* of that word that you could discuss instead of repeating the word. This is what you are asked to do in several of the questions following the essay on city life and in the exercise below. You can also consult a thesaurus for different words. See the work in Unit 6 with this other kind of word book.

Writing Assignment 20.4

Below is a list of general nouns. Next to each, write down three more specific nouns that are *examples* of what is named by the general noun. Be sure the examples you write down are nouns.

EXAMPLE: a car *a convertible, a sports utility vehicle, a Thunderbird*

1. a tool

_____

2. housework

_____

3. stores

_____

(Continued)

4. the wonders of nature

_____

5. a hat

_____

6. happiness

_____

7. public transportation

_____

8. fruit

_____

9. violent crime

_____

10. vacation excitement

_____

See Chapter 22 for more work with adjectives in a piece of writing.

Copyright © 2002 by Addison Wesley Longman, Inc.

21

Varying Verbs

Besides improving a piece of writing by varying its nouns, you can also consider its verbs. In the essay on city life in the last chapter, most of the verbs—*like, love, want, do, live, go*—could be used in any other essay because they have such wide meanings and uses. It may seem more difficult to improve verbs because it is harder to think of actions apart from their sentences than it is to think of people, objects, and qualities apart from their sentences. Nonetheless, just as with nouns and adjectives, there are many ways to improve the verbs in the sample essay just as there are in your own writing:

Word in Focus
love

> Use your dictionary as we did for *thing, good,* and other words in the last chapter. Think of particular examples to illustrate what the verb means.
> Form a mental picture of the verb: What might people performing the action look like or feel? What might happen to them as a result?

Let's see how the last piece of advice might play out. Sentences 11 and 12 in the sample essay in the last chapter, page 268, say people *love* the city and all the good things it has to offer. Think about the verb *love* for a moment.

- How does someone who *loves* something act? For example, someone who *loves* art, for example, wants to own works of art and enjoys looking at art and talking about it. Does a person who *loves* a city act similarly?
- What other feelings might a person who *loves* a city have? He may feel safe and comfortable in it, fascinated by it, unable to live happily outside it. A city may attract and hold him as securely as a woman he loves. Perhaps you could discuss people who live in a city as having a love affair with it.
- Let your imagination play with this possibility. How do lovers act? Are they always happy with each other? What other feelings come in, anger? Possessiveness? Irritation? Can a person be angry with his beloved city? Possessive about it when others attack it? Irritated with it?

- What happens to a person as a result of his love for a city? Does he learn to put up with its irritating features? Does he always come back to it with relief when he has been away? Does he try to live in it when he grows old?

As you can see, thinking about one verb can lead in many different directions. Are these all digressions from your topic? They can be, but on the other hand, they could help you write a more engaging paragraph or even revise a whole essay so that it has a more narrowly focused and more original point. But you don't have to change an entire essay to improve its verbs. You can simply replace general verbs like *love* with more vivid, precise verbs. People don't simply *love* a city; they can also *praise* it, *work to improve* it, *compare* it favorably with other places, and so on. All these actions come from the love.

Vocabulary Exercise 21.1

In the blank following each sentence below, replace the italicized words in the sentence with a verb or verb phrase that conveys the same meaning. But choose a verb like those in the example that gives a *more vivid* and *specific* picture of what is going on. Reread each sentence with its new verb to be sure it makes sense. You may want to work with a classmate here.

EXAMPLE: The rain *fell* on the roof. pattered, drummed, danced, tapped

1. The little boy *was happily eating* an ice cream cone.

   _____

2. I jogged till I couldn't go any farther, and then I *sat down* on the grass.

   _____

3. Some teenagers *talk* on the phone for hours.

   _____

4. Let's go to the beach and *lie* on the sand.

   _____

5. The sun *shone brightly* on the sea.

   _____

Copyright © 2002 by Addison Wesley Longman, Inc.

(Continued)

6. The old man *fell* on the sidewalk.

_____

7. Several people *walked* by without stopping to help.

_____

8. I was *going up* the library stairs when I *saw* Joe coming down. (2 verbs)

_____

9. During the earthquake, our building *shook* and all our bookcases *fell down*. (2 verbs)

_____

10. All the chickens *ran away* when the dog *ran* into the barnyard. (2 verbs)

_____

Vocabulary Exercise 21.2

In this exercise, replace the verb with another, more vivid verb. But this time, in addition to the verb also add an adverb or a phrase that answers the question *how?* as in the example. Adverbs usually end in *-ly*. When you put your verb and adverb/phrase into each sentence, you may have to separate the adverb/phrase from the verb.

EXAMPLE: The rain *fell* on the roof. pattered lightly, drummed like fingers, danced furiously

1. I think writing is hard work and I always *spend a lot of time on* an essay.

_____

2. Art students should *look carefully at* important paintings.

_____

3. The motor of the old Ford *made a funny noise* and then died.

_____

(Continued)

4. The critic *really loved* the new play at the Strand Theater.

   _____

5. Most graduate students *want* to be successful in their work.

   _____

6. He *worked* day and night to get through college.

   _____

7. My aged mother *has* a little car that gives her greater mobility than her friends who do not drive.

   _____

8. Nobody *makes* adults watch television.

   _____

9. This sweet child *has brought* tremendous joy to his family.

   _____

10. The manufacturer is supposed *to tell* consumers the contents of the cereal box.

   _____

For more work with adverbs, see Chapter 22.

Writing Assignment 21.1

Reread an essay you have written recently looking at the verbs you have used. For every page of your essay, replace three very common verbs, such as *is/are, see, tell,* and the verbs in the two preceding Vocabulary Exercises with verbs that give a more specific or vivid idea of what is going on. You may also need to change other words as well so that a sentence makes sense. ■

Copyright © 2002 by Addison Wesley Longman, Inc.

22

Using Modifiers

We have discussed adjectives in Chapter 20 and adverbs briefly in Chapter 21. This chapter explores these words more thoroughly because you can improve the precision, clarity, and vividness of your writing by using more, carefully chosen adjectives and adverbs, also called *modifiers*.

Word in Focus
modifier

- A modifier is any word, phrase or clause that *limits* or *narrows* another word, phrase, or clause in some way.
- Adjectives, which modify nouns, tell us the *color, size, shape, sound, texture, kind, number, age, temperament, or other qualities* of the nouns.
- Adverbs, which modify verbs, tell us *when, where, how,* or *why* the verbs happened. Adverbs can also modify adjectives and other adverbs. Sometimes, a group of words acts like an adverb. For example, *at noon* tells us *when,* and a *because* clause would tell us *why.*

Here is a very general sentence:

Many people love living in the city.

Besides replacing its general nouns and verbs (*people, love, city*) for more specific ones, as we did in Chapters 20 and 21, we can improve the sentence by modifying all the nouns and verbs:

- What *kinds* of people? Both old and young people, middle-class people, only the rich, people who have come to the city from small towns, and so on.
- *How many* is *many?* Two million, far too many people, many more people than fifty years ago, not as many people as you'd think at rush hour, and so on.
- *How* do they *love* it? Steadfastly, wholeheartedly, sometimes but not always, crazily, as if no other place existed, with their eyes open to its faults, and so on.
- What *kind* of city? The concrete and steel city; the soft-hearted city; the noisy, dirty, dangerous, fascinating city; the city surrounded by blue

mountains and blessed with mild weather; the city throbbing with new life; the city of a thousand disguises, and so on.

As you can see, modifiers can be:

- Single words *(steadfastly, wholeheartedly)*
- Phrases and clauses *(far too many, throbbing with new life, as if no other existed)*
- Lists and combinations *(noisy, dirty, dangerous, fascinating; surrounded with blue mountains and blessed with mild weather)*

Remember, then, that a good way of improving sentences that are too general or trite is to add adjectives and adverbs.

> Use modifiers to make nouns and verbs more precise, vivid and interesting.

Vocabulary Exercise 22.1

Here are some nouns. Modify each one to give a reader a more specific and vivid mental picture of a particular example of the noun: Add two or three adjectives that describe its color, size, shape, sound, texture, kind, number, age, temperament, or other qualities. The modifiers can be single words, phrases, clauses, lists, and combinations.

EXAMPLE: a pen *an old ball-point pen that always leaked onto his shirt*

1. a house _____

2. a newspaper _____

3. a tree _____

4. a lawyer _____

5. a restaurant _____

6. a teenager _____

7. a question _____

8. a proposal _____

9. admiration _____

10. communication _____

Copyright © 2002 by Addison Wesley Longman, Inc.

Vocabulary Exercise 22.2

Here are some adjectives that could be used to describe a person's physical appearance. Next to each write three or four other adjectives in the same category, following the example. Think of parts of the body to help you.

EXAMPLES: squeaky (voice) _cheerful, roaring, sobbing, jubilant_

long-limbed (size) _short, pint-sized, towering, huge_

1. skinny (shape)_____

2. auburn-haired (color)_____

3. pimply (texture)_____

4. elderly (age)_____

5. sentimental (temperament)_____

Vocabulary Exercise 22.3

Now return to the specific nouns you thought up for Writing Assignment 20.4 on page 272, and choose one noun each from five of the lists you wrote. Jot down in the spaces below three or four adjectives that could be used to make each noun more vivid and precise. Try to use adjectives from different categories for each noun, following the example. (Remember: Categories include color, shape, size, sound, quantity, texture, age, temperament, and so on.)

EXAMPLE: convertible _pink, sporty, streamlined, battered_

1. _____

2. _____

3. _____

4. _____

5. _____

Now that you have practiced making nouns more specific by adding adjectives to them, try doing the same activity for verbs by adding adverbs to them. Review the description of adverbs above, page 278, before continuing.

Vocabulary Exercise 22.4

Make the following verbs, in italics, more specific by adding to each two or three adverbs, phrases, or adverbial clauses (those beginning with *because, as, while, when,* and so on). Remember that adverbs tell us *when, where, how,* or *why* the verb occurs.

EXAMPLE: A bird *chirps*. A bird gaily chirps as the sun rises.

1. The German shepherd *barked*.

_____

2. The doorbell *rang*.

_____

3. This sociology professor *lectures*.

_____

4. My mother's car *stalls*.

_____

5. A bystander *reported* the accident.

_____

6. The new budget *was defeated*.

_____

7. The need to conserve energy *is growing*.

_____

8. Juanita says she *tells* the truth.

_____

Copyright © 2002 by Addison Wesley Longman, Inc.

(Continued)

9. A new gas furnace *heats* my home.

_____

10. A new study *has revealed* the importance of vitamin C.

_____

Vocabulary Exercise 22.5

Team up with a partner for this exercise. Working alone, both you and your partner should find and underline the adjectives and adverbs in any one of the sentences below. Each of you then replace two of these modifiers with different adjectives/adverbs so as to create a very different idea of what is happening in the sentence. Then exchange sentences. You should then add a few more sentences that continue the idea of the first sentence as suggested by your partner's adjective and adverb. Your partner should do the same with your sentence. Be sure you both continue to use appropriate modifiers as you compose. When you are done, exchange paragraphs, and discuss what difference two words made. Repeat with the other sentences.

This exercise is even more interesting when several pairs all work on the same sentence to produce multiple versions, or when writers in groups of three pass around the same sentence, each adding another sentence and other modifiers till a long paragraph has been composed.

EXAMPLE: The <u>birch</u> tree <u>that we planted ten years ago</u> has grown <u>well</u>.

<u>The OAK tree that we planted ten years ago has grown POORLY.</u> OR

<u>The birch tree THAT WE TRANSPLANTED LAST YEAR has grown well.</u> OR. . . .

1. Record high temperatures have made people unusually irritable.

2. The author's first novel was surprisingly successful.

3. Miriam, who lived nearby, had a small dog who always barked when the phone rang.

4. A fat envelope addressed by hand had been quietly slipped under Victor's apartment door.

5. A long black car drove silently up to the darkened pier.

Dictionary Exercise 22.1

Look up the meanings and Latin origins of the words *modify*, *moderate*, and *modulate* when they are used as verbs. How is the meaning of the Latin root *modus*, meaning *measure*, present in the current meanings of all three? Write a sentence for each word, making this connection clear. If these words are unfamiliar to you, think of a way to remember them now. Other English words from the same root include *modest*, *modern*, and *mode*. Use your own paper.

Copyright © 2002 by Addison Wesley Longman, Inc.

23

Varying Parts of Speech

> One mark of a strong writer is the ability to phrase the same idea in several
> different ways.

Such a writer has more to choose from as he works to make his writing clear, concise, and varied. One way to practice saying the same idea in different ways is to switch a word from one part of speech to another as you draft or revise sentences. In Chapters 16, 17 and 18 in the last unit, you practiced changing words from one part of speech to another, verbs to nouns, nouns to adjectives, and so on. The emphasis then was on learning new words in all their forms. The emphasis here is on using words you already know to play with different phrasings of an idea till you find one you like. You can exchange nouns and verbs with related meanings—*warmth/to warm, care/to care for*—as well as most single-word adjectives and adverbs—*warm/warmly, careful/carefully.*

Another way to practice saying the same idea in different ways is to move words to different parts of a sentence. Here are alternate versions of the same idea illustrating both practices. Which version of each do you prefer?

The Dutch gave us a warm welcome.
The Dutch welcomed us warmly.

Amy tended the plants with a careful sprinkle from the watering can.
With a careful sprinkle from the watering can, Amy tended the plants.
Amy carefully sprinkled the plants with the watering can.
With the watering can, Amy carefully sprinkled the plants.

Vocabulary Exercise 23.1

Practice changing the italicized nouns in the sentences below first to adjectives and then to adverbs by rewriting each sentence twice. Then check the one sentence in each set of three that you prefer.

As in the work in Unit 4, you may have to add an adjective suffix to a noun, or replace a noun suffix with an adjective suffix. Remember that an adjective is a word that can fill this blank: a/an _____ thing/person. (a *pretty* thing, an *elegant* lady). An adverb is a word that says *how* something happened, or sometimes *why, when, where*. (He danced *merrily*. She sang *well*.) Many adverbs are adjectives with the suffix *-ly*. If you do not know how to make a particular noun into an adjective or adverb, look it up in your dictionary, and find an entry near it for the corresponding adjective/adverb.

EXAMPLES: Hollywood assumes that women like *emotion* in a movie. (noun)

Hollywood assumes that women like an EMOTIONAL movie.   (adjective)

Hollywood assumes that women like movies that are EMOTIONALLY satisfying.   (adverb)

Carlos appreciated his father's *wisdom*.   (noun)

Carlos appreciated his father as a WISE man.   (adjective)

Carlos appreciated the fact that his father acted WISELY.   (adverb)

So Carlos gave his father *respect*.   (noun)

So Carlos was RESPECTFUL to his father.   (adjective)

So Carlos treated his father RESPECTFULLY.   (adverb)

1. There was slick *ice* on the road.

   The road was slick and _____.

   The road was _____ slick.

2. MADD warns us about the *hazard* of drunk driving.

   MADD warns us that driving while drunk is _____.

   MADD warns us that drunks drive _____.

3. Maria dresses with *style*.

   Maria wears _____ clothes.

   Maria dresses _____.

Copyright © 2002 by Addison Wesley Longman, Inc.

(Continued)

4. They shouted obscenities filled with *hate*.

   They shouted _____ obscenities.

   They shouted obscenities _____.

5. Mr. Rufo looked down at his dog with *pride*.

   Mr. Rufo gave his dog a _____ look.

   Mr. Rufo looked down at his dog _____.

6. The children begged with *persistence* for ice cream.

   The children made _____ demands for ice cream.

   The children begged _____ for ice cream.

7. Our new neighbors have made our move a *pleasure*.

   Our new neighbors have made our move _____.

   Our new neighbors welcomed us _____.

8. He gazed in the bakery window with *hunger*.

   He looked through the bakery window with a _____ gaze.

   He gazed in the bakery window _____.

9. The portrait captured Mathilda's personality to *perfection*.

   The portrait was a _____ depiction of Mathilda's personality.

   The portrait captured Mathilda's personality _____.

10. The groom said the wedding vows with great *calm*.

    The groom was very _____ when he said the wedding vows.

    The groom said the wedding vows very _____.

Vocabulary Exercise 23.2

In the blank following each sentence below, change the italicized phrase in the sentence into an adverb ending in *-ly*. Then say the sentence out loud several times, placing the adverb in a different position each time. Use arrows to show the different positions in the sentence where the adverb could be placed. Many can be placed in only one spot.

EXAMPLES: He looked at my new car *with envy.* <u>enviously</u>_____
^He looked ^at my new car ^*with envy.*

In an impulsive way, I fell in love at first sight. <u>Impulsively</u>_____
^*In an impulsive way,* I fell in love ^at first sight.

1. Greg was able to run the three miles *with ease.*

   _____

2. The women were dressed *in elegant outfits* for the gala concert.

   _____

3. *All of a sudden,* the child burst into tears.

   _____

4. The problem can be solved *in a simple way.*

   _____

5. The problem can be solved *in a very simple way.* (Don't eliminate *very* here.)

   _____

6. My brother, who is a chef, always tips waiters *a generous amount.*

   _____

7. On my vacation I ate breakfast *at my leisure.*

   _____

Use two adverbs in each of the next four sentences.

8. The defense counsel read her statement *in a loud and clear voice.*

   _____

9. *With nervousness and hesitation,* Timmy sat on the edge of his seat and told his story.

   _____

Copyright © 2002 by Addison Wesley Longman, Inc.

(Continued)

10. The news reporters pursued the senator *in an aggressive and determined manner.*

   _____

11. *With vigor and energy* the dog bounced into the yard.

   _____

12. Greg was able to run the three miles *without effort.* (Hint: replace *without* with the suffix *-less,* and then add *-ly.*)

   _____

13. *By instinct* squirrels start collecting and hiding nuts in the autumn. (Hint: the noun *instinct* has two adjective/adverb forms, one with the suffix *-ual,* the other with *-ive.*)

   _____

14. The new machine works *with such efficiency* that I can spend more time writing. (Change *such* to *so.*)

   _____

15. The teacher nodded *with approval* when Tommy started to read aloud. (Hint: First change the noun *approval* to an adjective ending in *-ing.*)

   _____

For more work changing nouns to adjectives, see Chapters 16 and 18 in Unit 4, pages 176 ff. and 225 ff.

24

Using Words Figuratively

Another way to vary your word choices and to make your meanings more precise and more vivid is to use words *figuratively*.

Words in focus

figurative
cliché
personification

> Figurative language is language in which we say that one thing IS something else because it is LIKE something else. A *figurative* meaning is the opposite of a *literal* meaning. Metaphors and similes are kinds of figurative language.

For example, *stars* are the bright heavenly bodies we can see in a night sky. This is the *literal* meaning of *stars*. When we say that someone *has stars in her eyes,* we are using the word *figuratively.* Her eyes are so bright and shiny, perhaps with happiness, that they *seem* to have stars in them, so we say that she actually *does* have stars in them.

We are so used to figurative expressions that we may not even recognize them as metaphors. When you say, for example, that a name is *on the tip of your tongue,* you do not mean that your tongue has actual letters printed on it. A *coldhearted* or *hardhearted* person has a real heart that is as full of warm blood as yours is. No real plow made the furrow in a *furrowed* brow.

In their book *Metaphors We Live By,* the linguists George Lakoff and Mark Johnson outline metaphors that are so basic we hardly notice them, but that show some of our cultural values. For example, we use many expressions that illustrate the metaphor *time is money.*

I spent *an hour on these problems.*
What's your time worth? *Do you have any* free *time?*
How many days of vacation have you earned?
He is living on borrowed *time.*

Copyright © 2002 by Addison Wesley Longman Publishers

Vocabulary Exercise 24.1

Here are some verbs we might use when discussing *money*. Together with a classmate, make up sentences that use them to discuss *time*, as in the examples above.

1. to waste:_____

2. to save:_____

3. to cost:_____

4. to invest:_____

5. to budget:_____

6. to borrow:_____

7. to lose:_____

8. to spare:_____

9. to gain:_____

10. to run out of:_____

We use many other metaphors to describe the complex emotion love. For example, we often describe *love* as if it were *madness:*

I'm crazy *(or* mad) *about you.*
You drive me out of my mind *(or* crazy).
He raves *on and on about her.*
She is obsessed *with him.*

What other metaphors do we use when we talk about love? Note those in the next exercise.

Vocabulary Exercise 24.2

In the left-hand column below are some remarks we might make about love. Match each to whichever metaphor in the right-hand column is being used in it.

1. Their marriage is on its last legs._____

2. She played him for a fool._____

3. She cast a spell over me._____

4. He's a real lady-killer._____

5. What does she see in him?_____

6. You broke my heart._____

7. Are we going anywhere in this relationship?_____

8. This is a sick relationship._____

9. He pursued her for months and finally won her hand in marriage._____

10. I hear they're breaking up._____

11. I lost my heart to her that day._____

12. After four years of marriage, they came to a parting of the ways._____

13. Some see marriage as a battle between the sexes._____

14. My love for you has died._____

15. She was shattered when he left her._____

a. Love is war.

b. Love is magic.

c. Love is sickness.

d. Love is fragile.

e. Love is a journey.

f. Love is a game.

g. Love is blind.

Copyright © 2002 by Addison Wesley Longman, Inc.

Writing Assignment 24.1

Choose a popular love song that you think uses figurative language to talk about love. Write a long paragraph in which you explain what metaphor or metaphors the song uses and why. (Keep in mind that there are other metaphors for love besides the ones in the preceding exercise.) Refer to particular parts of the song in your discussion.   ■

If you let your imagination roam freely, you will find that you can make your writing more vivid and original, as well as more precise, if you use figurative language.

> But beware of exchanging one overused word or expression for another just because the other is a metaphor or simile.

Many figurative expressions are just as tired from overuse as the words *people, nice,* and *interesting*. They have become *clichés*. That is, we use them so often and so automatically that they have lost their metaphorical energy. You can see some clichés in the next exercise.

Vocabulary Exercise 24.3

To see for yourself how worn out are the following figurative expressions, note how easily you can complete the end of each. Then think of a more unusual but vivid way of saying the same thing. Write your more original expression next to the clichéd one.

EXAMPLE: as quiet as *a mouse—as quiet as a cemetery at midnight*

1. eats like a_____

2. drinks like a_____

3. at the drop of a_____

4. as strong as_____

5. hit the nail on_____

(Continued)

6. as wise as_____

7. a needle in a_____

8. as deep as the_____

9. handed to him on a silver_____

10. like a bull in a_____

How can you tell if a metaphorical expression is a cliché or not?

> One rule of thumb is to avoid the first expression that enters your mind.
> Tell another person the first words of the phrase you want to use, for example, "He hit the nail. . . ." If the person can finish the phrase, it is probably too trite to use. Instead answer these questions: What is my subject *like?* In what ways does it *resemble* something else?

For example, instead of saying that someone is *very fat* or *as fat as a pig,* you could compare him to something huge besides the proverbial pig: he might be *elephantine,* or *mountainous,* or *as wide as a doorway.* You could picture his flesh as *overflowing like a washing machine with too much soap,* or his clothes as *sausage skins stuffed with flesh.*

When should you try figurative language?

> If you are explaining a complex process, try comparing it to something simpler.
> If you want to make an abstract issue more immediate and real, try turning it into a person. This kind of figurative language is called *personification.* If this issue were a person, how would it act?
> If you feel that the topic you must write about is dull, try injecting some life into it by using figurative language.
> If you are describing an unusual person, scene or event, try comparing it to something more familiar to your readers.

Here is some practice in thinking figuratively.

Copyright © 2002 by Addison Wesley Longman, Inc.

Writing Assignment 24.2

Use your own paper to write the following sentences and short paragraphs using figurative language.

1. Write a sentence describing an angry person, using the word *storm* figuratively.

2. In two or three sentences, describe a telephone as if it were human. Pretend that it has human feelings.

3. In a sentence or two, describe a math problem as a maze or labyrinth. First look up *maze* and *labyrinth* in your dictionary and think of a good way to remember their meaning.

4. Pretend that the wind has invisible hands. Describe two or three things, such as grass, through which you can see those hands moving.

5. People sometimes refer to the country in which they were born and grew up as their *fatherland*. How is one's country a father? Would it be more appropriate to call one's country the *motherland*? Defend your choice in a few sentences. ■

Writing Assignment 24.3

Look up the word *temperament* in your dictionary. How does it differ in meaning from a person's *temper*? Then describe the *temperaments* of two members of your family (one paragraph each) by comparing each to a kind of weather. To start, jot down a brief description of one person's temperament. Then make a list of words you might use to describe the weather that is similar to that temperament. For example, is the person calm, like a clear blue sky on a sunny day, or easily angered, like a biting winter storm? ■

Writing Assignment 24.4

In your view, what does the education of a child most resemble?

   a. filling a vase
   b. training a vine to grow on a trellis

(Continued)
   c. carving a chunk of wood into a statue
   d. building a house

Write a paragraph about 8–10 sentences long defending your choice. Then consider one of the actions listed above that you rejected. What is one way in which it *is* similar to educating a child? In what ways is that action *not* similar? Write a second paragraph of explanation. ■

Writing Assignment 24.5

Think of the many animal words we use to describe people. For example, a rough, violent man is a real *brute*. A quiet, shy person is *mousy*. In two or three sentences each, describe the people listed below in terms of the animals paired with each. You can describe the person's appearance and action too so that you create a picture of the animal as well as of the person you are describing.

   a. a woman leaving a beauty parlor—a clipped poodle
   b. a pickpocket—a snake
   c. a group of small children—puppies or kittens
   d. businessmen at a convention—penguins ■

Writing Assignment 24.6

Proverbs like "A bird in the hand is worth two in the bush" are popular because they express bits of common wisdom in a *figurative* saying that is easy to remember. Listed below are some proverbs. Explain what each one means in a few sentences. Look them up in a regular dictionary or a dictionary of proverbs if you are unsure. Then choose one proverb, and expand your explanation of it into a two- or three-paragraph essay by (a) discussing how you think the proverb originated in practical experience, and then (b) illustrating its use today by narrating your own or someone else's personal experience.

   a. Make hay while the sun shines.
   b. Let sleeping dogs lie.
   c. Every cloud has a silver lining.
   d. A stitch in time saves nine. ■

Copyright © 2002 by Addison Wesley Longman, Inc.

Review Exercise I

Here are some sentences using very common nouns, verbs, adjectives, and adverbs that could be improved. Rewrite each sentence, adding words and/or exchanging some or all of its common words for more vivid and specific words. Draw on all the work you have done in this unit. For further help, ask yourself questions like those in the example.

EXAMPLE: A car came around the corner. (Ask yourself questions about the words: What kind of car? Color? Age? Appearance? What kind of action is its coming? Did it *race, speed, cruise, creep, inch, slide*? How did it come? Try an *-ly* adverb like *carelessly*, or a prepositional phrase like *with a roar*, or figurative language such as *like a mad elephant*. Which corner? What was on or near the corner?)

A battered, dusty blue van loaded with boxes inched slowly around the corner of the supermarket.

OR

The sports car, low and sleek like a panther, shot out of the parking garage and swung around the corner.

1. Two women were sitting and talking on a park bench.

   _____

2. The children had a really good time.

   _____

3. The plant grew very tall.

   _____

4. Her friend is a nice person.

   _____

5. I like this book because it is very interesting.

   _____

6. Many people today are too dependent on machines.

   _____

7. Throughout the years, America has had an important place in world affairs.

   _____

(Continued)

8. Violence on TV is bad for children.

_____

9. Traffic in the city is a really big problem.

_____

10. There were lots of flowers in the room. (You may wish to rewrite this sentence by removing *There were* and starting with the subject instead.)

_____

Review Exercise II

Return once again to the essay on city life in Chapter 20, page 268, that you examined and then revised. Considering all the work in this unit on verbs, adding modifiers, varying parts of speech, and using words figuratively, revise the essay one last time.

Review Exercise III

Using everything you have learned in this unit about improving words in your writing to make them more precise, more varied, and more engaging to read, revise each of the following paragraphs. You may do anything with a paragraph (add, delete, substitute, reorder words), anything that you think will improve it, except for changing its basic ideas. Make good use of your dictionary. Use your own paper.

1. A real friend is someone whose advice you can trust. A real friend knows you better than most other people because he has gone through the same experiences you have. Furthermore, if he is the same age as you, he understands your feelings because he has sometimes felt the same way. A real friend is someone who wants the best for you and would do as much as he could to see that you get it. So if you have a problem with your boyfriend, girlfriend, or spouse, or with your work, or with anything else, talk it over with a good friend to help you decide what to do.

Copyright © 2002 by Addison Wesley Longman, Inc.

(Continued)

2. Age is a big thing to consider when dealing with teenagers who commit crimes. If a teenager commits a crime, he or she should not be subjected to the same punishment as an adult. Adults are fully mature and have more of a sense of responsibility than teenagers. Secondly, most teenagers are victims of a lot of peer pressure. They are constantly trying to do what their friends are doing. Adults deal with peer pressure better than teenagers. Finally, teenagers do not always realize the seriousness of their crimes. They have not experienced enough to be held responsible for their crimes.

3. Some people set standards for themselves. They know what they want out of life, and they believe that they will get it. They let nothing stand in their way. People such as these are willing to die for a cause. When my grandmother was working, she always said, "I'm going to keep on working. I'm going to make sure that my children and grandchildren are always clothed and fed. If I die today or tomorrow, I'll know my family will be all right." She was willing to die, in the literal sense, working for her family's well-being.

    Other people, however, are not willing to die for a cause, no matter what it is. Even if a person is not willing to die for a cause, she is not necessarily a selfish person. She may be a person with a worthwhile goal, but she may feel that, if she has to die for it, then the goal isn't worth it. She may feel that she has achieved nothing if she is dead.

Reading 5a

Here are some poems that talk about trees metaphorically, in terms of human life. In the first, the 19th-century British poet Alfred, Lord Tennyson, advises the reader to imitate an oak tree. In the second, the American poet Robert Frost talks to the tree outside his bedroom window as in some ways a counterpart or duplicate for himself and his own feelings. In the last poem, the British poet Philip Larkin tries to figure out what trees in spring are trying to express, as if they too were people.

The Oak
by Alfred, Lord Tennyson

Live thy Life,
    Young and old,
Like yon oak,
Bright in spring,
    Living gold;

Summer-rich
    Then; and then
Autumn-changed,
Soberer-hued
    Gold again.

All his leaves
    Fallen at length,
Look, he stands,
Trunk and bough,
    Naked strength.

Tree at My Window
by Robert Frost

Tree at my window, window tree,
My sash is lowered when night comes on;
But let there never be curtain drawn
Between you and me.

Vague dream-head lifted out of the ground,
And thing next most diffuse to cloud,
Not all your light tongues talking aloud
Could be profound.

But, tree, I have seen you taken and tossed,
And if you have seen me when I slept,
You have seen me when I was taken and swept
And all but lost.

That day she put our heads together,
Fate had her imagination about her,
Your head so much concerned with outer,
Mine with inner, weather.

Copyright © 2002 by Addison Wesley Longman, Inc.

The Trees
by Philip Larkin

The trees are coming into leaf
Like something almost being said;
The recent buds relax and spread,
Their greenness is a kind of grief.

Is it that they are born again
And we grow old? No, they die too.
Their yearly trick of looking new
Is written down in rings of grain.

Yet still the unresting castles thresh
In fullgrown thickness every May.
Last year is dead, they seem to say,
Begin afresh, afresh, afresh.

Mastery Exercises

Tennyson

1. Why do you think the poet holds up the oak tree as a model for humans to imitate? Support your answer by referring to words in the poem. Then write a few sentences saying how a person's life might be *bright in spring*, *Summer-rich*, *Autumn-changed*, and *Naked* in winter.

2. Tennyson creates several compound words to describe the oak tree: *Summer-rich*, *Autumn-changed*, *Soberer-hued*. What other adjectives would be appropriate to pair with each of the seasons to create other compound words? Jot down several below:

   Spring-_____
   Summer-_____
   Autumn-_____
   Winter-_____

3. Choose one of the four seasons, and write a few paragraphs elaborating various ways in which this season is like a time in a person's life. For example, in spring, everything in nature puts out new life, so in a person's springtime—childhood—everything in the child's life is new.

(Continued)

Frost

1. In what ways is Frost's tree like a person? What does he say they have in common? In the poem's last line, what do you think "inner weather" might refer to?

2. Frost uses the adjectives "diffuse" and "profound" to describe the tree in the second stanza. Look up the adjective *diffuse* in your dictionary; how are its two meanings both appropriate to Frost's tree? Look up *profound*. Then using one of its meanings, explain why you think that nothing the tree "says" can be "profound." Now consider the other meanings of *profound*. Is there anything a tree might "say" that is *profound* in one of these other meanings?

3. Think of two other ways in which different kinds of weather (for example, a hurricane) can affect a tree. What events in a person's life might affect the person in a similar way? Write a paragraph comparing the tree in such weather to the person.

Larkin

1. The poet imagines that the trees in spring are "almost" saying something, and by the end of the poem, he has worked out what they "seem" to be saying. Imagine trees in a different season; what might they "almost" be saying then? Why?

2. The poet calls the trees "unresting castles." How are trees like castles? Why are the trees described as "unresting"? What does the word "thresh" mean? What is a tree doing when it is "threshing"?

3. Larkin says that the trees' "greenness is a kind of grief." What color(s) do you think of when you think of grief? In a paragraph or two, talk about the meanings you attach to one or two colors. (Like Larkin, we often use colors as metaphors for these meanings.) Or write a brief poem that is a list of what the color you choose means to you, for example, "White is innocence, white is . . ."

All

In what other ways is a tree like some aspect of humanity or of human life? Consider a particular tree, as Tennyson and Frost do, or consider some part of a tree, or consider all trees, as Larkin does. You might also start from the

Copyright © 2002 by Addison Wesley Longman, Inc.

(Continued)

human side of the comparison: How is this or that aspect of human life or action by a person like this or that aspect of trees? For example, some people are flexible enough to continue to struggle even when disaster strikes, as palm trees bend in a storm. Write a paragraph explaining your comparison.

Reading 5b

Here is an essay that originally appeared in *The Colorado Springs Gazette* on May 7, 1999. In it, Scott Smith writes about clichés by using ONLY clichés, one after another. How many can you identify? After reading it once, get together with two other students to make a list of the clichés you spotted. Then see the questions following the reading.

Assignment Lets Him Hit the Nail on the Head
by Scott Smith

1   Write about clichés, the editors said.

2   When pigs fly, I thought. I'd rather try to squeeze blood out of a turnip. It's the kind of assignment that makes me feel like my back's against the wall and there's no tomorrow. Like I'm looking for a needle in a haystack, up the creek without a paddle, caught between a rock and a hard place, skating on thin ice, barking up the wrong tree and have bitten off more than I can chew. The whole shebang. Get my drift?

3   Please forgive me if this purple prose sounds like a broken record. But, really, I need to write a story on clichés like I need a hole in my head. It's just not my cup of tea. I have other fish to fry, thanks. Deep down, I really hate clichés. Avoid 'em like the plague.

4   Plus, my understanding of clichés is as clear as mud. I can't make heads nor tails out of which ones are the real deals and which are not worth a red cent or a plugged nickel. You'd think they would stick out like a sore thumb, but to me, they all seem like six of one, half-dozen of the other.

5   Trying to comprehend clichés makes me feel like climbing a wall or throwing in the towel. They're as confusing as a wild goose chase to where the grass is always greener on the other side of the tip of the iceberg.

6   Of course, the editors have turned a deaf ear to my whining. Easy to do when you work in an ivory tower and have grand delusions about the pen being mightier than the sword. However, they made it crystal clear that they'll support me through thick and thin, although I take those words with a grain of salt.

7   The story will be a piece of cake, easy as pie, the greatest thing since sliced bread, they say. More fun than a barrel of monkeys. You'll be in seventh heaven. Happy as a lark, a clam or a pig in slop. Just put your nose to the grindstone and place your best foot forward. Give it 110 percent. It'll be like taking candy from a baby, as easy as shooting fish in a barrel.

8   That said, I'm still prepared to give it my best shot. I promise to leave no stone unturned, rolling or otherwise. It's time to get down to brass tacks, take the gloves off and put my best foot forward. Hey, every Tom, Dick and Harry speaks in clichés, anyway. They're a dime a dozen, more of 'em out there than you can shake a stick at. Should be a breeze, a walk in the park. It's made in the shade.

9   Now it's just a matter of, by hook or by crook, narrowing the story's focus. Because, let's face it, it would take the patience of Job to write the book on clichés—you know, the whole shootin' match. But since necessity is the mother of invention, it's time to shift into high gear.

10   Maybe I should just focus on weather-related clichés: the calm before the storm, which includes a bolt from the blue from every cloud that has a silver lining.

11   Or food. But that would be like putting all your eggs in one basket or comparing apples and oranges until you bring home the bacon and don't spill the beans.

12   Or classics, the kinds of clichés that hit the nail on the head, are par for the course and make you want to party till the cows come home.

13   Whatever. All I know is that when it's over and done, I'll thank my lucky stars that I can say: Been there, done that. And last but not least, don't forget: It ain't over till it's over. Or is that until the fat lady sings?

Copyright © 2002 by Addison Wesley Longman, Inc.

Mastery Exercises

1. Smith manages to compose an essay almost entirely of clichés. Why do we find this funny? Do you think Smith approves of clichés? Explain in a paragraph.

2. Sometimes, the words in a cliché rhyme or begin with the same letter, like the h's in the cliché *like I need a hole in my head*. Find in the reading six examples of rhyming clichés or of clichés that repeat the same initial letter. Why do you think clichés often repeat sounds? Explain in a sentence or two.

3. Near the end of his essay, Smith lists some clichés by themes (weather, food). Find several clichés in his essay with another theme, animals. Then list four or five other clichés that he does not use and that also refer to animals. (We used some in Vocabulary Exercise 24.3 and Writing Assignment 24.6.)

4. In many spots in his essay, Smith manages to stuff two, three, or even more clichés into the same sentence. Which of these stuffed sentences do you find especially amusing?

5. Together with one or two other classmates, write a paragraph of nothing but clichés on a clichéd topic, such as realizing the American dream. Or write a television ad full of advertising clichés. If you like, all three of you can write a single paragraph or advertisement so that you have three heads instead of one to think up clichés.

Unit 5

Post-Test 1

Replace the italicized verbs in the following sentences with other, more specific, vivid verbs. If necessary, you may also change other parts of the sentences or add other words to fit with the new verbs.

EXAMPLES: The child *was playing* in the sand.

The child WAS BUILDING A CASTLE in the sand.

He *cried* when it was time to leave.

He WHIMPERED (or HOWLED, WHINED, BAWLED, etc.) when it was time to leave.

1. The dog next door always *barks* when left alone.

    _____

2. In the seminar room, the students *sat* at a long, broad table.

    _____

3. We all *wrote* in our notebooks, including the professor.

    _____

4. Because of its shifting currents, the river *is* very difficult to navigate.

    _____

5. Clouds *covered* the sun for much of the day.

    _____

6. Various fishermen *watched* the boat of tourists *come* into the harbor.

    _____

7. Leafy houseplants *will not grow* unless they *get* some sunlight.

    _____

8. Many people *do not like* the month of April because it is income tax time.

    _____

9. My cell phone *rang* just as the concert began.

    _____

10. I *was embarrassed* and quickly turned it off.

    _____

Copyright © 2002 by Addison Wesley Longman, Inc.

Unit 5

Post-Test 2

Now return to the sentences in the preceding exercise, and make one more change in each one to make it even more vivid and specific. You could change a general noun or adjective, add modifiers, change words from one part of speech to another, or use figurative language.

EXAMPLES: The child was building a castle in the sand.

The child WEARING A FLOPPY HAT was building a castle in the sand.

He howled when it was time to leave.

He howled LIKE A WOUNDED ANIMAL when it was time to leave.

_____

_____

_____

_____

_____

_____

_____

_____

_____

_____

Unit 5

Post-Test 3

Replace the italicized clichés in the following sentences with words that are more direct and not as trite. You may also revise other parts of the sentences if necessary or desirable. Look up in your dictionary any clichés you do not completely understand. And be careful not to replace one cliché with another.

(Continued)

EXAMPLES: They stayed married *through thick and thin.*
They stayed married when they had no money and when they had some.
In this day and age, some people still believe in astrology.
Even today some people still believe in astrology.

1. I *haven't seen hide nor hair* of the landlord since I moved into this apartment.

   _____

2. Rather than just saying what he wanted, Jaime *beat around the bush.*

   _____

3. *Slowly but surely,* I realized that he wanted to take another day off.

   _____

4. If you don't keep up with the course reading, you will have to *face the music* on the final exam.

   _____

5. When I received the letter of acceptance into law school, I *felt light as a feather.*

   _____

6. *Come hell or high water,* we will all be there to celebrate your retirement.

   _____

7. My uncle, who is *as honest as the day is long,* was offered a bribe to lie about the quality of construction in the building.

   _____

8. *Last but not least,* take this medication only as prescribed by your doctor.

   _____

9. Thompson bustled around the kitchen *as busy as a bee.*

   _____

10. *Roses are red, violets are blue. . . .*

   _____

Copyright © 2002 by Addison Wesley Longman, Inc.

UNIT 6

What Help Is a Thesaurus?

In this Unit, You Will Learn How to Improve Your Writing Vocabulary By:

For Skills Practice, You Will Read:

Introduction: The Thesaurus: A Different Word Book

> Use all word books wisely.

Up to this point, the only word book that we have referred to is the dictionary. As you have seen, there is much more information in a college dictionary than simply the meanings and spellings of words. Another word book, the thesaurus, a collection of synonyms and antonyms, can also be useful when you are writing to find alternatives for an overused word. But as you will see in this unit, a thesaurus can be helpful to a writer in other ways as well.

308

The word *thesaurus* comes from the Greek word for *treasure* (in fact, *thesaurus* and *treasure* are cognates); it is a treasury of synonyms and antonyms. Peter Roget compiled and published the first English thesaurus in 1852; Roget grouped words in categories according to their meanings. But because it is complicated to use, Roget's version of the thesaurus is now very difficult to find in print. Newer thesauruses arrange synonyms, not by category, but alphabetically, like the words in a dictionary, with synonyms and antonyms arranged under each word according to its meanings. If you write on a computer using a word-processing program such as WordPerfect or Word, you are probably also familiar with the thesaurus inside your program.

In this unit we shall use examples from both an alphabetical thesaurus and a word processor's thesaurus. You may think that any thesaurus is really easy to use, but, unfortunately, they all have limitations that you should be aware of.

Copyright © 2002 by Addison Wesley Longman, Inc.

©The New Yorker Collection 1981 Charles Barsotti from cartoonbank.com. All Rights Reserved.

25

The Limits of a Thesaurus

You may think that words listed in a thesaurus as synonyms are interchangeable. But be careful: Synonyms may be close in meaning, but they are not identical. Synonyms may:

Word in Focus
connotation

- Have different feelings, or connotations, associated with them.
- Refer to different classes of things.
- Be used in different idiomatic phrases.

For example, the short English adjective *fat* is not as dignified in sound or feeling as its synonym *corpulent*. Furthermore, we can use *fat* to refer to things other than people or animals having flesh. We can say that a *wallet* is *fat,* or that someone just got a *fat promotion*. But we can use *corpulent* correctly only for creatures having a body (*corpu-* means *body*): *a corpulent judge, a corpulent child*. And the short word *fat* appears in several idioms in which the longer, more Latinate *corpulent* could not be substituted: *fatty acids, the fatted calf, fathead,* and the slang expression, *to chew the fat*.

So there are reasons why English speakers have kept in the language so many words that seem, at first glance in a thesaurus, to have the same meaning. The variety of the English vocabulary often makes possible many subtleties and distinctions not possible in other languages. So if you use a thesaurus, remember that

> Words listed together as synonyms may differ quite widely in meaning, connotation, and usage.

How can you be sure you are using correctly a synonym with which you are unfamiliar? Look it up in a dictionary and read through its meanings to get a fuller sense of its uses. College dictionaries also offer many brief comparisons of synonyms that are sometimes confused. These comparisons are excellent sources of information about connotations and usage. For example, if you were to look up the word *foible* in *Merriam Webster's*

Collegiate Dictionary, you would find after its definition "*syn* see FAULT." If you looked up *fault,* after its definitions, you would find an explanation of the differences between *fault* and its synonyms *failing, frailty, foible,* and *vice.* Whenever your dictionary offers an explanation like this one of the subtle differences among a group of synonyms, grab the opportunity to learn more about their connotations and usage.

Dictionary Exercise 25.1

Read through each of the following explanations of synonym differences from *Merriam Webster's Collegiate Dictionary.* Then fill in the blanks of the sentences after each with the appropriate synonym from the explanation. Not all the synonyms of each explanation are used in the sentences. Use a synonym only once.

> *syn* DEAD, DEFUNCT, DECEASED, DEPARTED, LATE mean devoid of life. DEAD applies literally to what is deprived of vital force but is used figuratively of anything that has lost any attribute (Such as energy, activity, radiance) suggesting life <a *dead,* listless performance>. DEFUNCT stresses cessation of active existence or operation <a *defunct* television series>. DECEASED, DEPARTED, and LATE apply to persons who have died recently. DECEASED is the preferred term in legal use <the estate of the *deceased*>. DEPARTED is usually used as a euphemism <our *departed* sister>. LATE is used esp. with reference to a person in a specific relation or status <the company's *late* president>.

1. The library committee, which has been _____ for the past three years, will be reconstituted next fall.

2. Because I stupidly left the light on inside my car, the battery is now _____.

3. As the sign on the desk of the _____ President Harry Truman used to say, "The buck stops here."

> *syn* ESTIMATE, APPRAISE, EVALUATE, VALUE, RATE, ASSESS mean to judge something with respect to its worth or significance. ESTIMATE implies a judgment, considered or casual, that precedes or takes the place of actual measuring or counting or testing out <*estimated* the crowd at two hundred>. APPRAISE commonly implies the fixing by an expert of the monetary worth of a thing, but it may be used of any critical judgment <having their house *appraised*>. EVALUATE suggests an attempt to determine relative or intrinsic worth in terms other than monetary <*evaluate* a student's work>. VALUE equals APPRAISE but without implying expertness of judgment <a watercolor *valued* by the donor at $500>. RATE adds to ESTIMATE the notion of placing a thing according to a scale of values <a highly *rated* restaurant>. ASSESS implies a critical appraisal for the purpose of understanding or interpreting or as a guide in taking action <officials are trying to *assess* the damage>.

Copyright © 2002 by Addison Wesley Longman, Inc.

(Continued)

4. At the end of his first year of work, Tomas's boss _____ his performance and awarded him a raise.

5. The taxes _____ on this property will rise substantially if you build an office building on it.

6. If your house was on fire and you could save only three things, the things you would choose to save are those you _____ most.

7. The contractor _____ that it would cost $10,000 to remodel the kitchen.

8. The jeweler _____ Margarethe's necklace as worth at least $400.

syn GIFT, FACULTY, APTITUDE, BENT, TALENT, GENIUS, KNACK mean a special ability for doing something. GIFT often implies special favor by God or nature <the *gift* of singing beautifully>. FACULTY applies to an innate or less often acquired ability for a particular accomplishment or function <a *faculty* for remembering names>. APTITUDE implies a natural liking for some activity and the likelihood of success in it <a mechanical *aptitude*>. BENT is nearly equal to APTITUDE but it stresses inclination perhaps more than specific ability <a family with an artistic *bent*>. TALENT implies a marked natural ability that needs to be developed <has enough *talent* to succeed>. GENIUS suggests impressive inborn creative ability <has no great *genius* for poetry>. KNACK implies a comparatively minor but special ability making for ease and dexterity in performance <a *knack* for getting along>.

9. Once you heard the boy play, you knew he had tremendous _____ that deserved to be nurtured and supported.

10. Students with a/an _____ for languages can choose to live in one of the language houses, where only French, Italian or German is spoken.

11. Perfect pitch is a/an _____ that many musicians are born with, but proper pitch is so important in music that those not born with perfect pitch must learn at least to approximate it when they play or sing.

12. Miguel really has a/an _____ for making friends.

13. Though they are twins, Courtney is interested in public affairs and plans to attend law school, while Mavis has an artistic _____.

syn ASSENT, CONSENT, ACCEDE, ACQUIESCE, AGREE, SUBSCRIBE mean to concur with what has been proposed. ASSENT implies an act involving the understanding or judgment and applies to propositions or opinions <voters *assented* to the proposal>. CONSENT involves the will or feelings and indicates compliance with what is requested or desired <*consented* to their daughter's going>. ACCEDE implies a yielding,

(Continued)

often under pressure, of assent or consent <officials *acceded* to the prisoners' demands>. ACQUIESCE implies tacit acceptance or forbearance of opposition < *acquiesced* to his boss's wishes>. AGREE sometimes implies previous difference of opinion or attempts at persuasion <finally *agreed* to come along>. SUBSCRIBE implies not only consent or assent but hearty approval and active support < *subscribes* wholeheartedly to the idea>.

14. After his children told him about the effects of second-hand smoke, especially on the young, George _____ to their pleas to quit smoking altogether.

15. The mayor fully _____ to the idea of the accountability of all elected officials to the voters.

16. After his third proposal, Carla _____ to marry Eduardo, but not until she graduated high school.

17. Since she is still not an adult, her parents had to _____ to the marriage too.

18. In all matters having to do with the interior of their house, Mr. Egan _____ to his wife's decisions.

syn HARD, DIFFICULT, ARDUOUS mean demanding great exertion or effort. HARD implies the opposite of all that is easy <Farming is *hard* work>. DIFFICULT implies the presence of obstacles to be surmounted or puzzles to be resolved and suggests the need of skill, patience, or courage < the *difficult* ascent of the main face of the mountain>. ARDUOUS stresses the need of laborious and persevering exertion <the *arduous* task of rebuilding>.

19. After many years of _____ training, Svetlana qualified for the Olympics gymnastics team.

20. Jamal's climb to the status of Grand Master was long and filled with many _____ matches against other equally masterful chess players.

Thesaurus Exercise 25.1

Here are the synonyms for *fat* listed in the *New American Roget's Thesaurus in Dictionary Form:*

plump, stout, corpulent, obese, portly, chubby; fertile, profitable, fruitful, rich; greasy, unctuous.

In this thesaurus, semicolons separate the synonyms for different senses of words, so note the semicolons after *chubby* and *rich* in this list.

Copyright © 2002 by Addison Wesley Longman, Inc.

(Continued)

First look up *fat* in your dictionary and read through its meanings carefully, noting the kinds of nouns with which each meaning can be used. Also look up in your dictionary any synonyms or other words that are unfamiliar to you to note not only their meanings but also their uses.

After each sentence using *fat* below, write the synonyms from the list above that could be substituted for it in the sentence. For two of the sentences, NONE of the synonyms for *fat* seem appropriate. Write *None* after these.

1. The little girl's *fat* cheeks broke into a wide grin.

_____

2. The airline industry grew *fat* on domestic air travel during the 1960s and 1970s.

_____

3. The cook prepared a *fat* beef stew for the cowboys on the cattle roundup.

_____

4. My brother the stockbroker received a *fat* bonus for bringing in so much new business.

_____

5. The old man leaned back and rested his hands on his *fat* paunch.

_____

6. *Fat* pine yields a great deal of resin, so dry it thoroughly before burning it in your fireplace.

_____

7. The woman was so *fat* that she could not sit in a regular seat at the movie theater.

_____

8. Walt Whitman's *Leaves of Grass* is a *fat* volume of poetry that he revised several times.

_____

9. The song *America* celebrates the nation's *fat* farmland in such phrases as "amber waves of grain" and "the fruited plain."

_____

(Continued)

10. A *fat* lot of good it did Tom to practice running sprints all summer: He finished fourth in yesterday's meet.

_____

Thesaurus Exercise 25.2

Now here are the synonyms for *thin* listed in the *New American Roget's Thesaurus in Dictionary Form:*

slender, lean, narrow; watery, weak, diluted; attenuated; faint, dim, threadlike; fine, delicate; poor, lame (as an excuse); flimsy, sheer, filmy.

As shown by the semicolons, this thesaurus recognizes seven meanings for *thin*. In the spaces below, use *thin* in a sentence for each of these seven senses. Then decide which synonyms for that meaning could be substituted for *thin* in your sentence. Write these at the end of each sentence. Look up any unfamiliar synonyms. The first one is done as an example.

1. slender, lean, narrow:

   The ulna is the THIN bone in the forearm. SLENDER, NARROW

2. watery, weak, diluted:

   _____

3. attenuated:

   _____

4. faint, dim, threadlike:

   _____

5. fine, delicate:

   _____

6. poor, lame:

   _____

7. flimsy, sheer, filmy:

   _____

Copyright © 2002 by Addison Wesley Longman, Inc.

Let's look at another entry in the *New American Roget's Thesaurus in Dictionary Form,* the one for the common adjective *perfect.* This thesaurus combines alphabetized words and their synonyms, like *fat* and *thin* above, with many of Roget's original categories, which are alphabetized among the words, but set apart from them in boxes. *Perfection* is one of these categories. Other categories you might also look up, such as *Goodness,* are capitalized in the listings. We find *perfect* under the adjectives in the entry:

PERFECTION

Nouns—**1,** perfection, perfectness, indefectibility; impeccancy, impeccability, faultlessness, excellence. See GOODNESS.

2, paragon; ideal, paradigm; nonpareil; pink *or* acme of perfection; *ne plus ultra;* summit, model, standard, pattern, mirror; masterpiece; transcendence, transcendency, SUPERIORITY; quintessence.

3, perfectionist, idealist.

4, see COMPLETION, IMPROVEMENT.

Verbs—be perfect, transcend; bring to perfection, perfect, ripen, mature, consummate, complete, culminate.

Adjectives—perfect, faultless; indefective, indeficient, indefectible; immaculate, spotless, impeccable; unblemished, sound, scatheless, unscathed, intact; right as rain; consummate, finished, best, model, standard, state of the art; inimitable, unparalleled, nonpareil; superhuman, divine; *sans peur et sans reproche.*

Adverbs—to perfection, to a fare-thee-well; perfectly, *etc.;* to a T, to a turn, to the letter.

Antonyms, see IMPERFECTION.

While this thesaurus does separate the different senses of *perfect* with semicolons, remember that

> A thesaurus does not define the different meanings of a word.

It is up to you the user to decide which meaning of the word you want. Under *perfect* is the word *immaculate,* meaning either *perfectly clean,* as in *an immaculate, white tablecloth,* or *perfectly correct,* as in *an immaculate record of service.* But it does not mean *complete, total,* as in this sentence, *He was a perfect stranger to me.* An **immaculate stranger* in that sentence would be incorrect. In fact, none of the synonyms listed above for *perfect* would fit in that sentence.

The thesauruses in word-processing programs organize synonyms in different ways, but you still must decide which meaning of a word you want.

Some electronic thesauruses, like that in Microsoft Word, separate the different meanings of a word more clearly than do the semicolons in the entries above. MS Word lists four meanings for *perfect,* each of which can be accessed separately. Here they are with the other synonyms you can access through them:

finished (adj.)   complete, completed, consummate, full
faultless (adj.)   flawless, excellent, matchless, impeccable, exquisite, taintless, pure, immaculate
expert (adj.)   accomplished, adept, adroit, skilled
exact (adj.)   precise, pure, sharp, sound, distinct, thorough, definite, typical

MS Word's thesaurus also separates the verb synonyms for *perfect* from the adjectives. The thesaurus in WordPerfect 8 does not organize synonyms at all until you have found one close to the meaning you want. For the adjective *perfect,* for example, it lists over fifty synonyms without identifying which are adjectives and which are verbs. You scroll through the list to find the synonym closest to the meaning you want. Then highlighting that synonym leads to other synonyms, mostly from the list of over fifty, that are somewhat close in meaning. Through the synonym *faultless,* for example, you can see sixteen synonyms, most of which are in the original list for *perfect.*

Like *Roget's,* these electronic thesauruses do not provide dictionary definitions or usage information for the listed synonyms. And not all the synonyms of a word may be listed in a thesaurus. Even in the long list found in WordPerfect 8, some of the synonyms for *perfect* that we see in the entry from *Roget's* are not included. Even more frustrating is the fact that no thesaurus lists synonyms for all the words in a dictionary, only the most common. So as you use a thesaurus, in book form or on line, remember that

> No thesaurus lists all the words or all the meanings of a word like a dictionary.

Copyright © 2002 by Addison Wesley Longman, Inc.

Dictionary Exercise 25.2

Look up in your dictionary and list briefly on your own paper the different meanings of the adjective *perfect.* Then next to each write *Roget* if that meaning appears in the *New American Roget's Thesaurus* entry on page 316 and Word if that meaning also appears in the thesaurus entry of Word, above. Write *Neither* if a meaning appears in neither thesaurus.

Besides not giving you definitions of words, a thesaurus usually does not offer you much help with a word's usage or connotations. The *New American Roget's Thesaurus,* for example, does give some information about usage; it tells you if a word is *colloquial, slang, dialectal,* or *archaic.* But it does not tell you about more subtle aspects of usage for all the other words. For example, as we noted on page 310 above, *fat* can be used in ways that its synonym *corpulent* cannot. Note that in the thesauruses from the two word-processing programs discussed earlier, no information at all is given about usage. So you would be smart not to use an unfamiliar word you find in a thesaurus until you have looked it up in a dictionary or asked a more knowledgeable person about the ways that the word is used and the feelings that it carries. If you know how and when to use a word, you will avoid being unintentionally humorous! Remember that:

> A thesaurus gives incomplete information about usage or none at all, so check out an unfamiliar synonym's usage and connotations before using it yourself.

Here is an exercise to help you understand *connotation* more fully. The names of many common animals can be made into various adjectives describing humans and human activities. You worked with some of these words in Unit 5, Chapter 24, pp. 292 and 295. Animal adjectives with the suffix *-ish* and/or *-ey, -y* are often negative in connotation, as if resembling animals or acting like them were contemptible. Those ending in *-like,* however, carry a neutral connotation. (Before filling out the grid below, remind yourself about adding a suffix to a word ending in a consonant. Refer once more to the Spelling Box on page 186.)

Dictionary Exercise 25.3

Fill in the blanks of the following grid by turning the animal nouns in the left-hand column into adjectives ending in *-ish, -ey/-y,* and *-like.* Look up five of these adjectives whose meaning you are unsure of, and jot down their meanings in the grid. Then write a sentence using each of the five, remembering the word's connotation. An X appears in any blank of the grid when no such adjective exists. For example, there is no such word as *cattish.*

EXAMPLE: pig: <u>piggish</u>   <u>piggy</u>   <u>piglike</u>
             <u>greedy</u>

<u>My roommate has such a PIGGISH appetite that he will eat anything I leave in</u>
<u>the kitchen.</u>

Animal Noun	-ish Adjective	-ey/-y Adjective	-like Adjective
cat	X		
dog	X		
bear		X	
mule		X	
snake	X		
horse	X		
rabbit	X		
mouse	X		
rat	X		
wolf		X	
fish	X		

Another way to check a word's connotation is to ask yourself if you would feel flattered or insulted or neither if a word were used to describe you or something of yours. For example, note the different feelings each of the following questions would arouse in you:

Why are you hesitating?
Why are you unsure?
Why are you ambivalent?
Why are you on the fence?
Why are you so torn?
Why are you so indecisive?
Why are you so doubtful?
Why are you so wishy-washy?
Why are you so cowardly?

Vocabulary Exercise 25.1

Work with one or two classmates to make a list of questions like the list above. Ask questions about a different human trait, perhaps someone's faithfulness (Are you being true to me?) or someone's nervousness (Why are you jittery?).

First decide what attribute you will ask about. Then think of as many synonyms or near-synonyms as you can for the attribute, both formal and informal, both positive and negative in connotation. Then look up one or two of the words in a thesaurus to make your list even fuller. Finally, arrange your questions from the most positive to the most negative. Questions containing words with a neutral connotation should go in the middle of your list.

Copyright © 2002 by Addison Wesley Longman, Inc.

Dictionary Exercise 25.4

Here are some words that may be unfamiliar to you. In a college dictionary, read the entire definition of each one. Do you think the word has more of a positive, approving connotation or more of a negative, disapproving connotation? Or does it seem neutral? Why? Would you mind if the word were applied to you? Write your answers in the spaces provided.

EXAMPLE: craven: means COWARDLY, suggesting a negative connotation. No, I wouldn't want to be called craven.

1. lackey

2. whimsical

3. vacillate

4. dispassionate

5. querulous

6. bombast

7. indefatigable

8. charlatan

9. opulent

10. astute

Thesaurus Exercise 25.3

Make a context for learning the ten words in Dictionary Exercise 25.2 by looking up each one in a thesaurus (in book form or on line) and matching each with a synonym that you think is closest to it in connotation, that is, in the feelings it carries. If a synonym is unfamiliar, look it up in your dictionary also, and then learn both words for the "price" of one!

EXAMPLE: craven <u>base (meaning treacherous or contemptible) or sneaking</u>

1. lackey (noun)_____

2. whimsical_____

3. vacillate_____

4. dispassionate_____

5. querulous_____

6. bombast_____

7. indefatigable_____

8. charlatan_____

9. opulent_____

10. astute_____

Thesaurus Exercise 25.4

Working with one or two classmates, test for yourself the different connotations of synonyms by replacing the italicized words in the following paragraphs with synonyms from a thesaurus. Try your replacements for the italicized words one at a time, rereading the sentence to see if the new synonym makes a difference. Try substituting slang or colloquial synonyms as well as more formal kinds. Experiment. If you find a synonym you prefer, jot it down above the word. For example, for the first word, *amicable* in its meaning *friendly*, MS Word lists the synonyms, *affable, neighborly, amiable, agreeable, kindly, genial, sweet, peaceful.* Which of these words would YOU choose for *amicable*?

1. The customers who bring out the worst in even the most [1]*amicable* salesperson are the [2]*rude* individuals who seem not to have [3]*smiled* or said

Copyright © 2002 by Addison Wesley Longman, Inc.

(Continued)

a [4]*kind* word in years. So [5]*arrogant* and [6]*insistent* are they on the [7]*wrong* prices that one often [8]*fears* bodily harm. It is quite [9]*frightening* when an old lady, who gives the impression of being a [10]*sweet* grandmother, suddenly turns into a [11]*raging* witch with [12]*gleaming* red eyes.

2. Cowardice is nothing more than a self-preservation mechanism triggered whenever a person has to make a decision involving a [1]*certain* amount of [2]*risk*. In the [3]*armed forces* of all nations, soldiers [4]*are made* to march in formation so that they will learn to follow orders [5]*quickly* and in a [6]*mechanical,* unquestioning fashion. A military officer [7]*knows* that following orders is essential during [8]*war*. If men are allowed to [9]*think about* the consequences of [10]*storming* an enemy stronghold or of holding their ground in the face of [11]*overwhelming* odds, they would most likely disobey orders and [12]*flee.*

3. My first and last day as a waitress was one of my more [1]*upsetting* experiences. My [2]*employer,* of course, was under the impression that I had experience, that is, until I started working. Although I was [3]*polite* and friendly, I began to realize there was more to waiting on tables than a smile. Since I did not know how to [4]*carry* six plates at once, or how to speak restaurant [5]*lingo,* which was like Chinese to me, serving the customers their [6]*correct* orders was a very [7]*slow* process. Everything went wrong; [8]*plates* broke, orders were late, bills were incorrect. Worst of all, my feet were [9]*killing* me, and I was on the verge of tears. When I [10]*spilled* a cup of [11]*hot* coffee on a customer's lap, the boss [12]*yelled,* and I ran from the restaurant, vowing never again to submit myself to such a [13]*degrading* job.

Thesaurus Exercise 25.5

Each sentence below is followed by a list of some synonyms from the *New American Roget's Thesaurus* for the italicized word in the sentence. Which synonyms could appropriately be substituted for that word? Underline those that could. Before you decide, look up in a dictionary the meanings and uses of any synonyms you do not know.

EXAMPLE: Their marriage was the result of their *happy* encounter in an economics class. He needed her help with the math for the course, and she needed his help with the term paper.

fortunate, lucky; gay, contented, joyous, ecstatic; felicitous, apt; glad.

(Continued)

1. Grandma was so *happy* to see us all that she clapped her hands and beamed.

   fortunate, lucky; gay, contented, joyous, ecstatic; felicitous, apt; glad.

2. The separation of the lovers during the war was *painful* for them.

   hurting, hurtful; dolorous; cutting, consuming, racking, excruciating, searching, grinding, grating, agonizing.

3. When she first entered college, Margaret wanted to become a doctor. But later her poor grades in science made her *change* her plans.

   alter, vary, wax and wane; temper, modulate, tamper with; turn, shift, veer, tack, swerve; change one's tune, whistle *or* sing another tune, dance to another tune, reconsider, work a change, modify.

4. Lack of funds for advertising on television *hurt* the congressman's chances for re-election.

   ache, pain, throb; injure, wound; damage, harm; offend, distress, grieve, bruise.

5. The *savagery* of the Iroquois Indians against white men was sometimes instigated by other white men.

   1, violence, vehemence, intensity, impetuosity; boisterousness; turbulence, riot, row, rumpus, devil to pay, the fat in the fire; turmoil, DISORDER; AGITATION; . . . .

   2, SEVERITY, ferocity, ferociousness, fierceness, rage, fury; fit, frenzy, convulsion, paroxysm, orgasm; force, brute force; outrage, strain, shock, spasm, convulsion, throe; hysterics, tantrum, passion, EXCITEMENT.

6. The weather was perfect for a day on the *beach*, hot and sunny.

   shore, coast[line]; strand, sands, shingle.

7. It must be *difficult* to be a major league baseball umpire, especially at an important game.

   1, difficult, not easy, hard, tough, troublesome, toilsome, irksome, laborious (see EXERTION); onerous, arduous, demanding, Herculean, formidable; sooner *or* more easily said than done; difficult *or* hard to deal with; ill-conditioned.

8. Many ancient cultures knew how to *produce* glass by melting sand and then blowing it into various hollow shapes or pouring it into molds.

   Verbs—produce, perform, operate, do, make, FORM, construct, fabricate, frame, contrive; mass produce, hammer out, manufacture, turn out; weave, forge, coin, carve, chisel; build, raise, rear, erect, put together; set up, run up, establish, constitute, compose, organize, institute; achieve, accomplish, complete, perfect.

Copyright © 2002 by Addison Wesley Longman, Inc.

(Continued)

9. Salmon hatch in rivers and then travel downstream to the sea; when they are mature, they return to their spawning grounds by travelling upstream, *exhausting* themselves against swift currents and over rapids and falls.
   exhaust, *v.t.* drain, empty, let out, deflate; weaken, deplete, overtire, prostrate, fag, fatigue; spend, consume, USE, expend; develop, finish, end.

10. Before class began, a student *pleaded with* the professor for more time to hand in her paper since her computer had lost her document.
    plead, *v.* allege, assert, state; take one's stand upon; beg, petition, urge, REQUEST.

    REQUEST:
    Verbs—**1,** request, ask, beg, crave; sue, pray, petition, solicit; invite, beg, beg leave, crave *or* ask a boon; speak for, apply to, call upon, call for, commandeer, enlist, requisition, ask a favor; coax (see FLATTERY).
    2, entreat, beseech, plead, conjure, supplicate, implore, adjure, cry to, kneel to, appeal to; invoke, ply, press, urge, beset, importune, dun, cry for help; raise money; hound; whistle for. *Colloq.,* buttonhole. *Slang,* put the bite, sting, *or* touch on; fly a kite.

Thesaurus Exercise 25.6

Look up the italicized words in the following sentences in the thesaurus of a word-processing program, such as WordPerfect or MS Word. Jot down in the blank provided two synonyms that could be substituted for each word. You may have to search more than one list in the thesaurus to find appropriate synonyms. You may also have to change the part of speech of a synonym in the on-line thesaurus and remove or add function words, like *it, for,* or *to,* to fit the words in the sentence. Follow the example. Be sure to look up in your dictionary any synonyms with which you are unfamiliar.

EXAMPLE: Chlorophyll, the substance that makes plants green, *enables* them to make food for themselves and all plant-eating animals. makes it possible for, lets (omit "to"), permits

(Continued)

From MS Word:
  enable
  MEANINGS:
  provide the means (verb) set up
                      implement
                      <u>make possible</u>
  empower (verb) capacitate
                 sanction
                 qualify
                 <u>let</u>
                 <u>permit</u>
                 license

1. Birds often fly thousands of miles south to get to *warmer* places for the winter. _____

2. Roses are difficult plants to grow because they are *susceptible* to many diseases and pests. _____

3. Many college students suffer from eating disorders or from other psychological problems that *hurt* their performance. _____

4. Some scientific journals have *discovered* that publishing articles on line is a way to cut costs. _____

5. In prehistoric times, a land *bridge* existed between Siberia and Alaska that allowed humans and animals to enter the American continents. _____

6. The Smiths *defied* their neighbors by allowing the land in front of their house to fill with weeds. _____

7. The French painter Claude Monet *often* painted the same scene many times at different times of the day to capture changes in light. _____

8. Plants that can *live* in a desert, such as the saguaro cactus, are able to absorb and save what little moisture there is. _____

9. It is *unsafe* to use lead-based paint in any room where young children will spend time because they can eat the paint chips and develop lead poisoning. _____

10. A business letter should be written in clear, concise *words* so that the recipient won't waste time figuring out what it says. _____

Copyright © 2002 by Addison Wesley Longman, Inc.

26

Making the Thesaurus Work for You

Use a thesaurus for more than synonyms.

When a thesaurus does not have the meaning of a word you want to replace, don't reject it automatically. Use it to help you with *invention*, that is, the process by which you come up with ideas for a piece of writing and then develop the ideas. Spend a minute or two considering the meanings the thesaurus does list for your word. Sometimes, you will discover a meaning that you had not thought of but that is appropriate for what you are writing about. Other times, the antonyms of the word you looked up will give you more ideas for your writing. They may also help you think of other synonyms not listed in that entry. So if you keep your mind open, a thesaurus can help you make your writing:

Word in Focus
invention

- More precise, for it forces you to think about the exact meaning of a word, and
- More varied and fuller by suggesting ideas that had not occurred to you.

Thesaurus Exercise 26.1

Here are some common words, each followed by a list of phrases that use the word in different ways and with somewhat different meanings. Use your thesaurus to make each phrase more precise by replacing it with a synonym for the word that most closely matches its use and meaning in that phrase. If more than one synonym would work, choose the one you think is most suitable, and try to explain why. If no synonym seems appropriate, write NONE.

EXAMPLE: thin: a. *thin* hair <u>fine</u>

b. a *thin* girl <u>slender "Slender" seems better than "lean" because "thin" &</u>
<u>"slender" suggest delicacy, but "lean" suggests an athletic girl rather than a</u>
<u>delicate one.</u>

1. thick:
   a. a *thick* head of hair _____
   b. a *thick* layer of insulation _____
   c. The park was *thick* with people. _____

2. fault:
   a. My biggest *fault* is lack of patience. _____
   b. A *fault* in the wiring caused the fire. _____
   c. the San Andreas *Fault* in California _____

3. deliver:
   a. Railway Express *delivers* dependably. _____
   b. *Deliver* me, O Lord, from my enemies. _____
   c. The senator *delivered* a long speech. _____

4. home:
   a. The Arctic is *home* to timber wolves. _____
   b. a *home* for the aged _____
   c. We can't afford to buy our own *home*. _____

5. common:
   a. a *common* soldier _____
   b. The parks are *common* property. _____
   c. Jesse James was a *common* horse thief. _____

Just as with the trips you take to the dictionary, allow yourself to browse a bit when you visit a thesaurus. With a bit of practice, you can use the thesaurus as a source of ideas even BEFORE you start writing a paper. All you need are a few key phrases or a sentence whose words you can look up.

For example, suppose you want to write about the bad effects of prison on young criminals. You have written a sentence saying that prison *hardens*

Copyright © 2002 by Addison Wesley Longman, Inc.

young offenders, meaning it *mentally toughens* them by increasing their ability to endure suffering. You decide to look up *harden.* The *New American Roget's College Thesaurus* lists these synonyms:

> anneal, fire; steel; congeal, thicken (see HARDNESS); accustom, inure, blunt. See HABIT, INSENSIBILITY.

None of these words has the sense of *toughen mentally,* but the words *accustom, inure,* and *blunt* make you think of another way in which prison *hardens* young criminals: it *accustoms* them to living with other, older criminals and to thinking and talking about crime.

If you follow the thesaurus's suggestion to "See HARDNESS," you would find under the noun other words that you could apply to your topic: *rigidity, inflexibility, temper.* Young criminals could become *rigid* and *inflexible* in their attitudes toward the law and toward authority, thus making them much more likely to commit more crimes later. The word *temper* may lead you to write that prison doesn't teach the young how to control emotions such as anger that may have led them to commit crime.

Besides using a word's synonyms to spark new ideas for your writing, you can also check out a word's antonyms. The antonyms for HARDNESS in the *New American Roget's College Thesaurus* are SOFTNESS and ELASTICITY. If you look up the first, you find words that suggest what young criminals lose in prison: *sensitivity, responsiveness, mellowness, relaxation.* Under the second, you find *resilience* and *adaptability.* These words suggest another paragraph or two for your essay on what prison does not do for young criminals. Remember that

> The words in a thesaurus can give you ideas for your writing.

Thesaurus Exercise 26.2

Imagine that each of the following sentences is the first one you have written for an essay on the topic preceding it. Look up in a thesaurus the italicized word in each sentence, and follow the word's various meanings, from one entry to another, including both synonyms and antonyms, to come up with at least three ways in which the topic could be developed. Write these ways as phrases or complete sentences in the spaces provided.

(Continued)

EXAMPLE: Ways to discipline children: My parents were very *strict* with me when I was growing up. <u>My parents were RIGID because no rules could be broken. They were CONSCIENTIOUS parents who wanted only what was good for me. But they were not HEAVY-HANDED or HARD AS NAILS when I did break a rule. They weren't NEGLIGENT.</u>

1. Conserving natural resources: We shouldn't *waste* our natural resources, especially oil.

   _____

   _____

2. The value of reputation: Some people think of their reputation as their most *valuable* possession.

   _____

   _____

3. Buying on credit: It's so easy to buy on credit these days that many people *yield* to the temptation of spending more money than they can afford.

   _____

   _____

4. Scrooge in Dickens's *A Christmas Carol:* Scrooge is a very *cold* and *selfish* miser.

   _____

   _____

5. The benefits of sports for children: Playing *team* sports can teach children the value of *fair* play.

   _____

   _____

Copyright © 2002 by Addison Wesley Longman, Inc.

Writing Assignment 26.1

Choose two of the topics from the preceding exercise, and on a separate piece of paper, write short paragraphs further developing each of the phrases or sentences that you wrote from words you found in the thesaurus. Imagine that you are writing the draft of an essay on the chosen topic with your classmates as your audience, so use examples and details illustrating your remarks to make a reader interested in what you have to say.   ■

Thesaurus Exercise 26.3

Imagine that the following is a first, rough draft of an essay on whether or not twelve years of schooling for American children is too much. After reading it, use your thesaurus to come up with ideas for developing the essay further. Some of the words whose synonyms and antonyms you might look up are italicized. But don't limit yourself to looking up only these words. When you find synonyms or antonyms that suggest to you a way of developing the essay further, jot them down together with a brief sentence for each to remind yourself of the idea it suggested to you. As in Thesaurus Exercise 26.2, try to come up with at least three ways to develop this essay further.

I don't think that twelve years is too *long* for students to be *required* to attend school. My twelve years at *school* meant a great deal to me not only because I *learned* a lot, but also because school took my mind off many other less *valuable activities*. Even though my *experiences* in school were not always *pleasant,* I still learned a lot. Another point in favor of twelve years of school is that even if students could learn in half the time everything that their teachers could teach, they would *waste* the *time* they had left. The *extra* time would not be spent in extra learning, but in less valuable activities.

Writing Assignment 26.2

Now that you have accumulated some ideas for developing the rough draft in the preceding exercise, rewrite the draft in any way you like, using some of the ideas your thesaurus helped you think of. As you write, remember the work done in Unit 5, and make your writing more precise, vivid and clear by

(Continued)
using examples; by varying nouns, adjective, and verbs; by adding modifiers; by manipulating parts of speech; and by using figurative language. Think of your readers as your fellow classmates. Write at least 400 words. ■

Besides making your writing more precise, more varied and more fully developed, learning to use a wider vocabulary in your writing can also help you develop your own personal writing style because an important aspect of any writer's style is the kinds of words and expressions he or she prefers. Besides taking advantage of the help your thesaurus and dictionary can offer you with word choice, you can also try out other ways of expressing yourself by imitating the style of other writers you admire. In the following exercises, you can examine the words, phrases, and sentences of other writers and then try out other ways of expressing the same ideas, using your thesaurus as a source. You can also practice playing with the synonyms of some of the words introduced in earlier units of this book as you move closer to writing in your own mature style.

Thesaurus and Writing Exercise 26.4

Use your thesaurus, and your dictionary when needed for unfamiliar words, to choose alternatives for the italicized words in the following passages, some from passages quoted in earlier units. Which of these synonyms are closest to those in the original sentences? Then compose your own versions of the sentences, following directions in each case. Use your own paper for the sentences.

1. Here Anna Quindlen contrasts herself and her mother:
   "For all of my life my mother had been the other: I was *aggressive*, she was *passive*. (Perhaps simply *reserved*?) . . . I was *gregarious*, she was *shy*. (Perhaps simply more *selective* in her attachments?)"
   Quindlen, p. 100

   Write two or three sentences contrasting yourself with one of your relatives or friends, as Quindlen contrasts herself with her mother above. Start by looking up synonyms for the italicized adjectives, and then choose other adjectives that more accurately describe you and your relative/friend. Be sure that the pairs of adjectives you choose are antonyms, like the pairs in the passage. Check in your dictionary the meaning and usage of any unfamiliar word before using it.

Copyright © 2002 by Addison Wesley Longman, Inc.

(Continued)

2. Here is a summing up of a description of people with brain damage:
   Each of [these patients] suffers from damage to a specific part of the brain
   that leads to bizarre but highly characteristic changes in behavior. . . . Yet
   for the most part they are *lucid, rational* and *no more insane* than you or I.
                              Ramachandran & Blakeslee, p. 2

   Describe another group of people whom the ordinary reader would
   consider "bizarre." Use three adjectives that are similar in meaning, or
   two that are similar in meaning and one opposite in meaning, like those
   italicized in the passage above.

3. Here, Deborah Tannen tells of a relative who broke a *stereotype:*
   "My great-aunt, for many years a widow, had a love affair when she was
   in her seventies. *Obese,* balding, her hands and legs *misshapen* by arthritis,
   she did not fit the *stereotype* of a woman romantically loved. But she
   was—by a man, also in his seventies, who lived in a nursing home but
   occasionally spent weekends with her in her apartment."
                              Tannen, p. 113

   Describe someone or something else that does not "fit the stereotype"
   we expect. Write one sentence in which you follow the structure of
   Tannen's second sentence: two adjectives ("Obese, balding"), a clause
   ("her hands and legs misshapen by arthritis"), then the subject and
   predicate of the sentence.

4. How Jefferson as president used persuasion:
   "[Thomas] Jefferson made effective use of his close supporters in
   Congress, and of Cabinet members as well, in persuading Congress to go
   along with his proposals. His state papers were *models* of sweet reason,
   minimizing conflicts, stressing areas where all honest people must agree."
                              Garraty & Carnes, p. 173

   Whom do you know who can use "sweet reason" to get other people to
   agree with him/her? Write a few sentences describing this person's style
   of persuasion. Somewhere in the sentences, use two *-ing* participles like
   "minimizing . . . stressing" in the description of Jefferson above. (If you
   don't know of anyone who uses "sweet reason," make up such a person.)

5. Here, Robert Hughes describes the first time he caught a good-sized fish
   as a child:
   "Only once did I catch anything resembling a game fish, when by the
   sheerest fluke a small passing bonito grabbed my bait just as it hit the
   water. It couldn't have weighed more than four or five pounds, but I still
   have the faint white scars on my index finger left by the hand line. Fifty

(Continued)

years later they have faded to near invisibility, but I can still see them. I couldn't have been more *pleased* if they had been dueling scars. Sucking my cuts, admiring the dying fish as its colors faded on the dock, surrounded by a ring of *awed* kids my own age, I felt the first surge of *triumph* in my life."
Hughes, pp. 5–6

What other word instead of *pleased* might you use to describe how you felt as a child after some great success? How else might you describe "a ring of *awed* kids" watching another child's, or your own, "*triumph*"? After finding synonyms for *pleased, awe* and *triumph,* write your own sentences, similar to Hughes's, about a childhood success and beginning with "I have never forgotten. . . ." You can make up the event you "have never forgotten." Imitate the way Hughes in the last sentence puts three descriptions of himself first and then his subject and verb, "I felt. . . ."

6. Here, the Roman historian Tacitus describes the valor in battle of the ancient Germans:
   "In the field of battle, it is *disgraceful* for the chief to be surpassed in valor; it is *disgraceful* for the companions not to equal their chief; but it is *reproach* and *infamy* during a whole succeeding life to retreat from a field surviving him."
Tacitus, p. 99

   After looking up definitions and synonyms for *disgraceful, reproach* and *infamy,* think of some other action besides not fighting well in battle that would be *disgraceful.* Write a brief description of such action, repeating your synonym for *disgraceful* as Tacitus repeats, and then ending with a "but" clause saying what action would be even worse, using other words besides *reproach* and *infamy.*

7. Here is a description of a certain kind of body language:
   "If a man sees a woman whom he wants to attract, he tries to present himself by his posture and *stance* as someone who is *self-assured*. He moves *briskly* and confidently. When he catches the eye of the woman, he may hold her glance a little longer than normal. If he gets an encouraging smile, he'll move in close and engage in small talk. As they converse, his glance shifts over her face and body. He, too, may make *preening* gestures—straightening his tie, smoothing his hair, shooting his cuffs."
Edward Hall & Mildred Hall, "The Sounds of Silence,"
in Spradley & McCurdy, p. 68

   Look up the italicized words in your dictionary to be sure you know what they mean, and then find synonyms for them in your thesaurus. Finally, write a brief description of the body language of a particular man

Copyright © 2002 by Addison Wesley Longman, Inc.

(Continued)

or boy trying to attract a woman or girl. Follow the general description above. The man/boy could be yourself, someone you know, or a character in a film, book, or TV show.

8. Here are remarks about the role of money in political elections:
"'The mother's milk of politics!' That is how the late Jesse Unruh of California once described money's *role* in politics. And an *apt* description it is. A lot of money is needed to produce the bumper stickers, put out the brochures, hire the pollsters, buy the advertisements, pay for the television time, and do all the other things necessary to run an effective campaign today."

Harrigan, pp. 125–26

Think of something else that requires "a lot of money," such as getting a higher education or buying a house. Write a sentence imitating the last sentence in the quote above, which lists six specific things money is needed for when paying for an education, a house, or whatever else you choose.

9. This passage notes how little attention we pay to old age:
"Though we have begun to examine the socially *taboo* subjects of dying and death, we have leaped over that long period of time preceding death known as old age. In truth, it is easier to *manage* the problem of death than the problem of living with an old person. Death is a dramatic, one-time crisis while old age is a day-by-day and year-by-year confrontation with powerful external and internal *forces,* a bitter-sweet coming to terms with one's own personality and one's life."

Robert Butler, quoted in Schaefer, p. 438

Illustrate this passage with an example of a death and/or day-to-day life of an old person you know or know about. Let your example show that living in old age is harder than dying.

10. Here, Machiavelli contrasts various qualities men can possess:
"Let me say that whenever men are discussed (and especially princes because they are prominent), there are certain qualities that bring them either praise or blame. Thus some are considered generous, others stingy; some are givers, others grabbers; some cruel, others merciful; one man is treacherous, another faithful; one is feeble and effeminate, another fierce and spirited; one humane, another proud; one lustful, another chaste; one straightforward, another sly; one harsh, another gentle; one serious, another playful; one religious, another skeptical, and so on."

Machiavelli, in Kishlansky, p. 224

Choose any two pairs of contrasted words (you may choose two from the above passage), and look up synonyms for them in your thesaurus. Choose a synonym for each word that has a similar positive or negative connotation. For example, "generous" has a positive feeling, so a synonym like "charitable" would be a good substitute, but "lavish," which has a negative note of excess, would be less suitable.

Then write a brief description of the possible qualities you might find in someone or something else besides men in general, for instance, in students or professors, in TV shows or movies, in dogs or cats. In your description, pair antonyms as Machiavelli does.

Copyright © 2002 by Addison Wesley Longman, Inc.

Review Exercise I

Each italicized word in the following sentences was chosen from a thesaurus's synonyms for the word in parentheses. For example, *chubby* in the example was chosen from the synonyms for *fat*. Look up each italicized word in your dictionary to see if it is being used properly. (Be especially careful about connotation.) If it is being used properly, write OK next to it. If it is not, look up the word in parentheses in your thesaurus to find a better synonym.

> **EXAMPLE:** Haines got a promotion for signing a very *chubby* (fat) contract with the airlines for new jet engines. <u>A better synonym for fat here would be PROFITABLE.</u>

1. In the 1960s, many young men fled to Canada to *eschew* (avoid) the draft for the army fighting in Vietnam. _____

2. Just by playing with his older sister, the swimming instructor gradually *wheedled* (coaxed) the little boy into the shallow end of the pool.

    _____

3. State law *inhibits* (limits) the size of trucks permitted on state roads.

    _____

4. Whether or not I attend the state university *hinges* (depends) on how much money I can borrow. _____

5. It would be *fallacious* (wrong) for an airline to fly a plane that had not passed every inspection. _____

6. A college education can open the doors to a more *appeasing* (satisfying) career.

    _____

7. & 8. The *expenditure* (price) of success in law school is *uniform* (constant) studying.

    _____

9. & 10. To end her *skirmish* (fight) with the town council over zoning, the mayor offered a *contingent* (possible) compromise for the downtown renewal plan.

    _____

Review Exercise II

The following words are listed as synonyms in *The New American Roget's College Thesaurus in Dictionary Form*. But they do not all have the same connotations. Some carry a positive feeling or connotation, while others are more negative. Some are very casual, slangy words, while others are more formal. Rearrange the words so that they are listed either from the most positive word to the most negative, or from the most formal to the most slangy. Look up in your dictionary any synonyms whose meanings, connotations, or levels of usage you are unsure of. You and your classmates will disagree about these words because the feelings attached to words are often very difficult to pin down.

> **EXAMPLE:** Positive to negative: intellectual, whiz, brain, nerd
> Most to least formal: powder room, restroom, toilet, john

1. nitwit, jerk, fool, ass, simpleton _____
2. gang, pack, clique, buddies, mob _____
3. boisterous, loudmouthed, noisy, loud _____
4. sidekick, pal, intimate, friend, chum _____
5. sexy, suggestive, racy, risqué _____
6. shack, hut, cabin, hovel, shanty _____
7. bribe, payola, grease, hush money, graft _____
8. close-mouthed, reserved, taciturn, reticent _____
9. rascal, scoundrel, reprobate, black sheep _____
10. attic, loft, penthouse, garret _____

Review Exercise III

In a famous picture book for small children called *Goodnight Moon* by Margaret Wise Brown, a small bunny (a child) goes to sleep by first listing all the things and creatures in the bedroom. The list of objects includes things that a child would most notice in a room, from objects on the bureau—"a comb and a brush"— to pictures of children's stories on the wall, to "two little kittens/And a pair of mittens." Each is also pictured, as if the child were surveying each item in turn. Then, the bunny (child) goes through the list

Copyright © 2002 by Addison Wesley Longman, Inc.

again, carefully repeating the objects one by one, bidding goodnight to each thing and creature, as well as to things beyond the room. This time, the pictures show that the creatures (the kittens, a little mouse) are asleep. At the end, after saying goodnight to each thing and creature, the bunny's (child's) imagination goes beyond the room to say, "Goodnight noises everywhere," and the bunny is asleep as well. The objects in the list rhyme, and together with the repetition of each object, these rhymes make for a very soothing and soporific book, sure to send small children off to dreamland.

How could such a list be rewritten with a DIFFERENT speaker and for a DIFFERENT audience? Instead of a child (bunny), imagine that the speaker is one of the following, and rewrite the text for an ADULT audience in any way you like to make it suit its new speaker. Consider, for example, whether the new speaker would say the list twice, once merely to list familiar objects, and then a second time to bid them farewell. If such repetition seems too childlike for your speaker, use your thesaurus and dictionary to avoid the repetition of objects and creatures in the picture book by finding alternate ways of saying the same thing or by adding modifiers to the objects the second time around. Also decide what particular objects and creatures in the room your speaker would be likely to notice. Probably not everything in the room would be included. While you might want not to repeat your list, you might want to retain the repetition of "Goodnight" or "Goodbye" before each object to allow readers to recognize your version as an imitation of Goodnight Moon. And even though the bunny's list has almost no punctuation, an adult would use commas, periods, etc., and so should your imitation.

POSSIBLE SPEAKERS:

- A sick person in a feverish state bids goodnight to what he/sheTHINKS is in the room.

- A rapper or singer bids goodnight to the audience and whatever else is in the room.

- An adult who has just fallen in love lies in bed alone and bids goodnight to things in the bedroom and to the beloved, who is present only in his/her imagination.

- An insomniac says goodnight to what is in the bedroom as a way to fall asleep.

- Someone who is leaving home for a long time bids farewell to the things in his/her bedroom, perhaps where he/she grew up.

Review Exercise IV

Return to the essay on clichés by Scott Smith in Unit 5, pp. 302-03. "Translate" his clichéd sentences into sentences without clichés that make the same point as his original sentences. That is, substitute for the clichés words of your own that mean almost the same thing. Then make your sentences even less trite and humdrum by looking up in your thesaurus synonyms for some of your words. While you are browsing through the thesaurus, consider what else you might say in your "translation" about the difficulty of writing without using clichés by looking at synonyms you reject and at antonyms for the words you do use. Here, for example, are Smith's first few sentences, followed by one way to "translate" them. The italicized word in the "translation" would be a good one to look up in a thesaurus:

Write about clichés, the editors said.
When pigs fly, I thought. I'd rather try to squeeze blood out of a turnip. It's the kind of assignment that makes me feel like my back's against the wall and there's no tomorrow....

Write about clichés, the editors said.
That's *impossible*, I thought. I'd rather try to catch a fish without a hook. It's the kind of assignment that makes me feel helpless and hopeless....

Reading 6

Here are three descriptions of the same place, the marketplace, or *souk,* of the Moroccan city Marrakesh in North Africa. The first is by the American novelist Edith Wharton, who visited Morocco in 1917, the last year of World War I, and only five years after the sale of slaves there was made illegal. Though hers was a quick trip by car through Morocco, she wrote her impressions of the country because she wanted to give English-speaking readers a sense of its "mystery and remoteness" before it was overrun by tourists. As a guest of the French authorities in Morocco, she gained access to sights that another traveler, especially if a woman, would not have seen. Her travelogue is called simply *In Morocco.*

The second description of the Marrakesh *souk* is by Elias Canetti, a writer, scientist and sociologist who won the Nobel Prize for literature in 1981. He visited Marrakesh in 1966 and wrote about his visit in *Die Stimmen von Marrakesch (The Voices of Marrakesh).* As a man, Canetti was able to travel

Copyright © 2002 by Addison Wesley Longman, Inc.

much more freely than Wharton through the city and to see small details of its life that Wharton may have been too pressed for time to notice. Canetti wrote in German, and the translation here is by J.A. Underwood.

The third reading is from a modern guidebook for American tourists traveling in North Africa. Since its purpose is to help tourists find their way through the crowded marketplace, it gives general directions rather than individual impressions of the *souk*.

As you read, pay attention not only to the details of the *souk* that each writer chooses to describe, but also to the words used. Both the choice of details and of words create the impression that each writer is striving to make. You will be asked to consider these in more detail after the readings. Also, because the emphasis here is on word *choice* rather than word *meaning*, difficult words not studied in other units of this book are underlined and defined in the margins.

"Marrakesh: The Bazaars"
from *In Morocco* by Edith Wharton

1   Marrakech is the great market of the south; and the south means not only the Atlas with its **feudal** chiefs and their wild clansmen, but all that lies beyond of heat and savagery: the Sahara of the veiled Touaregs, Dakka, Timbuctoo, Senegal and the Soudan. Here come the camel caravans from Demnat and Tameslout, from the Moulouya and the Souss, and those from the Atlantic ports and the confines of Algeria. The population of this old city of the southern march has always been even more mixed than that of the northerly Moroccan towns. It is made up of the descendants of all the peoples conquered by a long line of Sultans who brought their trains of captives across the sea from Moorish Spain and across the Sahara from Timbuctoo. Even in the highly cultivated region on the lower slopes of the Atlas there are groups of varied ethnic origin, the descendants of tribes transplanted by long-gone rulers and still preserving many of their original characteristics.

feudal: land-owning & requiring service from tenants

2   In the bazaars all these peoples meet and mingle: cattle-dealers, olive-growers, peasants from the Atlas, the Souss and the Draa, Blue Men of the Sahara, blacks from Senegal and the Soudan, coming in to trade with the wool-merchants, silk-weavers, **armourers,** and makers of agricultural implements.

armourers: makers of armor and weapons

3   Dark, fierce and **fanatical** are these narrow *souks* of Marrakech. They are mere mud lanes roofed with rushes, as in

fanatical: excessively enthusiastic & devoted

South Tunisia and Timbuctoo, and the crowds swarming in them are so dense that it is hardly possible, at certain hours, to approach the tiny raised kennels where the merchants sit like idols among their wares. One feels at once that something more than the thought of bargaining—dear as this is to the African heart—animates these **incessantly** moving throngs. The *souks* of Marrakech seem, more than any others, the central organ of a native life that extends far beyond the city walls into secret **clefts** of the mountains and far-off oases where plots are hatched and holy wars **fomented**—farther still, to yellow deserts whence negroes are secretly brought across the Atlas to the inmost **recess** of the bazaar where the ancient traffic in flesh and blood still **surreptitiously** goes on.

4   All these many threads of the native life, woven of greed and lust, of **fetichism** and fear and blind hate of the stranger, form, in the *souks,* a thick network in which at times one's feet seem literally to stumble. **Fanatics** in sheepskins **glowering** from the guarded thresholds of the **mosques,** fierce tribesmen with inlaid arms in their belts and the fighters' tufts of camel's-hair turbans, . . . lusty slave-girls with earthen oil-jars resting against swaying hips, almond-eyed boys leading fat merchants by the hand, and bare-legged Berber women, tattooed and **insolently** gay, trading their striped blankets, or bags of dried roses and irises, for sugar, tea or Manchester cotton—from all these hundreds of unknown and unknowable people, bound together by secret **affinities,** or intriguing against each other with secret hate, there **emanates** an atmosphere of mystery and menace more stifling than the smell of camels and spices and black bodies and smoking fry which hangs like a fog under the close roofing of the *souks.*

5   And suddenly one leaves the crowd and the **turbid** air for one of those quiet corners that are like the **back-waters** of the bazaars: a small square where a vine stretches across a shop-front and hangs ripe clusters of grapes through the reeds. In the patterning of grape-shadows a very old donkey, **tethered** to a stone post, dozes under a pack-saddle that is never taken off; and near by, in a matted **niche,** sits a very old man in white. This is the chief of the Guild of "morocco" workers of Marrakech, the most accomplished craftsman in Morocco in the preparing and using of the skins to which the city gives its name. Of these sleek moroccos, cream-

incessantly: without stopping

clefts: openings, cracks

fomented: stirred up

recess: secret part inside

surreptitiously: secretly

fetichism: belief in magical objects

Fanatics: people filled with irrational zeal

glowering: glaring angrily

mosques: Islamic temples

insolently: boldly & contemptuously

affinities: relationships

emanates: comes out of

turbid: thick, heavy

back-waters: isolated, backward parts

tethered: tied

niche: hollow in a wall

Copyright © 2002 by Addison Wesley Longman, Inc.

white or dyed with **cochineal** or **pomegranate** skins, are made the rich bags of the Chleuh dancing-boys, the embroidered slippers for the **harem,** the belts and harnesses that figure so largely in Moroccan trade—and of the finest, in old days, were made the pomegranate-red morocco bindings of European bibliophiles.

6   From this peaceful corner one passes into the barbaric splendor of a *souk* hung with innumerable plumy bunches of **floss** silk—**skeins** of **citron** yellow, crimson, grasshopper green and pure purple. This is the silk-spinners' **quarter,** and next to it comes that of the dyers, with great **seething** vats into which the raw silk is plunged, and ropes overhead where the rainbow masses are hung out to dry.

7   Another turn leads into the street of the metal-workers and armourers, where the sunlight through the thatch flames on round flanks of beaten copper or picks out the silver **bosses** of ornate powder-flasks and pistols; and near by is the *souk* of the plough-shares, crowded with peasants in rough Chleuh cloaks who are waiting to have their **archaic** ploughs repaired, and that of the smiths, in an outer lane of mud huts where negroes squat in the dust and **sinewy** naked figures in tattered **loin cloths** bend over blazing coals. And here ends the maze of the bazaars.

"The souks"

from *The Voices of Marrakesh* by Elias Canetti

translated from the German by J.A. Underwood

1   It is spicy in the *souks,* and cool and colourful. The smell, always pleasant, changes gradually with the nature of the merchandise. There are no names or signs; there is no glass. Everything for sale is on display. You never know what things will cost; they are neither **impaled** with their prices, nor are the prices themselves fixed.

2   All the booths and stalls selling the same thing are close together—twenty or thirty or more of them. There is a bazaar for spices and another for leather goods. The ropemakers have their space and the basketweavers have theirs. Some of the carpet dealers have large, spacious vaults; you stride past them

cochineal: red dye from dried insects

pomegranate: red fruit

harem: secluded women in an Islamic house

floss: soft thread

skeins: lengths of yarn

citron: lemon

quarter: section

seething: boiling

bosses: raised studs

archaic: antiquated

sinewy: muscular

loin cloths: cloths worn around one's middle

impaled: pierced, fixed

as past a separate city and are meaningfully invited inside. The jewelers are grouped around a courtyard of their own, and in many of their narrow booths you can see men at work. You find everything—but you always find it many times over.

3   The leather handbag you want is on display in twenty different shops, one immediately adjoining another. A man squats among his wares. There is not much room and he has them all close around him. He need hardly stretch to reach every one of his leather handbags, and it is only out of courtesy that, if he is not a very old man, he rises. But the man in the next booth, who looks quite different, sits among the same wares. And it is like that for perhaps a hundred yards, down both sides of the covered passage. It is as if you were being offered all at once everything that this largest and most famous bazaar in the city, indeed in the whole of southern Morocco, possesses in the way of leather goods. There is a great deal of pride in this exhibition. They are showing what they can produce, but they are also showing how much of it there is. The effect is as if the bags themselves knew that they were wealth and are **flaunting** themselves in their excellence before the eyes of the passers-by. It would come as no surprise if the bags were suddenly to begin moving rhythmically, all of them together, displaying in a gaily-coloured, **orgiastic** dance all the seductiveness of which they were capable.

flaunting: proudly displaying

orgiastic: frenzied

4   The guild feeling of these objects, their being together in their separation from everything different, is re-created by the passer-by according to his mood on each stroll through the *souks*. "Today I'd like to explore the spices," he says to himself, and the wonderful blend of smells is already in his nostrils and the great baskets of red peppers before his eyes. "Today I feel like some dyed wools," and there they hang, crimson, deep blue, bright yellow, and black, all around him. "Today I want to see the baskets and watch them being woven."

5   It is astounding what dignity they achieve, these things that men have made. They are not always beautiful; more and more trash of **dubious** origin finds its way in here, machine-made imports from the northern countries. But they still present themselves in the old way. In addition to the booths that are only for selling there are many where you can stand and watch the things being manufactured. You are in on the process from the start,

dubious: doubtful

Copyright © 2002 by Addison Wesley Longman, Inc.

and seeing it makes you feel good. Because part of the desolation of our modern life is the fact that we get everything delivered to the door ready for **consumption** as if it came out of some horrid **conjuring** device. But here you can see the rope-maker busy at his work, and his stock of finished ropes hangs beside him. In tiny booths hordes of small boys, six or seven of them at a time, operate **lathes** while youths assemble the pieces the boys have turned for them into little low tables. The wool with its wonderful, glowing colours is dyed before your eyes, and there are boys sitting about everywhere knitting caps in gay, attractive patterns.

consumption: use

conjuring: magical

lathes: machines for shaping wood

6   Their activity is public, *displaying* itself in the same way as the finished goods. In a society that conceals so much, that keeps the interior of its houses, the figures and faces of its women, and even its places of worship jealously hidden from foreigners, this greater openness with regard to what is manufactured and sold is doubly seductive.

7   What I really wanted to do was to find out how bargaining worked, but whenever I entered the *souks* I temporarily lost sight of the bargaining for the things that were its objects. To the naive observer there seems to be no reason why a person should turn to one morocco merchant in particular when there are twenty others beside him whose wares hardly differ from his own. You can go from one to another and back again to the first. Which stall you will buy from is never certain in advance. Even if, say, you have made up your mind to this or that, you have every opportunity of changing it. . . .

8   It is desirable that the toing and froing of negotiations should last a miniature, incident-packed eternity. The merchant is delighted at the time you take over your purchase. Arguments aimed at making the other give ground should be far-fetched, involved, emphatic, and stimulating. You can be dignified or eloquent, but you will do best to be both. Dignity is employed by both parties to show that they do not attach too much importance to either sale or purchase. Eloquence serves to soften the opponent's resolution. Some arguments merely arouse scorn; others cut to the **quick.** You must try everything before you surrender. But even when the time has come to surrender it must happen suddenly and unexpectedly so that your opponent is thrown into confusion and for a moment lets you see into his heart. Some disarm you with **arrogance,** others with charm. Every trick is admissible, any slackening of attention **inconceivable.**

quick: inmost, sensitive life

arrogance: conceited pride

inconceivable: unthinkable

9   In the booths that are large enough to walk around in the **vendor** very often takes a second opinion before yielding. The man he consults, a kind of spiritual head as regards prices, stands in the background and takes no part in the proceedings; he is there, but he does not bargain himself. He is simply turned to for final decisions. He is able, as it were against the vendor's will, to **sanction** fantastic **deviations** in the price. But because it is done by *him,* who has not been involved in the bargaining, no one lost face.

vendor: seller

sanction: allow

deviations: changes

"Marrakesh: The Souks"
from *Berlitz Morocco Pocket Guide*
Text by Neil Wilson, revised by Robert Ullian

1   The *souks,* or markets, of the medina occupy a maze of narrow streets to the north of Djemaa al Fna. They are at their busiest in the early morning and late afternoon, the most interesting times to visit. A guide is not really necessary, but having one will make things easier if your time is limited. Official guides can be hired from the tourist office or any of the larger hotels.

2   The main entrance is at the opposite end of the square from the Koutoubia Minaret. The alley directly opposite the Café de France and just left of the Restaurant al Fath, will take you through the potters' *souk* to the **Rue Souk Smarine**—the main thoroughfare, striped with sunshine and shadow, and lined with the most expensive craft and antiques shops.

3   Where the street forks, take the right-hand branch. Immediately on the right, a narrow lane leads into a small square where you will find the wool market and the **apothecaries'** *souk.* Here, stall-holders will demonstrate the spices, roots, and herbs used in medicine, magic, and cosmetics: mandrake root is used for **aphrodisiacs;** argan oil for massage; the mineral ammonite, finely ground, makes kohl to outline the eyes; and countless jars hold **arcane** objects used in magic spells.

apothecaries: druggists

aphrodisiacs: love potions

arcane: secret, mysterious

4   Back on the main street, Souk el Kebir, you soon reach the **Kissarias** (covered markets) in the heart of the *souk,* where a variety of goods are for sale. Farther on, follow your nose to the luxurious smells of the **Souk Cherratin** (leather market), where shops are packed with jackets, bags, purses, sandals, and boots.

Copyright © 2002 by Addison Wesley Longman, Inc.

5   Head toward the left through the leather *souk,* then turn right to reach a small open space with a domed shrine on the right. This is the 11th-century Koubba Baddiyin, the only surviving Almoravid building in the city.

6   The next street on the right leads along the wall of the Ben Youssef Mosque; turn left at the far end to find the inconspicuous entrance to the **Medersa Ben Youssef.** Founded in the 14th century, this school was rebuilt in the Andalusian style by the Saadians in the 16th century. It is the largest medersa in Morocco, and the courtyard is bordered on two sides by delicate **arcades,** reminiscent of the Alhambra Palace in Granada.

arcades: covered walkways

7   On your return trip to the Djemaa al Fna, keep to the right of the Kissarias, continuing through the **Souk des Babouches** (slipper market). Off to the right, use your nose again to track down the **Souk Chouari** (woodworkers' souk), where the heady scent of thuya wood and cedar perfumes the air. Turning left along Rue Souk Attarine, you soon pass the **Souk des Teinturiers,** or dyers' *souk,* hung with brightly colored skeins of freshly dyed wool. Rue Souk Attarine then merges with Souk Smarine, which leads back to the Djemaa al Fna. A less-used entrance to the *souk,* **Rue Mouassin,** starting from the corner of Djemaa al Fna near the Café Argana, is lined with quality craft and antiques shops with better prices than those in the Souk Smarine.

Mastery Exercises

1. At the end of Wharton's fourth paragraph, she describes "an atmosphere of mystery and menace." Find in pars. 3 and 4 at least five words and/or phrases that help her create this feeling of both secrecy and danger. Then write a sentence or two discussing why you think she wanted to convey this feeling about the *souk*.

2. Look up synonyms for these underlined words in Wharton's third paragraph. Then for three of them, explain what difference it makes to use Wharton's word or its synonym.

   "<u>Dark</u>, <u>fierce</u>, and <u>fanatical</u> are these narrow *souks* . . . the crowds <u>swarming</u> in them . . . the tiny raised <u>kennels</u> . . . far beyond the city walls into <u>secret clefts</u> . . . where the <u>ancient traffic</u> in flesh and blood still <u>surreptitiously</u> goes on."

3. Find three or more places in Wharton's description where she uses a list of people or things like the one at the end of her first sentence. Then say in a sentence or two why you think she uses these lists.

4. Wharton uses at least three metaphors to help her describe the *souk*. They are "the central organ of a native life"(par. 3); "a thick network" (par. 4); and "the maze of the bazaar" (par. 7). In a few sentences, discuss her use of one of these metaphors: How does she elaborate it? Why do you think she uses it? What effect does it have on the reader?

5. The marketplace as Canetti describes it seems like a different place than the one of Wharton's description. By looking at what Canetti decides to describe, what do you think is his main interest in the *souk*? What feeling(s) or idea(s) about the *souk* does his description arouse in you, the reader?

6. Canetti's description is rather plain—only a few, common adjectives, hardly any metaphors, no lists. Look up synonyms you might substitute for the following underlined words and then explain how three of these substitutions would change his description.

   Par. 2: "Some of the carpet dealers have <u>large, spacious vaults</u>."

   Par. 3: "A man <u>squats</u> among his wares. . . . The effect is as if the bags themselves knew that they were wealth and are <u>flaunting</u> themselves . . ."

   Par. 5: "The wool with its <u>wonderful</u>, <u>glowing</u> colours is dyed before your eyes, and there are boys <u>sitting</u> about everywhere knitting caps in <u>gay</u>, <u>attractive</u> patterns."

Copyright © 2002 by Addison Wesley Longman, Inc.

(Continued)

7. What does Canetti leave OUT of his description that Wharton includes? What does Wharton leave out that Canetti includes? Write a paragraph of explanation.

8. Consider the words Canetti chooses to describe bargaining in par. 8. Make a list of some of his words there that show he ADMIRES the whole bargaining process.

9. Given what the *Berlitz Morocco Pocket Guide* chooses to describe, especially what the *Guide* says in the first paragraph, what do you think is the *Guide*'s main purpose in writing this description?

10. The marketplace of Marrakesh seems in all three descriptions an extremely varied place. Write a long paragraph explaining the different ways in which each writer conveys this variety. You may use material you have already written for earlier questions.

Unit 6

Post-Test 1

Below are some unfinished analogies arranged according to the words' connotations. Finish each analogy with the word from the list following it that relates to its partner in connotation in the same way that the other two words are related. Thus if the first word is a formal word and its partner is slangy, then the third word will be formal, so its partner should be slangy. Or if the first word has a positive connotation and the second also has a positive connotation, then the third should be paired with a synonym that also has a positive connotation. Look up in a dictionary any words you do not know.

EXAMPLE: powder room : john :: midden : _dump_ (sanitation station, junkyard, dump)
"Powder room" is a rather formal term, while "john" is informal, so the rather formal word "midden" should be contrasted with the informal word "dump."

1. famous : notorious :: brave : _____ (courageous, foolhardy, dauntless)

2. country : fatherland :: house : _____ (domicile, dwelling, home)

3. to butcher : to kill :: to brawl : to _____ (squabble, fight, scrap)

4. crazy : delusional :: sick : _____ (under the weather, asthmatic, laid up)

5. skinflint : tightwad :: big spender : _____ (sport, profligate, prodigal)

6. frosty : bitter cold :: warm : _____ (mild, sweltering, summery)

7. crook : criminal :: punk : _____ (kid, young man, squirt)

8. fearsome : scary :: mysterious : _____ (enigmatic, spooky, inscrutable)

9. glutton : gourmand :: drunk : _____ (wino, bon vivant, sot)

10. yucky : uncouth :: cranky : _____ (crabby, touchy, irascible)

Copyright © 2002 by Addison Wesley Longman, Inc.

Unit 6

Post-Test 2

Use your thesaurus to rewrite the following simple descriptions twice, once replacing the italicized words with synonyms that have positive connotations, and once replacing them with synonyms having negative connotations. If you need to find more words than the first entry gives you, look up entries for related words as well.

EXAMPLE: The *big* tree *moved* in the *wind*. The great tree swayed in the breeze.
The monstrous tree twitched in the gale.

1. The *baby cried loudly.*

   _____

   _____

2. We saw the *car speed* around the corner.

   _____

   _____

3. Suddenly, a cell phone *sounded* in the *quiet* auditorium.

   _____

   _____

4. The fog *slowly came in* till it *filled* the harbor streets.

   _____

   _____

5. This book is written in a *difficult, ornate* style.

   _____

   _____

Unit 6

Post-Test 3

Look up the following common, italicized words in your thesaurus, and choose two synonyms for each, one that could be used in the first phrase and another in the second. But choose synonyms that could not be interchanged in the two phrases. In other words, one should work well in one phrase but be inappropriate for the other.

EXAMPLES: deep: a.   a *deep* voice—a <u>SONOROUS</u> voice
              b.   *deep* thought—a <u>PROFOUND</u> thought

          heart: a.   a *heart* full of love—a <u>SOUL</u> full of love
              b.   the *heart* of the problem—the <u>CENTER</u> of the problem

1. light (adj.):   a.   a *light* heart _____
                     b.   a *light* blue _____

2. strength   a.   the *strength* of ten men _____
                     b.   the *strength* of her courage _____

3. orderly (adj.)   a.   an *orderly* arrangement of books _____
                     b.   an *orderly* group of children _____

4. stain (noun)   a.   a *stain* on the carpet _____
                     b.   a *stain* on his reputation _____

5. high   a.   *high* prices _____
                     b.   *high* priest _____

6. cheap   a.   *cheap* tickets _____
                     b.   a *cheap* miser _____

7. preserved   a.   peaches *preserved* in jars _____
                     b.   a few possessions *preserved* from the fire _____

8. blind (adj.)   a.   a *blind* beggar _____
                     b.   a *blind* rush to success _____

9. stand (verb)   a.   My offer still *stands.* _____
                     b.   I can't *stand* prunes. _____

10. fight (noun)   a.   the *fight* over taxes _____
                     b.   an old boxer still full of *fight* _____

Copyright © 2002 by Addison Wesley Longman, Inc.

UNIT 7

Appendix: Additional Word Families

In this Unit, You Can Learn Words in the Following Word Families:

corp-, "body"   354
dexter, "the right hand" and *sinister,* "the left hand"   355
unda-, "wave"   357
rap-, rav-, "to snatch, seize"   358
negat-, null-, nihil-, "make nothing, none, nothing"   360
cand-, "to shine; glowing, white, burning purely"   362
cred-, "to believe"   364
voc-, -voke, "voice, call"   366
viv(a)-, "life"   368
greg-, "a flock, herd"   370
integer, "whole, entire"   371
prob(a)-, prove, "to test, prove"   373
ped-, "foot" and *ped-*, "child"   375
cast-, chast-, "pure"   379
tort-, "to twist"   381

Introduction: More Latin Roots

The following word lists are developed from word parts that can be traced back to Latin roots, some new to this book and some encountered earlier. Each list starts with words you probably already know and continues with less familiar ones. To help you learn and remember these new words, connect them to the word part they contain, as well as to the more familiar words. The exercises accompanying each word list will help you learn how to use some of the words, as well as to remember them. To help your memory further and to introduce you to still more new words, synonyms of the unfamiliar words will sometimes appear in the lists as well. The more connections you make between known and new words and the more times you use new words, the more likely they are to enter your active vocabulary.

Despite what Humpty Dumpty says below, you can't *make* words mean what they don't mean, but the more you use new words with the meanings and uses they do have, the more mastery you gain over them, even the verbs!

"When *I* use a word," Humpty Dumpty said in rather a scornful tone, "it means just what I choose it to mean–neither more nor less."

"The question is," said Alice, "whether you *can* make words mean so many different things."

"The question is," said Humpty Dumpty, "which is to be master–that's all."

Alice was too much puzzled to say anything, so, after a minute, Humpty Dumpty began again.

"They've a temper, some of them–particularly verbs, they're the proudest: adjectives you can do anything with, but not verbs. However, *I* can manage the whole lot of them! Impenetrability! That's what *I* say!"

Copyright © 2002 by Addison Wesley Longman, Inc.

WORD PART: *corp-*, "body"

As In

corpse, n., a dead body
corpuscle, n., a blood cell (literally, a *little body*)
corporation, n., a group of people acting as one legal body
corporate, adj., relating to a business company or corporation
incorporate (*in-,* into + *corp-*), v., to combine into one
incorporeal, adj., (*in-,* not + *corp-*), nonmaterial, spiritual
corpus, n., a complete body or collection of work on one subject or by
   one writer
corpulent, adj., fat

SYNONYMS FOR *CORPULENT:* besides *fat* include *obese, stout, portly, rotund, plump,* and *chubby.* All these words refer to an excess of flesh. *Fat, obese,* and *corpulent* have negative overtones. The other words have somewhat pleasant overtones: *Stout* implies strength and is also used for a short fat person. Use *portly* for someone who is imposing in size, like a great ship coming into *port. Rotund* means rounded, as in *rotunda,* a large, round room. *Plump* and *chubby* suggest a pleasing, even lovable excess of flesh.

Vocabulary Exercise A.1

Fill in the blanks below with one of the five words above that contain *corp-,* using the words' meanings and parts of speech as clues. Use each word only once.

1. Santa Claus is usually depicted as a _____ old man in a red, fur-trimmed suit.

2. In many children's fairy tales, _____ fears assume physical shape in such characters as witches, trolls, and flesh-eating giants.

3. Three large housing developments on the outskirts of the city want to _____ themselves into a separate town.

4. The whole _____ of John Keats's poetry fits into one small volume.

5. I have just read a book that offers good advice to employees of large companies who want to get ahead in _____ life.

Writing Assignment A.1

Think of three different people or fictional characters who are fat. Which of the synonyms for *fat* would best describe each? Write a 400-word essay in which your topic is the various synonyms for *fat*. Explain their similarities or differences by describing the three people or characters you have chosen. ■

WORD PARTS: *dexter,* "the right hand" and *sinister,* "the left hand"

As In

dexterity, n., skill in the use of one's hands
dexterous or *dextrous,* adj., skilled with one's hands, nimble-fingered

SYNONYMS FOR *DEXTEROUS: deft, nimble, handy, adroit* (French for *by the right hand*).

All these words have a positive connotation and can be used to describe both physical and mental skills. *Dexterous* is associated with hands that can do many things well, hands that are versatile. *Deft* implies sure, quick, light movement. *Nimble* means quick and accurate and can be used for leg and body movements too, as in the nursery rhyme, "Jack, be nimble, Jack, be quick." We use the word *handy* to describe a person who is able to perform many manual tasks easily and well, while *adroit* suggests that a person is naturally skillful under pressure.

sinister, adj., bearing evil or bad luck. In the Middle Ages, when noblemen had coats of arms, a *bar sinister* on their shield meant that the person was born out of wedlock, *on the wrong side of the sheets.*

SYNONYMS: *ominous, baleful, dire, malign, malignant*

All these adjectives have a negative connotation of threat or evil intent. *Sinister* suggests that a person means to do evil or a thing could turn out evil; the smile of a movie "bad guy" could be called *sinister. Ominous,* from the noun *omen,* suggests something menacing that is coming soon; distant thunder is an *ominous* sign of a coming storm. *Baleful* is more intense than *ominous* and *sinister* and suggests that the evil or the threatening person or thing is already present, while *dire* can refer to the effects of the event or thing itself that has caused trouble, such as the *dire* consequences of damage to the earth's ozone layer. *Malign,* more often

Copyright © 2002 by Addison Wesley Longman, Inc.

used as a verb meaning to slander someone by telling lies, is also related to *malignant* from the prefix *mal-,* bad. Both adjectives suggest active evil or injury. In Shakespeare's *Othello,* Iago is *malign* as he sets up Othello for a fall; and a cancer that will spread and kill a person is called *malignant.* (Find more about *mal-* in Chapter 5.)

Writing Assignment A.2

Think of someone you know or have seen perform who is very skilled at some physical activity like dancing or playing a sport. In a paragraph about 8–10 sentences long, describe this person in action, using two or three of the synonyms for *dexterous* above.   ■

Writing Assignment A.3

For a paragraph about 8–10 sentences long, choose one of the following topics. Use two or three of the synonyms for *sinister* above to describe the causes or effects of the topic you choose.

- neglecting your health
- a large oil spill close to a shore
- smoking tobacco   ■

Writing Assignment A.4

The majority of human beings are right-handed, so the world is geared in many ways to right-handed people. For example, left-handed people cannot cut paper with ordinary scissors. If you yourself are not left-handed, talk to at least one left-handed person about how left-handers have to adjust themselves to a right-handed world. Then write an essay of about 400 words describing these adjustments, using the Latin roots *dexter* and *sinister* and the English words that come from them to show the world's prejudice against left-handers.   ■

WORD PART: *-unda-*, "wave"

As In

abound, abundant, abundance, v., adj., n. (from *ab-* + *unda,* flow from, overflow), to be more than enough; adj., plentiful; n., an ample supply

surround, v., to enclose on all sides (literally, to *flow over*)

undulate, v., to move in waves

inundate, v., to flood, pour in

redundant, adj., more than is necessary; superfluous (literally, *waves flowing back on*); often used of speech or writing that is wordy and repetitious.

redound, v., to have an effect; to return, recoil, as in "The students' hard work producing this newspaper *redounds to* their credit."

Vocabulary Exercise A.2

Fill in the blanks in the following sentences with the appropriate word from the above list. Use each word only once.

1. Medieval castles were often _____ by a wide moat filled with water.

2. As soon as I installed a FAX machine, I was _____ with unwanted ads, mostly from local businesses.

3. The typical Thanksgiving table is filled with an _____ of food, from the roast turkey to the pumpkin pies.

4. The final victory over their toughest opponents _____ to the glory of the basketball team and their coach.

5. The dancer moved gracefully across the floor, her long dress _____ behind her.

6. Many of the prepositions in this essay are _____ because they repeat the meaning of their verbs, for example, *retreat from* and *ascend up*.

7. At the start of a new year, dieters _____ because everyone wants to shed the pounds gained over the holidays.

Copyright © 2002 by Addison Wesley Longman, Inc.

Writing Assignment A.5

Write a few sentences each answering the following questions:

1. What animal moves in a way that could be called *undulating*?

2. Why would a first-year college student be upset if she had to take courses that seem *redundant* because she took them in high school? What might her college advisor tell her about such courses?

3. Would a popular singer be happy or sad if he was *inundated* with requests to give concerts? Explain.   ■

WORD PART: *rap-, rav-,* "to snatch, seize"

As In

rapid, adj., moving quickly, fast, swift

rape, v. & n., to force someone to engage in sex; n., forced sexual intercourse

rapt, adj., caught up in strong, lofty emotion; totally engrossed

rapture & rapturous, n. & adj., ecstasy, a state of overwhelming joy; adj., feeling great emotion

rapacious, adj., taking by force, greedy

surreptitious, adj., sneaky, doing something in a secret, stealthy way (The prefix *sur-,* another spelling of *sub-,* which usually means under, here means secret, as in another word for *surreptitious,* <u>underhand</u>. What is literally *under your hand* is secret.)

SYNONYMS FOR *SURREPTITIOUS: secret, stealthy, covert, clandestine, surreptitious, furtive, underhand*

All these adjectives describe actions that are purposely kept hidden. *Secret* is neither negative nor positive and has the largest variety of uses; *stealthy* implies actions done undercover for a particular purpose. *Covert,* which means literally *covered,* implies any action not done in the open. Another expression for spying is *covert* operations. The opposite of *covert* is *overt,* open. *Clandestine,* which is related to the word *intestines,* implies that the actions being hidden are somehow illegal or improper. *Surreptitious* implies quick, as well as improper, action, and *furtive,* from the Latin root for thief, suggests the slyness and stealth of a thief. Finally, *underhand* or *underhanded* implies that the actions are not only hidden but also unfair and fraudulent.

> *ravenous,* adj., very hungry; also, greedy for something other than food
> *ravish & ravishing,* v. & adj., to seize and take away by force or to enrapture; adj., entrancing, very delightful
> *ravage,* v. & n., to destroy or devastate; n., great damage or destruction

WATCH OUT! The roots in the words *raveling* and *rave* are different from this one!

Vocabulary Exercise A.3

Fill in the blanks in the following sentences with the appropriate word from the above list. Use each word only once.

1. Marilyn Monroe was said to have _____ beauty and great sex appeal.

2. Many college campuses have become alert to the possibility of date _____, a crime that often occurs when the man and woman involved have been drinking heavily.

3. The Huns, coming out of Asia under their great leader Attila, _____ Europe during the fourth and fifth centuries.

4. In Shylock, Shakespeare created a _____ moneylender who wanted to collect a pound of flesh from his debtor if he couldn't collect his money.

5. After the soccer game, the children were so _____ that they ate everything we served, even the vegetables.

6. At the end of the tragedy, the audience sat silent, _____ with emotion, and then burst into loud applause.

7. The burglar made a _____ entry into the bedroom, took all the valuables and left without waking anyone.

8. When he saw his new bicycle, the one he had "always" wanted, the little boy's face lit up with _____.

Copyright © 2002 by Addison Wesley Longman, Inc.

Writing Assignment A.6

After reading over the differences among the synonyms for *surreptitious,* compose a sentence using each one. If you need additional help in using a word, consult your dictionary for a fuller explanation of its meaning and use. If you like, you may use the words, which are all adjectives, as adverbs by adding the suffix *-ly.* ∎

> **WORD PART:** *-negat-, -null-, -nihil-,* **"make nothing, none, nothing"**

As In

negate, negation, v. & n., to deny (literally, *to say no to something's existence*); n., the denial or opposite of something positive

negative, adj. & n., opposite of something positive; n., a drawback, also, numbers below zero and a photograph before it is developed

abnegate, abnegation, v. & n., to deny, renounce, surrender something; n., a denial or surrender

renege, v., to revoke, go back on a promise (*re-* means *back*)

null, adj., invalid, amounting to nothing, as in the idiom *null and void* (*void* means *empty*), usually referring to laws, regulations, and other legal documents

nullify, v., to make invalid or *null*

annul, v., literally, to reduce to *nothing,* it means to make invalid

nil, n. & adj., *nothing,* zero

nihilist, n., someone who believes in *nothing,* who believes that traditional values are unfounded and life is meaningless

annihilate, v., to reduce to *nothing,* destroy, kill, or totally conquer

All these words share the Latin negative prefix *ne-,* which, like *non-,* means not.

SYNONYMS FOR *ANNIHILATE: nullify, invalidate, negate, annul*

All these verbs mean to deprive something of effect or of existence, usually by legal or official means. *Nullify* means to counteract the power or value of something completely, as when a referee says that a touchdown, goal or basket doesn't count because of a penalty or foul. *Invalidate* has the same general meaning, but adds the idea that something is *invalid* because it hasn't met a legal or official requirement. *Negate* suggests that one thing has made something opposite to it ineffective or nonexistent, as when one argument *negates* the opposing argument. *Annul* implies that something is being made ineffective or is being destroyed by legal means, as when a marriage is *annulled* (literally, made nothing).

Vocabulary Exercise A.4

Fill in the blanks in the following sentences with the appropriate word from the above list. Use each word only once.

1. My mother, who always told me never to smoke, _____ her own advice by smoking a pack a day for years.

2. At the end of *The Merchant of Venice,* Shylock is forced to _____ his religion.

3. Bombing during World War II almost totally _____ the historic city of Dresden.

4. The contractor had to _____ on paying back the bank loan to expand his business, and that led to his filing for bankruptcy.

5. Voting taxes in the South that kept many poor people from voting were _____ by the Voting Rights Act of 1965.

6. I have nothing to wear to your party—nada, zilch, _____ .

7. A pessimist is someone who always expects the worst and who has a generally _____ view of life.

8. They fell in love in high school and ran away to get married in Reno, but when they returned home, their marriage was _____ by the town clerk because they were both too young to get married.

Writing Assignment A.7

Write a few sentences each answering the following questions:

1. What are some reasons why his children might be secretly happy when their father has to *renege* on his promise to take them camping?

Copyright © 2002 by Addison Wesley Longman, Inc.

2. When one sports team defeats another by a very large score, you might say that one *annihilated* the other. In what ways is such a statement both true and false?

3. Consider the idiomatic expression *null and void*. In what sense is it *redundant*? In what sense is it not?   ∎

WORD PART: *cand-*, "to shine; glowing, white, burning purely"

As In

candle, n., a stick of wax and string that burns to give light

candidate, n., a person running for a political position or office (from the wearing in ancient Rome of *white* togas by political *candidates*)

candelabrum, sing. n., *candelabra*, plur. n., a branched candleholder

incandescent, adj., glowing brightly (from *in-* as an intensifier. See Chapter 4.)

incandescence, n., the visible light emitted by something shining; brilliance, intensity

candor, n., honesty, openness, sincerity

candid, adj., open, honest, sincere; unrehearsed (as in *candid* photographs or the TV show *Candid Camera*)

WATCH OUT! The word *candy* comes from a different root!

SYNONYMS FOR *CANDID: frank, open, outspoken, plain*

All these words suggest free and bold words. *Candid* suggests the speaker is being sincere, honest and impartial. ("The mayor asked her advisors for a *candid* assessment of her chances for re-election.") *Frank* suggests a straightforward, even tactless expression of your opinions or feelings, and it often implies that the words described as *frank* are unwelcome for some reason. (When someone says, "Let me be *frank*," be prepared for some unpleasant truth!) *Open* suggests that nothing is being hidden, but the speaker is less earnest than someone who is speaking *candidly.* ("The town meeting provides an *open* microphone for residents to say what they want about the new tax proposal.") *Outspoken* means someone is talking boldly and freely, even when it is inappropriate. ("Marcia often lost friends because she was so *outspoken* about her love life.") *Plain* talk is simple, honest, and free—nothing subtle or fancy. ("She sat her daughter down and in *plain* English told her to get serious about her studies.")

Vocabulary Exercise A.5

Fill in the blanks in the following sentences with the appropriate word from the above list of synonyms. Use each word only once.

1. The typical cowboy hero of movies in the 1950s was a tall, mysterious, but basically simple stranger known for _____ talk or no talk at all.

2. The report was a _____ appraisal of the advantages and drawbacks of the plans for the new bridge.

3. Caspar Milquetoast (pronounced milk toast) was a comic strip character in the 1950s who was very meek and mild and who responded with fear and apprehension to any aggressive, passionate or _____ person.

4. Eleanor couldn't be _____ with Marco in person, so she sent him a "Dear John" letter telling him about her true feelings and breaking their engagement.

5. The council set up a town meeting so that all the residents could express their opinions _____ about the proposed tax hike. (Note: Add the adverb ending -ly to the synonym.)

Writing Assignment A.8

Think about the different kinds of conversations you can have with different friends of yours—or with different co-workers of yours. Since there are probably different degrees of closeness between you and different friends or co-workers, your talk with each is probably also more or less free. Choose three friends or co-workers and write a long paragraph in which you use some of the five synonyms above to describe the different amounts of freedom with which you can talk to each person. Come to some conclusion at the end about conversation. ∎

Copyright © 2002 by Addison Wesley Longman, Inc.

WORD PART: *cred-*, "to believe"

As In

creed, credo, n., a set of beliefs, especially religious beliefs

credence (say **cree´**-dence), n., acceptance as true, believability (give *credence* to someone's theory)

credential, n., something that gives you a title to *credit* or trust ("A degree in library science is a necessary *credential* for a chief librarian.")

credible, incredible, adjs., believable & unbelievable

credit, n., & v., reliance on the truth of something ("give no *credit* to rumors"); financial term for money or time at your disposal to spend or pay what you owe; esteem or a source of honor ("She was a *credit* to her school"); recognition for work done; v., to believe ("Don't *credit* what he tells you"); to give someone goods on *credit;* to consider someone favorably because of something he/she has done ("The chairman *credited* Ralph with getting the new customers.")

creditor, n., someone to whom you owe money or other debts, that is, someone who has given you *credit*

credulity, credulous, n. & adj., readiness, willingness to believe something despite lack of adequate evidence; adj., ready to believe something despite lack of adequate evidence

incredulity, incredulous (*in-* = not), n. & adj., unwillingness to accept something as true, skepticism; adj., unwilling to believe, skeptical

(See Chapter 17, page 219, for more examples of the difference between *incredulous* and *incredible,* as well as *credulous* and *credible.*)

accredit, v. (literally, *to give credit to*) to approve, usually officially; to recognize as outstanding

discredit, v. & n., to refuse to believe, to cause disgrace to; n., loss of reputation, disgrace

SYNONYMS FOR *CREED*: *belief, faith, credence, credit, conviction*

All refer to your agreeing to the truth of something offered for your acceptance. *Belief* is a general word meaning accepting something as true, though you may not have seen proof of it for yourself ("a *belief* in holistic medicine"). *Faith* implies that you believe something important deeply and for sure, even without proof ("*faith* in the power of love"). *Conviction* is a strong, deep acceptance of something as true, without doubt and usually because you have strong proof; you are *convinced* ("The prosecutor is filled with the *conviction* that it is right to try this defendant for murder, not manslaughter"). *Credence* usually refers to less significant things that you may believe, though without proof ("to lend *credence* to gossip"). It usually implies that whatever you are giving *credence* to is untrue or unworthy of belief. *Credit* implies that you accept something as true on the basis of something else, like another person's say-so, though it never implies certainty ("Because she is a friend of yours, I gave her *credit* for being honest, but she disappointed me").

Vocabulary Exercise A.6

Fill in the blanks in the following sentences with the appropriate word from the above list of synonyms. Use each word only once.

1. Don't give _____ to anything he says about me; he has always despised me.

2. The writers of the United States Constitution put their _____ in the ability of ordinary citizens to vote for representatives who would run the government.

3. Even though the movie failed to make a lot of money, I have to give the producers and director _____ for daring to make such a daring film.

4. Dina, moved by the deep _____ that every adopted child should be able to find out who her birth parents were, struggled to get the state to open adoption records to any adopted person who asked.

5. Galileo was brought to trial because he did not accept the _____ that the earth traveled around the sun, not the sun around the earth.

Writing Assignment A.9

Think about reasons why so many people are taken in by get-rich-quick schemes. Why are they so *credulous*? Are such schemes at all *credible*? Write a paragraph in which you explore the *credulity* of such people, using examples if you know any. Use some of these *cred-* words in your paragraph. ∎

Copyright © 2002 by Addison Wesley Longman, Inc.

WORD PART: *voc-, -voke*, "voice, call"

As In

vocal, vocalize, adj. & v., spoken, can be heard; v., to say aloud
vocabulary, n., a list or set of words
vocation, n., your *calling* or life's work
vociferous, adj., noisy, loudly speaking, protesting, literally, *carrying (-fer) the voice*

SYNONYMS FOR *VOCIFEROUS: clamorous, blatant, strident, boisterous, obstreperous*

All these words mean something/someone is conspicuously loud, even annoying. *Vociferous* is for vehement shouting and protesting. *Clamorous* adds to *vociferous* the idea that the protesting is long and insistent. *Blatant* means the noisiness is coarse, rude, offensive; it can also refer to something that is obvious and offensive, like a *blatant* lie. *Strident* has an idea of harshness and shrillness, like the screeching of a violin that's out of tune. *Boisterous* implies that the noisemakers are full of good spirits, enjoying their noise. *Obstreperous* implies that there's some aggressiveness in the noise-making and an unwillingness to stop.

advocate, v., & n., to speak for, in favor of; n., someone who takes up your defense, a supporter
advocacy, n., active support
convoke & convocation, v., & n., to *call together,* usually for an official meeting; n., a formal, official gathering, like a *convocation* of bishops
evoke, evocative, v., & adj., to *call forth* something ("The taste of chicken soup *evokes* for me memories of my mother"); adj., *calling forth* a memory, feeling, image ("The words of the Declaration of Independence are very *evocative* for many Americans.") (See the synonyms of *evoke* on page 382 below.)
invoke & invocation, v., & n., to pray to, appeal to, literally, to *call into;* n., an opening prayer
provoke, provocation, provocative, v., to stir up someone to action, to incite, arouse, literally, to *call for;* n., something that arouses or irritates you; adj., stimulating, exciting; also, sexually arousing
revoke, v., to cancel or repeal, literally, to *call back*

These words are excellent examples of a family of words like those in Chapter 15: one root combining with several prefixes (*ad-, ex-, in-, pro-, re-*) to make several different English words, all with the original Latin meanings still present in English.

Vocabulary Exercise A.7

Fill in the blanks in the following sentences with the appropriate word from the above list of synonyms for *vociferous*. Use each word only once.

1. The huge crowd in Times Square to watch the ball drop on New Year's Eve was _____ and happy, not at all nasty or crude.

2. The voice over the loudspeaker was _____ and hard to understand. None of the people waiting on the train platform could understand it.

3. Animal-rights protestors at the fashion show made _____ outcries every time a model came down the runway wearing anything made out of fur.

4. Children who talk in class when they should be working are not usually aware that their behavior is considered _____ by their teachers, who sometimes treat them like criminals.

5. The use of four-letter words in ordinary conversation with one's grandparents shows a _____ disregard for the older folks' sense of propriety.

Writing Assignment A.10

Discuss in a sentence or two the meanings of the Latin prefixes and roots in each of the following italicized words in order to answer these questions:

1. What sorts of activities might an *advocate* of homeless people engage in? Why is it fitting to call him an *advocate*?

2. Some people think that neither politics nor religion is a safe topic for polite conversation. In what ways might politics and religion be *provocative* topics? What might each call forth?

Copyright © 2002 by Addison Wesley Longman, Inc.

3. Why might a senator making a speech about personal freedom *invoke* the name of Thomas Jefferson? What effect do you think he hopes that *invocation* will have on his listeners?   ■

WORD PART: *-viv(a)-,* "life"

As In

Words you probably already know:

vivid, adj., *live*ly, bright, intensely colored (used more of things than people)

revive, revival, v., & n., to bring back to *life,* restore; n., a returning to *life,* recovery

survive, survival, survivor, v., & n., to continue *living,* to *live* and prosper despite obstacles; n., continued *living;* someone who continues to *live* after ("Evelyn Mackey, 92, died yesterday in the city; her only *survivor* is her son John, with whom she lived.")

Other less familiar words:

vivacious (vī-**vā**-shus), *vivacity* (vī-**vă**-si-tē), adj. & n., *live*ly and high-spirited; n., *live*liness, being *vivacious* ("Kathleen was a *vivacious,* charming woman with many friends.")

vivify, v., to give *life* to, to energize

revivify, v., to give new *life,* restore to *life*

convivial, adj., fond of eating and drinking with friends, sociable, jolly

SYNONYMS FOR *VIVIFY: quicken, animate, enliven*

All these verbs mean to give life to something. *Quicken* means something has been suddenly renewed, like trees breaking into leaf in spring. *Animate* is used when speaking of giving *life* to artificial or mechanical things: Cartoons are called *animation* because the drawings seem to come *alive. Enliven* means to arouse something or someone dull, as a good storyteller can *enliven* a party. *Vivify* suggests that you are giving renewed vigor, making more *live*ly something that once was lively, as a blood transfusion can *vivify* someone who has lost blood in an accident.

RELATED SYNONYMS: *excite, pique, provoke, quicken, stimulate, stir*

All these verbs refer to arousing someone to life or to take action by pricking. *Provoke* is the most general; it emphasizes the response called forth (see *-voke* words above) and usually has an object. When used to describe a noun or pronoun, it often means *irritated, irritating: The motorists, provoked by the traffic, blew their horns.* To *excite* means to stir someone deeply, especially emotionally. *Pique* (say pēk) means to stir up with something irritating ("Her casual remark about her affair with the poet *piqued* the audience's curiosity, but she wouldn't say anything more"). It is related to the adjective *piquant* (say pēkənt), which describes sharp, lively, spicy flavors or qualities ("The chili sauce was *piquant*." OR "His *piquant* humor even made fun of the people present.") *Quicken* has a positive connotation, usually referring to a good stirring up, and it can be used without an object ("Love *quickened* her heartbeat" OR "Her heartbeat *quickened* when her lover approached."). The verb *stimulate* usually causes a brief response and is related to *stimulus,* the thing that gets you going. *Stimulate* usually means rousing someone or something that was lazy or deadened before, so final exams can be the *stimulus* that *stimulates* you to study hard. *Stir* usually refers to longer, deeper responses ("The death of Lincoln *stirred* in the nation deep mourning not just for him but for all the Civil War dead.")

Vocabulary Exercise A.8

Fill in the blanks in the following sentences with the appropriate word from the two lists of synonyms above. Use each word only once.

1. Standing on the corner with a phone pressed to his ear, Tomas carried on a(n) _____ conversation with his girlfriend. (Add *-ed* to the synonym.)

2. The third-graders were all _____ by the prospect of going to the zoo together and getting to touch some of the animals.

3. Whenever I see a drum and bugle corps marching in a parade and hear them play a patriotic song, my pulse _____.

4. For the first time all semester, the physics professor gave a lively demonstration of the principle he was teaching that _____ the students to ask lots of interested questions.

5. Even before I opened your letter, your return address, Fort Moresby, Papua-New Guinea, _____ my curiosity.

6. In his essay "A Hanging," George Orwell tells of a lively dog bursting into the prison courtyard to _____ the dreary scene.

Copyright © 2002 by Addison Wesley Longman, Inc.

7. The surprise attack on Pearl Harbor in December, 1941, _____ such anger and fear that thousands of Americans rushed to induction centers to join the armed forces.

8. With so many men overseas, American women, _____ by the nation's need for workers to make weapons for the men in the war, went to work in munitions factories for the first time. (Add *-ed* to the synonym.)

9. America's entry into the war _____ the European nations struggling to stop the advance of Hitler's troops and often badly losing.

Writing Assignment A.11

Do you know anyone who is *convivial*? Do you know anyone who is *vivacious*? Do you think it's possible for the same person to possess both these traits? In your response, describe briefly both a *convivial* person and a *vivacious* person to show these two qualities. ∎

WORD PART: *-greg-*, "a flock, herd"

As In

Some words you may already know:

congregate, congregation, v., & n., to come together as a group, crowd; n., a gathering of people, especially as a religious community

segregate, segregation, v., & n., to separate or isolate from others; n., such a separation, usually referring to isolation of a group of people by race or ethnicity

Other less familiar words:

gregarious, adj., tending to be with others; enjoying the companionship of others, sociable

aggregate, n., An *aggregate* is something formed by a cluster of units, like concrete, which is made of sand and rock held together by cement. It is the sum total of all the units mixed together. The word can also be used as an adjective, meaning clustered together, or a verb, meaning to cluster together ("The *aggregate* sale of houses by all the realtors in the state showed a marked increase over last year's sales.")

ANTONYMS OF *SEGREGATE, SEGREGATION: integrate, integration,* v., & n., to unite or blend separated parts into a single whole; n., the uniting with the general society of groups formerly isolated because of their race or ethnicity.

> **WORD PART: for *integrate: integer,* "whole, entire"**

As In

integer, n., any *whole* number
integral, adj., essential to being *whole,* complete ("Learning self-control is an *integral* part of growing up to be a healthy adult.")
integrity, n., strong moral convictions. A person with *integrity* always does what he thinks is right, even when that is difficult.

SYNONYMS FOR *INTEGRITY: honesty, honor, integrity, probity*
All these words refer to moral uprightness and strength of character. *Honesty* means the absence of all fraud or deceit in anything you do. *Honor* suggests that you stick closely to a moral code in which you firmly believe and by which you act, even though it may not be a code that everyone agrees with. *Integrity* emphasizes your moral soundness or *whole*ness; a person of *integrity* has no weak spot and is incapable of betraying a trust or responsibility. The word *probity* implies a moral steadiness that has been put to the test; it has been *probed* and found to be strong and true. (See next entry for an example.)

Vocabulary Exercise A.9

Which of the synonyms above could be used to describe the quality that each of the following possesses? Write the appropriate synonym in the blank following each example. Then explain your choice. You may use each synonym more than once.

1. The man who found your wallet and returned it to you with all your money inside

_____

Copyright © 2002 by Addison Wesley Longman, Inc.

2. Men who fought duels in the seventeenth century to protest insults to their family

_____

3. The company treasurer, who prides herself on accounting for every penny of the company's money

_____

4. A building inspector who has been offered many bribes, but has never taken one

_____

5. A lawyer who refuses a job with a prestigious law firm to work as a public defender because she has always felt that such work is more important than making money

_____

6. A candidate for mayor in a really tough race who returns a big donation to his campaign because it came from a company whose business he doesn't approve of

_____

7. A woman who returns to a department store to give back ten dollars because she paid that much less than the amount shown on her receipt

_____

8. A prisoner in a state prison who refuses to tell the guards who started a widespread protest among the prisoners over poor living conditions

_____

Writing Assignment A.12

Humans are social beings, but are we always pleased to be mixed in with the crowd? The nouns *segregation* and *integration* and their respective verbs have been used mostly to describe separating or bringing together people by race and ethnicity. But we also separate and come together in many other ways (think, for example, of the people with whom you like to eat lunch, or the people who join a specific club). What are some examples of ways other than racially in which ordinary people *segregate* themselves into smaller social groups? What are some larger social groups in which people are more *integrated*? Use these highlighted words in your response.   ■

WORD PART: *prob(a)-, prove,* "to test, prove"

As In

You may already know all but a few of the English words that come from this root. Only the least common are defined for you here.

probe, v., & n., to search into thoroughly, to investigate; n., any medical or other instrument that goes someplace that a person can't go and gathers information, like a space *probe* sent beyond our solar system to explore a distant comet

probity, n., moral character and uprightness that has been tested and *proven* sound. A judge who has made many sound decisions over the years might be described as possessing judicial *probity*.

probate, n., the process of *proving* before a law court that some document, often a will, is authentic and valid

probation

probable, probability/improbable, improbability

prove, proof

disprove, disproof

approve, approval

disapprove, disapproval

improve, improvement

reprove, reproof, v., & n., to scold gently to correct someone's fault; n., such criticism for a fault

reprobate, n., & adj., a depraved, unprincipled person, literally, *someone who has been reproved;* adj., condemned by God, depraved, corrupt

SYNONYMS FOR *REPROVE: reprove, rebuke, reprimand, admonish, reproach, chide*

All these verbs mean to criticize someone so as to correct a fault. When we *reprove* someone, we scold gently and offer constructive criticism; we might *reprove* a small child who chews his food with his mouth open to teach him better table manners. *Rebuke* and *reprimand* suggest sharp, even angry scolding and criticism; *reprimand* can also refer to a severe official criticism of

Copyright © 2002 by Addison Wesley Longman, Inc.

a public employee who hasn't done his/her job and often carries an implication of punishment. *Admonish* means literally to warn about, so when we *admonish* someone, we are also cautioning the person about the dangers of the fault committed. A professor might *admonish* a student who has innocently plagiarized a research paper to warn the student not to plagiarize again. When we *reproach* someone, we are scolding out of a sense of hurt, as if we were saying, "How could you do that and disappoint me so much?" When we *chide* someone, we do so also in anger and disappointment, as when we *reproach,* but also with the hope of improving the person criticized. The verb *chide* comes from an earlier English word meaning quarrel.

Vocabulary Exercise A.10

Which of the synonyms above could be used to criticize each of the following? Write the appropriate synonym(s) in the blank following each example. Then explain your choice. You may use more than one synonym for one example, and you may use each synonym more than once.

1. A city architect hiring a relative of his to do a job for which the relative is not qualified

   _____

2. A flute player in a high school band who continually plays out of tune

   _____

3. Your teenage daughter, who drove the family car too fast and had a minor accident

   _____

4. Your patient who has still not given up smoking two packs of cigarettes a day

   _____

5. Your nine-year-old, who did not do his homework

   _____

6. Your nine-year-old, who did not do his homework—again

   _____

7. A valued employee who treated a rude customer rudely

_____

8. An army general accused and found guilty of sexual harassment

_____

9. An old friend, who forgot to meet you for lunch as planned

_____

10. Yourself when you sleep through the alarm and miss your bus to work

_____

Writing Assignment A.13

What qualities would a thoroughly *reprobate* person have? How might such a person act? Explain in a paragraph, using any example(s) you like, but remembering the meaning of the word *reprobate*.   ■

WORD PART: *ped-*, "foot" AND *ped-*, "child"

Of course a child is very different from a foot! But despite their similar spellings, these two roots are still worth knowing. Soon you'll be able to distinguish the words that developed out of one from the words that developed out of the other.

ped-, "child"

As In

    pediatrics, pediatrician, n., the medical specialty that deals with the care of *children;* a doctor who cares for *children*

    pedagogue, n., a teacher, literally, *leader (-agogue) of children*

    pedagogy, n., the art of teaching

    pedant, pedantry, n., someone who pays too much attention to book learning and rules and ignores practical experience, also someone who shows off his learning; the habit of paying too much attention to rules and details

Copyright © 2002 by Addison Wesley Longman, Inc.

pedantic, adj., narrowly, boringly, and often showily learned. If you went to a baseball game with someone *pedantic,* you would probably be bored in the first half hour by his dreary recitation of facts about the game. He might be called a baseball *pedant.*

ped-, "foot"

As In

Some words you may already know (but note the last adjectival meaning of *pedestrian*):

pedal, n., part of a machine that is operated with a *foot,* like a car's gas *pedal*

pedestrian, n., & adj., a person walking, usually near car traffic; adj., related to walking OR commonplace, ordinary. A writer's style might be described as *pedestrian.*

Other, less familiar words:

pedestal, n., the base of a column; a statue or other ornamental device may be placed on it. "Putting someone on a *pedestal*" means that you hold that person in high esteem.

pedicure, n., care of the *feet* and toenails

pedometer, n., a small machine that measures how far you've walked by counting the number of steps you've taken

biped, n., an animal with two *feet*

centipede, millipede, n., insects with so many legs and *feet* that one seems to have a hundred (*centi*), and the other a thousand (*mille*)

expedite, v., to hurry something along, help; literally, *to get the feet out of,* to free them

expedition, expeditious, n., & adj., a group of people organized to take a journey with a definite destination, like an *expedition* to Mars; adj., done smoothly and quickly. Delivery services have to be *expeditious.* Their *feet* really have to move!

expedient, adj. & n., good for a purpose; also, serving your own interest; n., whatever serves a purpose, a means to an end; also, whatever is to your advantage. We can distinguish between a plan that is *expedient* because it gets a necessary job done and one that is *expedient* because it gives you an advantage over others.

expediency, n., suitability; also, adherence to *expedient* means. Someone who always uses the quickest and most suitable way of getting things done, without considering whether it's right or not, uses *expediency.*

impede, impediment, v. & noun—to slow someone's progress, to hinder, block, from the Latin verb meaning to shackle, chain the *feet;* n., something that hinders you, blocks your progress

impedimenta, plural n., things that are carried, like baggage, that slow or hinder your progress. The equipment and provisions needed to house and feed an army are referred to as *impedimenta.*

SYNONYMS FOR *IMPEDE*: *impede, hinder, hamper, trammel, clog, obstruct, block*

All these verbs refer to slowing down or stopping someone's forward progress. *Impede* suggests a delay that clogs the *feet,* like a muddy path. *Hinder* and *hamper* suggest anything that holds you back, physical or otherwise, causing harmful or annoying delay. For example, a herd of sheep crossing a road may *hinder* cars from proceeding past them, and a witness to a crime can *hamper* an investigation by refusing to talk about the crime. *Trammel* as a noun refers to a kind of fishing net, so something that *trammels* your progress does so by entangling you. Caring for small children might *trammel* a woman's progress in a career. *Clog,* as a *clog* in a sink suggests, means that there is too much of something that shouldn't be there or of something that would not stop you if there were less of it. Rush-hour traffic can *clog* a road that is normally easy to drive, and fatty deposits can *clog* your arteries. The verb *obstruct* means literally to *build against,* so it means that obstacles in your way are stopping or slowing you down. Billboards on a highway *obstruct* your view of the scenery. *Block,* as the noun meaning of it suggests, means to *obstruct* completely. Police set up *roadblocks* to stop every car to question their drivers.

Vocabulary Exercise A.11

Which of the synonyms above could be used to describe each of the following actions? This time, use only one synonym per example, though you may use a synonym more than once. Briefly explain your choices.

1. A pillar in front of your seat at the theatre lets you see only part of the stage.

Copyright © 2002 by Addison Wesley Longman, Inc.

2. Deep snow makes it difficult to walk your dog.

   _____

3. Several bystanders catch a mugger and prevent his escape till the police arrive.

   _____

4. A small toy that your child put down the sink won't let the water drain.

   _____

5. The great number of cases scheduled for family court ahead of yours will delay your own hearing many months.

   _____

6. Icebergs slow down the progress of ships that must pass through that part of the ocean.

   _____

7. A child's butterfly net won't let a butterfly fly away.

   _____

8. Huge waves caused by a hurricane make it difficult for lifeguards to rescue a surfer who can't swim to shore on his own.

   _____

9. A senator makes an endless speech called a filibuster to keep the other senators from voting on a bill he does not want passed.

   _____

10. Your inability to speak or read French makes getting around Paris difficult.

   _____

Writing Assignment A.14

It is often *expedient* to use any means available to achieve a good end. But is it always right to do so? For example, you have a paper due tomorrow, but you haven't even started writing it yet, so you surf the internet and download an essay you find somewhere, put your name on it, and hand it in. Discuss this situation in terms of what is *expedient* vs. what is honest. Use the word *expedient* in your discussion.   ■

WORD PART: *cast-, chast-,* "pure"

As In

> *caste,* n., one of the four hereditary classes into which Hindu society is divided and by which its members are restricted from certain professions and associations; any sharply defined social class. Literally, the *castes* are kept unmixed and thus *pure.*
>
> *castigate,* v., to punish or criticize someone publicly for a wrongdoing ("*purify*" someone morally). A newspaper editorial may *castigate* a public official by sharply criticizing him/her. See the synonyms below.
>
> *incest, incestuous,* n., & adj., literally, *not (in-) pure*; sexual union between close relatives that is forbidden or illegal because they are too closely related; adj., involving *incest*

WATCH OUT! The English word *cast* (*throw*) and the Latin root of *castle* are different!

> *chaste* (say chāst), *chastity* (say **chăs´**-tə-tē), adj. & n., *pure,* modest, never having had sex; also, simple; n., the state of being *pure* or virginal or celibate
>
> *chasten* (say **chăs´**-tən), v., to punish, literally, to make *chaste;* also, to refine something, to make someone more humble, often used as an adjective, *chastened* ("He was *chastened* by his father's scolding.") See the synonyms below.
>
> *chastise* (say **chăs-tiz´**), *chastisement,* v., & n., to punish severely, as with whipping; n., any severe punishment. See the synonyms below.

SYNONYMS: *punish, chastise, discipline, castigate, penalize, chasten*

All these verbs are about the inflicting of pain or loss onto someone because of a wrongdoing. The first word seems the most general; *punishing* someone usually involves a penalty, like the loss of freedom or money, or the giving of pain. *Chastise* suggests severe punishment, often through physical pain, but can also mean a strong verbal condemnation. To *discipline* means to control the wrongdoer and to try to correct that individual's behavior; it comes from the word *disciple* or pupil, so it has kept the idea of teaching. *Castigate* is now used mostly for public condemnation and punishment. The word *penalize* is weaker than these others because it involves not scolding or

Copyright © 2002 by Addison Wesley Longman, Inc.

physical pain, but a demand for money or a loss of privilege (a *penalty*) as a way to punish someone for breaking the rules. Finally, *chasten,* which also means to punish, is more used to imply the desire of the punisher to perfect the one punished and the humbling and subduing effects of a punishment. You are more likely to see it as the adjective *chastened,* describing the receiver of a reprimand or punishment, than the verb *chasten,* describing the act of punishing.

Vocabulary Exercise A.12

Which of the synonyms above could be used to describe each of the following actions? Use only one synonym per example, though you may use a synonym more than once. Briefly explain your choices.

1. A referee saying that a score doesn't count because a player was in the wrong spot

   _____

2. A young woman telling her boyfriend that his vulgar jokes embarrass her

   _____

3. A mother making her teenager stay home all weekend because he failed a big test

   _____

4. A candidate for public office in a debate calling her opponent the enemy of poor people

   _____

5. A seventeenth-century sea captain ordering a crewman whipped for stealing rum

   _____

6. A teacher sending a child to the principal's office for hurting a classmate

   _____

7. The federal government fining a company for polluting a river

   _____

8. A cure for her cancer making a woman seriously and quietly reconsider what is really important to her in life

_____

9. A judge imposing a mandatory jail sentence on someone caught selling heroin

_____

10. A novelist writing a story about the horrible conditions in the meat-packing industry

_____

Writing Assignment A.15

The Latin root of the words *castigate, chastise,* and *chasten* suggests a connection between punishment and purifying the one punished (*castus* meant *pure* in Latin). Do you think there is such a connection? That is, can punishment make the person punished better? Does it depend on the punishment? On the person being punished? On the wrongdoing? On the punisher? Use one example of punishment to explore this matter fully.   ■

WORD PART: *-tort-*, "to twist"

As In

> *torture,* n. & v., agony, something that causes unbearable pain; v., to inflict unbearable pain. Various instruments of *torture,* like the thumb screw, *twist* the body into painful shapes.
>
> *torment,* n. & v., the repeated infliction of pain, persecution; v., to inflict pain repeatedly, to persecute
>
> *torsion,* n., the twisting or wrenching of a body in a spiral so that one end moves to the right and the other end to the left
>
> *torque,* n., a force that produces *twisting* or *torsion*
>
> *tort,* n., a legal term for any wrongdoing for which you seek payback in court. Literally, a *tort* is a *twisted*—or illegal—act.
>
> *contort, contortion, contortionist,* v. & n., to *twist* or deform into a strange, unnatural shape, as when you *contort* your face into a grimace; n., any

Copyright © 2002 by Addison Wesley Longman, Inc.

such strange *twisting;* someone who is so flexible that he/she can *twist* the body into shapes not possible for normal people

distort, distortion, v. & n., to *twist* out of true shape or meaning; literally, to *twist away;* n., any such *twisting.* A cartoonist may *distort* the features of a public official in a political cartoon to make fun of him, but the drawing would still be natural and recognizable enough so that it is a *distortion* rather than a horrible *contortion.*

extort, extortion, extortionist, v. & n., to get something from someone by force or intimidation; literally, to *twist out of;* n., any such *extorting,* especially for money; someone who *extorts* money

retort, v. & n., to pay back, reply, answer, especially to answer sharply; literally, to *twist* or hurl *back;* n., any sharp, quick, witty response

These words are excellent examples of a family of words like those in Chapter 15: one root combining with several prefixes (*con-, dis-, ex-, re-*) to make several different English words, all with the original Latin meanings still present in English.

SYNONYMS FOR *EXTORT*: *extort, extract, elicit, evoke, educe*

All these verbs contain the prefix *ex-* or *e-*, meaning *out of;* they all refer to drawing out something that is hidden or secret. They are arranged from the most forceful to the least forceful. To *extort,* as the root *-tort* shows, means to *twist* or wring something out of someone who resists; the *extortionist* may use violence, intimidation, or other illegal power to get what he wants from the victim. The verb *extract* emphasizes the force used to drag something out; a dentist uses force to *extract* a tooth, and the root *-tract,* as we saw in Unit 4, means *dragged, drawn.* When you *elicit* something, you use skill and effort to get it out, as when careful questioning of a crime victim *elicits* a true account of the crime. *Evoke* usually involves something strong that arouses an immediate feeling or memory or image; for example, the smell of a certain perfume may *evoke* from you the memory of a woman you knew who wore it. *Educe,* which is a cognate of *educate,* contains the root *duc-,* to lead. It implies that some hidden potential is being brought out, or *led out.* No force is involved at all.

Vocabulary Exercise A.13

Answer the following questions by using the information about the five synonyms above.

1. By what means might a child *extract* from his mother a promise to take him to the movies on the weekend?

   _____

2. By what means might a child *elicit* from his mother a promise to take him to the movies on the weekend?

   _____

3. What might *evoke* sweet memories of home in a homesick child away at summer camp?

   _____

4. Give one reason why someone would give a lot of money to a man who was *extorting* him.

   _____

5. Which of the following might a teacher of third graders do to *educe* their hidden potential as readers? Explain.

   a. quiz them on their knowledge of word sounds
   b. let them choose books to take home
   c. read stories aloud to them

   _____

6. If a politician running for the Senate is making a speech before a crowd of retired people, what might *elicit* applause from the listeners? Explain.

   _____

7. How might a wealthy grandmother use the making of her will to *extort* regular visits from her grandchildren?

   _____

8. How might demolition experts clearing a piece of land for the construction of a new building *extract* a tree stump from the ground?

   _____

9. What feeling might the smell of a doctor's office *evoke* in you? Explain.

   _____

Copyright © 2002 by Addison Wesley Longman, Inc.

10. What might a person holding up a sign that says, "Homeless—Will work for food" be trying to *elicit* from passersby?

_____

Writing Assignment A.16

We can use the words *torture* and *torment* to refer to nonphysical pain as well as to physical. For example, if your child got lost on the way home from school, you might *torture* yourself emotionally for not picking her up at school. Not knowing what happened to her would be mental *torment* also. In what way(s) are mental or emotional *torture* and *torment* similar to physical *torture* and *torment*? How are they also *twisting*? In your discussion, use the example above, or think of another. ∎

Glossaries

Word Parts

Greek and Latin Roots

Here is a list of Greek and Latin roots from Units 2, 4, and 7, together with page numbers where they are featured and words containing each. How many can you now identify?

-anim(a)-,	p. 151	*anim*osity, *anim*ation
-anthrop(o)-,	p. 57	*anthrop*ology, phil*anthropy*
auto-,	p. 57	*auto*mobile
ben(e)-,	p. 57	*bene*fit
biblio-,	p. 57	*biblio*graphy
bio-,	p. 57	*bio*logy
cand-,	p. 362	*cand*le
cast-, chast-,	p. 379	*cast*igate, *chast*ity
-centr-,	p. 57	*centr*alize, con*centr*ic
-cept, -ceive,	p. 169	ac*cept,* re*ceive*
chrom(o)-,	p. 57	*chrom*osome
-chron(o)-,	p. 57	*chron*ology, syn*chron*ize
-claim, -clam-,	pp. 169, 180	ac*claim,* ex*clam*ation
-cor(d)-,	p. 153	ac*cord*
corp-,	p. 354	*corp*se
-cosm(o)-,	p. 58	*cosm*os, *cosm*etics
-cracy,	p. 57	demo*cracy*
-crat,	p. 58	demo*crat*
cred-,	p. 364	*cred*ulous
dexter, sinister,	p. 355	*dexter*ous, *sinister*
-dic(t)-,	p. 151	*dict*um, bene*dict*ion
domest-, domin-,	p. 152	*domest*ic, *domin*eering
-duc(t)-,	pp. 168, 178	se*duct*ive, con*duc*ive

385

-fect,	p. 192	per*fect*, af*fect*ion
-fer, -fere,	pp. 168, 176	suf*fer*, in*fere*nce
-fid(e)-,	p. 152	*fid*elity, *fid*uciary
-grad(e), -gress,	p. 153	*grad*ual, *grade*, di*gress*
-gram-,	p. 58	*gram*mar, kilo*gram*
-graph(y),	p. 58	*graph*ic, bio*graphy*
-greg-,	p. 370	con*greg*ate
heter(o)-,	p. 58	*hetero*sexual
homo-,	p. 58	*homo*sexual
hydr(o)-,	p. 58	*hydro*electric power
integer,	p. 371	*integr*al
-ject-,	pp. 161-62, 172	de*ject*ed, in*ject*
-latry,	p. 58	ido*latry*
-lay,	p. 168	al*lay*, re*lay*
-log(o)-, -logy, -logue,	p. 58	cata*log*, mono*logue*, neuro*logy*
macro-,	p. 58	*macro*cosm
-man(u)-,	p. 154	*man*ual, *man*ifest
-mand-, -mend-,	p. 154	*mand*ate, com*mend*
-metr-, -meter, -metry,	p. 58	iso*metr*ic, thermo*meter*, geo*metry*
micro-,	p. 58	*micro*scope
-miss-, -mit-,	pp. 168, 172	e*miss*ion, inter*mit*tent
multi-,	p. 58	*multi*colored
-negat-, -null-, -nihil-,	p. 360	*negat*ive, *null*, *nihil*ism
omni-,	p. 58	*omni*bus
orth(o)-,	p. 58	*ortho*pedist
pan-,	p. 58	*pan*orama, *Pan*-American
-path(o)-,	p. 58	*path*etic, sym*path*y, *path*ology
ped-,	p. 375	*ped*estrian, *ped*iatrician
-pel-, -puls(e)-,	pp. 168, 184	dis*pel*, com*puls*ive
-pend,	p. 192	de*pend*, inde*pend*ence
-phil(o)-,	p. 58	*philo*sophy, Anglo*phile*
-phobia or -phobe,	p. 58	claustro*phobia*, Anglo*phobe*
-phon(o or e)-,	p. 58	*phon*ograph, tele*phone*
-photo-,	p. 58	*photo*graph, tele*photo* lens
poly-,	p. 58	*poly*gon
-port-,	pp. 168, 182	*port*able, sup*port*
-pos(e),	p. 192	pro*pos*ition, sup*pose*
prob(a)-, -prove,	p. 373	*prob*e, ap*prove*
proto-,	p. 58	*proto*type

pseudo-,	p. 58	*pseudo*nym
psych(o)-,	p. 58	*psycho*logy, *psych*ic
-pung-, -punct-,	p. 151	*pung*ent, com*punct*ion
rap-, rav-,	p. 358	*rap*ture, *rav*ishing
sati(s)-,	p. 151	*satis*fy, *sati*ate
-scop-,	p. 58	*scop*e, micro*scop*e
-scrib(e)-, -script-,	p. 153	*scrib*ble, circum*scrib*e, con*script*ion
-sist-,	pp. 169, 188	con*sist*ent, sub*sist*ance
-spect-,	p. 153	*spect*er, per*spect*ive
-struct-,	p. 169	con*struct*, de*struct*ion
-tain-,	p. 168	con*tain*, at*tain*able
tel(e)-,	p. 58	*tele*vision
-tend,	p. 192	in*tend*, pre*tend*
the(o)-,	p. 58	*theo*logy
-tort-,	p. 381	con*tort*
-tract,	p. 192	at*tract*, dis*tract*ion
-unda-,	p. 357	red*unda*nt
-vert,	p. 192	con*vert*, di*vert*
-viv(a)-,	p. 368	*viva*cious, re*viv*e
voc-, -voke,	p. 366	*voc*ation, pro*voke*

Prefixes

Here is a list of the prefixes featured in this book, together with the pages where they may be found and examples of words containing them. How many prefix meanings do you now know?

ab-, abs-, a-,	p. 161	*ab*ject, *abs*tract, *a*version
ad-, ac-, af-, ag-, al-,		*ad*join, *ac*cept, *af*fair, *ag*gravate, *al*lure,
an-, ap-, ar-, as-, at-,	p. 161	*an*nihilate, *ap*prove, *ar*rive, *as*sociate, *at*tain
ante-,	p. 65	*ante*date
bi-,	p. 70	*bi*monthly
cent-,	p. 70	*cent*ury
circum-,	p. 65	*circum*stantial
com-, con-, col-,	p. 161	*com*bine, *con*duct, *col*lect, *cor*rect, *co*operate
cor-, co-		
contra-, counter,	p. 65	*contra*dict, *counter*balance
de-,	p. 161	*de*ceive, *de*frost
dec-, deca-,	p. 70	*deca*de

Copyright © 2002 by Addison Wesley Longman, Inc.

demi-,	p. 70	*demi*tasse
dis-, di-,	p. 161	*dis*miss, *dis*honest, *di*vide
du-,	p. 70	*du*al
equi-,	p. 65	*equi*poise
ex-, ec-, ef-, es-, e-,	p. 161	*ex*pel, *ec*centric, *ef*fect, *es*cape, *e*lect
extra-,	p. 65	*extra*marital
hemi-,	p. 70	*hemi*sphere
hyper-,	p. 65	*hyper*critical
in-, en-, il-, im-, ir-,	p. 72	*in*tent, *en*trance, *il*lusion, *im*mense, *ir*responsible
inter-,	p. 65	*inter*play
intra-, intro-,	p. 65	*intra*mural, *intro*duction
mal-,	p. 65	*mal*feasance
mille-, milli-,	p. 70	*mille*pede, *milli*second
mis-,	p. 65	*mis*understand
mono-,	p. 70	*mono*gram
non-,	p. 66	*non*committal
ob-, oc-, of-, op-, o-,	p. 161	*ob*tain, *oc*cur, *of*fer, *op*pose, *o*mit
oct-,	p. 70	*oct*agon
pent-,	p. 70	*pent*angle
per-,	p. 162	*per*ceive, *per*suade
post-,	p. 162	*post*graduate, *post*nasal
pre-,	p. 162	*pre*suppose, *pre*cedent
pro-,	p. 162	*pro*noun, *pro*gress
quadri-,	p. 70	*quadri*lateral
quin(t)-,	p. 70	*quin*tuplets
re-,	p. 162	*re*bound, *re*pay
retro-,	p. 66	*retro*grade
semi-,	p. 70	*semi*circle
sept-,	p. 70	*Sept*ember
sext-,	p. 70	*sext*et
sub-, suc-, suf-, sug-,		*sub*division, *suc*ceed, *suf*fer, *sug*gest,
sum-, sup-, sur-, sus-,	p. 162	*sum*mon, *sup*port, *sur*rogate, *sus*pend
sym-, syn-,	p. 66	*sym*phony, *syn*thetic
trans-,	p. 162	*trans*port, *trans*act
tri-,	p. 70	*tri*angle
un-,	p. 72	*un*likely, *un*tie
uni-,	p. 70	*uni*verse

Suffixes

Here is a list of the suffixes featured in this book. Since a suffix is a sign of a word's part of speech, the suffixes are arranged by parts of speech. Also included are page numbers where they are featured and examples of words in which they appear. Which ones give a specific meaning to the words they end?

Verb

| -fy, | p. 75 | beauti*fy*, glori*fy*, terri*fy* |

Nouns

-ability, -ibility,	pp. 75, 208	dur*ability*, cred*ibility*
-acity,	pp. 208, 235	ten*acity*
-ance, -ancy,	p. 208	endur*ance*, ten*ancy*
-ard, -art,	p. 75	drunk*ard*, bragg*art*
-ation, -tion, -sion,	pp. 201, 203, 208	gener*ation*, addi*tion*, ver*sion*
-cide,	p. 75	homi*cide*, parri*cide*
-dom,	p. 208	king*dom*
-ee,	p. 75	employ*ee*, goat*ee*
-ence, -ency,	p. 208	independ*ence*, leni*ency*
-er, -ar, -or, -eer,-ier, -yer, -ster,	p. 75	employ*er*, begg*ar*, don*or*, volunt*eer*, law*yer*
-ery,	p. 208	win*ery*
-hood,	p. 208	child*hood*
-ification,	p. 75	glori*fication*, beauti*fication*
-ics,	p. 76	opt*ics*, phys*ics*, acrobat*ics*, characterist*ics*
-ism,	p. 208	optim*ism*
-ment,	pp. 199, 208	fer*ment*
-mony,	p. 208	ali*mony*
-ness,	p. 208	happi*ness*
-onym,	p. 76	syn*onym*, ant*onym*
-ship,	p. 208	friend*ship*
-tude,	p. 208	atti*tude*
-ty, -ity,	pp. 208, 231	beau*ty*, scar*city*
-ure,	p. 208	meas*ure*

Copyright © 2002 by Addison Wesley Longman, Inc.

Adjectives

-able, -ible,	p. 76	dur*able*, cred*ible*
-acious,	pp. 76, 235	cap*acious*, aud*acious*
-fic,	p. 76	terri*fic*, horri*fic*
-ish, -like,	p. 76	child*ish*, child*like*
-less,	p. 76	home*less*, defense*less*
-onymous,	p. 76	an*onymous*, syn*onymous*
-ous,	p. 229	fam*ous*, fabul*ous*
-ose,	p. 76, 229	verb*ose*, grandi*ose*
-ward, -wards,	p. 76	home*ward*, back*wards*

Word List with Pronunciation Key

Pronunciation Key:

\ə\ **a**but \ər\ **fur**ther \a\ **a**sh \ā\ **a**ce \ä\ **mo**p, m**ar** \au̇\ **ou**t \ch\ **ch**in
\e\ b**e**t \ē\ **ea**sy \g\ **g**o \i\ h**i**t \ī\ **i**ce \j\ **j**ob \ŋ\ si**ng** \ō\ g**o**
\ȯ\ l**aw** \ȯi\ **b**oy \th\ **th**in *th*\ **th**e \ü\ l**oo**t \u̇\ f**oo**t \y\ **y**et \zh\ vi**s**ion
The syllable in **boldface** receives the heaviest stress in a word.

Word pairs that are often confused because they have similar beginnings but
different suffixes, such as *appreciative, appreciable,* are listed together.

abashed   (ə-**basht**), p. 13
abject   (**ab**-jekt), p. 161
abnegate   (**ab**-ni-gāt), p. 360
acclaim   (ə-**klām**), pp. 170, 180
accredit   (ə-**kre**-dit), p. 364
accrue   (ə-**krü**), p. 127
acrimonious   (a-crə-**mō**-nē-əs), p. 230
acrimony,   (**a**-crə-mō-nē) p. 230
admonish   (ad-**mä**-nish), pp. 373-374
adroit   (ə-**droit**), p. 355
advocacy   (**ad**-və-kə-sī), p. 366
advocate   (verb, **ad**-və-kāt; noun, **ad**-və-kət), p. 366
aggregate   (**a**-gri-gət), pp. 370-371
alienation   (ā-lēə-**nā**-shən), p. 50
alignment   (ə-**līn**-mənt), p. 20
allude   (ə-**lüde**), p. 160
allusion   (ə-**lü**-zhən), p. 166
amateurish
   (**a**-mə-tər-ish or -tùr- or -chùr-), pp. 44, 47
ambiguity   (am-bə-**gyü**-ə-tē), p. 231
ambiguous   (am-**bi**-gyə-wəs), p. 231
amenable(to)   (ə-**mē**-nə-bəl or ə-**me**-nə-bəl), p. 20
amuse   (ə-**myüz**), p. 166
analogous   (ə-**na**-lə-gəs), p. 50
animate   (verb, **a**-nə-māt; adj., **a**-nə-mət), p. 368
animosity   (a-nə-**mä**-sə-tē), p. 151
annul   (ə-**nəl**), pp. 360-361

apocalypse   (ə-**pä**-kə-lips), p. 113
appeal   (to) (ə-**pēl**), pp. 184-185
appreciative, appreciable
   (ə-**prē** -shə-tiv, ə-**prē** -shə-bəl), p.218
apropos   (a-prə-**pō)**, p. 113
artifacts   (**är**-ti-fakts), p. 52
ascertained   (a-sər-**tānd**), p. 47
assure   (ə-**shur**), p. 167
astute   (ə-**stüt** or a-**stüt**), p. 320
atrophy   (**a**-trə-fē), p. 98
atypical   (ā-**ti**-pi-cəl), p. 21
audacious   (ȯ-**dā**-shəs), p. 235
audacity   (ȯ-**da**-sə-tē), p. 235
authoritative, authoritarian
   (ə-**thär**-ə-tā-tiv, ȯ-thär-i-**ter**-ē-ən), p. 222
avail   (oneself of) (ə-**vā**(ə)**l**), p. 214

baleful   (**bā**(ə)l-fəl), p. 355
barbarity   (bär-**bar**-ə-tē), p. 231
barbarous,   (**bär**-bə-rəs), p. 231
barter   (**bär**-tər), p. 213
belladonna   (be-lə-**dä**-nə), p. 9
bellicose   (**be**-li-kōs), pp. 97-99
bemuse   (bi-**myüz**), p. 166
benediction   (be-nə-**dik**-shən), p. 151
benign   (bi-**nīn**), p. 60
blatant   (**blā**-tənt), p. 366

Copyright © 2002 by Addison Wesley Longman, Inc.

\ə\ **abut** \ər\ **further** \a\ **ash** \ā\ **ace** \ä\ **mop, mar** \aú\ **out** \ch\ **chin**
\e\ **bet** \ē\ **easy** \g\ **go** \i\ **hit** \ī\ **ice** \j\ **job** \ŋ\ **sing** \ō\ **go** \ò\ **law**

---

boggle (**bä**-gəl), p. 122
bombast (**bäm**-bast), p. 320
bombastic (bäm-**bas**-tik), p. 98
bottleneck (**bä**-təl-nek), p. 14
briskly (**brisk**-lē), p. 333
bullheaded (**bul**-hedəd), p. 48
byword (**bī**-wərd), p. 48

calabash (ka-lə-bash), p. 16
camaraderie (käm-**rä**-də-rē), p. 128
candelabrum (kan-də-**lä**-brəm), p. 362
candid (**kan**-dəd), p. 362
candor (**kan**-dər or -dòr), pp. 120, 362
caprice (kə-**prēs**), p. 229
capricious (kə-**pri**-shəs or kə-**prē**-shəs) p. 229
captive, captious (**kap**-tiv, **kap**-shəs), p. 217
carouse (kə-**raùz**), p. 115
caste (kast), p. 379
castigate (**kas**-tə-gāt), p. 379
cavil (**ka**-vəl), p. 215
censor, censure (**sen**-(t)sər, **sen**-(t)-shər), p. 218
charlatan (**shär**-lə-tən), p. 320
chaste (chāst), p. 379
chastise, chasten
    (chas-**tīz**, **chā**-sən), pp. 219, 379–380
chide (chīd), pp. 373–374
chortle (**chòr**-tl), p. 122
circumscribe (sər-kəm-**skrīb**), p. 153
circumspect (**sər**-kəm-spekt), p. 153
clairvoyant (klar-**vòi**-ənt), p. 227
clamor (**kla**-mər), pp. 180-181
clamorous (**kla**-mər-əs) pp. 180-181, 366
clandestine
    (klan-**des**-tən or -tīn or -tēn), p. 358
clichés (klē -**shāz**), pp. 292-293, 302–304
cloister (**klòi**-stər), p. 127
cloy (klòi), p. 127
cognate (**käg**-nāt), p. 124
cognizance, cognition
    (**käg**-nə-zəns, käg-**ni**-shən), p. 131
commend (kə-**mend**), p. 154
comport (kəm-**pōrt** or -**pòrt**), pp. 169, 182-183

compulsive, compulsory
    (kəm-**pəl**-siv, kəm-**pəls**-rē or -**pəls**-sə-rē), p. 185
compunction (kəm-**pəŋ**(k)-shən), p. 151
(in) concert (with) (**kän**-sərt), p. 17
conducive, conductive
    (kən-**dü**-siv, kən-**dək**-tiv), pp. 178-179
confident, confidant(e)
    (**kän**-fə-dənt, **kän**-fə-dänt), p. 216
congenial, congenital
    (kən-**jē**-nē-əl, kən-**je**-nə-təl), p. 219
connotation (kä-nō-**tā**-shən), pp. 310, 318
conscription (kən-**skrip**-shən), p. 153
consistent (kən-**sis**-tənt), p. 189
contemptible, contemptuous
    (kən-**tem(p)**tə-bəl, kən-**tem(p)**-chə-wəs), p. 221
contentment, contention
    (kən-**tent**-mənt, kən-**ten**-shən), p. 219
context (**kän**-tekst), pp. 3, 33, 97-99,
    105-106, 115, 119
contiguous (kən-**ti**-gyə-wəs), p. 12
contort (kən-**tòrt**), pp. 381-382
conventionally (kən-**ven**-shən-ə-lē), p. 10
convivial (kən-**viv**-yəl or -**vi**-vē-əl), p. 368
convocation (kän-və-**kā**-shən), p. 366
convoke (kən-**vōk**), p. 366
corpulent (**kòr**-pyə-lənt), pp. 150, 157, 310, 354
corpus (**kòr**-pəs), p. 354
council, counsel (**kaùn**(t)-səl, **kaùn**(t)-səl), p. 217
countenance, continence
    (**kaùn**-tən-ənts, **kän**-tən-ənts), p. 130
counterbalance
    (noun: **kaùn**-tər-ba-lənts;
    verb: kaùn-tər-**ba**-lənts), p. 51
coursing (**kōr**-səŋ), p. 20
covert (kə-**vərt** or **kō**-vərt), p. 358
cowed (kaùd), p. 9
craven (**krā**-vən), p. 320
credence (**krē**-d(ə)nts), p. 364
credible, credulous
    (**cre**-də-bəl, **cre**-jə-ləs), pp. 219, 364
creditor (**kre**-di-tər or -**tòr**), p. 364
credo (**krē**-dō or **krā**-dō), p. 364

\ȯi\ **boy** \th\ **thin** *th*\ **the** \ü\ **loot** \u̇\ **foot** \y\ **yet** \zh\ vi**si**on
The syllable in **boldface** receives the heaviest stress in a word.

credulity   (kri-**dü**-lə-tē or -**dyü**-lə-tē), p. 364

cuttingly   (**kə** -tiŋ-lē), p. 51

cynical   (**si**-ni-kəl), p. 122

dearth   (dərth), p. 98

decline   (di-**klīn** or dē-**klīn**), p. 214

deduct   (di-**dək**t), pp. 178–179

deduction   (di-**dək**-shən) pp. 178–179

deductive   (di-**dək**-tiv), pp. 178–179

deference   (**de**-fər-əns), pp. 107–108, 176

deft   (deft), p. 355

dejected   (di-**jek**-təd), p. 162

demoniacal   (dē-mə-**nī**-ə-kəl), p. 50

demur   (di-**mər**), p. 111

demure   (di-**myu̇r**), p. 111

denunciation   (dē-nən-sē-**ā**-shən), p. 98

depleted   (də-**plē**-td), p. 22

deportment, deportation
    (di-**pōrt**-mənt or -**pȯrt**-,
    di-pōr-**tā**-shən or -pȯr-), pp. 182-183

designated   (**de**-zig-nā-təd), p. 54

desist   (di-**sist** or dē-**sist**), p. 188

deter   (di-**tər** or dē-**tər**), p. 128

dexterity   (dek-**ster**-ə-tē), p. 355

dexterous or dextrous   (**dek**-st(ə)-rəs), p. 355

diatribe   (**dī**-ə-trīb), p. 98

dichotomy   (dī-**kä**-tə-mē), p. 111

dictum   (**dik**-təm), p. 151

didactic   (dī-**dak**-tik), p. 111

diffidence   (**di**-fə-dən(t)s), p. 152

diffusion   (di-**fyü**-zhən), p. 9

digress   (dī-**gres**), p. 154

dimension   (də-**men**-shən or dī-**men**-shən), p. 50

dire   (dīr), p. 355

directive   (də-**rek**-tiv or dī-**rek**-tiv), p. 53

disclaim   (dis-**klām**), p. 180

discredit   (dis-**kre**-dət), p. 364

discrepancy   (di-**skre**-pə-sē), p. 12

disgruntled   (dis-**grən**-təld), pp. 23–24

disheartened   (dis-**här**-tənd), p. 46

disinterested   (dis-**in**-trəs-təd), p. 167

disparity   (dis-**par**-ə-tē), p. 8

dispassionate   (dis-**pa**-shə-nət), p. 320

dispel   (di-**spel**), p. 184

disport   (di-**spōrt** or -**spȯrt**), pp. 148, 171, 182, 190

dissipated   (**di**-sə-pā-td), pp. 22, 120

dissipation   (di-si-**pā**-shən), p. 22

diversity, diversion
    (də- or dī-**vər**-sə-tē, də- or dī-**vər**-zhən), p. 220

domicile   (**dä**-mə-sīl), p. 152

domineering   (dä-mə-**nir**-iŋ), p. 152

dominion   (də-**min**-yən), p. 152

dupe   (düp), p. 213

ebb   (eb), p. 213

eccentric   (ik-**sen**-trik or ek-**sen**-trik), p. 120

educe   (i-**düs** or -**dyüs**), pp. 178, 382

efficacious   (e-fi-**kā** -shəs), p. 235

efficacy   (**e**-fi-kə-sē), p. 235

eject   (ē-**jekt**), p. 162

elicit   (i-**li**-sət), pp. 166, 382

elixir   (i-**lik**-sər), p. 17

elongation   (ē-loŋ-**gā**-shən), p. 48

elude   (ē-**lüde**), p. 160

emission   (ē-**mi**-shən), p. 173

enormousness, enormity
    (ē-**nȯr**-məs-nəs, ē-**nȯr**-mə-tē), p. 222

ensure   (in-**shu̇r**), p. 167

epicurean   (e-pi-kyu̇-**rē**-ən), p. 228

epigram, epigraph   (**e**-pə-gram, **e**-pə-graf), p. 223

epitome   (i-**pi**-tə-mē), p. 109

equanimity   (ē-kwə-**ni**-mə-tē), p. 152

ethnocentric   (eth-nō-**sen**-trik), p. 7

evocative   (i-**vä**-kə-tiv), p. 366

evoke   (i-**vōk**), pp. 366, 382

exacerbate   (ig-**za**-sər-bāt), p. 15

exactitude   (ig-**zak**-ti-tüd), p. 48

expedient   (ik-**spē**-dē-ənt), pp. 227, 376-377, 378

expedite   (**ek**-spə-dīt), p. 376

expeditious   (ex-spə-**di**-shəs), p. 376

exploit
    (verb: ik-**splȯit**; noun: **ek**-splȯit), pp. 25–27, 213

exploitation   (ek-splȯi-**tā**-shən), pp. 25–26

extort   (ik-**stȯrt**), p. 382

Copyright © 2002 by Addison Wesley Longman, Inc.

\ə\ **abut** \ər\ f**ur**ther \a\ **ash** \ā\ **ace** \ä\ mop, mar \aů\ **out** \ch\ **chin**
\e\ bet \ē\ **easy** \g\ go \i\ hit \ī\ **ice** \j\ **job** \ŋ\ si**ng** \ō\ go \ȯ\ law

extortion   (ik-**stȯr**-shən), p. 382

fallacious   (fə-**lā**-shəs), pp. 50, 235
fallacy   (**fa**-lə-sē), p. 235
fiasco   (fē-**äs**-kō or fē-**as**-kō), p. 124
fidelity   (fə-**de**-lə-tē), p. 152
fiduciary   (fə-**dü**-shē-er-ē), p. 152
figurative   (**fi**-gyə-rə-tiv), pp. 289, 292-293
filibuster   (**fi**-lə-bəs-tər), p. 121
finesse   (fi-**nes**), p. 128
fixative   (**fik**-sə-tiv), p. 50
fledgling   (**flej**-liŋ), p. 226
fleeting   (**flē**-tiŋ), p. 13
flout   (flaůt), p. 127
foible   (**fȯi**-bəl), pp. 310-311
fortuitous   (fȯr-**tü**-i-təs), p. 51
freakishly   (**frē**-kish-lē), p. 46
fulminate   (**fůl**-mə-nāt), p. 122
furtive   (**fər**-tiv), pp. 358-359

garrulity,   (gə-**rü**-lə-tē), p. 231
garrulous   (**gar**-ə-ləs), pp. 156, 231
gentrification   (jen-tri-fi-**kā**-shən), p. 8
germane   (jər-**mān**), p. 126
gnash   (nash), p. 113
gnome   (nōm), p. 113
gregarious   (gre-**gar**-ē-əs), pp. 18, 331, 370
guerrilla   (gə-**ri**-lə), p. 110
guise   (gīz), pp. 110, 242
gull   (gəl), p. 215

hamlet   (**ham**-lət), p. 50
hassle   (**ha**-səl), p. 122
hatchery   (**ha**-chə-rē), p. 48
heinous   (**hā**-nəs), p. 112
heir apparent   (ar or er ə-**par**-ənt), p. 112
hermit   (**hər** -mit), p. 121
hierarchy
    (**hī**-ər-är-kē or **hi**-ər-är-kē),
    pp. 112, 241-242, 246-247
hieroglyphics   (hī-rō-**gli**-fiks), p. 112
histrionic   (hi-strē-**ä**-nik), p. 98

humor   (**hyü**-mər or **yü**-mər), p. 214

ill-timed   (il-**tīmd**), p. 54
illicit   (i-**li**-sət), p. 166
illusion   (ē-**lü**-zhən), p. 167
impassioned   (im-**pa**-shənd), p. 47
impede   (im-**pēd**), p. 377
impediment   (im-**pe**-də-mənt), p. 377
impetuosity   (im-pe-chə-**wä**-sə-tē), p. 232
impetuous
    (im-**pech**-wəs or im-**pe**-chə-wəs), p. 232
importune   (im-pər-**tün**) p. 129
importunities   (im-pər-**tü**-ni-tēz), p. 17
impugn   (im-**pyün**), p. 113
incandescence   (in-kən-**de**-sən(t)s), p. 362
incest   (**in**-sest), p. 379
incestuous   (in-**ses**-chə-wəs- or in-**sesh**-), p. 379
incorporate   (in-**kȯr**-pə-rāt), p. 354
incorporeal   (in-kȯr-**pōr**-ē-əl or -**pȯr**), p. 354
incredible, incredulous
    (ən-**cre**-də-bəl, ən-**cre**-jə-ləs), pp. 24, 219, 364
incrustation   (in-crəs-**tā**-shən), p. 50
indefatigable   (in-di-**fa**-ti-gə-bəl), p. 320
indigent, indigenous
    (**in**-də-jənt, in-**di**-jə-nəs), pp. 17, 218
indignation, indignity
    (in-dig-**nā**-shən, in-**dig**-nə-tē), p. 220
induce   (in-**düs**), pp. 178, 197
inducement   (in-**düs**-mənt), pp. 178, 197
induct   (in-**dəkt**), pp. 171, 178, 197
induction   (in-**dək**-shən), pp. 178, 197
ineffable   (i-**nef**-ə-bəl), p. 54
infamy   (**in**-fə-mē), p. 333
infer   (in-**fər**), pp. 176–177
inference   (**in**-fə-rən(t)s), pp. 176–177
infidel   (**in**-fə-del), p. 152
initiate   (i-**ni**-shē-āt), p. 17
initiative   (i-**ni**-shə-tiv), p. 17
inject   (in-**jekt**), p. 162
insidious   (in-**si**-dē-əs), p. 120
insular   (**in**-sů-lər or **in**-syů-lər), p. 18
insupportable   (in-sə-**pōr**-tə-bəl or -**pȯr**-), p. 183

\ȯi\ **boy** \th\ **thin** *th*\ **the** \ü\ **loot** \u̇\ **foot** \y\ **yet** \zh\ vi**si**on
The syllable in **boldface** receives the heaviest stress in a word.

insure   (in-**shu̇r**), p. 167
intangible   (in-**tan**-ji-bəl), p. 19
integer   (**in**-ti-jər), p. 371
integral   (**in**-ti-grəl), p. 371
interject   (in-tər-**jekt**), p. 162
intermittent   (in-tər-**mi**-tənt), p. 174
interpolate   (in-**tər**-pə-lāt), p. 109
intrigue   (noun: **in**-trēg; verb: in-**trēg**), p. 214
inundate   (**i**-nən-dāt), p. 357
invalidate   (in-**va**-lə-dāt), pp. 360-361
invention   (in-**ven**-shən), p. 326
invocation   (in-və-**kā**-shən), p. 366
invoke   (in-**vōk**), p. 366
irresistible   (ir-i-**zis**-tə-bəl), pp. 188-189

jaunty   (**jȯn**-tē), p. 125
jeopardy   (**je**-pər-dē), p. 121
jockeying   (**jä**-kē-iŋ), pp. 24-25
jovial   (**jō**-vē-əl or **jō**-vyəl), p. 122
juggernaut   (**jə**-gər-nȯt), p. 122
juxtapose   (**jək**-stə-pōz), p. 26-27

kowtow   (kau̇-**tau̇**), p. 122

labyrinth   (**la**-bə-rinth), p. 294
lackadaisical   (la-kə-**dā**-zi-kəl), pp. 54, 122
lackey   (**la**-kē), p. 320
laggard   (**la**-gərd), p. 53
lampoon   (lam-**pün**), p. 213
lapse   (laps), p. 213
largess   (lär-**zhes** or lär-**jes**), p. 51
lassitude   (**la**-sə-tüd), p. 53
latecomer   (**lāt**-kə-mər), p. 53
Latinate   (**la**-tən-āt), pp. 150, 160, 174
legacy   (**le**-gə-sē), p. 51
lethargy   (**le**-thər-jē), p. 120
literal   (**li**-tə-rəl), p. 289
luminosity,   (lü-mə-**nä**-sə-tē), p. 232
luminous   (**lü**-mə-nəs). p. 232

magnanimous   (mag-**na**-nə-məs), p. 152
malapropism   (ma-lə-**prä**-pi-zəm), p. 257

malice   (**ma**-ləs), p. 229
malicious   (mə-**li**-shəs), p. 229
malign   (mə-**līn**) p. 355
malignant   (mə-**lig**-nənt), pp. 355-356
mandate   (**man**-dāt), p. 154
manditory   (**man**-də-tōr-ē or -tȯr-ē), p. 154
manifest   (**ma**-nə-fest), pp. 50, 120, 154
manipulate   (mə-**ni**-pyə-lāt), p. 119
manumission   (man-yə-**mi**-shən), p. 19
marginal   (**märj**-nəl or **mär**-jə-nəl), p. 46
marketable   (**mär**-kə-tə-bəl), p. 48
materialistic   (mə-tir-ē-ə-**lis**-tik), p. 55
maze   (māz), p. 294
meander   (mē-**an**-dər), p. 98
mendacious   (men-**dā**-shəs), p. 235
mendacity   (men-**da**-sə-tē), p. 235
meretricious   (mer-ə-**tri**-shəs), p. 121
metaphor   (**me**-tə-fȯr or **me**-tə-fər), pp. 120, 289
missive   (**mi**-siv), p. 190
mnemonic device   (nə-**mä**-nik də-**vīs**), p. 108
moderate
   (noun & adj.: **mä**-də-rət; verb: **mä**-də-rāt), p. 283
modifier   (**mä**-də-fī-ər,), pp. 278, 283
modify   (**mä**-də-fī), pp. 278, 283
modulate   (**mä**-jə-lāt), p. 283
momentary, momentous
   (**mō**-mən-ter-ē, mō-**men**-təs), pp. 222, 229
muse   (myüz), p. 125

naive   (nä-**ēv**), p. 110
naivete   (nä-ēv-**tā** or nä-ēv-ə-**tā**), p. 110
negate   (ni-**gāt**), pp. 360-361
negligent, negligible
   (**ne**-gli-jənt, **ne**-gli-jə-bəl), p. 217
nihilist   (**nī**-(h)ə-list), p. 360
nimble   (**nim**-bəl), p. 355
nonchalant   (nän-shə-**länt**), p. 120
noncommittal   (nän-kə-**mi**-təl), p. 175
nostalgia   (nə-**stal**-jə or nä-**stal**-jə), p. 121
noteworthiness   (**nōt**-wər-*th*ē-nes), p. 48
novel   (**nä**-vəl), p. 226
null   (nəl), p. 360

Copyright © 2002 by Addison Wesley Longman, Inc.

\ə\ abut \ər\ further \a\ ash \ā\ ace \ä\ mop, mar \aù\ out \ch\ chin
\e\ bet \ē\ easy \g\ go \i\ hit \ī\ ice \j\ job \ŋ\ sing \ō\ go \ȯ\ law

nullify   (nə-lə-fī), pp. 360

obese   (ō-bēs), pp. 157, 332, 354
objection   (əb- or äb-jek-shən), p. 172
objective   (əb- or äb-jek-tiv), p. 172
obstreperous   (əb-stre-p(ə)-rəs, or äb-) p. 366
obstruct   (əb-strəkt), pp. 170, 377
official, officious   (ə- or ō-fi-shəl, ə-fi-shəs), p. 216
offshoots   (ȯf-shüts), p. 56
ominous   (ä-mə-nəs), p. 355
opportune   (ä-pər-tün or -tyün), pp. 55, 129
oppressive   (ō-pre-siv), p. 47
opulent   (ä-pyə-lənt), p. 320
orient (themselves)   (ōr-ē-ənt or ȯr-ē-ənt), p. 20
ostentatious, ostensible
    (ä-stən-tā-shəs, ä-sten-sə-bəl), p. 221
ostracize   (äs-trə-sīz), p. 121
overawe   (ō-vər-ȯ), p. 13
overindulgent   (ō-vər-in-dəl-jənt), pp. 45-46

pacific   (pə-si-fik), p. 127
painstaking   (pān-stā-kiŋ), p. 51
panacea   (pa-nə-sē-ə), p. 113
paradigm   (par-ə-dīm), p. 113
pariah   (pə-rī-ə), p. 121
parsimonious   (pär-sə-mō-nē-əs), p. 230
parsimony   (pär-sə-mō-nē), p. 230
passive   (pa-siv), p. 18
patent   (pa-tənt or pā-tənt,
    depending on meaning), pp. 53, 227
pathos   (pā-thäs or -thȯs), p. 106
patronymics   (pa-trə-ni-miks), p. 55
paucity   (pȯ-si-tē), p. 10
pavilion   (pə-vil-yən), p. 121
pedagogue   (pe-də-gäg), p. 375
pedagogy   (pe-də-gō-jē or -gä-jē), p. 375
pedantic   (pi-dan-tik), p. 376
pedestal   (pe-dəs-t(ə)l), p. 376
pediatrics   (pē-dē-a-triks), p. 375
pedicure   (pe-di-kyùr), p. 376
perceptive, perceptible
    (pər-sep-tiv, pər-sep-tə-bəl), p. 220

peril   (per-əl), p. 229
perilous   (per-ə-ləs), p. 229
persecute   (pər-sə-kyüt), p. 166
personal, personnel   (pər-sə-nəl, pər-sə-nel), p. 216
pertinent, pertinacious
    (pər-tə-nənt, pər-tə-nā-shəs), p. 220
photosynthesis   (fō-tō-sin-thə-səs), p. 4
physiognomy   (fi-zē-äg-nə-mē), p. 113
pique   (pēk), pp. 213, 368–369
pittance   (pi-təns), p. 20
plebeian   (pli-bē-ən), p. 23
polemic   (pə-le-mik), p. 98
pomposity   (päm-pä-sə-tē), p. 232
pompous   (päm-pəs), p. 232
portly   (pōrt-lē or pȯrt-), p. 354
precarious   (prē-kar-ē-əs), p. 20
precautionary   (pri-kȯ-shə-ner-ē), p. 47
precede   (pri-sēd), p. 166
precept   (prē-sept), pp. 31, 170
precipice   (pre-sə-pis), p. 112
precipitous   (pri-si-pə-təs), p. 112
preening   (prēn-iŋ), p. 333
preferable, preferential
    (pre-fər-ə-bəl, pre-fə-ren(t)-shəl), pp. 176, 216
prejudiced, prejudicial
    (pre-jə-dəst, pre-jə-di-shəl), p. 215
preponderance   (pri-pän-də-rənts), p. 98
probate   (prō-bāt), p. 373
probity   (prō-bə-tē), pp. 371, 373
problematical   (prä-blə-ma-ti-kəl), p. 48
proceed   (prō-sēd), p. 166
proclivities   (prō-kli-və-tēz), p. 13
profligate   (prä-fli-gət), p. 227
projectile   (prə-jek-təl or -tīl), p. 113
proletariat   (prō-li-ter-ē-ət), p. 9
prosecute   (prä-sə-kyüt), p. 166
proselytize   (prä-sə-lə-tīz), p. 6
provocative   (prə-vä-kə-tiv), p. 366
provoke   (prə-vōk), pp. 366, 368-369
pterodactyl   (ter-ə-dak-təl), p. 111
ptomaine   (tō-mān), p. 111
pugnacious   (pəg-nā-shəs), pp. 113, 235

\òi\ **boy** \th\ **thin** *th*\ **the** \ü\ **loot** \u̇\ **foot** \y\ **yet** \zh\ **vision**
The syllable in **boldface** receives the heaviest stress in a word.

---

pugnacity   (pəg-**na**-sə-tē), p. 235

punctilious   (pəŋk-**ti**-lē-əs), p. 151

pungent   (**pən**-jənt), p. 151

punitive   (**pyü**-nə-tiv), pp. 53, 127

purport
   (noun: **pər**-pȯrt or -pȯrt;
   verb: pər-**pȯrt** or -**pȯrt**), pp. 182-183

pusillanimous   (pyü-sə-**la**-nə-məs), p. 152

quay   (kē or kā), p. 110

querulous   (**kwer**-yə-ləs or **kwer**-ə-ləs), p. 320

queue   (kyü), p. 110

quibble   (**kwi**-bəl), p. 213

quietus   (kwī-**ē**-təs or kwī-**ā**-təs), p. 51

rankle   (**raŋ**-kəl), p. 126

rapacious   (rə-**pā**-shəs), pp. 235, 358

rapt   (rapt), p. 358

ravage   (**ra**-vij), p. 359

ravish   (**ra**-vish), p. 359

rebuff   (ri-**bəf**), p. 213

rebuke   (ri-**byük**), pp. 373–374

reconnaissance   (ri-**kä**-nə-zənts), p. 112

reconnoiter   (rē-kə-**nȯi**-tər), p. 112

recouped   (ri-**küpt**), p. 14

recreant   (**re**-crē-ənt), p. 112

redoubtable   (ri-**daù**-tə-bəl), p. 98

redound   (ri-**daùnd**), p. 357

redundant   (ri-**dəən**-dənt), pp. 129, 357

refurbish   (ri-**fər**-bish), p. 98

regalia   (ri-**gāl**-yə), p. 55

reliable, reliant   (ri-**lī**-ə-bəl, ri-**lī**-ənt), p. 216

remit   (rē-**mit**), pp. 169, 173

renege   (ri-**nig** or -**neg**), p. 360

repel   (ri-**pel**), pp. 184–185

repellent   (ri-**pe**-lənt), pp. 18, 184–185

repress   (ri-**pres**), p. 129

reprieve   (ri-**prēv**), p. 130

reprimand   (**re**-prə-mand), pp. 129, 373–374

reprisal   (ri-**prī**-zəl), p. 130

reproach   (ri-**prōch**), pp. 333, 373–374

reprobate   (**re**-prə-bāt), pp. 112, 373

reproof   (ri-**prüf**), p. 373

reprove   (ri-**prüv**), pp. 373–374

resistant   (ri-**zis**-tənt), pp. 188-189

respectable, respective
   (ri-**spek**-tə-bəl, ri-**spek**-tiv), p. 218

responsible, responsive
   (ri-**spän**(t)-sə-bəl, re-**spän**(t)-siv), p. 216

restitution   (res-tə-**tü**-shən), p. 54

retort   (ri-**tȯrt**), p. 382

retrograde   (**re**-trə-grād), p. 153

revivify   (rē-**vi**-və-fī), p. 368

revoke   (ri-**vōk**), p. 366

ribald   (**ri**-bəld), p. 51

ritual   (**ri**-chə-wəl or **rich**-wəl), p. 227

riverine   (ri-və-**rīn** or ri-və-**rēn**), p. 48

rotund   (rō-**tənd**), pp. 150, 157, 354

rotunda   (rō-**tən**-də), p. 354

ruminations   (rü-mi-**nā**-shənz), p. 13

sacrilege   (**sa**-krə-lij), p. 229

sacrilegious   (sa-krə-**li**-jəs), p. 229

salacious   (sə-**lā**-shəs), pp. 131, 235

salient   (**sā**-lyənt or -li-ənt), p. 131

sally   (**sa**-lē), p. 131

salutary, salubrious   (**sal**-yə-terē, sə-**lü**-brē-əs), p. 131

sanctimonious   (saŋ(k)-tə-**mō**-nē-əs), p. 230

sanctimony,   (**saŋ**(k)-tə-mō-nē), p. 230

satiate   (**sā**-shē-āt), p. 151

satire   (**sa**-tīr), pp. 122, 215

scandalmonger   (**skan**-dəl-məŋ-gər), p. 50

scavengers   (**ska**-vən-jərz), p. 8

scruple   (**skrü**-pəl), p. 120

scrupulosity   (skrü-pyə-**lä**-sə-tē), p. 232

scrupulous   (**skrü**-pyə-ləs, p. 232

scrutinize   (**skrü**-tə-nīz), p. 100

scrutiny   (**skrü**-tən-ē or **skrüt**-nē), p. 100

seductive   (sə-**dək**-tiv), pp. 178-179

segregate   (**se**-gri-gāt), p. 370

segregation   (se-gre-**gā**-shən), pp. 7, 370

self-assertive   (self-ə-**sər**-tiv), p. 48

sentinel   (**sent**-nəl or **sen**-tən-əl), p. 54

shibboleth   (**shi**-bə-ləth), p. 121

Copyright © 2002 by Addison Wesley Longman, Inc.

\ə\ abut \ər\ further \a\ ash \ā\ ace \ä\ mop, mar \aů\ out \ch\ chin
\e\ bet \ē\ easy \g\ go \i\ hit \ī\ ice \j\ job \ŋ\ sing \ō\ go \ȯ\ law

---

shortfall (**short**-fȯl), p. 54

sinister (**si**-nəs-tər), p. 355

skulking (**skəl**-kəŋ), p. 14

slake (slāk), p. 126

snub (snəb), p. 215

sonority (sə-**nȯr**-ə-tē or -**när**-ə-tē), p. 231

sonorous
  (sə-**nōr**-əs or sə-**nȯr**-əs or **sä**-nə-rəs), p. 231

soporific (sä-pə-**ri**-fik), p. 228

special, specious (**spe**-shəl, **spē**-shəs), p. 216

specter (**spek**-tər), p. 153

stealthiness (**stel**-thē-nis), p. 46

stealthy (**stel**-thē), p. 358

stereotype (**ster**-ē-ə-tīp or **stri**-), p. 332

stimulus, stimulant
  (**stim**-yə-ləs, **stim**-yə-lənt), pp. 221, 369

stoic (**stō**-ik), p. 228

straitlaced (**strāt**-lāsd), p. 18

stratagem (**stra**-tə-jəm), pp. 21, 28, 31

strident (**strī**-d(ə)nt), pp. 110, 366

subjection (səb-**jek**-shən), p. 172

subjective (səb-**jek**-tiv), p. 172

sublime, subliminal
  (sə-**blīm**, sə-**bli**-mə-nəl), pp. 221-222

submissive (səb-**mi**-siv), p. 173

subordinating (sə-**bȯr**-də-nā-tiŋ), p. 14

subsistence (səb-**sis**-tən(t)s), pp. 188-189

sufferance (**sə**-fə-rən(t)s), pp. 176-177

supercilious (sü-pər-**si**-lē-əs or -**sil**-yəs), p. 121

supposition (sə-pə-**zi**-shən), p. 10

surcease (sər-**sēs** or **sər**-sēs), p. 51

surreptitious (sər-əp-**ti**-shəs), pp. 358-359

taboo (ta-**bü**), pp. 8, 334

tactics (**tak**-tiks), p. 5

taint (tānt), pp. 130, 213

tangible (**tan**-ji-bəl), p. 19

tawdry (**tȯ**-drē), p. 122

temper (**tem**-pər), p. 213

temperament (**tem**-pə-rə-mənt), p. 294

tenacious (tə-**nā**-shəs), p. 235

tenacity (tə-**na**-sə-tē), p. 235

testimonials (tes-tə-**mō**-nē-əls), p. 55

thesaurus (thi-**sȯr**-əs), pp. 308-309

throes (thrōz), p. 128

tinge (tinj), p. 130

torque (tȯrk), p. 381

torsion (**tȯr**-shən), p. 381

tort (tȯrt), p. 381

trammel (**tra**-məl), p. 377

transgression (tranz-**gre**-shən), p. 154

trenchant (**tren**-chənt), p. 125

tribute (**tri**-byüt), p. 19

trite (trīt), pp. 263-264

truncated (**trən**-kā-təd), p. 126

ubiquitous (yü-**bi**-kwə-təs), p. 231

ubiquity (yü-**bi**-kwə-tē), p. 231

unabridged (ən-ə-**brijd**), p. 100

unanimity (yü-nə-**ni**-mə-tē), p. 110

undulate (**ən**-jə-lāt or -dyə-lāt), pp. 129, 357

unformulated (ən-**fȯr**-myü-lā-td), p. 50

uninterested (ən-**in**-trəs-təd), p. 167

unsportsmanlike (ən-**spȯrts**-mən-līk), pp. 50, 52

vacillate (**va**-sə-lāt), p. 320

venerate (**ve**-nə-rāt), p. 129

venereal (və-**nir**-ē-əl), p. 129

vicariously (vī-**ker**-ē-əs-lē), p. 266

vivacious (və-**vā**-shəs or vī-**vā**-shəs), p. 368

vivacity (və-**va**-si-tē), p. 368

vivify (**vi**-və-fī), p. 368

vociferous (vō-**si**-f(ə)-rəs), p. 366

vulnerability (vəl-nər-ə-**bi**-lə-tē), p. 14

wafts (wäfts), p. 19

(be) wary (of) (**wa**-ri or **we**-ri), p. 13

whimsical (**hwim**-zi-kəl or **wim**-zi-kəl), p. 320

wrangle (**raŋ**-gəl), p. 111

wreak (rēk), p. 126

writhe (rī*th*), p. 124

zealous (**ze**-ləs), p. 126

ziggurat (**zi**-gə-rat), p. 4

Answer Key

Unit 1:

Vocabulary Exercise 1.3, pp. 7–9 (answers will vary in wording):

1. One group feels superior to another group and treats it badly.
2. His own way of acting and doing things, as opposed to other ways, is the best way.
3. eat things that are dying or dead, as well as garbage
4. difference
5. Neighborhoods are changed into more appealing places to live.
6. Someone thought that doing it caused bad things to happen.
7. a worker who owned no tools, except your body
8. spread through that area
9. drug that makes the eyes glisten
10. silenced, unwilling to speak

Vocabulary Exercise 2.1, pp. 12–14:

1. discrepancy: b) difference; congruity: c) agreement
2. contiguous: b) adjoining
3. be wary of: c) be on the lookout for; overawe: a) scare
4. proclivities: a) inclinations
5. abashed: c) embarrassed
6. fleeting: c) passing; ruminations: b) thoughts
7. skulking: a) sneaking around
8. vulnerability: b) weakness; bottlenecked: c) greatly slowed down
9. recouped: c) got back
10. subordinating: b) placing lower

Vocabulary Exercise 3.1, pp. 16–18:

1. An *elixir* is something you drink that makes you feel wonderful.
   Importunities are words that plead with someone.
2. When we act *in concert* with others, we are not acting alone.
3. *Indigent* people are those who are poor.
4. & 5. introduce new laws.
   To take the *initiative* means to take the lead, to do something first.

Copyright © 2002 by Addison Wesley Longman, Inc.

6 & 7. If a *passive* person got caught up in an argument, she/he would not argue or would apologize and then be quiet.

At a party, a *gregarious* person would go out, meet, and talk well with people just met.

8. A person who is *straitlaced* would never do the following: have an affair, drink until drunk, or stay up all night partying.

9. A person who lived an *insular* life would be unlikely to meet new people or go new places.

10. A sweater in a *repellent* color is one that you find disgusting, even nauseating.

Review Exercise I, pp. 19–21:

1. manumission: freeing, releasing
2. tribute: extortion, protection money
3. wafts: floats
4. tangible: visible, physical; intangible: abstract, spiritual
5. pittance: very little money
6. amenable: suited, appropriate
7. oriented: arranged, positioned; alignment: arrangement
8. coursing: racing, pulsing, moving
9. precarious: unsteady, insecure, doubtful
10. atypical: not typical, unusual

For answers to Review Exercise II, pp. 21–27, students should see their instructor.

Unit 2:

Vocabulary Exercise 4.1, p. 41:

Combinations include backache, backrest, backside, bed light, bed rest, bedside, bedtime, daylight, daylong, daytime, headache, headlight, headline, headlong, headrest, heartache, heartburn, lifeline, lifelong, sunburn, sunlight.

Vocabulary Exercise 4.2, pp. 42:

Combinations include bare-back, bare-chested, bare-faced, threadbare; bluebottle, blueberry, bluebell, bluegrass, blueprint, true-blue; brown-bag, brownnose, brownout, brownstone; deep-freeze, deep-sea, deep-seated, skin-deep; high-pitched, highlight, highjack, sky-high; hotblooded, hotheaded, hothouse, hotcakes; newborn, newcomer, newfangled, brand-new; red-hot, redhead, redwood, red-handed; soft-spoken, software, softball, softshell; strong-arm, stronghold, strong-minded, headstrong.

Vocabulary Exercise 4.3, p. 44:

1. margin	8. drama	15. person
2. amateur	9. poise	16. strain
3. position	10. relate	17. river
4. essential	11. period	18. acid
5. passion	12. long	19. polar
6. physical	13. certain	20. infant
7. normal	14. merit	

Vocabulary Exercise 4.4, p. 45:

1. after thought
2. oppress press
3. freak freakish
4. establish establishment
5. dishearten heart hearten
6. dew lap
7. steal stealth stealthy
8. fool hard hardy
9. precaution caution
10. premeditate premeditated meditate meditated
11. brow beat
12. extinguish extinguishable
13. overindulge indulge indulgent
14. half half-wit wit
15. develop development
16. manage manager
17. log head heads
18. untrustworthy trustworthy trust worth worthy
19. harp chord
20. Oriental Orient

Vocabulary Exercise 4.5, pp. 46–47 (the wording of answers may differ):

1. marginal: unnecessary, extra
2. disheartened: discouraged
3. freakishly: strangely, oddly
4. stealthiness: secrecy, quiet, unobtrusiveness
5. overindulgent: treating very leniently or generously
6. precautionary: taking care ahead of time
7. oppressive: restricting, burdensome
8. ascertained: made certain or sure
9. impassioned: full of feeling, passion
10. amateurish: unprofessional, like an amateur

Vocabulary Exercise 4.6, p. 48:

1. c) fit to be sold
2. c) a lengthening
3. a) stubborn
4. c) uncertain, questionable
5. b) the quality of being precise
6. b) aggressive
7. c) the quality of being outstanding
8. c) a place where fish or poultry eggs are hatched
9. b) near the banks of a river
10. b) a familiar saying

Copyright © 2002 by Addison Wesley Longman, Inc.

Vocabulary Exercise 5.1, pp. 50–51
(Yes and No here stand for circled roots and crossed-out roots):

1. Yes	8. Yes	15. Yes
2. No	9. Yes	16. No
3. No	10. Yes	17. Yes
4. Yes	11. No	18. Yes
5. No	12. Yes	19. No
6. Yes	13. Yes	20. Yes
7. No	14. No	

Vocabulary Exercise 5.2, pp. 52–56 (wording of answers may differ):

1. *Art* is things people make for the sake of beauty, and pottery is something people make that could have been made partly to be beautiful, so *artifacts* could be the things people make at least partly for beauty.
2. *pun* No
3. *Lag* means to be behind, to be late, and the hare lost because he stayed behind to rest, so he was a *laggard,* one who tarried behind.
4. *lass* No
5. *pat* No
6. *Direct* means to tell someone what to do, so a *directive* could be the orders issued by the general.
7. *Late* and *come* mean to come late, and people who come after a play has started are late or *latecomers.*
8. *sent* No
9. *fable* No
10. *Ill* and *timed* (*time*): *Ill* means poor, bad, so something that is *ill-timed* comes at a poor or bad time.
11. A *design* is something that is deliberately planned, so a *designated* hitter is the player that the manager deliberately plans to be only a batter.
12. *rest* No
13. The roots *short* and *fall* suggest that a *shortfall* is something that falls short, that is not enough, like the salary mentioned in the sentence.
14. *port* No
15. *pat* No
16. *Regal* means having to do with kings and queens, and the costume or *regalia* worn by the guards probably comes from the fact that they serve the monarch of England.
17. *test* No. But *testimony* would work because it is something that someone swears is true about someone else, and letters of reference could be *testimonials* because they say something the writers swear is true about your good character and strong work habits.
18. *Lack* suggests that Jimmy lacks something in his attitude toward reading, maybe interest or enthusiasm, so *lackadaisical* could mean uninterested or bored..

19. *Material* suggests that Yolanda likes material things, like money and nice clothes, so that's what *materialistic* probably means.
20. *Shoot* means to send out, like a bullet from a gun, and, together with *off*, suggests that an *offshoot* is something that comes from or out of something else.

Vocabulary Exercise 6.1, pp. 59–61:

1. because he/she loves people
2. He can have many wives.
3. because they make the features of a face more harmonious with each other
4. because we eat just about everything
5. They can speak many languages.
6. to straighten them
7. because what we see (*vision*) has been sent from a faroff studio somewhere
8. It can land on and take off from water.
9. The person him/herself writes the story of his/her own life.
10. because it measures distances from far away
11. The god dwells in everything.
12. because it has plants in many different countries
13. books
14. microscopic (very tiny) forms of life
15. all the power
16. benign because it is a "good" tumor
17. the mind or soul
18. that they were afraid of strangers, or at least didn't like strangers
19. one that stays around most of the time
20. because it's her false name
21. He acts (2) bossily because he wants to rule everyone himself (*auto-*).
22. A *psychopath* is sick in the mind, insane, crazy.
23. small islands and many islands
24. because all together, they form the circle in which all life lives
25. She would be studying the ideas of Communism.

Vocabulary Exercise 6.2, pp. 61–62:

1. c) eager reader
2. b) madman
3. c) pen name
4. b) almighty
5. a) speaks many language
6. c) set of concepts
7. a) harmless
8. b) afraid of the foreign
9. a) long-lasting
10. c) dictator

Copyright © 2002 by Addison Wesley Longman, Inc.

Vocabulary Exercise 6.3, p. 63:

Students devise their own new inventions.

Vocabulary Exercise 7.1, pp. 66–68:

1. all around the world
2. that he is not a happy man
3. It is fed directly into a person's veins.
4. because such a person would be excessively critical
5. to think of the event by looking back or remembering it
6. tasks to fight against terrorists
7. that some people from each tribe have married people from the other tribe
8. someone more interested in his or her own feelings
9. that it occurred before the sinking of the Titanic
10. because the night hours of an *equinox* are equal to the daylight hours
11. to set all their watches to the same exact time
12. that taxes are not an issue, not something to be discussed
13. that it goes against the law
14. because they all occur at the same time as, or together with a cold
15. pranks that were intended to be bad or do harm
16. They have agreed not to be aggressive toward the other, that is, not to invade the other.
17. the sorts of things that are outside of the senses or not felt by the senses
18. that the raise will be paid as if it had been in effect *back* on January 1
19. at an equal distance from each of the two bright stars
20. because she had made a bad marriage, or made a poor choice of husband

Vocabulary Exercise 7.2, p. 69:

1. b) unicorn, unicycle, unity
2. e) bifocals, bicycle, biweekly, and k) dual, duplicate, duet
3. h) triangle, triplets, trio
4. f) quadrangle, quadrilateral
5. a) quintuplets, quintet
6. j) sextuplets, sextet
7. g) septet, septuagenarian
8. d) octagon, octopus, octave
10. i) decade
100. c) century, centipede, centigrade

Vocabulary Exercise 7.3, pp. 70–71:

1. four; a square, a rectangle, a parallelogram, a trapezoid
2. It would be half the size.
3. because a unicycle has only one wheel, not two
4. five
5. six; a septet
6. one-thousandth of a meter
7. one hundred
8. biathlon: two; pentathlon: five; decathlon: ten
9. three

10. two
11. duplex: two; triplex: three
12. monogamist: one; bigamist: two
13. two, each one-half of the globe

14. $500
15. because they are the ninth, tenth and twelfth months, not the seventh, eighth and tenth

Vocabulary Exercise 7.4, p. 73:

1. in-: not flexible
2. un-: not certainty
3. un-: the opposite of *pack*
4. im-: not modest
5. im-: to plant within, inside
6. un-: not decided
7. ir-: not religious
8. il-: not logical
9. un-: the opposite of *fold*
10. ir-: to water within

Vocabulary Exercise 7.5, pp. 73–74:

1. inequality: not equality
2. immigrate: migrate into
3. insubstantial, unsubstantial: not substantial
4. intangible: not tangible
5. uncover: the opposite of *cover*
6. unworkable: not workable
7. illiterate: not literate
8. impressed, unpressed: pressed (touched, moved) within, not pressed (ironed)
9. untouched: not touched
10. entangle, untangle: tangle inside, the opposite of *tangle*

Vocabulary Exercise 8.1, pp. 76–77:

1. fratricide
2. washability
3. durability
4. dullard
5. hairless
6. trainee
7. anonymous
8. modification
9. accessibility
10. skyward

Vocabulary Exercise 8.2, pp. 77–78:

1. a name or word that is somehow the same as another word
2. the killing of a baby
3. to make straight, or set to rights
4. not able to be conquered
5. full of hunger
6. to make into nothing, to make ineffective
7. someone who walks heavily and slowly, like a slug
8. able to be angered easily
9. the name of one's father
10. full of wisdom
11. like a wasp
12. to make holy
13. killing one's mother
14. not able to be examined carefully, unknowable
15. to make peaceful

Copyright © 2002 by Addison Wesley Longman, Inc.

Vocabulary Exercise 8.3, p. 78:

1. irascible and waspish
2. pacify, invincible

3. rectify, voracious
4. sanctified, sagacious, inscrutable

Vocabulary Exercise 8.4, pp. 79–80:

1. irate, ire
2. sage
3. carnivore,
   herbivore

4. sanctimony,
   sanctuary
5. convince
6. maternal, matriarchy

7. correct, rectitude
8. scrutiny, scrutinize
9. infantile, infancy
10. pacifist, pacifier

Spelling Exercise 8.1, pp. 80–81:

1. creditor
2. auctioneer
3. laborer
4. trickster
5. liar
6. conqueror
7. engineer

8. foreigner
9. cashier
10. investor
11. financier
12. visitor
13. charioteer
14. gangster

15. pamphleteer
16. actor
17. carrier
18. New Yorker
19. executor
20. juror

For Dictionary Exercise 8.1, students use their own dictionaries, so answers will vary.

Review Exercise I, p. 84:

1. equity: c
2. symbiosis: g
3. nonconformist: d
4. telephoto lens: j

5. phonetics: h
6. orthography: b
7. homogenized: f
8. photomicrograph: a

9. hydrophobia: e
10. pentangle: i

For answers to Review Exercises II-IV, pp. 84–87, students should ask their instructor.

Unit 3:

For all the Dictionary Exercises in this unit, students use their own dictionaries and, in some cases, their imaginations, so their answers will vary.

Vocabulary Exercise, pp. 98–99:

Students create their own mental pictures for remembering the highlighted words.

Vocabulary Exercise 12.1, pp. 119–120:

Students make up their own imaginative explanations for how the highlighted words developed from the foreign words to which they can be traced.

Unit 4:

Vocabulary Exercise 14.1, pp. 151–52:

Students devise their own connections between the highlighted roots and words.

Vocabulary Exercise 14.2, pp. 152–54:

Students devise their own connections between the highlighted roots and words, and on their own, think of other words with the same roots.

Vocabulary Exercise 14.3, p. 158:

1. see, look at: prospect, spectator, etc.
2. body: corpse, corpulent, etc.
3. write, written: scribe, scripture, etc.
4. hand: manufacture, manifest, etc.
5. say, tell: dictator, diction, etc.
6. faith, belief; to trust, rely on: fidelity, infidel, etc.
7. to prick; point, dot: punctual, compunction, etc.
8. word: verb, verbal, etc.
9. entrust, order; literally, put into the hands of: mandate, mandatory, etc.
10. step, walk, go: gradual, transgression, etc.
11. mind, spirit: animate, animosity, etc.
12. heart: cordial, discordant, etc.
13. enough: satisfy, satiate, etc.
14. house, head of house: domestic, dominion, etc.

Vocabulary Exercise 14.4, pp. 158–59:

1. wordy
2. a sin, breaking a law, literally, going against a rule
3. point of view, a view from a certain point
4. shyness, literally, a lack of faith in oneself
5. calm, composure, an even temper (spirit)
6. active hatred, literally, great feeling
7. a strong opinion, something said that is laid down as a rule, law
8. exact, very careful about behavior
9. going backward, retreating
10. to enclose, restrict, limit with rules, literally, to write around
11. careful, literally, looking all around
12. an order, literally, something handed down
13. talkative, pouring out words
14. residence
15. to show, clear, easy to see
16. to satisfy fully
17. an unbeliever

Copyright © 2002 by Addison Wesley Longman, Inc.

18. a blessing, literally, a saying that prays you will be well
19. uneasiness caused by guilt, literally, feeling the prick (of conscience)
20. worn out with age

Spelling Exercise 15.1, p. 164:

The prefixes are underlined here.

1. accustomed
2. sufficient
3. committee
4. occasion
5. appearance
6. irresistible
7. efficient
8. supplement
9. oppression
10. illiterate

Vocabulary Exercise 15.1, p. 164:

1. immature
2. correction
3. efface
4. assurance
5. occupation
6. illusion
7. supplant
8. allusion
9. colloquial
10. opportunity

Dictionary Exercise 15.1, p. 165:

Because students use their own dictionaries for this exercise, their answers will vary.

Dictionary Exercise 15.2, pp. 166–67:

Because students use their own dictionaries for this exercise, their answers will vary.

Dictionary Exercise 15.3, p. 167:

1. allusions
2. elicit
3. descent
4. imminent
5. proceed
6. prosecute
7. bemused
8. disinterested
9. assures
10. insure

Vocabulary Exercise 15.2, pp. 168–69:

1. admit, commit, emit, omit, permit, remit, submit, transmit
2. conduct, deduct, induct, product
3. confer, defer, infer, interfere, offer, prefer, proffer, refer, suffer, transfer
4. comport, deport, disport, export, import, report, support, transport
5. compel, dispel, expel, impel, propel, repel
6. abstain, attain, contain, detain, entertain, obtain, pertain, retain
7. acclaim, declaim, disclaim, exclaim, proclaim, reclaim

8. assist, consist, desist, exist, insist, persist, resist, subsist
9. construct, destruct, instruct, obstruct
10. accept, concept, except, intercept, precept; conceive, deceive, perceive, receive

Vocabulary Exercise 15.3, pp. 169–71:

Student answers may vary.

1. send
2. brought, gave
3. carried (herself), behaved
4. washed away
5. drive away, push away

6. replaced
7. shouts, applause, praise
8. principles, rules of conduct
9. block

10. everyday, informal, conversational
11. calling out, reciting
12. sends out
13. playing
14. survived
15. admitted, taken into

Vocabulary Exercise 16.1, pp. 174–75:

Students create their own sentences for the highlighted words.
For all Grid Exercises, student answers may vary from those below.

Grid I Exercise, pp. 176–77:

1. They have double consonants.
2. treatment that favors (prefers) some over others. In college admissions, talented athletes, students with perfect SAT scores, and children of alumni are some who might be given *preferential* treatment.
3. implied; inferred
4. *dis-*, away from; *-fer*, carry, bear. One thing *differs* from another because your mind bears it away or separates it from the other.
5. A *referee* is *referred* to for a judgment in a game when it isn't clear what an action means.
6. On Saturday mornings, children at home might watch cartoons all morning, or a tired student in the back row of a class might sleep during class.

Grid II Exercise, pp. 178–79:

1. He might offer scholarships, a new car, dinners at a restaurant, athletic equipment, etc.
2. People are brought into an organization, such as an honor society.
3. productive
4. A bribe is a *seduction* because its purpose is to lure someone into doing something bad or illegal.
5. a hot bath, warm milk, soft music, dim lights, etc.
6. deductive

Copyright © 2002 by Addison Wesley Longman, Inc.

Grid III Exercise, pp. 180–81:

1. To *disclaim* means to disown something or someone, to shout it apart from yourself. To *proclaim* something means to shout it forth to others, to announce.
2. (Here, the syllable with the heaviest stress is indicated by capital letters; the syllable with secondary stress is underlined.)
   <u>ex</u> cla MA tion   <u>de</u> cla MA tion
   ex CLAM a <u>to</u> ry   de CLAM a <u>to</u> ry

The position is different to make stressed syllables alternate with unstressed syllables.
3. She is denying that the rumor is true.
4. because it makes words that it follows shout out with importance or feeling
5. They are supposed to be restoring the land to the way it was before the mining.
6. 1) The two words rhyme. 2) The heaviest stress falls on the next-to-last syllable in each (Emanici PA tion Procla MA tion). 3) They are each four syllables long.
7. Since *claim* derives from the root *clam-*, meaning to call, cry out, then you could say that what you call out for is what you want to be yours, and after calling for it long enough, you start calling for it as if it were yours by right.
8. c) crying out urgently and insistently

Grid IV Exercise, pp. 182–83:

1. export, import, purport, <u>report</u>, <u>support</u>, transport
2. Both can be used with *-self* words like *oneself, themselves,* to mean "behave in a certain way, or according to some code of behavior."
3. important
4. *Deportation* means to send (carry) someone officially out of a country.
5. No. meaning, gist, substance
6. It is not (*in-*) able (*-able*) to be supported. There is no evidence to carry (*-port*) or *support* his claim.

Grid V Exercise, pp. 184–86:

1. Students write their own sentences using *dispel* and *repel.*
2. compulsive, compulsory
3. because there are two vowels before the *l.* The sound of these vowels is already *ē.*
4. Our *pulse* is the rhythmic pushing of our blood through our veins by the heart.
5. Something *water-repellent* pushes away water. An insect *repellent* drives away insects.
6. Something *attractive* seems to be calling out to us to see and admire it.
7. Some *push* idioms of things or actions that *push* are
   to push your luck   when push comes to shove
   to push around   to push up daisies

   Some *push* idioms of things or actions that get *pushed* are
   push broom   pushcart
   pushover   push-up

Spelling Exercise 16.1, p. 187:

1. flatten, flatter
2. paired, purring
3. occurred, occurrence
4. dispairing, disheveled
5. admittedly, adopting
6. propeller, prosperous
7. forgetful, forgetting
8. controllable, convertible
9. topless, topping
10. redness, reddening

Grid VI Exercise, pp. 188–89:

1. assist, subsist
2. They both mean to stop, but *desist* suggests that something has MADE you stop, while *cease* can mean you stopped on your own.
3. The parts of *assist* mean to stand next to, which is where you might be to help, or *assist,* someone.
4. inconsistent, irresistible. *In-* means not.
5. A person's behavior can be *consistent* if the person's actions are all similar, all in harmony with one another.
6. The family is barely surviving. They are literally standing below an adequate lifestyle.
7. resistant, resistible

Vocabulary Exercise for Grids I-VI, pp. 190–91:

1. He is saying that he was not associated with that company.
2. a letter
3. Whatever you do to have fun, like dance, go to a movie, visit another country, etc.
4. because you cannot stand to be around the child; he/she cannot be endured.
5. a blood vessel
6. No, because a *compulsive* person is forced to act a certain way by uncontrollable feelings, while an *impulsive* person can choose not to act impulsively.
7. because they are unexpectedly thrown into our speech because of a sudden feeling like pain or surprise
8. They would be setting up a continuous noise, probably of protest, outside the place where men were taken or drafted into the armed forces.
9. Columbus reasoned *deductively* because he started with a general theory and drew a particular conclusion from it. Newton, however, reasoned *inductively,* going from one example of one apple falling to the general theory of gravity by which all things fall.
10. Sentences a and d because both verbs *claims* and *purports* imply that Mario is not REALLY a friend of the governor. These verbs imply that he is lying, or at least exaggerating the truth.

Copyright © 2002 by Addison Wesley Longman, Inc.

Review Exercise I for Chapters 14–16, p. 192:

1. avert, advert, convert, divert, invert, pervert, revert, subvert
2. attend, contend, distend, extend, intend, pretend
3. affect, infect, perfect, effect
4. compose, depose, dispose, expose, impose, oppose, propose, repose, suppose, transpose
5. abstract, attract, contract, detract, distract, extract, protract, retract, subtract

For Answers to Review Exercises II-VI for Chapters 14–16, pp. 192–95, students should ask their instructor.

Vocabulary Exercise 17.1, pp. 199–200:

1. endorsement
2. embodiment of the unalienable rights that Jefferson wrote about in the Declaration of Independence
3. embellishment
4. abridgement
5. disparagement
6. Her friends the Scarecrow, the Tin Man, and the Cowardly Lion felt total disillusionment when they found that the celebrated Wizard of Oz...
7. engagement
8. harassment
9. entrapment
10. aggrandizement

Vocabulary Exercise 17.2, p. 201:

1. supporting
2. gives form to
3. dressed up
4. shortened
5. make little of
6. freed from a false idea
7. fought with
8. persecuted
9. lured into danger
10. make greater

Spelling Exercise 17.1, p. 202:

1. enticing
2. believable
3. careless
4. caring
5. judging
6. judgment (though this word is sometimes spelled *judgement*)
7. civilization
8. receding
9. legalization
10. isolation

Spelling Exercise 17.2, p. 202:

1. outrageous
2. allegiance
3. judicious
4. knowledgeable
5. embraceable
6. elegant
7. vengeance
8. financial
9. religious
10. eligible

Spelling Exercise 17.3, p. 203:

1. soft
2. hard
3. soft
4. hard
5. soft
6. soft
7. soft
8. hard
9. hard
10. hard

Vocabulary Exercise 17.3, pp. 203–06

1. *evaporation* of water
2. *cultivation* of olive trees
3. *imitations,* there will never be *duplications*
4. *delineates* some little understood aspects of George Washington's personality
5. *generate* enough electrical power for...
6. the *mediation* of disputes and misunderstandings between...
7. *speculation* about the possibility of humans traveling to Mars, not my *advocation* of our doing it next week or even next year
8. *proliferated* so much in recent years that libraries are having trouble...
9. The *articulation* of his fear of death in Hamlet's "To be or not to be" speech is a fear we all share but seldom express openly. But he speaks it...
10. *compensate* for the loss of her husband in a traffic accident. The money should help the *mitigation* of her sense of loss.
11. Calling each other names *exacerbates* your bad feelings for each other. Why not call in a third person to *arbitrate* your dispute?
12. *commiseration.* But I find it hard to sympathize with you because of your *procrastination* of studying....
13. People go to expensive spas to *rejuvenate* for a few days, even though they have not paid attention to their health in years. But the *purgation* from the body of cholesterol and the effects of years of smoking and drinking takes a lot longer than a few days.
14. The first suspect was released because of the *corroboration* by two co-workers of his alibi for the night of the robbery. The time on his timecard was a further *substantiation* of his alibi.
15. Because the governor is *vacillating* over whether or not to run for re-election, he is *alienated* from the rest of the Democrats, who want a more committed candidate.

Copyright © 2002 by Addison Wesley Longman, Inc.

Vocabulary Exercise 17.4, p. 206:

1. accurate description
2. production
3. settle
4. considering
5. supporting
6. rapid increase
7. expresses in words
8. payment
9. lessen
10. aggravating
11. resolution
12. feel sorry for
13. put off
14. restoration of youth
15. cleanse
16. supported
17. proven
18. wavering
19. separation

Vocabulary Exercise 17.5, p. 207:

1. relax
2. reveal
3. adapt
4. occupy
5. sterilize
6. improvise
7. provoke
8. denounce
9. insinuate
10. inflate

Vocabulary Exercise 17.6, p. 208:

1. friendship
2. commandment
3. deliverance
4. election
5. martyrdom
6. alcoholism
7. bakery
8. exactitude
9. authenticity
10. correctness, correction, correctitude

Spelling Exercise 17.4, p. 209:

1. hastily
2. laziness
3. trying
4. conveying
5. conveyance
6. worried
7. prettier
8. rallied
9. rallying
10. delaying

Spelling Exercise 17.5, p. 210:

1. care
2. tar
3. tarry
4. part
5. party
6. curtsey
7. eye
8. grip
9. gripe
10. cute

Vocabulary Exercise 17.7, pp. 210–11:

1. reliance
2. alliance
3. compliance
4. defiance
5. trial
6. denial
7. espial
8. defilement
9. revilement
10. derailment
11. connivance
12. contrivance
13. revival
14. survival
15. submersion
16. conversion
17. diversion
18. immersion
19. convergence
20. divergence
21. emergence
22. resurgence
23. acquiescence
24. coalescence
25. effervescence

Vocabulary Exercise 17.8, pp. 213–14:

1. quibbled
2. lapsed
3. tempered
4. bartered

5. pique
6. duped
7. exploit
8. ebb

9. lampoon
10. rebuffed

Vocabulary Exercise 17.9, pp. 214–15:

Students' answers may differ depending on their dictionaries.
1. Both can mean one's disposition, temperament, or usual state of feelings.
2. Both can mean to make use of.
3. Both can mean to arouse.
4. Both can mean an exchange.
5. Both can mean to fall away, die down.
6. Both can mean to push away, reject with contempt.
7. Both can mean a small mistake.
8. Both can mean to fool, deceive, or hoodwink someone.
9. Both can mean a harsh, witty criticism.
10. Both can mean to bicker, raise trivial objections.

Vocabulary Exercise 17.10, pp. 215–17:

Students write their own sentences using the more familiar words highlighted here.
1. meddlesome, obtrusive, nosy
2. quick to answer, sensitive to
3. dependent on
4. the person to whom you tell secrets, your intimate friend
5. seeming true, plausible
6. employees, workers, staff
7. quick to find fault, hypercritical, carping
8. advised
9. showing preference to, giving priority to
10. small, trivial

Copyright © 2002 by Addison Wesley Longman, Inc.

Vocabulary Exercise 17.11, pp. 217–23:

1. deleted as objectionable; officially criticized
2. grateful, appreciating; noticeable, considerable
3. poor, impoverished, without income; native, born in a particular place
4. punished; subdued, humbled
5. pleasant, favorable; hereditary, inherited
6. *incredible:* unbelievable; *incredulous:* skeptical, unbelieving
7. *credible:* believable; *credulous:* gullible, easily tricked
8. pleasure, satisfaction; controversy, argument
9. scornful anger, rage; insult, injury
10. variety, heterogeneity; distraction
11. insightful, discerning; noticeable

12. relevant, appropriate; obstinate, annoyingly persistent
13. despicable, detestible; disdainful, disrespectful
14. incentive, catalyst; substance that wakes you up
15. showy, flashy, gaudy; apparent, overt
16. lofty, grand, majestic; subconscious, unnoticed
17. huge size, immensity; outrageousness, viciousness
18. short, brief; important, significant
19. official, definitive; strict, (a manner) favoring total obedience
20. short, witty sayings, aphorisms; short, introductory quotation, quoted one-liner

Vocabulary Exercise 17.12, p. 223:

1. flirtation
2. discoloration
3. visitation
4. consultation
5. fixation
6. computation
7. foundation
8. conservation
9. dramatization
10. authorization

Vocabulary Exercise 17.13, p. 224:

1. fulfill
2. isolate
3. deport
4. construct
5. continue
6. empower
7. enunciate
8. drudge
9. extend
10. glorify

Vocabulary Exercise 17.14, p. 224:

Corrections are underlined.
1. courag*e*ous
2. fortunat*el*y
3. tru*l*y
4. Correct
5. arg*um*ent
6. definit*el*y
7. Correct
8. manag*e*able
9. Correct
10. sincer*el*y

Vocabulary Exercise 18.1, pp. 226–28:

1. c) new
2. b) obvious
3. a) unusually perceptive
4. b) ceremonial
5. b) one-sided
6. a) advantageous
7. b) wildly extravagant
8. c) sleep-causing
9. a) calm
10. c) pleasure-seeking

Vocabulary Exercise 18.2, pp. 229–30:

1. momentous
2. perilous
3. advantageous
4. spacious
5. gracious
6. malicious
7. capricious
8. sacrilegious
9. famous
10. disastrous
11. ridiculous
12. virtuous

13. wondrous
14. envious
15. harmonious
16. ceremonious
17. acrimonious
18. parsimonious
19. sanctimonious
20. piteous

Vocabulary Exercise 18.3, pp. 230–31:

1. malicious, sacrilegious
2. acrimonious
3. parsimonious
4. piteous
5. momentous
6. perilous
7. sanctimonious
8. capricious
9. malicious
10. advantageous

Vocabulary Exercise 18.4, pp. 231–32:

1. enormity
2. ambiguity
3. barbarity
4. continuity
5. garrulity
6. hilarity
7. sonority
8. ubiquity
9. curiosity
10. generosity
11. impetuosity
12. luminosity
13. monstrosity
14. nebulosity
15. pomposity
16. scrupulosity

Vocabulary Exercise 18.5, pp. 232–33:

1. ambiguous
2. impetuosity
3. barbarity, monstrosity, enormity
4. garrulity
5. luminous
6. nebulous
7. ubiquitous
8. barbarous, monstrous
9. sonorous
10. continuity

Vocabulary Exercise 18.6, pp. 233–35:

Students write their own imaginative answers to these questions.

Vocabulary Exercise 18.7, p. 235:

audacity
efficacious
fallacious
pugnacity
rapacious
perspicacity
salacious
tenacity
veracious
mendacity

Vocabulary Exercise 18.8, pp. 236–37:

1. ability, potential
2. position, office
3. power (to do good), effectiveness
4. effective
5. boldness, nerve
6. faulty, illogical
7. aggressiveness, belligerence
8. greedy, grasping
9. perceptive, astute, shrewd
10. lewd, pornographic
11. truthfulness
12. lying, deceitfulness
13. persistent, tough

Copyright © 2002 by Addison Wesley Longman, Inc.

Review Exercise I for Chapters 17–18, p. 238:

1. g) whatever stirs to action
2. j) disowning, rejection
3. i) impulsiveness
4. f) alleviate, moderate
5. a) speak badly of
6. b) persecution
7. h) snub, push aside
8. e) waver, hesitate
9. c) go along with
10. d) one who endures calmly

For answers to Review Exercises II–IV, pp. 238–39, students should ask their instructor.

Unit 5:

Vocabulary Exercise 19.1, p. 257:

absurd instead of *a bird*
inane instead of *a plane*
creped crusader instead of *caped crusader*
hi-trek instead of *high-tech*
flaptop computer instead of *laptop computer*
inflammation instead of *information*
Windex 98 instead of *Windows 98*

knee-mail instead of *e-mail*
smell instead of *spell*
food instead of *word*
smurf instead of *surf*
ciderspace instead of *cyberspace*
carpool instead of *carpal*
loser-friendly instead of *user-friendly*

Vocabulary Exercise 19.2, pp. 257–58:

1. obliterate
2. prodigy
3. artistry?
4. superficial
5. geography
6. contiguous
7. orthography
8. comprehend
9. superfluous
10. pinnacle
11. hysterics
12. desisted
13. intercepted
14. alligator
15. comparisons

Vocabulary Exercise 19.3, pp. 259–61:

Tortoise is a pun for *taught us.*
Reeling is a pun for *Reading.*
Writhing is a pun for *Writing.*
Ambition, Distraction, Uglification, and Derision are puns for *Addition, Subtraction, Multiplication, and Division.*
Mystery is a pun for *History.*

Seaography is a pun for *Geography.*
Drawling is a pun for *Drawing.*
Stretching is a pun for *Sketching.*
Fainting in Coils is a pun for *Painting in Oils.*
Laughing and Grief is a pun for *Latin and Greek.*
Lesson is a pun for *lessen.*

Vocabulary Exercise 19.4, p. 262:

Students compile their own lists of words and phrases significant to a particular field.

Vocabulary Exercise 20.1, p. 264:

Depending on the dictionary they use, students' responses to this exercise will vary.

Vocabulary Exercise 20.2, pp. 265–66:

Below are synonyms derived from the definitions of *good* in *Merriam Webster's Collegiate Dictionary* (10th ed.).

1. suitable, fit
2. wholesome, salutary
3. choice
4. deserving of respect, honorable
5. virtuous, commendable
6. kind, benevolent
7. close
8. agreeable, pleasant
9. competent, skillful, complete
10. full

Vocabulary Exercise 20.3, p. 267:

Below are synonyms derived from the definitions of *bad* in *Merriam Webster's Collegiate Dictionary* (10th ed.).

1. disagreeable, unpleasant
2. spoiled, rotten
3. incorrect, faulty
4. sorry, unhappy
5. invalid, void
6. wicked, immoral
7. ill, in pain
8. severe, violent, intense
9. dangerous, harmful
10. inadequate, poor

Vocabulary Exercise 20.4, pp. 268–70:

1. people, excitement
2. Students provide their own rewordings.
3. Students write their own sentences.
4. disagreeable, unpleasant
   For *crowds of people,* disagreeable, unpleasant
   For *garbage,* spoiled, rotten
   For *noise,* disagreeable, unpleasant
5. Students make their own lists.
6. agreeable, pleasant; wholesome, salutary
7. Students make their own lists.
8. Students make their own lists.

Vocabulary Exercise 20.5, pp. 271–72:

Students write their own suggestions.

Vocabulary Exercise 21.1, pp. 275–76:

Students choose their own vivid, specific verbs.

Vocabulary Exercise 21.2, pp. 276–77:

Students think of their own vivid verbs and adverbs or adverbial phrases.

Vocabulary Exercise 22.1, p. 279:

Students think of their own adjectives.

Copyright © 2002 by Addison Wesley Longman, Inc.

Vocabulary Exercise 22.2, p. 280:

Students think of their own adjectives.

Vocabulary Exercise 22.3, p. 280:

Students think of their own adjectives.

Vocabulary Exercise 22.4, pp. 281–82:

Students think of their own adverbs, phrases, or adverbial clauses.

Vocabulary Exercise 22.5, p. 282:

Here are the modifiers that students should underline and replace, but they think of their own replacements and additional sentences on their own.
1. Record, high, unusually, irritable
2. first, surprisingly, successful
3. who lived nearby, small, who always barked when the phone rang (also, "always" modifies "barked")
4. fat, addressed by hand, quietly, apartment
5. long, black, silently, darkened

Vocabulary Exercise 23.1, pp. 285–86:

1. icy, icily
2. hazardous, hazardously
3. stylish, stylishly
4. hateful, hatefully
5. proud, proudly
6. persistent, persistently
7. pleasant, pleasantly or pleasurable, pleasurably
8. hungry, hungrily
9. perfect, perfectly
10. calm, calmly

Vocabulary Exercise 23.2, pp. 287–88:

1. easily: Greg was ^ able to run the three miles ^. (That is, we could say "Greg was *easily* able to run the three miles" or "Greg was able to run the three miles *easily*.")
2. elegantly: The women were ^ dressed ^ for the gala concert.
3. suddenly: ^ the child burst ^ into tears ^.
4. simply: The problem can be solved ^.
5. very simply: The problem can be solved ^.
6. generously: My brother, who is a chef, always ^ tips waiters ^.
7. leisurely: On my vacation I ^ ate breakfast ^.
8. loudly and clearly: ^ the defense counsel ^ read her statement ^.
9. nervously and hesitantly: ^ Timmy sat ^ on the edge of his seat and ^ told his story ^.
10. aggressively and determinedly: ^ the news reporters ^ pursued the senator ^.

11. vigorously and energetically: ^ the dog bounced ^ into the yard ^.
12. effortlessly: Greg was able to run the three miles ^.
13. instinctively or instinctually: ^ squirrels ^ start ^ collecting and hiding nuts in the autumn ^.
14. so efficiently: The new machine works ^ that I can spend more time writing.
15. approvingly: The teacher nodded ^ when Tommy started to read aloud.

Vocaulary Exercise 24.1, p. 290:

Students make up their own sentences speaking of time metaphorically.

Vocabulary Exercise 24.2, p. 291:

1. c	6. d	11. f or a
2. f	7. e	12. e
3. b	8. c	13. a
4. a	9. f	14. c or d
5. g	10. d	15. d

Vocabulary Exercise 24.3, pp. 292–93:

1. pig	5. the head	9. platter
2. fish	6. an owl	10. china shop
3. hat	7. haystack	
4. an ox or a bull	8. sea or ocean	

Review Exercises I–III, pp. 296–98:

Students write their own versions of the sentences, paragraphs, and essay in these Review Exercises.

Some Answers to Mastery Exercises for Reading 5b, pp. 303–04:

2. Some other rhyming clichés and clichés that repeat the same initial letter are purple prose, other fish to fry, stick out like a sore thumb, the grass is always greener, crystal clear, through thick and thin, place your best foot forward, a dime a dozen, more than you can shake a stick at, it's made in the shade, by hook or by crook, a bolt from the blue, last but not least (The last one also almost rhymes).
3. Some animal clichés in the essay: when pigs fly, barking up the wrong tree, more fun than a barrel of monkeys, happy as a lark, a clam, or a pig in slop, party till the cows come home. Other animal clichés from Vocabulary Exercise 24.3 include fat as a pig, timid as a mouse, wise as an owl, etc.

Copyright © 2002 by Addison Wesley Longman, Inc.

Unit 6:

Dictionary Exercise 25.1, pp. 311–13:

1. defunct	8. appraised	15. subscribed
2. dead	9. talent	16. agreed
3. late	10. aptitude	17. consent
4. evaluated	11. gift	18. acquiesced
5. assessed	12. knack	19. arduous
6. value	13. bent	20. difficult
7. estimated	14. acceded	

Thesaurus Exercise 25.1, pp. 313–15:

1. plump, stout, chubby
2. profitable, rich
3. rich, greasy
4. profitable, rich (though neither of these words sounds as idiomatic with bonus as *fat*)
5. plump, stout, portly (*Chubby* seems inappropriate for a paunch, and *corpulent* and *obese* usually refer to the whole body.)
6. greasy
7. stout, corpulent, obese (*Portly* seems too dignified a word for the sentence, and *chubby* too "cute.")
8. None
9. fertile, fruitful, rich
10. None

Thesaurus Exercise 25.2, p. 315:

Students write their own sentences.

Dictionary Exercise 25.2, p. 317:

Students' answers here will vary, depending on the dictionaries they use.

Dictionary Exercise 25.3, pp. 318–19:

cat: catty, catlike
dog: doggy, doglike
bear: bearish, bearlike
mule: mulish, mulelike
snake: snaky (or snakey), snakelike
horse: horsey (or horsy), horselike

rabbit: rabbity, rabbitlike
mouse: mousy (or mousey), mouselike
rat: ratty, ratlike
wolf: wolfish, wolflike
fish: fishy, fishlike

Vocabulary Exercise 25.1, p. 319:

Students make up their own lists of questions.

Dictionary Exercise 25.4, p. 320:

Students supply their own explanations of the connotations below.

1. lackey: negative
2. whimsical: can be positive if used to mean "lightly fanciful," but might also be negative if used to mean "erratic"
3. vacillate: neutral
4. dispassionate: positive
5. querulous: negative
6. bombast: negative
7. indefatigable: positive
8. charlatan: negative
9. opulent: can be positive if it means "wealthy, rich," though it can be somewhat negative when it means a "lavish display of wealth"
10. astute: positive

Thesaurus Exercise 25.3, p. 321:

Students may find other appropriate synonyms besides those below, depending on the dictionary they use.

1. lackey: toady
2. whimsical: capricious
3. vacillate: hesitate
4. dispassionate: imperturbable, detached
5. querulous: crotchety, peevish, complaining
6. bombast: pomposity
7. indefatigable: tireless, persistent
8. charlatan: fake, fraud, quack
9. opulent: wealthy, affluent
10. astute: perspicacious, perceptive

Thesaurus Exercise 25.4, pp. 321–22:

Students experiment with their own synonym replacements.

Thesaurus Exercise 25.5, pp. 322–24:

1. joyous, ecstatic, glad
2. excruciating, agonizing
3. alter, reconsider, modify
4. damage, harm
5. violence, ferocity, ferociousness, fierceness, rage, fury
6. shore, coast, sands
7. hard, tough, demanding
8. make, form, manufacture
9. drain, weaken, overtire
10. beg, petition, ask, entreat, beseech, implore, cry to, appeal to, press

Thesaurus Exercise 25.6, pp. 324–25:

Answers here are from the program MS Word.

1. more temperate, milder
2. sensitive, vulnerable
3. harm, damage, impair, mar
4. learned, determined, ascertained
5. link, connection, span
6. braved, challenged, or resisted, opposed, withstood
7. frequently, regularly, oftentimes, repeatedly
8. exist, subsist
9. hazardous, dangerous
10. expressions, statements

Copyright © 2002 by Addison Wesley Longman, Inc.

Thesaurus Exercise 26.1, p. 327:

Students find synonyms on their own and provide their own explanations of the synonyms they choose.

Thesaurus Exercise 26.2, pp. 328–29:

Students work out their own ways of developing the topics.

Thesaurus Exercise 26.3, p. 330:

Students work out their own ways of developing the essay.

Thesaurus and Writing Exercise 26.4, pp. 331–35:

Students work out their own answers to the questions.

Review Exercise I, p. 336:

1. A better synonym for *avoid* would be *dodge, elude* because *eschew* means to avoid something habitually, but the young men wanted to avoid the draft only once.
2. OK
3. A better synonym for *limits* here would be *restricts, defines. Inhibits* means to stop someone from doing something.
4. OK
5. A better synonym for *wrong* here would be *immoral* because *fallacious* means that something is not logical or is factually wrong, rather than morally wrong.
6. A better synonym for *satisfying* here would be *rewarding* or *fulfilling* because *appeasing* means calming, allaying, pacifying, that is, bringing peace and quiet, not happiness.
7 & 8. A better synonym for *price* here would be *cost* because *expenditure* means the act of spending or something that is paid out, like money, rather than what the thing (success) costs. A better synonym for *constant* here would be *regular* because *uniform* means always having the same form (*uni-*, one), rather than going on over a period of time.
9. OK
10. A better synonym for *possible* here would be *feasible* because something *contingent* depends on something else. *Possible* has a wider meaning.

For answers to Review Exercise II, students should ask their instructor.

UNIT 7—Appendix

Vocabulary Exercise A.1, p. 354:

1. corpulent
2. incorporeal
3. incorporate
4. corpus
5. corporate

Vocabulary Exercise A.2, p. 357:

1. surrounded
2. inundated
3. abundance
4. redounded
5. undulating
6. redundant
7. abound

Vocabulary Exercise A.3, p. 359:

1. ravishing
2. rape
3. ravaged
4. rapacious
5. ravenous
6. rapt
7. surreptitious
8. rapture

Vocabulary Exercise A.4, p. 361:

1. negated
2. abnegate
3. annihilated
4. renege
5. nullified
6. nil
7. negative
8. annulled

Vocabulary Exercise A.5, p. 363:

1. plain
2. candid
3. outspoken
4. frank
5. openly

Vocabulary Exercise A.6, p. 365:

1. credence (credit is acceptable here too)
2. faith
3. credit
4. conviction
5. belief

Vocabulary Exercise A.7, p. 367:

1. boisterous
2. strident
3. clamorous
4. obstreperous
5. blatant

Copyright © 2002 by Addison Wesley Longman, Inc.

Vocabulary Exercise A.8, pp. 369–70:

1. animated
2. excited
3. quickens

4. stimulated
5. piqued
6. enliven

7. provoked
8. stirred
9. vivified

Vocabulary Exercise A.9, pp. 371–72:

Students' explanations may vary somewhat from those below.
1. honesty: The man acted without fraud.
2. honor: They observed a moral code that was often illegal.
3. integrity: She is careful not to betray the trust the company places in her.
4. probity: He has been tested and found to be morally steady.
5. integrity: She has always acted according to her own beliefs, which others admire.
6. integrity: He remains true to his own admirable belief, but the word *honor* might work here also because a lot of people might think his code was simply foolish.
7. honesty: She shows an absence of fraud, even when she's the only one who knows the truth.
8. honor: He follows a code of behavior that those outside the prison might not agree with.

Vocabulary Exercise A.10, pp. 374–75:

Students' explanations may vary somewhat from those below.
1. reprimand: He deserves a public criticism.
2. reprove: Unless the bandleader is really upset, she/he would scold the player and suggest how to assure being in tune. If angry, she/he might *chide* the flute player.
3. rebuke, reprimand or admonish: If you are angry with the girl, you'd *rebuke* or *reprimand* her, but if you had cooled down first, you'd *admonish* her about the dangers of driving too fast.
4. admonish: As a doctor, you would warn the patient again about the dangers of smoking.
5. reprove or rebuke: If you think he is unaware of the importance of the homework, you might gently *reprove* him, but if you think he does understand, you might be angry and would scold him with a *rebuke*.
6. rebuke, reprimand, or chide: Now you ARE angry and might punish the child. You might also *chide* him because, besides being angry, you also want him to improve.
7. reprove: You value the employee so you don't want to criticize him/her harshly.
8. reprimand: Criticism of the general would be official and public.
9. reproach or rebuke: If you are angry, you might *reproach* your friend for forgetting you, but if you were only mildly annoyed, you might only *rebuke* your friend.
10. reproach: If you are criticizing yourself, you are no doubt angry with yourself and even disappointed.

Vocabulary Exercise A.11, pp. 377–78:

Students' explanations may vary somewhat from those below.
 1. obstruct: An obstacle prevents you from seeing the whole stage.
 2. impede: Your feet are slow because they have to drag through the snow.
 3. trammel: The crowd's arms entangle the thief's arms and legs, preventing escape.
 4. block: The toy is totally obstructing the water flow.
 5. clog: There are too many cases for there to be easy progress through family court.
 6. impede, hinder or hamper: If you emphasize the progress of the ships' hulls through the water, then the icebergs *impede* them like mud on feet, but if you emphasize their lack of progress, you might use *hinder* or *hamper.*
 7. trammel: The net entangles the butterfly's wings.
 8. impede: It is not impossible to rescue the surfer, so *block* is not suitable, and the lifeguards can get through the waves, so *clog* and *obstruct* are not suitable, but their progress is slowed by them.
 9. obstruct or block: If the filibuster eventually stops, he is just *obstructing* the bill, but if he successfully gets the bill removed, he has *blocked* it completely.
10. hinder or hamper: Your lack of French causes annoying delays and may even get you into trouble.

Vocabulary Exercise A.12, pp. 380–81:

Students' explanations may vary somewhat from those below.
 1. penalize: A player has broken the rules and so loses a score.
 2. chasten: She criticizes him but also wants to make him act better.
 3. discipline: She keeps him home as punishment but also so he will study.
 4. castigate: She is publicly condemning him.
 5. chastise: Whipping is a severe punishment.
 6. punish or discipline: If the teacher merely wants the child to suffer, use *punish,* but if she also wants to improve the child's behavior, use *discipline.*
 7. penalize: The fine is the punishment.
 8. chasten: Cancer has humbled and subdued her.
 9. punish: The jail sentence means the loss of freedom.
10. castigate: The novelist is publicly criticizing the industry.

Vocabulary Exercise A.13, pp. 382–84:

Students' explanations may vary somewhat from those below.
 1. He might accuse her of being a bad mother if she doesn't.
 2. He might promise to do special chores for her or to study hard in school all week or to do something else she'd approve of.
 3. A letter from home, a goody box from home, seeing something at camp that's very similar to something at home, like a dog, etc.

Copyright © 2002 by Addison Wesley Longman, Inc.

4. He was afraid he'd get hurt or be killed.
5. b) to get their own interests involved, or c) to show them how much fun reading is
6. The politician might support keeping Social Security strong or providing better health care for the retired person.
7. She could say she plans to leave her money to those grandchildren who pay attention to her now.
8. They might use a bulldozer to pull it out.
9. fear, if I expected bad news or pain; anxiety, if I were uncertain
10. pity or sympathy and the offer of a job or money

Index